POLITICS AND THE RIGHT TO WORK

ROB JENKINS
JAMES MANOR

Politics and the Right to Work

*India's National Rural Employment
Guarantee Act*

HURST & COMPANY, LONDON

This edition published in the United Kingdom in 2017 by
C. Hurst & Co. (Publishers) Ltd.,
41 Great Russell Street, London, WC1B 3PL
© Rob Jenkins & James Manor, 2017
All rights reserved.
Printed in India

The right of Rob Jenkins and James Manor to be identified as the
authors of this publication is asserted by them in accordance
with the Copyright, Designs and Patents Act, 1988.
A Cataloguing-in-Publication data record for this book is available
from the British Library.

ISBN: 9781849045704 *paperback*

This book is printed using paper from registered sustainable
and managed sources.

www.hurstpublishers.com

To the memory of our friend,
E. RAGHAVAN

CONTENTS

ACKNOWLEDGEMENTS

We are grateful to the British Economic and Social Research Council, which drew upon funds provided by the UK Department for International Development, for a grant in support of the extensive field research undertaken for this book. Crucial assistance in the field was provided by the Institute of Development Studies (IDS), Jaipur, and by Samarthan in Bhopal. The late Professor Surjit Singh, IDS Director during the period of field research in Rajasthan, gave especially valuable support, as did Yogesh Kumar and Vishal Naik, whose work at Samarthan was invaluable to the study's research in Madhya Pradesh.

We learned much from discussions in New Delhi with analysts and administrators at the Ministry of Rural Development (the key supervisory agency for this programme), and at India's Planning Commission. We received important assistance from senior civil servants during field research in Madhya Pradesh and Rajasthan—from R. Parasuram and his colleagues in Bhopal, and from Ashok Pande in Jaipur. It is impossible to mention each of the many other officials who provided help of one kind or another by name, but we thank them nonetheless. We were also aided immensely by the insights and knowledge of countless journalists, academics, retired civil servants, and representatives of both development NGOs and social movements.

Important observations concerning NREGA's origins, formulation, implementation and impact—including the politics surrounding all of these processes—have come from interviews conducted with a wide range of people who were closely engaged with the programme throughout the entire period covered in this book. The authors interacted with some of these people for years prior to the adoption of NREGA, providing an extremely valuable longer-term perspective, especially with respect to issues of human rights and accountable governance.

ACKNOWLEDGEMENTS

Among the institutions the authors would like to thank for their indirect support for this project are the Department of Political Science and the Roosevelt House Public Policy Institute at Hunter College, City University of New York, and the Institute of Commonwealth Studies at the University of London. We also thank our families for their support during the completion of this book.

While we have benefited greatly from all of these forms of assistance, the analysis in this book represents our independent assessment, unencumbered by any institutional constraints. We alone are responsible for its content.

RJ & JM, New York

LIST OF ABBREVIATIONS

AAP	Aam Aadmi Party
ASCI	Administrative Staff College of India
AIMIM	All India Majlis-e-Ittehadul Muslimeen
BDO	Block Development Officer
BJP	Bharatiya Janata Party
BPL	Below Poverty Line
BSP	Bahujan Samaj Party
CAG	Comptroller and Auditor General
CEGC	Central Employment Guarantee Council
CEO	Chief Executive Officer
CM	Chief Minister
CSO	Civil Society Organisation
CII	Confederation of Indian Industry
DC	District Collector/Deputy Commissioner
DMK	Dravida Munnetra Kazhagam
DPC	District Programme Coordinator
EAS	Employment Assurance Scheme
EFMS	Electronic Fund Management System
EGC	Employment Guarantee Council
EGS	Employment Guarantee Scheme
EPW	Economic and Political Weekly
FIRs	First Information Reports
FOIA	Freedom of Information Act
GCKS	Grameen Coolie Karmikara Sangathana
GMS	Grameen Mazdoor Sabha
GoM	Group of Ministers

GRB	Grievance Redressal Bill
IAC	India Against Corruption
IAS	Indian Administrative Service
ICDS	Integrated Child Development Services scheme
ILO	International Labour Organisation
IUML	Indian Union Muslim League
JADS	Jagrut Adivasi Dalit Sangathan
JMM	Jharkhand Mukti Morcha
JNNURM	Jawaharlal Nehru National Urban Renewal Mission
JRY	Jawahar Rozgar Yojana
KC(J)	Kerala Congress (Joseph)
LARRA	Right to Fair Compensation and Transparency in Land Acquisition, Rehabilitation and Resettlement Act
LJP	Lok Janshakti Party
MDMK	Marumalarchi Dravida Munnetra Kazhagam
MIS	Management Information System
MKSS	Mazdoor Kisan Shakti Sangathan
MLA	Member of the (state-level) Legislative Assembly
MP	Member of Parliament
MoRD	Ministry of Rural Development
MTA	Ministry of Tribal Affairs
NAC	National Advisory Council
NCP	Nationalist Congress Party
NCMP	National Common Minimum Programme
NDA	National Democratic Alliance
NEGF	National Employment Guarantee Fund
NFFWP	National Food for Work Programme
NFSA	National Food Security Act
NFSB	National Food Security Bill
NGO	Non-Governmental Organisation
NOMIS	NREGA Online Management Information System
NREGA	National Rural Employment Guarantee Act
NREP	National Rural Employment Programme
NTUI	New Trade Union Initiative
OBCs	Other Backward Classes
PAEG	People's Action for Employment Guarantee
PDP	People's Democratic Party
PDS	Public Distribution System

LIST OF ABBREVIATIONS

PIL	Public Interest Litigation
PMK	Pattali Makkal Katchi
PMO	Prime Minister's Office
PO	Programme Officer
PRIs	Panchayati Raj Institutions
PSC	Parliamentary Standing Committee
PUCL	People's Union for Civil Liberties
PRIA	Participatory Research in Asia
RESKAA	Rozgar Evum Suchana Ka Adhikar Abhiyan
RJD	Rashtriya Janata Dal
RPI(A)	Republican Party of India (Athvale)
RPI(G)	Republican Party of India (Gawai)
RTIA	Right to Information Act
SGRY	Sampoorna Grameen Rozgar Yojana
SCs	Scheduled Castes
STs	Scheduled Tribes
TRS	Telangana Rashtra Samithi
UNDP	United Nations Development Progamme
UPA	United Progressive Alliance

1

INTRODUCTION

India's National Rural Employment Guarantee Act 2005 (NREGA) sought, on a vast scale, to upgrade the country's relatively thin social welfare provision to something more in keeping with its growing economic and political profile.[1] The Act is both revolutionary and modest: it promises every rural household 100 days of employment annually on public works projects, but the labour is physically taxing and paid at the minimum wage.

The employment programmes established under NREGA have reached more people than almost any direct poverty reduction initiative in the developing world. The numbers are staggering. Between 2006, (when NREGA became operational) and early 2012, 251.84 million people participated. By early 2012, the total number of person-days worked was 11.52 billion, and women labourers accounted for roughly half of these.[2] The nearly nine billion dollars spent on NREGA in 2010–11 represented nearly three per cent of the national budget.

Since its inception, NREGA has become a staple of public discussion and political debate in India. The country's lively media frequently report on NREGA, taking particular relish in covering cases of corruption identified in official audits or revealed by civil society activists. The cost and the quality of the works produced by NREGA are frequently commented upon, often based on limited information. Popular protests demanding full implementation of the employment guarantee or increases in NREGA wage rates feature prominently in debates in India's parliament and state legislatures. Politicians and party leaders vie to claim credit for employment opportunities provided under NREGA, or to level blame against state-level ruling parties for failing to deliver on its promise.

Internationally, too, NREGA's merits and shortcomings are a familiar talking point among aid donors, multilateral development agencies, and non-governmental organisations (NGOs), as well as the governments of aid-recipient countries—all of which are on the lookout for new approaches to addressing poverty and economic vulnerability in an era of globalisation. Countless academic seminars and practitioner workshops have been devoted to analysing NREGA's impact, significance, and cost. NREGA is frequently compared to programmes as varied as contemporary Brazil's 'conditional cash transfer' initiative and the New Deal employment programmes that were used in the United States during the 1930s.[3] The degree to which such conversations are informed by an understanding of the actual functioning of NREGA varies considerably.

NREGA's statutory provisions and the regulations framed to govern its operation are exceedingly complex. They are described and analysed in detail in Chapter 2. The subsequent chapters examine how NREGA came into being, how it has operated in practice, and how efforts to reform it have fared. For the present, we confine ourselves to outlining certain key features of NREGA, and to explaining what the politics surrounding this huge, innovative, and important programme reveal about the prospects for using democratic institutions to make the state accountable to poor people. The manner in which NREGA has been conceived, executed, criticised, defended, and reconfigured provides an unparalleled window into the inner workings of Indian politics and the complex character of the Indian state. Poverty, and attempts to combat it, are always political. NREGA is no exception, though the unusual scale of its ambition hardly makes it the rule, either.

The Nature and Significance of NREGA

In describing NREGA, let us begin with its most basic characteristic: it is an Act of parliament, not merely a government programme. Public-sector anti-poverty schemes, of which India has seen many over the decades, can be withdrawn at the discretion of the government of the day, particularly in parliamentary systems such as India's, where the legislature is often unable to effectively check executive power. NREGA has translated the broad concept of an 'employment guarantee' into a series of specific legal entitlements, which amount to justiciable rights, the denial of which can be contested through official proceedings, including in a court of law.

NREGA departs from the predominant pattern, in and beyond India, by being demand-driven. Any person residing in a rural area can apply for work at their local government office, and must be offered employment within fifteen days. If a work assignment is not offered, an unemployment allowance is payable by the state. This model makes the Act's intended beneficiaries—the rural poor—the initiators of the official machinery. Job seekers need not await instruction from government bureaucrats. They start NREGA's fifteen-day clock ticking by staking their claim for employment. In doing so, they are demanding recognition of what has emerged as a limited yet profoundly important 'right to work'.

While NREGA seeks to address poverty, among other objectives, it is not a targeted programme. NREGA is open to any rural resident who, after weighing the opportunity costs, deems minimum wage manual labour an economically worthwhile prospect. Job applicants need not be poor, or from some other 'protected category' of beneficiary, which means they are liberated from the administrative requirements typically found in targeted programmes, such as supplying documentary evidence to prove their eligibility. For the large number of poor people who have been unfairly excluded from earlier anti-poverty initiatives because they were not officially classified as 'below poverty line' (BPL)—either because the criteria were badly designed or the process of applying them was plagued by incompetence, corruption, or both—NREGA's universality is highly welcome. Employment programmes of this type are 'self-targeting', offering payoffs that only people in very straitened circumstances would consider attractive given the low wages and physically demanding nature of the work. The potential 'errors of inclusion' that may result from NREGA's non-targeted model (spreading benefits to the non-poor) are considered by most NREGA supporters worth risking to avoid what they regard as more costly 'errors of exclusion' (denying benefits to those who need them).

The Act delineates not only the general nature of the job guarantee to which rural residents are entitled, but also an unusually specific set of procedural obligations faced by official actors, from the village level all the way up to the Government of India in New Delhi. NREGA requires each state to establish an employment scheme that conforms to minimum standards stipulated in the Act, while recognising the federal division of power under India's constitution by according state governments substantial latitude in designing mechanisms to fulfil the guarantee. The roles and responsibilities of various government entities—and the requirement to create new ones—are spelled out in considerable detail in both the Act and the regulations framed pursuant to it.

Among NREGA's defining features is the set of provisions designed to enhance transparency, combat corruption, and promote accountability. They are more extensive than those found in any comparable 'social protection' initiative anywhere on earth, though their effectiveness is open to question. NREGA's accountability provisions include requirements on various officials to publicise information concerning the operation of the scheme, to make transaction-level financial data publicly available, and to involve local communities in auditing programme functioning and performance. NREGA regulations, which are regularly revised and updated in response to performance assessments, call for the creation and maintenance of a sophisticated information-technology system, with searchable records for every person who seeks employment. The system is designed to record each step in an applicant's engagement with the state machinery: the date of programme registration, applications for employment, details on each day worked, the amount and timing of payments received, and so forth. The electronic data is supposed to match information recorded on each worker's paper 'job card' so that cross-checking can reveal false entries. Additional procedural requirements are intended to enhance transparency. For instance, details of public works projects must be posted in every locality, 'muster rolls' listing the names of workers on any site must be freely accessible, and the reasons for delayed payment of unemployment allowances must be published.

NREGA specifies a crucial role for India's system of elected local government, known as *panchayati raj*. At least half of NREGA funds must be expended on projects designed and implemented by village councils (*gram panchayats*). Elected officials at higher levels of the *panchayati raj* system—that is, at the 'block' (sub-district) and 'district' level—are also assigned specific roles in designing, approving, implementing, and monitoring the works projects on which employment is created. At the base of this system are the public meetings of all local residents of a *gram panchayat*, known as *gram sabhas* (village assemblies), which under NREGA also have specified functions, such as identifying local development priorities and monitoring the management of public works projects. For most parts of India, where grassroots democratic institutions have been severely neglected despite constitutional provisions that recognise them as an integral part of India's political structure, NREGA represents a massive increase in the level of resources to be managed by these bodies and the degree of decision-making authority they are permitted to exercise.

Concepts and Approach

This book does not provide a technical evaluation of NREGA. Many excellent analyses—and some more ill-informed ones too—are available. Instead, we concentrate on political dynamics: the variety of ways in which politics has shaped (and been shaped by) NREGA's legal and programmatic structure, the politics surrounding the process by which the Act came into being, the political factors that have shaped the range of approaches that state governments have taken to implementing it, and political debates that have accompanied efforts to redefine NREGA's purpose and refine its operation. By focusing on politics, it is possible to explain phenomena that otherwise remain obscure or puzzling.

We define 'politics' broadly as the interplay of actors, institutions, and ideas in the pursuit, distribution, and exercise of power. Politics in this sense involves not just matters connected to the state, but also interactions that are not specifically mediated by officials. Each of the terms contained within this conception of politics is open to multiple interpretations. We avoid clinging too closely to one or another definition of these terms, partly because to do so is to exclude the variety of meanings used by the subjects of this study. We are consistent, however, in attempting to make clear when we are employing a particular version.

At the centre of virtually any conception of politics is power, which as Charles Lindblom has argued, can be exercised in at least three ways: through coercion, persuasion, or exchange.[4] Where one draws the line between these three modes of power is often arbitrary. An actor's capacity to arrange deals often entails making an offer that others cannot refuse. The exercise of exchange power, in other words, often shades imperceptibly into coercion, just as one's willingness to be persuaded may require the application of incentives, making the process closer to a commercial transaction (or exchange) than a genuine intellectual conversion. The diverse array of actors examined in this book—official and non-official, individual and collective, elite and ordinary—tend to employ all three forms of power, depending on prevailing circumstances. The shifting repertoire of tactics, and the purposes to which each form of power is employed, are as much of interest as the type and volume of power, which can also be thought of in either relative or absolute terms.

What constitutes an 'institution' is a similarly tricky business. This book, again, adopts a broad definition which encompasses both formal organisations (ostensibly rule-bound entities populated by actors with designated functions and arranged into hierarchies) and informal relationships (in which the behavior of actors is guided, though not determined, by unwritten conventions). It is the interaction between both types of institution—the formal and the informal—that primarily concerns us here, not least because of our focus on politics, in which the exercise of power can tilt the balance between the two.

'Ideas' is another slippery term, particularly when it comes to political speech and action, or when the attractiveness of a particular idea is invoked to explain an observed outcome. Some ideas are defined in precise language. This is true for elements within NREGA statute, for instance. Others, such as freedom or community, are vague, connoting a general spirit and often deriving their potency from their tendency to mean different things depending on who is receiving them. Some ideas rise to the status of an ideology, encapsulating a moral worldview or theory of historical causation. Others are discrete contentions, bound by spatial, temporal, or functional context. When we refer in this book to 'ideas', a term incorporated into our working definition of politics, we generally mean those expressions of belief designed to serve a political purpose—that is, to distribute resources, to shape relations among actors, or to consolidate or reinvent institutional forms.

While political issues have surfaced in some accounts of NREGA, there has been a shortage of systematic political analysis. This book examines political factors that have contributed to NREGA's passage and to certain legislative design features, and analyses the varied political contexts in which NREGA-compliant initiatives have had to operate, with particular attention paid to differences between states and between regions within states. It examines how politics of different kinds—formal and informal, linked to movements and parties, manifested at the grassroots or at the apex of the political system—have affected NREGA's operation and performance, while also identifying the political considerations that are driving (and those that are obstructing) reform to the functioning of NREGA.

The political dynamics underlying NREGA's operation are examined in close detail in two states: Madhya Pradesh and Rajasthan. The research conducted in both states has involved a mapping of the mechanisms through which politics has impinged upon, or been affected by, the conception, enactment, implementation, evaluation, and refinement of NREGA and the employment programmes devised pursuant to it. Not only are these phases disaggregated, the analysis also distinguishes between different levels of the political system—national, state, district, sub-district, and village. Indeed, it is often conflicts between actors operating at different levels of the political system—based on conflicting incentives—that helps to explain why NREGA has worked differently in different places.

Understanding these interactions requires us to examine various forms of politics—for instance, the pursuit of power through formal state institutions and through relatively informal structures such as political parties. The seeking of bureaucratic turf by civil servants is a different form of political activity than the pursuit of electoral advantage by local politicians. While some of the goals might be the same—influence over decision-making, opportunities to skim public funds—there are usually substantial differences in terms of the time horizons adopted, the types of allies pressed into service, and the propensity to be concerned with public opinion.

In this study, we use a broad definition of 'poverty', one focused on human well-being in its widest sense. This is consistent with the intentions of those who conceived of NREGA, though it is always possible to identify differences of emphasis, sequence, and measurement, among other variables. Poverty, in the sense employed in this book, entails not just severe shortages of assets and incomes, but also a debilitating deficiency of opportunities (e.g., to go to school or enjoy good health) and capabilities (e.g., to secure a livelihood or participate in the life of one's community). In other words, our definition is not narrowly economistic or focused on material possessions, but instead includes the political and social dimensions of life. This understanding of poverty and the methods employed to reduce its incidence or severity is in keeping with the concept of human development. While we do not rely on the specific indicators that comprise the United Nations Development Programme's Human Development Index, we do situate the state-level case studies analysed in Chapters 4 and 5 in terms of their relative placement on similar indices.

In the interest of greater specificity, and because our analysis of NREGA is focused on politics, we pay particular attention to one key aspect of poverty—a lack of what has elsewhere been called 'political capacity'. In examining the empirical material, especially the dynamics prevailing in the local contexts where NREGA works take place, we distinguish between four dimensions of citizens' political capacity—that is, their awareness, connections, confidence, and skills. Political awareness refers to the knowledge that people possess concerning their rights, the obligations (and vulnerabilities) of various actors (official and non-official), the way that local political systems and dynamics work, the opportunities available to them, and the existence of competing courses of action. Political connections are the networks of people and institutions on which individuals and collectivities can draw in exchange for favourable treatment, whether in the form of direct benefits or changes to rules or institutions that will confer future advantages. Political confidence is the belief that people have in their own efficacy, which impels them to take risks in seeking to advance their interests in the public sphere. Political skills refers to the ability of people to build alliances that enhance their leverage over official and non-official actors, to calculate the possible payoffs from competing courses of action, and to utilise potentially unexploited (or even undiscovered) assets. Increases in each of these dimensions of political capacity can generate increases in others, though not always, and not necessarily in a linear or (even predictable) fashion.

Main Arguments of the Book

The chapters that follow provide a detailed analysis of how NREGA came into being, the politics of implementation at both state and local levels, the significance of efforts to reform and experiment with NREGA's operational modalities, and the ways in which it has figured in national political debates. Each of these topics involves a large range of subsidiary questions, which it would be premature to summarise here. But as the totality of the analysis is later deployed to support a series of six interconnected arguments concerning the relationship between politics and NREGA, it may be worthwhile to preview these claims before entering into the substantive discussion.

These arguments, spelled out at greater length in Chapter 8 (on 'Implications'), are of three main types, distinguished according to the breadth of their implications. The first, most narrow-gauged set of arguments engages with existing analyses of NREGA that characterise its significance or evaluate its performance. The second set links our analysis of how NREGA has been conceived and implemented—including the marked variations between jurisdictions and over time—to broader debates in the study of Indian politics and political economy. Third, we put forward arguments intended to address longstanding issues of theoretical concern that reach beyond the Indian case—particularly issues that arise in the comparative study of development politics. The book's six main claims—two assigned to each of the three categories outlined above—are summarised below.

Assessing NREGA's Performance

1. *The process of implementing NREGA, for all its faults, has improved the well-being of tens of millions of poor and marginalised people.*

The evidence surveyed in this book, including existing studies and our own mainly qualitative field research, confirms NREGA's positive impact—on a huge scale. NREGA has provided a vital lifeline to people living with persistent economic insecurity. It has done so by providing temporary employment and by increasing the bargaining power of many rural workers. The guarantee of work on demand, however imperfectly realised, is a significant milestone in the development of India's welfare state.

As we shall see, NREGA's shortcomings have led some ideologically inspired critics to argue, perversely, that NREGA actually harmed the poor—whether through hidden inflationary effects, by entrenching a 'dependency culture' among the poor, or by diverting the energies of India's bureaucrats. In fact, poor and marginalised groups, including Scheduled Castes (SCs) and Scheduled Tribes (STs), have gained disproportionately from this programme. While SCs and STs constitute less than a quarter of India's population, they undertook roughly half of the total work days created under NREGA during 2006–12. These are people that social programmes find notoriously hard to reach. Because NREGA is not 'means tested', it does not exclude the large number of poor people who have been unable to obtain the 'below poverty line' cards necessary to prove eligibility for many of India's 'targeted' programmes. We cite evidence to counter the claim that NREGA steered a majority of its benefits to the non-poor, while also noting that participation by the 'nearly poor' may have both salutary economic effects (by providing a form of insurance to people facing livelihood insecurity) and political benefits (by widening the constituency that supports entitlement-based welfare programmes).

Furthermore, we take issue with the claim that NREGA is too expensive, a luxury that India can ill-afford. The central government's buoyant revenues (see Table 8.1) during most of the 2000s meant that additional funds were available for a programme of NREGA's magnitude. And when tax revenue increases began to slow, from roughly 2010, it is not clear why fiscal hawks did not direct their ire at India's elite-oriented 'non-merit' subsidies. Instead, especially during the 2014 general election campaign, NREGA became the poster child of budgetary profligacy. This reflected prevailing ideological currents in India as much as an attempt to apply sound principles of public finance.

2. *NREGA's political aims and implications must be recognised in order to appreciate its significance as a development initiative.*

To arrive at a more accurate assessment of NREGA's performance, and to comprehend its larger significance as a human development intervention, one must grasp NREGA's essentially political nature. As one commentator observed: 'the politics of entitlement', under programmes like NREGA, 'becomes important not just as legislative rights which can be enforced and justiciable, but as a participative political process.'[5] In short, NREGA is part of an activist political agenda, rooted in a particular model of political change—one based on a commitment to progressive legal reform coupled with an ongoing pursuit of what one of NREGA's architects has called 'democratic struggle'.[6] NREGA's political implications in this respect are sufficiently far-reaching and radical to qualify it as an 'audacious reform', to use Grindle's term.[7] In approach, then, as well as with respect to many of our findings, this book adopts a perspective that is broadly consistent with the 'empowerment framework' found in Shankar and Gaiha's impressively careful study of NREGA implementation.[8]

NREGA gave all rural households the right to demand work, and tens of millions of people did so. This often resulted in at least some daily wage employment—for many people, more positive attention than they had ever received from the state, whose officials have widely been perceived as predatory. NREGA also explicitly sought to give poor people a voice in setting local development priorities and in the participatory public auditing of the works projects undertaken. Though they are supposed to facilitate public auditing of the *panchayat's* expenditures, local leaders are typically very reluctant to share information or expose themselves to anything that might resemble a cross-examination.[9] Village officials routinely submit false reports documenting fictitious public hearings to satisfy NREGA-imposed 'transparency' requirements. This leaves it to the highly corrupt cadre of state auditors to, in effect, audit the conduct of NREGA 'social audits', which is to say spot check local government activity reports to see whether public meetings listed in *panchayat* records actually took place. Of course, state auditors usually have no incentive to do anything of the sort, especially when not doing so is considered likely to result in professional advancement and personal enrichment. NREGA's architects were well aware that social audits and other transparency mechanisms built into the programme would work only imperfectly. Indeed, few Indians were better aware than the activists who conceived of NREGA of the array of deceptions, delays, and evasions that powerful actors at the local and district level engage in to ensure that such programmes serve their interests (some of these mechanisms are discussed in detail in Chapter 3). Still, NREGA's framers expected, or at least hoped, that the fiscal decentralisation aspect of NREGA—more money in the hands of local authorities—would make accounting irregularities and attempts by *panchayat* officials and middlemen to steal from workers' wages much more visible to poor villagers. The intention was to provide institutional means to channel the ensuing discontent into a process of continuous democratic struggle.

This may have been overly ambitious. But it did have unusual effects, many of which are discussed in Chapter 6, on NREGA's non-material impacts. For instance, NREGA labourers often had to visit work sites located away from their often caste- or community-segregated neighborhoods. They worked alongside people from different communities. In a number of documented instances, some of which we report on, NREGA workers from across ethnic divides discovered certain affinities. New perspectives, if not immediately meaningful relationships, could be formed. For members of other social categories, simply emerging from the domestic into the public sphere was a significant political step. Women have accounted for almost half of all NREGA person-days worked—and in some states well above this level. Many women found themselves, for the first time in their lives, participating in public activities unaccompanied by male relatives. They were holders of 'government jobs', however temporary. Many women held onto their wages, and kept in their possession the job card that could earn them more. Some studies have found that women NREGA workers fared better under women *sarpanches*, just as SCs and STs did under *sarpanches* elected through reservations.[10]

Critics who have argued that cash transfers should replace NREGA misperceive the initiative's political intent, which is to catalyse a kind of state-society chain reaction in which a government programme of this type, born of a popular movement, expands the constituency for social change and inculcates an orientation towards challenging government non-performance. Unfortunately, the most implacable of NREGA's critics tend to operate with a narrowly economistic definition of 'poverty'—as a severe shortage of incomes and assets—rather than the more encompassing definition outlined earlier in this chapter. NREGA does more than merely provide funds to poor people; it also targets other, political dimensions of poverty. Commentators who cast NREGA as 'only a subsidy'[11]—let us grant, for the moment, that despite being a wage, there is a subsidy dimension to payments made to NREGA workers—fail to grasp that the programme had other objectives beyond increased purchasing power: devolving substantial administrative decision-making, and collective oversight (however flawed), to elected local councils, and building collective solidarity among similarly situated—which is to say chronically underemployed—agricultural workers. All this was premised on the notion that non-performance under NREGA would trigger discontent and facilitate active claim-making against the state by a non-elite section of society constituted by NREGA workers, as well as by local residents who may demand action to improve the quality of public works created under NREGA, especially when poor workmanship or low-grade materials is reasonably thought to have resulted from corruption by *panchayat* officials. The intention to provide avenues for collective complaint among NREGA workers contrasts sharply with the political dynamic underlying cash transfer schemes, in which 'beneficiaries' are treated as passive, isolated, individual 'welfare recipients'. NREGA aimed squarely at enhancing workers' political awareness, confidence, skills and connections—in short, their 'political capacity'. Cash transfers have less of an impact on these fronts. If instituted in India, such schemes should supplement, not substitute for, NREGA.[12]

Debates Regarding India's Political Economy

Our next two claims connect aspects of the NREGA experience with important debates in the study of Indian politics and political economy.

3. *While the Indian state's porousness provides privileged access to business organisations and socially powerful constituencies, it also offers openings for voices seeking to effect progressive social change in the interests of non-elite groups.*

How to characterise the nature of the state—as weak, overdeveloped, predatory, developmental—is a longstanding question in the study of Indian political economy. NREGA offers a useful vantage point from which to assess the degree to which the Indian state can, under certain conditions, act with relative autonomy vis-à-vis dominant social forces. In this case, autonomy translates into the capacity of public authorities to pursue crucial human development goals in the face of opposition from powerful political constituencies. This capacity of the Indian state to override direct pressure from influential actors has usually been seen as extremely low.

The Indian state has in fact usually been described as a hybrid of sorts—as a 'weak-strong state',[13] for instance, where 'demand politics' and 'command politics' remain in unsteady equiliribum. Other writers have seen India's state as founded on a configuration of class interests that constituted an 'intermediate regime'.[14] More recently, however, the Indian state has been described in rather stark, all-or-nothing terms—as controlled by powerful interests, impervious to fundamental change, or aligned with a particular vision of the world. Some recent characterisations have cast the Indian state as all but captured by big business and in the thrall of a neo-liberal vision of development.[15] Atul Kohli goes so far as to say that a 'state-business ruling alliance' has been constructed.[16] The influence exerted by business groups is indeed a cause for concern, but the degree to which the state has forfeited its autonomy of action has been overstated. Would a government so completely dominated by a nexus of social elites and business interests have adopted the rights-based paradigm underlying NREGA? Highly unlikely. Indeed, the way NREGA came into being demonstrated that infiltrating government institutions to steer policymaking in a preferred direction has not been the sole preserve of elite interests. The 'porousness' of the Indian state can provide social activist constituencies, working with and on behalf of decidedly non-elite groups, the ability to shape important dimensions of the country's development paradigm. During the UPA government, key target institutions for this sustained effort to become 'institutionally embedded' included the National Advisory Council and the Planning Commission. The state's permeable membranes offered a 'political opportunity structure' that permitted civic organisations and other visible public actors to advance counter-hegemonic agendas. The demonstrated viability of this strategy has led other groups fighting for social justice to pursue similar efforts at infiltrating policymaking and implementation processes at the state level. For example, movement activists became deeply intertwined with the rural development bureaucracy in Andhra Pradesh during the period of Congress rule in the state (2004–14), as they assisted in devising and operating a NREGA monitoring system for the state.

Does all this imply that India has become—or is on the verge of becoming—a European-style 'welfare state'? Certainly not. Nor does it imply that India's capitalists have been politically neutered. But NREGA and other initiatives that have succeeded in making both growth and governance more 'inclusive' have created significant opportunities for poor people and their allies to make an impact within state structures—an important achievement that deserves to be built upon rather than abandoned as unrealistically ambitious.

4. *Various aspects of NREGA implementation—including efforts to make officials more accountable to poor and marginalised people—have demonstra-*

ted the complex process through which 'clientelist' politics in India is being transformed rather than eliminated.

Over the past decade, a lively debate has emerged over the extent to which India may have transitioned from 'clientelist' politics (in which government benefits are distributed to the supporters of a particular candidate, faction, or party) to 'programmatic' politics (in which political backing is driven not by anticipation of partial treatment by those who assume government office, but by the perceived wisdom and impacts of a party's policy positions and overall governance performance). The ambiguous context makes any such assessment hazardous: despite three decades of economic liberalisation, which is supposed to shrink the state's role in the economy, government decision-makers retain great discretion over many aspects of economic policy, including the implementation of social welfare programmes, which have grown and multiplied over the past fifteen years. The transparency and accountability mechanisms contained within NREGA were meant to undermine, to the highest degree possible, bureaucratic discretion in the selection of wage-earners, and to disincentivise corruption by making illegality more apparent to local communities and bureaucratic managers at various levels of the administrative hierarchy, all of whom would be empowered to take remedial action.

Though NREGA's architects did not expect an immediate end to the long-standing practice in India of political interference by patrons and the siphoning of workers' wages in jobs programmes—and, as we shall see, they were not proved wrong—there was a strong belief among the programme's early advocates that NREGA represented an important step in India's long journey toward post-clientelist politics—a system in which a government's performance in delivering impartially on the ruling party's stated objectives, and ensuring more effective mechanisms to hold appointed officials accountable, would increasingly influence its political fortunes. Key post-clientelist features of NREGA included its mechanisms for tracking the actions of individual officials—for instance, through the web-enabled Management Information System (MIS) designed for NREGA. In many places, the kind of brazen theft of workers' wages that had characterised precursor employment schemes became much rarer. Moreover, people's gradual awareness of the theoretical 'guarantee' of wage employment increased the need for politicians at the state level to be seen to be implementing the programme in a credible fashion. The networks of information that NREGA workers entered as a result of involvement in the programme made them aware of the key role played by state governments in determining whether NREGA was run relatively efficiently or whether it was operated purely for the benefit of local intermediaries, on whom parties sometimes rely to broker the delivery of votes at election time.

Recognising this degree of exposure, ruling-party leaders in several states—including Madhya Pradesh and Rajasthan, the two case-study states for this book—engaged in the practice of identifying a small number of districts (which we call 'worst case' districts) where systematic looting of NREGA could take place without endangering the party's electoral fortunes. Because this process was guided from the apex of each state's political system, it helped to swell the corpus of illicit funds available to party leaders—funds that could be used to buy the support of MLAs and other political actors. This form of patron-client politics, focused on relations between members of the political elite at different levels of the system rather than on exchanges directly with (often ethnically defined) voters, is an example of how clientelist politics was being transformed rather than eliminated.[17] Senior politicians have increasingly introduced post-clientelist programmes because they recognise that the distribution of patronage is insufficient to win re-election. They must supplement clientelism with programmatic initiatives that are at least somewhat shielded from local bosses (something increasingly found in 'best case' districts)—bosses who face strong incentives to overgraze the commons of patronage-based spending.

Implications Beyond the Indian Case

The third pair of arguments advanced in this book contributes to debates beyond India, particularly with respect to theory-building derived from the comparative study of development politics.

5. *NREGA is emblematic of a new category of rights, pioneered in India over the past decade—a category we term 'governance rights', characterised chiefly by their hybridity, both in terms of what is being guaranteed and how guarantees can be enforced.*

NREGA was the flagship in a flotilla of initiatives that represented a fundamental transformation in the nature of rights-based approaches to development in India, including (1) the Forest Rights Act (2006),[18] which accords traditional forest-dwellers conditional title to certain forest lands and rights to use forest products; and (2) the Right to Education Act (2010),[19] which entitles all children—aged fourten and under—the right to attend school, which under the statute was also made compulsory.

Three distinctive features of NREGA are significant in this context. First, it specifies a non-means-tested entitlement to advance a particular aspect of human well-being. Second, the Act requires the creation of special-purpose institutions to ensure that state commitments are fulfilled. Third, NREGA includes a range of mechanisms through which ordinary people and their associations can engage directly in the process of holding the officials who implement the act accountable for their actions and omissions. Taken together, these and other provisions amount to a novel hybrid of two categories of rights that are typically treated in isolation from one another: social and economic rights, and civil and political rights. The way in which NREGA has been conceived recognises that while these two categories may be theoretically distinct, in practice they are inseparable. To fulfil social and economic rights—such as the right to a decent livelihood—requires not just the general legal protections associated with liberal democracy, but institutional arrangements that permit—indeed encourage—citizens to participate in the procedures through which state programmes operate. The right to engage directly in mechanisms through which officials are held accountable for their performance in delivering programme entitlements represents a hybrid category that we call 'governance rights'.

This book makes the case that the conception of rights found in NREGA constitutes, in essence, the right to participate in purpose-built governance institutions to ensure the delivery of particular benefits essential to the fulfilment of basic social and economic rights. As manifestations of hybridity, governance rights are distinguished from civil and political rights in that they are not about choosing representatives, forming associations, or engaging in political speech. Instead, governance rights confer on citizens the right to engage directly in processes intended to ensure direct accountability of officials tasked with delivering on state 'guarantees'—mainly by making officials publicly answerable and legally sanctionable in ways that go beyond the delegated model found in most representative democracies.

While civil society is assigned a key role in realising the potential of rights-based initiatives such as NREGA, not every type of civic association is equally effective. Conventional advocacy, awareness-raising, or service-delivery NGOs rarely adopt the strategies or take the risks necessary to improve NREGA performance. As our field studies in Rajasthan and Madhya Pradesh have revealed, organisations that adopted a more overtly political stance—challenging local constellations of power through a constantly evolving repertoire of techniques—have been far more effective. Much of this success stemmed from the hybrid nature of these groups themselves: they combined efforts to mobilise people on the margins of society with a focus on concrete developmental activities—what Gandhians call 'constructive work'.

Our sixth, and final, argument also addresses a key theme in the international literature on development politics:

6. *The NREGA-prompted devolution of resources to elected local councils made* gram panchayats, *despite their shortcomings, a site where poorer people's demands for accountability were legitimated—a process aided in some states (e.g. Rajasthan) by particularly well-positioned civil society organisations and in others by committed, capable state bureaucracies (e.g. Tamil Nadu).*

NREGA represents the most significant injection of funds into elected local bodies in post-independence India. The Act requires at least half of programme funds to be channelled through local councils, and a few state governments have placed closer to 90 per cent under the (qualified, partial) control of *panchayats*.[20] The existence of corruption under NREGA at the district level and below has prompted, among other things, a renewed willingness among political analysts and development practitioners to dismiss the potential of *panchayats* as an instrument for empowering the poor and, ultimately, increasing government accountability to non-elites in a quasi-post-clientelist political environment.

There are at least two important reasons why such an easy dismissal of the NREGA experience is unwise. First, much of the corruption that accompanied the NREGA's implementation stemmed not from decentralisation as such, but from the incomplete form of decentralisation pursued. What was missing, at least in part, was sufficient devolution of authority to permit elected leaders to check the power of field-level bureaucrats over crucial steps in NREGA implementation process. Without this authority, even well-intentioned local leaders, including those competing for poor peoples' votes, had to skim from the programme to bribe bureaucrats to deliver the clearances required to keep works projects, and wage payments, moving through the administrative labyrinth. One crucial reason why this institutional imbalance (*de jure* devolution of political power, but *de facto* subordination of local elected officials to bureaucratic authority) was less damaging to NREGA than it might have been stems, again, from the political dynamics at work in much of rural India. Of particular significance are the incentives created by patterns

17

of partisan competition at the state level. Because state-level parties seek to draw electorally successful local faction bosses into their spheres of influence, more sophisticated *gram panchayat* leaders can exert considerable leverage in their battles with local and block-level officialdom. An MLA (a Member of the state-level Legislative Assembly) with whom a *sarpanch* (the local *panchayat* head) has joined forces has, at the very least, the ability to threaten a recalcitrant Block Development Officer (BDO) with a transfer to a grim job in an undesirable duty station, unless the BDO goes easy on the *sarpanch* who has called in this favour. This informal override mechanism helps to counteract the effects of incomplete decentralisation.

A second reason to reassess the received wisdom about decentralisation and elite capture concerns the *nature* of corruption under NREGA, which has in many localities been sufficiently visible to galvanise poor people to join in protest action. Our direct field observations in Madhya Pradesh and Rajasthan suggest that while many types of corruption have afflicted NREGA projects, the transparency and accountability mechanisms built into NREGA can deter the most brazen forms of corruption. In many places, the procedural requirements that NREGA imposed on local government institutions facilitated the asking of uncomfortable questions by workers and other people affected by corruption. Even when the answers from officials and political representatives were unconvincing, the culture of questioning began, in some places, to take hold.[21] Moreover, to misappropriate funds, NREGA guidelines (for instance, on wage payments through individual bank accounts) often required officials to enlist the reluctant collusion of workers. Corrupt officials could not rely on the traditional mechanism of invisible skimming, which can take place unilaterally.

Moreover, researchers in a broad cross-section of localities across India and in other countries have found that if elected local councils are allowed to function over extended periods, they can improve human development. Evidence has emerged from several studies that, over time, poor people grasp the opportunities that competitive *panchayat* politics offers. This means applying pressure on candidates in local elections to deliver concrete benefits—through NREGA and other programmes—rather than empty promises. Even leaders from elite social backgrounds are often forced to compete for the (usually abundant) votes of the poor, and to recognise that they are accountable to such people between elections as well.[22]

Project Scope and Research Process

This book was researched and written over the course of six years—from early 2008 through early 2014. Each of the authors brought to the research process wide-ranging experience in the study of Indian politics and political economy, including earlier work on anti-corruption movements, anti-poverty initiatives, rights-based approaches to development, regional politics, electoral analysis, the political economy of policy change, the functioning of political parties, and democratic decentralisation. All of these proved relevant to the issues addressed in this book.

The research entailed quantitative survey-based methods and qualitative investigations (both in the surveyed localities and beyond). The field surveys were carried out mainly in late 2008 and early 2009, with some additional surveys carried out later in 2009 and early 2010. Interviews with key informants continued during several subsequent visits to India. In addition to our own survey results, we obtained quantitative data from a wide range of government sources, including the government offices charged with compiling NREGA statistics at the state and national levels. We have also benefitted from numerous quantitative studies conducted by academics, policy analysts, and government entities such as India's Planning Commission and its comptroller and auditor general.

Much of the research focused on the mechanics of NREGA's operation, and how this has interacted with various manifestations of politics, in two states: Madhya Pradesh and Rajasthan. The political and developmental context in each state is provided in early sections of both Chapter 4 (Rajasthan) and Chapter 5 (Madhya Pradesh). It is worth noting that the two states are sufficiently similar to make the remaining differences between them—particularly those related to political conditions—potentially powerful explanatory variables. The two states resemble one another in terms of geographic location (they are both predominantly Hindi-speaking states in north India), size (the second and third largest states in terms of area), and economic profile (relatively low levels of industrialisation and per capita income). Both also have sizable tribal populations.

Beyond these family resemblances are a range of historical and political similarities. Both are close to Delhi, and the power dynamics emanating therefrom. Before independence, each state had much of its territory located in princely India—almost all of it in Rajasthan, hence the state's name, 'land of the Rajas'. Both states possessed a tradition of pursuing, at times, innovative anti-poverty schemes. Both states are essentially two-party systems, dominated by India's two main national parties: the Indian National Congress and the Bharatiya Janata Party (BJP). Both were ruled by the BJP during the first three years of NREGA's existence (from 2005 through 2008). A crucial difference emerged following state elections held in December 2008: in Rajasthan, the BJP lost power to the Congress, while in Madhya Pradesh the BJP was re-elected. This divergence of electoral outcomes enabled us to highlight, where relevant, the extent to which post-2008 differences between the ruling parties influenced the approach to NREGA by each of the state governments concerned. Ruling party alternation in Rajasthan allowed a comparison between the two parties within the context of a single state.

The two states were also selected because they represented similar yet distinct different points along the spectrum from success to failure in terms of the operation and impacts of NREGA. Rajasthan is certainly among the better performers in terms of the proportion of households participating in the programme, the proportion of women among NREGA workers, and to some degree, the extent to which the state's government and its civil society activists have sought to experiment with new ways of implementing NREGA. On most of these measures, Madhya Pradesh falls somewhere near the middle of the league table—and in some respects in the lower reaches. Both states contained considerable variation within their boundaries, containing extremely poorly performing districts (and blocks within districts) as well as some in which results were particularly impressive. As we have indicated, this book is not designed to evaluate NREGA's overall effects, or to highlight variables accounting for minutely observable differences in impact. But basing much of the direct empirical analysis on field investigations in two states that are marked by these similarities and differences opened up many avenues of inquiry that otherwise would not have been possible to explore.

During the field investigations in these two states, which were aided by support from the Institute of Development Studies, Jaipur, and the Samarthan organisation in Bhopal, we interviewed actors at all levels of the political system. This included social elites and middle-income, as well as poor, and in some cases very poor, people. Most had worked on NREGA projects. We also engaged with analyses from other states, with colleagues who had produced them, and with key policy actors from several states as well as those operating in New Delhi. We made field visits and intensively reviewed literature on four additional states: Andhra Pradesh, where an alternative approach to NREGA was a helpful contrast to our two primary case-study states; Karnataka where NREGA was never pushed by the state government to the degree found in most other states; Bihar, where NREGA was embraced by a reform-minded chief minister who saw its political potential, but could not be effectively implemented due to bureaucratic pathologies inherited from his predecessor; and Tamil Nadu, where NREGA accountability functioned mainly through the state bureaucracy rather than through participatory forums such as public hearings.

Sustained, if not intensive, attention to developments in these states also allowed our research to expand in geographic scope, from north India to India's south and east, and to examine states governed by regional parties rather than the two national parties (Congress and the BJP) that dominate politics in Rajasthan and Madhya Pradesh. Covering a broad range of state contexts also permitted us to examine the many different types of politics outlined earlier in this chapter, and to do so at multiple levels of the political system. At the national level, we consider the role of the United Progressive Alliance (UPA), the coalition government led by the Congress Party, which was elected in 2004, introduced a NREG Bill the same year, and passed NREGA in 2005. We examine the UPA's political inheritance; its leaders' calculations about the political utility and the financial feasibility of NREGA; the inclusion of civil society leaders in the National Advisory Council (NAC), the policy-development body that largely designed NREGA; and the complex process of passing the Act, including the role of parliamentary actors. This analysis is set forth in Chapter 2.

In examining responses to NREGA, we examine states governed by parties allied with the ruling UPA in New Delhi, and states governed by the UPA's opponents. State governments had to decide how (and how energetically) to implement NREGA; what regulations and processes to set in place; what elements of the programme to stress or de-emphasise; and how to respond to evidence of, and political reactions to, patterns of implementation. They had to consider how (and indeed whether) to foster awareness of NREGA's details among poor people, and what precisely to make them aware of; how assiduously to implement transparency mechanisms such as social audits; how much to draw civil society organisations into these processes; and what types of civil society organisations to work with. They also had to decide how NREGA funds would be divided between elected local councils (to achieve some bottom-up input) and line ministries (which tended to pursue top-down initiatives with far less transparency than local councils), and the degree to which (and where) NREGA should be 'milked' to enrich party coffers and satisfy political allies.

Within states, we encountered variations from district to district in the implementation of the programme. As indicated in our discussion of post-clientelism above, NREGA was well administered in a few districts ('best case' districts), while being systematically squeezed for illicit funds in others ('worst case' districts). Most districts were 'ambiguous' cases. Upon closer inspection, this pattern turned out to be the result of political calculations made at the state level. Variations among districts were more marked than at the next level down the administrative hierarchy—that is, between two or more 'blocks' within a district. Still, in several cases, contrasts even between blocks were far from trivial. Again, political dynamics largely explained this. Within any given district, some blocks might contain especially impoverished groups with very limited political capacity, while others contained residents who were better able to negotiate effectively with government actors involved in administering NREGA. Some blocks contained formidable chairpersons of elected local councils, while others lacked them. As noted above, some blocks were endowed with dynamic civil society organisations, while others sorely lacked such groups. All of these factors affected political dynamics within blocks and thus the workings of NREGA.

* * *

The remainder of the book is organised as follows. Chapter 2 outlines NREGA's most significant provisions, and analyses the political dynamics surrounding the Act's formulation and eventual passage. Chapter 3 unpacks the processes through which NREGA affects (and is affected by) 'local' politics, including the relations between the multiple levels of bureaucratic and elected officialdom that exist in rural India. State-level variations in the politics of NREGA implementation are the focus of Chapters 4 and 5, which look at our two primary case study regions, Rajasthan and Madhya Pradesh. Drawing on the findings of these field studies, as well as evidence produced by many other researchers and journalists, Chapter 6 examines the complex mechanisms through which NREGA's material and non-material impacts have strengthened the political capacity of poor and marginalised people, including women. Chapter 7 analyses the national political debates that have accompanied NREGA's implementation and efforts at the state and national level to revise and update the regulations that govern its operation. Chapter 8 discusses the implications of our analysis of NREGA's political dynamics—at the national, state, and local levels—for three kinds of debates: those concerning NREGA's impact and significance; longstanding disputes over the political economy of the Indian state; and the relevance of India's experience to issues arising in the comparative study of development politics.

* * *

This chapter has provided an overview of the book's analytical focus, conceptual approach, main arguments, and research process. It indicates that the story that we tell here is shot through with ambiguities and seeming contradictions. This is nothing new in the study of Indian politics. Deep investigations of contemporary India have long carried titles such as *The Indian Paradox*, *The Modernity of Tradition*, and *Poverty Amid Plenty*.[23] Our analysis, likewise, carries us deep into a world of startling dissonances. We have uncovered fundamentally important features of the state—some inspiring, others deeply depressing—that sit uncomfortably alongside one another. Our evidence concerning NREGA and the struggle that characterised its emergence and implementation does not suggest that the tension between the multiple dichotomies we uncovered will be settled anytime soon. In India, as elsewhere, incongruous hybrids often endure. Encounters between theses and antitheses often fail to resolve themselves into tidy syntheses.

2

ACT OF CREATION

THE CONTENT AND ORIGINS OF NREGA

In the process of introducing the book's analytical focus and central contentions, the previous chapter briefly identified certain key features of NREGA. The purpose was to highlight elements of NREGA that have shaped (or been shaped by) political actors and processes. We turn now to a closer examination of specific provisions found in the Act. Our aim is not to be comprehensive. Indeed, our preoccupation with the rights-based character of NREGA probably causes us to neglect many of its other legislative features.

The analysis of the legal and regulatory provisions (the Act's content) is followed by an examination of how NREGA came into being (its origins). The focus, again, is on the politics underlying this process. We do not explore, let alone definitively explain, the emergence of each of the Act's many provisions. Instead, we stress the importance of India's precursor employment programmes and various movements that have demanded that they operate more accountably. We also assess aspects of NREGA that became matters of intense debate—whether in committee rooms, on the floor of parliament, or in the media and public demonstrations. It is striking that each of these contested provisions would subsequently, in some form or other, play a role in the political battles surrounding NREGA's implementation, as we will see in Chapter 7, on national policy debates.

The Structure and Sinew of NREGA

NREGA passed into law on 5 September 2005 when it received the assent of the President of India.[1] It had passed in parliament the month before. It is a complex piece of legislation containing six Chapters, each consisting of numerous sections, sub-sections, and qualifying stipulations. The Act also contains two Schedules that, respectively, specify the 'Minimum Features of a Rural Employment Guarantee Scheme' (Schedule I), and set forth the 'Conditions for Guaranteed Rural Employment under a Scheme and Minimum Entitlements of Labourers' (Schedule II).[2]

NREGA's initial architects, and the many actors who subsequently contributed to its construction, sought to leave as little room for ambiguity as possible in specifying what the employment guarantee would actually consist of in practice. (Their attention to detail explains why this Act was, despite some disappointments, much more successful than the Forest Rights Act (FRA), which was passed into law the same year. The FRA has suffered severely from crippling ambiguities and imprecise wording.) Part of their agenda was to devolve as much decision-making authority as possible to local elected bodies. Unlike earlier generations of social-protection legislation in India and elsewhere, the granting of what amounted to a 'right to work' was accompanied by painstakingly detailed provisions relating to the scope of the entitlement, the methods by which it would be fulfilled, the techno-economic requirements for works projects, the administrative procedures to be followed, and much else besides. All this specificity reflected a determination to see NREGA succeed where so many earlier experiments had run aground. Activists pressing for a strong regime of accountability within NREGA knew that this was essential to the programme's chances of achieving even a moderate level of success.

While the key purposes of the Act were outlined in the previous chapter, here we draw attention to selected elements of the legislation specifically designed to ensure that these objectives were realised. The text contains many seemingly minor provisions that, as we will see in the second part of this chapter, were fiercely contested when the NREG Bill was being debated in parliament and the press.[3] For instance, NREGA specifies the multi-stage process by which the scheme would be rolled out across the entire country. It would begin with an assortment of 200 (particularly underprivileged) districts, but the entire country would be covered within five years of its enactment. The laborious negotiations that went into the wording of this provision are not reflected in the seeming simplicity of the statement. Nor were these evident at first glance in the provision limiting the Act to employment only in rural areas. This limitation is built into the Act's name, of course. But it is somehow only once the restriction is articulated—that is, that guaranteed employment would not be provided to people living in 'areas covered by any urban local body or a Cantonment Board'—that the sense of an unfinished agenda is conveyed.[4]

The mirror image of this phenomenon was also in evidence: provisions that one might have expected to attract political controversy, such as quotas for certain groups, were adopted without fanfare and consumed very little of the negotiators' time. Schedule II, Section 6 stipulates that at least one-third of NREGA beneficiaries must be women. This provision helpfully provides a 'floor', which creates an incentive for outreach to women by programme implementers at state, district, block, and village levels. This type of proactive provision was missing from earlier employment-generation schemes. Schedule II, Section 34 requires women and men to receive the same wage, again something that is counter-cultural to say the least. This wage-parity principle, encoded into the portion of the statute that sets out guidelines for the creation of federally mandated programmes at the state level, has incentivised women to participate in NREGA works. Wage parity was a very welcome development in places where agricultural wage rates were known to be especially discriminatory to women. Particularly egregious cases could be found, for instance, in parts of Kerala[5] and Tamil Nadu.[6] The nationwide increase in women's participation under NREGA compared with prior employment schemes is, in large measure, a reflection of these rules, which were wisely embedded in the legislation itself rather than in the subsequently framed regulations (which can be more easily amended).

The Nature of the Guarantee

The centrepiece of the Act was the guarantee of paid work. But there is a federal dimension to this foundational premise. Section 3(1) stipulates that state governments would be the duty-holders in this rights-fulfilment model. States were required, annually, to 'provide to every household whose adult members volunteer to do unskilled manual work not less than one hundred days of such work'. Workers are to be paid minimum wage—that is, 'the minimum wage fixed by the State Government under section 3 of the Minimum Wages Act, 1948 for agricultural labourers'.[7] There was an additional provision—6(1)—indicating that the central government could specify a separate wage rate for the purposes of the Act, as long as it was not less than Rs 60 per day. Wages were to be paid within fourteen days of when the work was carried out.[8]

Crucially, the entitlement included not just a specification of benefits and eligibility, but also the division of responsibilities among actors and a time-bound procedure through which they would make good on the state's promise. A prospective beneficiary was to 'apply' for work at a designated government office, and if employment was not provided 'within fifteen days of receipt of his application', the applicant would be 'entitled to a daily unemployment allowance'.[9] States were allowed to set this rate, and even to set 'terms and conditions of eligibility', as long as they were consistent with the Act, but these could not be less than one-fourth of the regular NREGA 'wage rate' for the first thirty days of the financial year, and no less than one-half of the wage rate for the remainder of the year.[10] This unemployment allowance would be payable until the applicant or another household member was offered work, or until 100 days of work had been supplied (or the equivalent amount of wages had been paid in unemployment allowance).[11] It would be up to state governments to specify the procedures for paying the allowance and to designate which local authority would authorise the payments. Whatever its arrangements, each state government would ultimately be responsible for ensuring that every eligible allowance was issued within 'fifteen days from the date on which it became due for payment'.[12] Section 8(1) states that if a Programme Officer (PO) cannot disburse the required unemployment allowance to a job applicant, the PO is not only required to notify the District Programme Coordinator, but also to specify in writing the reasons for non-payment 'in a notice on his notice board and the notice board of the *Gram Panchayat* [elected local council]'. Every case of non-payment or delayed payment of unemployment allowances was also to be included (along with specific reasons) in 'the annual report submitted by the District Programme Coordinator to the State Government'.[13] Cases of non-payment (or underpayment) at the local level would then become the responsibility of the state government.[14]

Chapter III of NREGA gave each state six months to establish a 'Scheme'— a duly constituted government programme—under which the 100-day guarantee would be fulfilled. Until such a scheme was put in place, two existing central government-funded employment programmes—the Sampoorna Grameen Rozgar Yojana (SGRY) and the National Food for Work Programme (NFFWP)—would be used to meet the requirements of the Act. State-level employment schemes constituted to comply with NREGA would need to adopt the transparency provisions found in the Act. In particular, state governments would need to devise administrative mechanisms for sharing the project information to which workers (and all other scheme stakeholders, for that matter) are supposed to have access.

Dedicated Structures

One of NREGA's distinguishing features as a mechanism for fulfilling economic rights is the specialised implementation and oversight apparatus stipulated in the Act. Among the bodies NREGA instructed the government to create was a Central Employment Guarantee Council (CEGC). The CEGC, whose members are appointed by the central government, must include Government of India officials at the level of Joint Secretary and above, and 'representatives of the State Governments'. The Council would also include up to fifteen 'non-official' representatives—a category that included both elected members of local bodies and non-governmental organisations 'representing workers and disadvantaged groups'. Two of these non-official members were to be elected Chairs of district-level local bodies.[15] The proportional balance between officials and non-officials was not specified. It was left to elected officials in the central government to determine the extent to which they might wish the CEGC to consist of senior civil servants over whom the elected officials have supervisory authority. But this is a rare lapse, and (again) the result of some of the hard bargaining over the NREG Bill that will be discussed later in this chapter. Even regarding the CEGC, NREGA's degree of specificity—concerning membership, rank, and route of appointment—is notable. Typically, legislative initiatives regarding rural development are more oriented toward the larger framework, leaving it to the bureaucracy to decide how it wants to organise itself for whatever executive tasks the legislature has assigned it.

The powers given to the CEGC were wide-ranging but potentially difficult to exercise. It could establish an 'evaluation and monitoring scheme', 'recommend improvements' to NREGA's 'monitoring and redressal mechanism', 'promote the widest possible dissemination of information' about employment schemes created pursuant to the Act, and prepare 'annual reports to be laid before Parliament' concerning the Act's implementation.[16] The CEGC was also permitted (but not required) to 'undertake evaluation' of the various schemes created under NREGA, and to 'collect or cause to be collected statistics pertaining to the rural economy and the implementation of the Schemes'.[17]

A similar employment council was to be established within each state.[18] Each state government would be free to decide what proportion of its state-level employment council should come from the bureaucracy over which this body is designed to exercise oversight. The number of non-official members was capped at fifteen. For both the CEGC and the state EGCs, the Act required that at least one-third of the non-official members be women, and one-third be members of the Scheduled Castes (SCs), Scheduled Tribes (STs), Other Backward Classes (OBCs), or religious minorities. The functions of the state EGCs were also similar to those conferred upon the CEGC: advising the state government concerned, monitoring the operation of grievance-redress mechanisms, promoting information-dissemination about the Act and relevant schemes, and preparing an annual report for the state legislature. State-level councils were expected to 'coordinate' with the CEGC to ensure that implementation did not suffer from conflicting directives or duplicative procedures. State EGCs were also expected to consult with the central Council in order to decide which kinds of works projects would receive 'preferred' status.[19]

The Act also directed the government to establish a National Employment Guarantee Fund (NEGF).[20] Appropriations passed by parliament would be lodged in the NEGF, and it would be up to the central government to determine, within the rules set forth in the Act, how such funds could be expended. States would be permitted, but not required, to establish similar funds, and could likewise impose stipulations on the use of such resources. However, NREGA stipulated that these funds could be used 'for meeting the administrative expenses in connection with the implementation of this Act'.[21] This was an important means of providing additional, relatively untied, funds to state governments. Another key financial provision of NREGA was that the central government would be responsible for meeting the cost of 'payment of wages for unskilled manual work' under any schemes created pursuant to NREGA,[22] whereas the state governments would bear 'the cost of unemployment allowance payable' as per the Act.[23]

NREGA required states to designate for each district an official responsible for overall implementation. This 'District Programme Coordinator' (DPC) could be the chief executive officer of the elected district-level *panchayat* body (an organ that goes by different names in different states) or the District Collector or Deputy Commissioner (DC), the officer traditionally in charge of revenue and law-and-order functions. Despite the intention of NREGA's architects to specify the nature of the powers to be exercised by the DPC, the Act did not state precisely what these might be in any given state. Section 14(4) of the

Act merely required state governments to 'delegate' to this official 'such administrative and financial powers ... as may be required to enable him to carry out his functions under this Act'. Determining which powers might or might not be 'required' would inevitably involve discretion by state-level political elites, who are typically loath to part with authority.

The Act called for the appointment of NREGA Programme Officers (POs) to 'function under the direction, control and superintendence of the DPC'.[24] The statute did, however, permit state governments to assign, at their sole discretion, 'any or all' of the PO's functions to the *gram panchayat* or another 'local authority'.[25] The DPC was 'to accord necessary sanction and administrative clearance wherever necessary', and to 'review' and 'monitor' each PO's 'performance'.[26] Both provisions offered DPCs considerable authority. If there was any doubt as to who was in charge, this was laid to rest in another provision, which stated that not only the PO, but 'all other officers of the State Government and local authorities and bodies', would be 'responsible to assist the District Programme Coordinator' in implementing the Act.[27] Nevertheless, while the DPC was in overall control, block-level officers, including the PO, were to be key figures in NREGA implementation. This inherent tension between village- and block-level stakeholders, both bureaucratic and political, is discussed in considerable detail in Chapter 3.

Democratic Decentralisation

Another institutional domain on which NREGA was quite specific was India's multi-tiered system of representative government known as *panchayati raj*. These constitutionally-recognised bodies, often referred to as Panchayati Raj Institutions (PRIs), are elected 'at district, intermediate and village levels'. The Act identified these institutions as 'the principal authorities for planning and implementation' of the employment schemes to be instituted by state governments pursuant to the directives contained in NREGA.[28] A set of enumerated functions was specified at each level, beginning at the bottom of the pyramid with the *gram panchayat*, or village council. Indeed, the *gram panchayat's* first role was to ensure that NREGA implementation was initiated at an even more foundational level, the *gram sabha* (or village assembly). In open *gram sabha* meetings, to which all local residents would be invited (with formal notification procedures specified in the relevant statutes and operational guidelines), 'recommendations' from local citizens were to be collected to help shape local priorities for NREGA public works. The *gram panchayat* was then to select projects based on these recommendations, consolidating them into a local 'development plan' that would consist of works that would be implementation-ready 'as and when demand for work arises'.[29] The elected *gram panchayat* would 'allocate employment opportunities among the applicants and ask them to report for work',[30] while also ensuring that projects 'meet the required technical standards and measurements' of each state's NREGA-compliant employment scheme.[31] A prioritised list of works would then be forwarded by the *gram panchayat* to the specially designated NREGA PO, a non-elected official at the block level. Blocks are the administrative equivalent to the 'intermediate tier' of the three-level *panchayati raj* system of elected bodies—above the *gram panchayat* but below the district *panchayat*.[32]

Block-level POs were charged with 'scrutiny and preliminary approval' of the project plans produced by the *gram panchayats*.[33] They were required to allocate at least half of the monetary value of approved NREGA projects to works that would be implemented through the *gram panchayats*, as opposed to projects administered by the line ministry offices represented within the district and block-level administrative apparatus—such as the departments of irrigation, forestry, sanitation, roads, and so forth.[34] The Act specified, moreover, that POs would hold an administrative rank equal to that of the Block Development Officer (BDO), an existing functionary.[35] The PO is also responsible for preparing a block-level plan of works projects 'by consolidating the project proposals prepared by the *gram panchayats* and the proposals received from intermediate *panchayats*'.[36] This would permit the PO to discharge the responsibility of 'matching the demand for employment with the employment opportunities arising from projects in the area under his jurisdiction'.[37] Logistically, POs were to ensure the payment of wages to workers and unemployment allowances to those eligible for them.[38]

The role assigned by NREGA to intermediate (or block) level *panchayats* is minimal, reflecting the weak nature of block-level elected bodies across India. Formally, however, intermediate *panchayats* must approve the block-level plan devised by the PO and 'forward it to the district *Panchayat* ... for final approval'.[39] At the district level, the elected bodies were accorded somewhat more power than their counterparts at the intermediate level. NREGA mentions the DPC's role in 'assisting' the district *panchayat* twice—in almost identical wording.[40] Still, even though district *panchayats* 'finalise and approve' each of the block-level plans within their respective jurisdictions, it was the (unelected) DPC who was made responsible for formulating the consolidated plan, a process that endows the DPC with great discretion and considerable agenda-setting advantages.[41] The PO, too, is expected under NREGA to play a key role in operationalising the Act's accountability systems by monitoring all projects, whether implemented by a *gram panchayat* or an administrative entity.[42] For instance, the PO is supposed to ensure that *gram sabhas* regularly conduct 'social audits', 'that prompt action is taken on the objections raised', and that 'all complaints that may arise' concerning implementation are dealt with in a timely fashion.[43]

Indeed, the linchpin of NREGA's system of popular accountability was the *gram sabha*, the local assembly that constitutes the institutional base of India's political pyramid. This entailed considerable risks because local-level mass meetings have seldom, in practice, been permitted real influence in India's system of democratic decentralisation (or in those used in most other countries). Through the *gram sabha*, political representation was to be supplemented by direct citizen participation in deliberative decision-making. Not only would the *gram sabha* formulate local NREGA plans; it would constitute the forum for collective social audits of all projects implemented within the *gram panchayat*'s area. These were to be conducted regularly and according to a prescribed set of procedures. (The periodicity was eventually stipulated in the NREGA 'Operational Guidelines' framed after the Act passed into law.) To facilitate the holding of social audits, the *gram sabha* was empowered to ask for and obtain from the elected *gram panchayat* 'all relevant documents—including muster rolls, bills, vouchers, measurement books, copies of sanction orders and other connected books of account and papers'.[44]

Despite these enumerated powers, it would nevertheless be up to officials—the PO and the DPC—to determine whether the *gram panchayat* leaders, with whom POs and other officials often acted collusively, had complied adequately with NREGA's transparency requirements. The PO and the DPC were also in charge of initiating further investigative action on *prima facie* cases of inappropriate or criminal behavior identified in NREGA social audits. Moreover, it was at the level of the state government that rules would be framed to 'determine appropriate grievance redressal mechanisms at the Block level and the district level for dealing with any complaint by any person' concerning implementation, and to establish a 'procedure for disposal of such complaints'. This was seen by one person closely involved with the Act's formulation as 'pretty much putting the fox in charge of the hen house'.[45]

While NREGA accords local elected institutions a large degree of authority with respect to both planning and auditing, its architects understood that, paradoxically, for decentralised implementation to achieve results a fairly radical centralisation of record-keeping functions would be required. This was to be combined with a nationwide system for storing and accessing programme implementation data. To make such a system work, NREGA rules required all programme records to be entered through a dedicated Management Information System (MIS), to be located on the website of the central government's Ministry of Rural Development (MoRD). This system would not only allow the collection of data on various dimensions of implementation; it would also act as a check on false record keeping by programme managers, while providing local citizen-auditors the disaggregated data they would need to highlight discrepancies. These and other rules concerning centralised record-keeping and management oversight were, paradoxically, crucial elements of NREGA's promise of decentralised accountability.

The Origins of NREGA

Where NREGA came from is a complicated question. Its origins can be found in a range of precursor programmes, including the many employment schemes that central and state governments have operated over the decades. The existence of near-precedents for NREGA does not, however, explain why (and how) political actors pursued this policy direction in the period leading up to its passage in 2005. Nor do policy legacies account for a government's ability to get such a statute enacted. The remainder of this chapter assesses various factors, structural and contingent, that contributed to NREGA's adoption.

Policy Legacies

NREGA's origins can be traced back to Maharashtra, which passed an Employment Guarantee Act in 1977, and funded it through a set of hypothecated taxes. (NREGA's more distant family tree goes back to the famine-relief works instituted under British colonial rule.) The resulting Maharashtra Employment Guarantee Scheme (EGS) was largely deemed a success during its first two decades in operation.[46] The key similarity to NREGA was the 'guarantee', the duty imposed on the state government to provide temporary work to those who applied. The Maharashtra EGS's self-targeting nature was particularly valued, and those who studied how it worked in practice identified important social capital-building effects.[47] In the early 1990s, World Bank economists pointed to the Maharashtra EGS as the type of programme that governments pursuing market-oriented policy reform should institute to shield the poor from the potentially adverse effects of 'economic adjustment'.[48] For all its achievements and renown, the Maharashtra EGS experienced chronic difficulties, notably the state government's failure to ensure replenishment of the state's dedicated Employment Guarantee Fund (from which resources for public works projects were to be drawn) or to make sufficient employment available in a timely fashion. The underpayment and late payment of wages was a common complaint among both workers and advocates for the rural poor. The ease with which government officials evaded accountability for non-fulfilment of the employment 'guarantee' spurred many efforts to increase oversight and triggered significant collective action among EGS workers in Maharashtra. At various times, workers and labour organisations created EGS 'unions' to protest malfeasance. They also participated in civil litigation against the state government.

Both before and after Maharashtra's EGS was created, many national programmes sought to provide temporary employment as a form of social protection. In the 1970s, there was the somewhat rashly titled 'Crash Scheme for Rural Employment'. This was followed, in the 1980s, by the far more institutionalised National Rural Employment Programme (NREP). Starting in 1989, a centrally sponsored scheme known as the Jawahar Rozgar Yojana (JRY) was a major component of India's social safety net. The Employment Assurance Scheme (EAS) was unveiled in 1993, partly in response to the findings of World Bank research on the Maharashtra EGS. In 1999, the Government of India introduced the Jawahar Gram Samridhi Yojana to complement the other initiatives. However, none of these central programmes, nor any of the schemes developed by various state governments over the years, contained the crucial guarantee provisions found in the Maharashtra EGS.

NREGA can also be traced back to Rajasthan, both conceptually and organisationally. Conceptually, NREGA's inclusion of dedicated institutions and detailed procedures to counter politicisation and corruption reflects the experiments in pro-poor governance undertaken by civic activists in Rajasthan during the prior decade and a half. It was in central Rajasthan that the Mazdoor Kisan Shakti Sangathan (MKSS), or Worker and Farmer Power Organisation, and other activist groups alternately fought against, worked with, upbraided, advised, and humiliated by force of counter-example the state's senior civil servants and leading politicians from across the political spectrum. Not only was Rajasthan home to the core of the movement that conceived of NREGA and lobbied successfully for its passage; the MKSS and its allies pioneered the social audit techniques that constitute one of NREGA's defining features. The MKSS's efforts to obtain and use government-held information to empower ordinary people—mainly workers on government-run employment programmes or people eligible (but not receiveing) benefits under 'targeted' schemes—was a crucial influence on the shape of India's Right to Information Act, the information-access provisions found in NREGA, and the detailed procedures found in the regulations that govern the implementation of both statutes.

Thus, while Maharashtra's government introduced the idea of guaranteed employment that would become a central NREGA feature, it was Rajasthan's civil society that developed the accountability mechanisms through which NREGA workers would, it was hoped, help to enforce that guarantee. During the 1990s, these were typically localised and piecemeal innovations devised by activists and sometimes conducted in partial partnership with state government officials, particularly the district- and block-level bureaucrats who wield great discretionary authority in rural India. But these experiments were more often pursued in the teeth of bureaucratic and political resistance—a process that fostered a struggle-based approach to better programme implementation that was a core principle of NREGA concept. In short, while Maharashtra can fairly claim partial parentage of NREGA, a fair amount of the Act's institutional and political DNA can be traced back to Rajasthan.

Jean Dreze, who was active with the MKSS from the 1990s, traces NREGA even further back, to the debates that produced the Indian Constitution in 1950. Dreze notes that BR Ambedkar, the Dalit political leader who chaired the Constituent Assembly's Drafting Committee, sought unsuccessfully to have the 'right to work' included among the Constitution's 'fundamental rights'—provisions that the state has an affirmative legal obligation to fulfil. Lacking sufficient political support for this step, Ambedkar was forced to place the right to work alongside the numerous other economic and social rights that ultimately made their way into the Constitution's Directive Principles of State Policy.[49] The Directive Principles were distinguished from Fundamental Rights by the explicit instruction that they were 'not to be enforced by any court'.[50] Still, they were 'fundamental to the governance of the country'.[51] The Constitution's Directive Principles amounted to national aspirations, a guide to future government action, but not 'rights' in the legal sense of the term. In Dreze's words, they 'were expected to be fought for, politically'.[52] Grassroots movements that over the past twenty years have sought to realise such rights—to food, to education, to work, to health—have proceeded on precisely this struggle-oriented understanding.

The Rajasthan-based movements for the right to information and the right to work were not only part of the conceptual background to the development of NREGA; they were integral to the process by which the Act entered the UPA government's agenda. While national-level employment guarantee legislation had long been discussed—and attempts to introduce legislation in parliament were made as early as 1990[53]—the genesis of what would become NREGA stemmed from the interrelation between economic realities in Rajasthan and political developments in Delhi. In 2001, several activist groups in Rajasthan, connected to but extending far beyond the MKSS, began articulating a demand that the state government pass an employment guarantee act. This took place in the wake of two actions by the Rajasthan government: the passage of flawed but substantial state-level right to information legislation, and the enactment of amendments to Rajasthan's local government statute that made popular auditing of village-level development expenditure the right of all citizens.[54]

In addition to their extensive experience with rural employment programmes, activist groups in Rajasthan had also long demanded that state governments observe the provisions of existing minimum wage laws. They were involved in a much-celebrated case (Sanjit Roy v Rajasthan) in 1983 in which the Supreme Court ruled that, contrary to widespread practice, state governments could not pay labourers less than the statutory daily minimum wage, even when administering so-called 'emergency' famine-relief works.[55] Though the state government provided statistics to show that it had been responding to drought conditions effectively and over an extended period of time, the court found that this very same data constituted evidence that relief works had become a regular feature of government policy, and therefore could not be exempted from the purview of minimum-wage legislation. Moreover, the court ruled that paying workers less than the minimum wage was a violation of Article 23 of the Indian Constitution, which outlawed forced labour. This very issue—of the relationship between minimum wage laws and the operation of employment programmes—would become a source of huge political controversy in 2009 and 2010, as NREGA implementation became a matter of intense public debate.[56]

Given this history, it was appropriate that the demand for employment guarantee legislation in Rajasthan emerged in the context of an extended drought in the state, which continued through almost the entire period of Congress Party Chief Minister Ashok Gehlot's term in office (1998–2003).[57] In late 2001, the Akal Sangharsh Samiti, an 'all-Rajasthan network of about

50 grassroots organisations', was formed 'to defend the rights of drought affected people, especially the right to employment', which many activists considered an important means of realising the right to food.[58] The Samiti's campaign involved 'action-based' research focused on 'living conditions in drought-affected areas, the government's response to the crisis, and corruption in relief works'.[59] By conducting surveys of people's well-being in drought-affected areas, the Samiti was able to counter the state government's assertions about the implementation of drought-relief programmes—'claims that were otherwise largely unchallenged', according to Dreze.[60] A defining moment in the Samiti's campaign was the June–July 2001 *dharna* held in the state capital of Jaipur demanding an extension of drought-relief employment programmes until the autumn harvest season.

During this period, the approximately fifty tonnes of foodgrains held in government warehouses throughout the country—amidst a nationwide crisis of food availability—became a symbol of government callousness and incompetence. Earlier in 2001, a coalition of activist groups (which came to be known as the Right to Food movement) had filed a Public Interest Litigation (PIL) at the Supreme Court. The lead petitioner was the People's Union for Civil Liberties (PUCL), whose Jaipur-based head was a key member of Rajasthan's activist network, closely involved in efforts to fight corruption as well as violence against women, Dalits, and religious minorities.[61] The activists' legal brief argued that several state governments were violating Article 21 of the Indian constitution, which guaranteed citizens the 'right to life', by not adequately implementing the food and nutrition programmes created and largely funded by the central government. The initial result of the PIL was an 'interim order' by the Supreme Court (issued in May 2001) that required state governments to change the way in which they fulfilled what activists had been calling the 'right to food', which the court designated a component of the right to life. Just as important as this jurisprudential advance was the organisational arrangements the court devised to ensure fulfilment of this basic right. In November 2001, the Supreme Court extended the coverage of its interim order across the entire country. From then on, the benefits distributed through government nutrition schemes would be treated as legally protected entitlements.[62] In May 2002, a year after its first interim order, the Supreme Court placed the implementation of all food- and nutrition-related programmes under the supervision of court-appointed 'commissioners', who would report back to the court regularly on the results of their monitoring efforts. India's nation-wide Public Distribution System (PDS) was by far the largest entity to be monitored, but seven other government programmes, representing a wide-range of sectors and models, were also within their purview: the Annapurna programme; the Antyodaya Anna Yojana; the Integrated Child Development Services programme; the National Family Benefit Scheme; the National Maternity Benefit Scheme; the National Old Age Pension Scheme; and the National Programme of Nutritional Support to Primary Education. For much of the period leading up to the passage of NREGA, the so-called 'food commissioners' consisted of retired officers of the Indian Administrative Service (IAS) with longstanding connections to important activist groups. (Such was the linkage between the commissioners and the right to food and right to work movements that two of the most high-profile food commissioners eventually ended up on the NAC, where the first official draft of NREGA was formulated.)[63] In October 2002, recognising the scale of the oversight mandate assigned to the commissioners, the Court decided that the commissioners would be aided by 'assistants to the Commissioners' (appointed by state governments), 'nodal officers' (to ensure execution of the orders within the civil service), and outside 'advisors' (which the commissioners themselves would be permitted to nominate).[64] This structure would prove enormously effective in channeling information to the court—information that could be used to ensure compliance with its orders in far-flung jurisdictions.

It was not long before these and other developments began filtering into the domain of electoral politics. Lakin and Ravishankar argue that the court's ruling had 'upped the ante' for parties contemplating new social welfare initiatives to address the food crisis. By putting public employment 'on the agenda', and presenting 'a set of opportunities and constraints for enterprising politicians', the court, prodded by movement-based activists, had redefined 'the parameters facing politicians'.[65] Lakin and Ravishankar's larger point was that, contrary to most theories of how redistributive policies emerge, it was civil society and the judiciary, not parties or bureaucrats, that set the stage for progressive change.[66] Still, Lakin and Ravishankar argued, for this conducive environment to result in actual legislation, it required another actor—a 'political entrepreneur' willing and able to seize the opportunity.

Electoral Competition and Party Politics

Throughout 2002, the Akal Sangharsh Samiti continued its campaign for state-level employment guarantee legislation. Its efforts accelerated as

Rajasthan's state assembly elections (scheduled for late 2003) drew near. Though activists were disillusioned with the failure of the Congress Party government to enact state-level legislation during its five years in office, they were even less optimistic about what a BJP government might do were it to win power in Rajasthan. The MKSS and like-minded civil society groups mounted protests and public demonstrations, calling on all parties to include in their manifestos a promise to enact employment-guarantee legislation. Such a pledge would provide leverage for activists after the elections. Despite remaining officially non-partisan, the activist community's ideological distaste for the BJP was evident. Indeed, as MKSS activists themselves would later concede, '[t]he movement for an Employment Guarantee Act also encompassed a larger politics'. It was 'presented as a counter to the divisive politics of the right wing, which was attempting to mobilise chauvinistic Hindu sentiment ... [in Rajasthan] through the aggressive distribution of tridents',[67] a religious symbol that had been adopted as a badge of militant Hindu identity—and which, in a pinch, could be used as a weapon.

While highly visible, the movement demanding a state-level employment guarantee in Rajasthan was not very effective. Chief Minister Gehlot showed little interest in committing the state Congress to the idea. The party's manifesto-drafting committee was similarly unenthused, and no promise of employment legislation was included. The state's other parties apparently saw no reason to outflank Congress on this issue. The BJP won the elections.

In mid-2004, however, the idea of a guaranteed-employment programme 'entered national policy debates in India', in Jean Dreze's memorable phrase, 'like a wet dog at a glamorous party'.[68] A sequence of 'unlikely events had catapulted it to the top of the political agenda'.[69] While the Rajasthan Congress Party had not adopted the employment-guarantee pledge, national party president Sonia Gandhi had been impressed by its potential after meeting with MKSS and other activists while on a campaign tour through Rajasthan during the state assembly elections. The 2003 Rajasthan election campaign had thus been an 'important prelude', an 'opportunity to create interest in a national Employment Guarantee Act among leaders of various political parties'—notably the Congress Party.[70] As MacAuslan points out, guaranteed employment was a unifying idea for activist organisations working on a diverse array of issues: 'Whether the goal was rural poverty reduction, women's empowerment, democratisation, or workers' rights, these actors perceived guaranteed employment as the most appropriate instrument.'[71]

Sonia Gandhi had in fact been quietly lobbied on the employment-guarantee concept as early as 2000 by at least one key figure in what would become the right to food campaign.[72] A year later, she 'took up the issue, writing to Congress chief ministers in 2001 to explore the idea'.[73] In a related move, in 2002 she committed Congress-ruled state governments (including Rajasthan's)[74] to investigating alleged famine-related deaths, which had stoked national political controversy.[75] The tenor of discussions at a July 2003 party meeting in Simla indicated that the Congress was moving towards a broadly 'rural' strategy for the general election scheduled for the following year.[76] From then onward, employment-guarantee activists repeatedly sought to win over two key Congress leaders responsible for framing the party's 2004 election manifesto: Manmohan Singh and Jairam Ramesh.[77] It is not clear when exactly Singh and Ramesh embraced the idea, though Ramesh claimed (in 2006, two years after the general election) that he had recognised its political potential well before the party came to power.

By early 2004, the promise of employment-guarantee legislation was in the Congress Party's national election manifesto. It was positioned in public rallies as part of a larger commitment to dealing with the crisis in rural areas, including the high rate of farmer suicides in states such as Andhra Pradesh, a major theme of Sonia Gandhi's campaign oratory.[78] Despite her endorsement, enthusiasm for the employment-guarantee pledge among senior Congress leaders was thin at best. Indeed, this commitment was said to have been included in the manifesto mainly because those who might have opposed it never thought Congress would form the next government. However, Congress's reluctant allies among the Left parties, according to Dreze, 'were strong advocates of the Employment Guarantee Act' idea, in part because the demand for the right to work legislation had been 'a long-standing demand of the labour movement' on which much of the Left parties' organisational strength was built.[79] Lakin and Ravishankar reject the claim that the employment-guarantee pledge in Congress's manifesto reflected a conscious attempt by party strategists to outflank the Left. Either way, the very first policy commitment found in the National Common Minimum Programme (NCMP) of the United Progressive Alliance, the Congress-led coalition of parties that won the 2004 elections,[80] was passage of an Employment Guarantee Act to cover rural areas as well as the poor and middle classes in urban areas.[81]

Following the UPA's surprise defeat of the ruling BJP-led alliance in 2004, many in the Indian and international media attributed the result to a revolt among India's rural poor against the National Democratic Alliance (NDA) government's continued liberalisation of the Indian economy.[82] These claims were inaccurate. Congress and its allies attracted greater support in urban rather than rural areas, and from prosperous groups who had benefited dispro-portionately from economic liberalisation rather than from the poor.[83] Congress leaders were well aware of this, but they chose not to challenge the myth of a revolt by the rural poor because it helped to burnish their pro-poor credentials, and—more importantly—to distinguish the Congress Party from the BJP. Their intention was to consolidate the image of a compassionate Congress so as to benefit the party in future electoral contests—both in state-level elections and at a subsequent general election, which many thought might not be far off, given the likelihood of dissonance within the hastily assembled UPA. As Lakin and Ravinshankar put it, the Congress's top leader-ship 'exploited the notion of a national mandate for rural development to pass a program that supported the party's long-term electoral strategy'.[84]

The NAC and the Citizens' Draft

After the election results were known, Sonia Gandhi, the leader of the Congress Party, declined the opportunity to become prime minister, opting instead to remain party president while former Finance Minister Manmohan Singh assumed the premiership. Mrs Gandhi pressed for the creation of a quasi-governmental entity, the National Advisory Council (NAC), over which she would ultimately preside as chairperson. The NAC was intended to serve as a policy-development forum for the UPA government on issues of social welfare—a body that would draw on actors from within and beyond government, including retired civil servants, academic researchers, and leading figures from India's vibrant civil society. A number of NAC members were both former civil servants and social activists in their own right. Aruna Roy, who had helped to found and guide the MKSS in Rajasthan for many years, including on issues of transparency in the conduct of public employment programmes, was on the NAC from the outset. A later entrant was Harsh Mander, who had left the civil service in protest against the government's inability to protect religious minorities from persecution and had become a powerful voice for inclusive governance. Mander and fellow former Indian Administrative Service (IAS) officer N.C. Saxena, whose career as an admin-istrator had combined with an interest in social science research to make him a formidable advocate for more sustainable and people-friendly approaches to rural development,[85] both served as Supreme Court-appointed commissioners on the right to food public interest litigation (PIL).

The NAC designed a number of new policies, programmes, and draft laws for the UPA government in New Delhi, but to say only that is to overlook something more striking. They brought a new perspective on the nature of 'poverty', and ways to tackle it, into the policy process at the very apex of power. Drawing on the work of Amartya Sen among others, and on the experiences of progressive civil society organisations like the MKSS, they broadened the government's working definition of poverty. They saw it as not merely a severe shortage of incomes, assets, and funds, but also as a severe shortage of opportunities, liberties, capabilities, and information. This perspective informed the NAC when it discussed the need for 'social protection' legislation that would augment India's lamentable 'safety net', the inadequacy of which was seen at the time as a major reason for the rural revolt that was (erroneously) said to have doomed the previous NDA government's electoral prospects. The focus very quickly turned to methods for operationalising the right to work, an idea that had grown up alongside the right to food movement—partly because many of the same activists were involved in both campaigns;[86] partly because access to some kind of paid employment was widely seen as a crucial means of improving household-level food security; and partly because the two ideas had long been integrated in government programmes, notably the 'Food for Work' programme, the essential components of which could be traced back to the British colonial administration's approach to 'famine relief'. The British Famine Codes, which Amartya Sen had analysed even earlier in his academic career, identified public works projects as a key element of the state's drought relief efforts. In Rajasthan and a number of other places, the right to information was seen as a crucial element in the ability of workers to make the right to work realisable.

In fact, the NAC, which was charged with translating the NCMP into concrete policy measures, took up the employment guarantee as its first piece of business. Dreze and Roy appeared at the NAC's first substantive meeting with draft legislation for an employment guarantee act. This initial text was built around a so-called 'citizens' draft' that had been prepared by civil society organisations, particularly those affiliated with the right to food campaign. Some of the civil society groups had members (or experts associated with them) on the NAC. The first NAC draft, issued in August 2004, incorporated extensive transparency mechanisms that were intended to combat corruption by enabling poor workers to see attempts by political actors to divert funds from the programme. Some NAC members were well aware that this would inspire discontent among workers, but welcomed this because it was seen as a way of catalysing collective action among poor people and strengthening their 'political capacity'.

Among the NAC's other early actions was a new Right to Information Act, which was, again, based on documents generated by the civil society organisations (CSOs) with which NAC members were linked. A Freedom of Information Act (FOIA) had been passed by the previous BJP-led government in 2002, but was widely seen as insufficient—full of exemptions and lacking clear procedural mechanisms. (The FOIA in any case never came into force.) The activists who joined the NAC had been among the most vocal critics of the FOIA. The purpose of the new RTI Act (RTIA), passed in 2005 in a form that closely resembled the draft text supplied by Dreze and Roy at an early NAC meeting, was to enable ordinary people to obtain the maximum possible information held by government institutions. The RTIA closed several loopholes, specified an institutional structure for government compliance (including an appellate authority), and instituted penalties for officials who refused to divulge information according to the procedures set forth in the Act. The RTIA put unprecedented pressure on bureaucrats and elected politicians to overcome their longstanding allergy to transparency and downward accountability. By opening up new channels for pressure from below, this created opportunities for both ordinary and poor people—and their activist allies—to proactively engage with a previously opaque system that was starting to become translucent. The NAC sought, in other words, to catalyse collective action by the poor by enhancing their political awareness, confidence, skills and connections—that is, building their 'political capacity'.

Inter-Ministerial Negotiation

The version of the Bill ultimately approved by the NAC became the basis for inter-ministerial consultation. The MoRD took the lead in coordinating the further development of the NAC draft, and was directed by the Prime Minister's Office (PMO) to ensure close collaboration with the ministries of finance, *panchayati raj*, and labour. The finance ministry—and the finance minister himself—was from the outset extremely concerned about the potential cost of the programme. To guardians of fiscal rectitude, the idea of a 'guarantee' was dangerously open-ended. The demand-driven nature of the Act appeared, from a fiscal perspective, like a 'blank cheque', as one critic in the finance ministry put it to a NAC member. Because the number of people who might apply for work under the proposed Act was unknown, it was impossible to place a precise upper limit on its cost. This caused uneasiness among cabinet members beyond the finance ministry, who were concerned at the effect this fiscal commitment might have on the availability of budgetary resources for their own initiatives. The NAC estimated that NREGA, when fully implemented (which it would not be in its first year), would amount to 1.3 per cent of GDP.[87] An independent assessment arrived at a figure of 1.7 per cent of GDP.[88]

The Finance Ministry obtained strong support from the Planning Commission—including its executive head[89]—in insisting on two key changes to the NAC draft. The first was a provision specifying that the guarantee of employment could be 'suspended' whenever the Government of India issued a formal order to this effect. The second proposed change was to limit employment under the Act to families officially classified as Below the Poverty Line (BPL). These changes were not acceptable to activists, some of whom later shared their belief that, when it came to ensuring that employment be both guaranteed and universally available, '[o]pposition came chiefly from sections of the corporate sector and its offshoots in the finance ministry and elsewhere.'[90]

Another worry, voiced by a wide range of political actors and commentators, involved the opportunity for massive corruption during the implementation of the programme. This sudden concern with corruption was puzzling to some observers, and downright suspicious to others, given the degree of corruption officials had long been willing to countenance in other government programmes, including those that involved investment and export 'incentives' to private-sector firms. A related issue was the possibility that, in part through the use of corrupt methods, funds would end up in the hands of the non-poor. Raghav's Gaiha's mid-1990s study of Maharashtra's EGS was seized upon, somewhat unfairly, by critics of the NREG Bill during legislative debates. Gaiha had found that in some parts of Maharashtra, EGS funds had not reached their intended beneficiaries to the degree hoped.[91]

NREGA's architects responded—both at the time and later—that critics 'who invoke corruption to argue against NREGA are unlikely to accept the same argument to discontinue, say, defence contracts or oil deals'.[92] Moreover, NREGA's opponents did not channel their concerns about the potential for corruption into concrete proposals to mitigate it. Instead, they 'took corruption as an immutable feature of these [public works] programmes and denied the possibility of transparent implementation.'[93] NREGA's architects agreed that, '[i]n refuting this argument, Rajasthan's experience played an important role, particularly the successful abolition of mass fudging in "muster rolls".'[94] The civil society-led improvements in accountability between 1987 and 2003 'showed that public vigilance is the most effective way of tackling corruption in employment programmes'.[95] This made the inclusion of rigorous transparency and social audit provisions 'the key to the possibility of a successful Employment Guarantee Act'.[96]

NREGA's supporters on the NAC clearly understood that, despite the complex accountability mechanisms inserted into the Act, corruption could not be completely eliminated and efforts to combat it would involve constant mobilisation by workers, as well as continuous refinement of the implementation modalities. The transparency measures would reveal to workers attempts by powerful actors to steal their wages, and would inevitably catalyse discontent among poor villagers. The intent was to provide 'a wage entitlement that would give people a measure of dignity and create space for their political mobilisation'.[97] The programme's architects recognised that there would be those who would 'threaten to derail the Act by indulging in corrupt practices'. But they also realised that its 'wide-ranging transparency safeguards' would offer new opportunities for 'social movements to build campaigns for people's empowerment'.[98] The ongoing struggle to realise the right to work would 'give the rural poor a chance to bring into play some of their creative energies'.[99] The process of collectively exposing abuses in NREGA would, in fact, 'also give birth to stronger citizens' movements to fight corruption'.[100]

In interviews, NAC members have stated plainly to us that this logic was well understood by Sonia Gandhi, though perhaps not by other NAC members—nor by all MPs, civil servants, or cabinet members who eventually voted for the Act. But those who did grasp this thinking fully expected people's awareness of precisely how funds were being stolen to drive demands for improved implementation. They also hoped that, in the process, poor people would become politicised, more proactive in defending their interests, and willing to make even greater demands of the state.[101]

A related issue, which has received much less attention in accounts of NREGA's passage, concerned what might be called the programme's 'political feasibility'. This was a particular preoccupation of senior Congress political strategists who were justifiably worried that the party organisation was incapable of ensuring that NREGA was implemented in ways that would pay electoral dividends. Congress leaders were well aware that the party's state and district level units were extremely weak, faction-ridden, and focused on very short-term priorities. As a result, key members of the Congress 'high command' in Delhi decided to make a virtue of necessity by ensuring that the implementation bureaucracy was, to the degree possible, insulated from the direct influence of party officials.[102] Congress chief ministers were instructed to inform party functionaries and elected legislators to adopt a hands-off policy when it came to the design and operation of NREGA works. Party activists at lower levels would be unhappy that they could not exploit such a huge programme for partisan purposes. But the leadership's calculation was that, by freeing the proposed employment guarantee from overt partisan manipulation, the Congress would be rewarded in the medium-term by voters fed up with local party bosses interfering in the operation of development programmes.

Another reason for the Congress leadership's restraint was its keen awareness that, for NREGA to flourish, it had to be made politically feasible in another sense as well. The programme's design had to ensure that rival parties, which held power in many of India's states, would implement it enthusiastically, even though NREGA had been devised by a Congress-led government in New Delhi. They therefore agreed that NREGA would be funded almost entirely from central government resources, with only modest investments from state government budgets. This, it was hoped, would make even non-Congress state governments eager to push the programme. Congress leaders in New Delhi also gave the programme a neutral, non-partisan name, in contrast to earlier programmes that Congress-led governments had created, such as the Indira Awas Yojana and the Rajiv Gandhi National Rural Health Mission. When the name of the programme was changed in 2009, to the Mahatma Gandhi National Rural Employment Guarantee Act, there were some complaints that a figure so closely associated with Congress was being linked to the programme. In general, however, the principle of neutrality was maintained. Gandhi, despite his roots in the Congress, was understood to belong to the nation. Voters' positive perceptions of NREGA at the 2009 general election made it far more likely to survive any future change of government in New Delhi.[103]

The MoRD consultation covered the period from August to December 2004. Many of the details of these consultations spilled into the public domain, including to the authors of the present book. While the finance ministry was identified as the main obstacle to preserving the original draft Bill's distinctive features, other insider accounts stress the role of the MoRD. Indeed, one disagreement was said to be between the MoRD, which preferred to see the programme implemented through line ministries in the state governments, and the Ministry of Panchayati Raj, which wanted a strong role for the *panchayats* specified in the Bill.[104] Whatever the truth of these claims, the complaints about 'watering down' that followed the introduction of the Bill that the MoRD-led process ultimately produced (that is, the version introduced in parliament) were routed informally through individual NAC members.[105]

The Parliamentary Process

The National Rural Employment Guarantee (NREG) Bill 2004 was submitted to parliament on 21 December 2004. The deliberations that had taken place throughout the autumn of 2004—in the cabinet and the bureaucracy, as well as in the press—had produced a bill that was significantly weaker than the NAC draft. The accountability provisions in the NREG Bill were less extensive. It was more limited in its geographic and temporal coverage, and more restrictive in the definition of beneficiaries. The Bill removed the provision in the NAC draft that called for extending the government's obligation to provide employment to the entire country over time. Even more importantly, the Bill gave the government the discretion—as the finance ministry had insisted—to opt out of the Act's requirements. The guarantee was gone in all but name. Moreover, the universal (self-targeting) nature of the NAC draft—rooted in deep suspicion of both the integrity and capacity of state bureaucracies—had been replaced with a means-tested approach, in which only families with BPL certificates (which many genuinely poor families had been unable to obtain) would be allowed to participate in NREGA works. Finally, the MoRD's excision of the NAC draft's minimum-wage requirement was seen by activists as brazen backsliding on earlier commitments.

The NREG Bill was immediately criticised by a range of civil society activists, including some NAC members, who of course had been in close proximity to the inter-agency deliberations that led to its watering down. What particularly alarmed many observers was that the NREG Bill no longer represented a rights-based approach in any meaningful sense. Having seen an advance copy of the Bill to be introduced in parliament, a leading figure in the process called it a 'travesty' and a 'betrayal' of what had been promised in 'innumerable' meetings.[106] Because so much was left to the central government's discretion—particularly when and where the Bill's provisions would apply—it was, in Dreze's view, 'so weak that it defeated the purpose of a legally enforceable employment guarantee'.[107]

Even as the MoRD was putting the final touches on the draft to be tabled in parliament, right to work and right to food activists continued operating on all fronts: lobbying elected politicians, feeding the press with insider accounts of the Bill's progress, imploring trade union leaders to mobilise their members, and staging protests in strategic locations. The public campaign began with a demonstration and signature campaign on the very day the Bill was introduced in parliament. The ensuing public debate, which continued throughout most of 2005, highlighted many issues that would continue to be debated in the years to come, as we shall see in Chapter 7.

NAC members and their allies in civil society were adamant that they would address what they saw as the NREG Bill's many shortcomings during the parliamentary process. Their strategy was to work with MPs from UPA parties as well as the Left parties that provided the government with outside support. They even decided to engage 'tactically' with BJP leaders, many of which were keen to embarrass the Congress for abandoning its campaign promises. BJP leader Venkaiah Naidu had called the government's Bill a 'betrayal' of its earlier commitment to cover all of India, including urban areas, where the BJP's electoral base was said to reside. Working with the BJP helped to position NREGA as an initiative that transcended partisan politics.

Soon after the NREG Bill was tabled in parliament, it was referred to a Parliamentary Standing Committee (PSC) on Rural Development. (On the government side, a 'Group of Ministers' was also constituted to ensure that all parties within the UPA reached a policy consensus).[108] The chair of the PSC, BJP leader Kalyan Singh, took little action on the Bill until March 2005. In fact, Singh 'boycotted meetings on NREGA for six months', though whether this was because he opposed the entire NREGA concept or merely the diluted bill is hard to determine.[109]

In BJP spokesman Arun Jaitley, one of India's leading lawyers, the Bill's activist supporters found perhaps their best conduit to party leaders. It was reportedly Jaitley who convinced Kalyan Singh to convene a series of meetings where the details of the proposed legislation could be discussed.[110] In the very first meeting, committee members agreed 'to open the bill to public amendment'.[111] The willingness of Dreze and his colleagues to engage with BJP leaders enraged senior figures in the Congress party. As one former minister recalled some years after the fact: 'Madam had given these people a platform'—the NAC—and when party leaders and the bureaucracy had acted 'responsibly' to avoid 'populism', these 'NGO wallahs had gone running to the BJP! It was really very shocking.'[112]

The degree of displeasure felt within the highest ranks of the Congress party is suggested by an episode that reportedly took place in April 2005. When NAC members went to discuss the progress of the Bill with Defence Minister Pranab Mukherjee, who headed the Group of Ministers (GoM) assigned to coordinate the cabinet's position on the employment guarantee issue, an unpleasant scene unfolded. After Dreze made the case for preserving the programme's rights-based nature, 'Mukherjee began berating Dreze', allegedly telling him: 'This is not your country, this is India, an act like this is not possible here'. The approach that Dreze and his civil society colleagues had proposed, Mukherjee insisted, would be 'a huge burden on the exchequer'. They would have to give up on 'the guaranteed employment clause and limit the scheme to poor households'.[113] NAC members then reportedly went to Sonia's residence, where she informed them that she could persuade Mukherjee to drop his opposition to the 'guarantee' element of the proposed legislation, but only if a key compromise was agreed: the guarantee would have to be limited to 100 days.[114]

Prime Minister Manmohan Singh, an economist by profession, was among those who expressed serious concern about the potential fiscal consequences of the employment guarantee. He raised the issue at an informal meeting with members of the NAC, who then realised that they had to address this anxiety. One NAC member, Dr. N.C. Saxena (a former 'Member-Secretary' of India's Planning Commission) worked with former colleagues in the civil service and policy-oriented economists to develop a set of comparative cost calculations. This involved estimating the likely scale of employment demand under NREGA based on data from earlier programmes and variables relating to India's current labour-market conditions. The calculations showed that the projected annual outlay for NREGA would not differ greatly from the combined expenditures for the existing rural development programmes that it would largely replace. At a key meeting between NAC members and the prime minister in early 2005, Saxena presented his calculations and persuaded Manmohan Singh that the programme was financially feasible.[115] One contingent factor that helped to convince the prime minister that NREGA was affordable was the increase in government revenues that had begun earlier in the decade and had accelerated from 2003.[116]

Despite assurances from Sonia and an important degree of buy-in from the prime minister, the hostility that NREGA's most ardent supporters were encountering within the cabinet (and throughout much of the bureaucracy) made their advocacy work in parliament all the more essential. Roy, Dreze, and other key activists such as Nikhil Dey were concerned with revised language indicating that the government would be responsible for providing employment only when its 'economic capacity' was deemed at an appropriate level. They had further complaints concerning the role assigned to PRIs (diminished in comparison with the original proposal), restrictions on the nature of works projects eligible for inclusion under NREGA (which would make local decision-making less meaningful), and the 'household'-based (as opposed to individual) nature of the employment entitlement (which was seen as bad for women in particular). These and other activists also had to contend with a newly floated proposal—a modification of a provision in Maharashtra's EGS—to require workers to apply for employment in groups of fifty to initiate a new works project. Roy and Dreze were also, not surprisingly, concerned with the structure of the legislation—acutely aware that the references to labourer entitlements had to be built into 'the body of the Act, rather than included merely in "Schedules"'.[117]

Activists also pressed MPs to insist on a *panchayat*-friendly form of legislation. Dreze and Roy, in their formal submission to the PSC—one of many submitted by a wide range of civil society organisations—argued that '[o]ne of the most important potential advantages of this legislation is that it can both strengthen Panchayati Raj Institutions and give them a mechanism to fulfill their constitutional role'.[118] Implementing the employment guarantee through local *panchayats* would 'strengthen grassroots democracy'.[119] Well after the Act had been passed into law, Dreze would continue to argue that reviving local democratic institutions was a key objective of NREGA's architects. By giving them 'a new purpose, backed with substantial financial resources', NREGA could help to 'activate and revitalise the institutions of local governance'.[120] (Insufficient funds are one of three problems that often cripple elected councils at lower levels across India and the world—along with insufficient powers and a lack of accountability.) When finally implemented, with generous provisions for *panchayats*, NREGA would represent the largest ever transfer of funds to elected local councils anywhere in the world.[121] Yet a central concern raised by Dreze and Roy was that the bill introduced in parliament would vest authority over NREGA operations 'with the implementing officer, and through him/her with the bureaucracy', thus providing 'only symbolic accountability to the *gram panchayat* and *Gram Sabhas*'.[122] And rather than restrict the range of public works that could be implemented under NREGA, Dreze and Roy advocated leaving it to state governments and PRIs to 'decide their own priorities'.[123] They proposed amending the text such that 'productive works' would refer to any project that 'in the opinion of the State Council [on Employment Guarantee], contributes directly or indirectly to the increase of production, the creation or maintenance of assets, the preservation of the environment, or the improvement of the quality of life'.[124]

Roy and Dreze opposed using the 'household' as the unit of entitlement under NREGA. They wanted the act to specify the provision of '100 days of guaranteed employment per adult per year' instead of '100 days of guaranteed employment per household per year'. They argued that '[i]f women have individual entitlements, they will be less vulnerable to being marginalised within the household'.[125] While the activists ultimately lost this particular battle, the PSC process allowed them to secure important improvements to the Bill. Among these were the detailed proposals regarding penalties for erring officials. Commenting on the December 2004 NREG Bill, Roy and Dreze advised PSC members that '[t]he provisions for penalising the implementing officials (in particular the PO) for dereliction of duty must be clearly spelt out'.[126] Moreover, because the courts were too cumbersome, administrative means—notably, 'an authority independent from the implementation hierarchy'—would need to be devised 'to enforce these penalties'.[127]

The PSC's Report, issued in July 2005, recommended restoring many of the provisions that NREGA Bill tabled by the MoRD had eviscerated. The PSC endorsed civil society's most important demands: guaranteed employment without exemptions, a national minimum wage 'floor' (below which state-level wages could not be lowered), no means-testing, gradual extension of the Act to cover the entire country, and detailed transparency and accountability requirements supported by penal provisions. Within the cabinet, the GoM became the crucial mechanism for translating the PSC's recommendations into policy changes. This required deal-making at the highest levels. For instance, it was reportedly agreed that the UPA's more pro-market parties would support the revised bill if Left-oriented parties agreed to withhold their opposition to the government's Special Economic Zone Bill.

Throughout the parliamentary process, the BJP found it convenient to complain about the limitations placed on the Act, echoing the position staked out by civic activists who certainly harbored no affection for the BJP. These maneuvers were opportunistic rather than rooted in principle—though Lakin and Ravishankar persuasively argue that the BJP-led NDA government's economic policy was more pro-rural in terms of expenditure than many had been willing to concede. BJP leaders regularly repeated the critical talking points emanating from the People's Action for Employment Guarantee (PAEG), an umbrella group consisting of the MKSS, the Right to Information campaign, and right to food activists. To maintain the momentum they had built up within the parliamentary process, PAEG undertook a *yatra* (a travelling awareness-raising campaign) through eleven states, drawing wherever possible on sympathetic local activist groups to host and organise public meetings.[128]

In early July 2005, just as the PSC's report was being released, activists held a 'people's convention' in Delhi. An address by former Prime Minister V.P. Singh was a highlight, and his consistent support for the cause of a strong NREGA was something activists would point to when recalling this campaign years later.[129] The event's organisers explicitly linked the right to food and the right to work, noting that 'more than half of the country's 100 crore [one billion] population is still deprived of employment, livelihood and food'. The organisers pledged 'that until this right is reflected in a full-fledged Employment Guarantee Act we shall struggle wholeheartedly'.[130]

While the parliamentary process was crucial, '[t]he most contentious issues were settled in August 2005, in a frantic round of bargaining between the constituent parties and supporters of the UPA government, with the Left parties extracting some major last-minute concessions' that restored some of the Act's important features.[131] On 18 August 2005, the government tabled a revised version of the NREG Bill in parliament. This version included no provisions on BPL targeting and no loopholes that would allow the government to suspend the employment guarantee on grounds of financial capacity. During cabinet deliberations, however, the finance ministry had extracted a new concession—in the form of a 'corruption' clause that permitted a state-level programme to be suspended if evidence of widespread corruption was unearthed. Activists, inside and outside the NAC, objected strongly. Not only could this provision be abused by government officials; it would also act as a disincentive for workers and civil society activists to expose abuses, a key element of the legislative design. NREGA, passed by parliament on 23 August 2005, included this provison.[132]

Another clause had been added at the behest of the minister of rural development,[133] who was otherwise seen as supportive of a strong NREGA. This stated that the central government could, at its discretion, supersede state 'minimum wages'—and institute the central minimum wage, which was then Rs 60 per day. At the time, some states had minimum wages above this level, while others were below it. The purpose of this provision was to guard against additional financial liabilities for the central government if state governments raised their minimum wages—a distinct possibility given the populist tendencies of many state governments and the fact that, under NREGA, the Government of India was to foot the wage bill. One account claimed that this provision was introduced by the minister of rural development as part of a deal with the finance ministry, which had by this point acquired a reputation for treating the poor in a 'step-motherly' fashion.[134] The question of how minimum wages would be calculated, and which wage levels would apply, would in the years ahead become part of national policy debates and high-profile litigation. These issues are discussed in Chapter 7.

Whatever the Left's claims about its part in passing NREGA,[135] its 'major contribution came in the later stages after the bill had been introduced in parliament, when it played a key role in protecting the draft legislation' from attempts to shrink its scope. Intense pressure from the Left parties, on which the UPA government relied for its parliamentary majority, helped NREGA's architects to stave off a final assault.[136] Left parties were also kept abreast of internal government negotiations by activists. For instance, activists learned (and then informed their allies in the Left parties) that some cabinet members had resisted including language that would specify the timeframe for extending the Act's coverage from India's poorest districts to the entire country.[137] The resulting pressure from the Left, already aggrieved at the omission of urban areas from the Act's purview, helped to ensure that a time-bound extension (within five years) of the employment guarantee throughout rural India was included in the Act. (As it happened, political exigencies led this extension to take place within less than three years.) During this legislative endgame, key regional parties within the UPA focused on the implications of the Act for state-level finances. Pressure from these parties—aided and abetted by activists within their respective states—ensured that the main costs to be borne by state governments would be for one-quarter of the cost of material for NREGA works (a reduction from the one-half proposed earlier) and the entire cost of the unemployment allowance, a provision designed as an incentive for states to deliver on the promise of employment within fifteen days.

Lakin and Ravishankar argue that in finalising the Bill, 'high-level wrangling over how much power to give local government' under NREGA was largely a 'turf' war between the MoRD and the Ministry of Panchayati Raj, which had been carved out of the MoRD just a year earlier. Both ministries, they claim, 'wanted control over the program'. Yet, the degree to which decision-making authority over programme implementation was devolved to elected *panchayats* (as opposed to district-level bureaucrats) had little direct bearing on which of the two central ministries would gain 'control'. The MoRD would play no direct role in implementation regardless of whether works projects were selected by *panchayats* or by officials from state-level departments such as irrigation, public works, and forestry. The only way the MoRD would suffer a loss of power was if an extreme form of *panchayat* empowerment was agreed—one in which *gram panchayats* were unconstrained in deciding what works could be undertaken with NREGA funds. No such proposal was then in play.[138] More importantly, even if *panchayats* were somehow given complete freedom of action to pursue works of any type, without reference to a prescribed list, this would not mean greater 'control' over NREGA by the Ministry of Panchayati Raj. It was clear by July 2005 that, whether it was an elected *panchayat* or bureaucratic officials at the block level that decided which projects would receive NREGA funding in a given locality, the works would still need to fall within one of the eligible categories to be defined by the MoRD. Whatever their merits, rules granting local political control would by definition mean less authority for bureaucratic officials at every level. If this form of decentralisation were subverted using illicit tactics, this would empower local officials, not those in the Ministry of Panchayati Raj in New Delhi.[139]

Theoretical Implications

There are many ways of interpreting the significance of the circuitous process through which NREGA entered the statute books. The lessons one might learn are in many respects dictated by one's preoccupations. Lakin and Ravishankar, while unearthing important parts of NREGA's creation story, nevertheless adopt an interpretive lens that leads them to a number of unwarranted conclusions. The first is their claim that concerns about cost and corruption reflected 'a conflict between competing conceptions of the Bill'. On the one hand, there were 'bureaucrats' who saw it as just another anti-poverty programme; on the other, activists (and some politicians) who saw it as an 'expansion of civil rights'.[140] But as we argued in Chapter 1, NREGA was not primarily seen as an expansion of 'civil' rights, even by those who embraced the programme's rights-based framework. Instead, it was the hybrid nature of the rights embodied in NREGA (both economic and political, substantive and procedural) that invested it with such significance. Moreover, political decision makers who supported the open-ended financial commitment implied by this demand-driven programme did not do so only, or even mainly, because they saw it as advancing 'the right to life, as articulated by the activists and the Supreme Court', but because they saw it as a winning political proposition— something that could help to nurture their political careers. Lakin and Ravishankar also claim that the reason why 'technocrats preferred to give the Centre more discretion over where and when the program should function' was their desire 'to reduce the scope for corruption in NREGA'.[141] The idea that giving 'discretion' to central government decision-makers over when and where to initiate NREGA works would undercut corruption is contrary to most theories of why corruption thrives.

A second shortcoming is Lakin and Ravishankar's tendency to construct straw men. Their account of NREGA's origins self-consciously contests the supposedly widely held view that election manifesto pledges inevitably reflect demands 'from below'. But who seriously claims that manifestos are always (or even mainly) the result of clearly articulated policy preferences from well-defined constituencies among non-elite social groups? Political scientists working from a rational-choice perspective surely do not subscribe to such a linear conception of policymaking. In fact, the commonsense understanding of how political commitments are generated would seem to be much closer to Lakin and Ravishankar's contention that politicians incorporate policy proposals 'into a national policy platform' when it suits 'their electoral interests and broader campaign strategy'.[142] Moreover, Lakin and Ravishankar argue that while civil society and the courts were crucial in bringing the issue of guaranteed employment into public discussion, efforts by these actors alone were insufficient. What was needed was a 'political entrepreneur' willing to seize the opportunity presented by this conducive environment.[143] But it is a stretch, to put it mildly, to cast Jairam Ramesh and Manmohan Singh as the kind of scrappy networkers generally associated with the term 'political entrepreneur'.

Another straw man emerges in Lakin and Ravishankar's claim that 'the principal mechanism driving NREGA was not a rising Left, but electoral competition between Congress and the BJP'. Why might anyone have assumed that it was fear of the Left that drove Congress's adoption of the employment guarantee promise? The passage of NREGA, according to Lakin and Ravishankar, is consistent with what Ruth Berins Collier has termed 'competitive support mobilisation'.[144] Quite clearly the main competition faced by Congress was from the BJP. Surely the far more important theoretical question is how forces working 'from below' influence (and are influenced by) those operating 'from above', and the extent to which the interaction between the two may affect policy and the success with which it is carried out—both of which turn out to be crucial aspects of India's experience with NREGA.

Third, Lakin and Ravishankar present a somewhat skewed vision of the roles played by various actors involved in NREGA's creation. While their observation that 'NREGA is not the bill that the Congress party would have produced in the absence of civil society pressure' is true, if unremarkable, it fails to recognise that civil society provided far more than pressure.[145] The civic activists who drove the adoption of NREGA furnished a fully articulated policy vision, born of direct engagement with state programmes over an extended period of time, and backed by quantitative research findings that grounded their claims in the social-scientific discourse that policymakers in India, as elsewhere, have come to find comforting. The encompassing nature of Lakin and Ravishankar's further conclusion—that 'NREGA was driven by a combination of electoral politics, elite political entrepreneurship, judicial activism, and pressure from non-partisan civil society organisations'—makes it hard to argue with. They accurately depict the basic chronology: that NREGA started as a demand from civil society; was picked up as a national electoral promise by party leaders; subsequently 'recast by high level politicians and bureaucrats in the government'; and 'reformed a final time in response to pressure from civil society activists and the organised Left'. But this tidy account of the sequencing ignores the feedback effects involved and the incentives created by a coalition government containing many largely regional parties.

Of greater consequence is Lakin and Ravishankar's tendency to ignore the eccentricities of party institutions in India. For instance, they seriously downplay the importance of Sonia Gandhi in the NREGA story, including her role in a long list of enabling factors. Yet, at many crucial stages, Sonia's backing for the activist camp was not only necessary, it was all but sufficient. By attributing the government's commitment to a strong NREGA to 'internal pressure from Sonia Gandhi and the wing of the Congress behind her', Lakin and Ravishankar misrepresent the inner-party dynamics of the time. There really was no other 'wing' of the party. The extreme centralisation of decision-making authority, particularly after the party's surprise election victory in 2004, meant that Congress leaders had little choice but to go along with Sonia's wishes. Cabinet ministers who opposed elements of the proposed legislation could do so only up to a point, and only in tandem with displays of abject loyalty to the party president. For most Congress MPs, the motivation for supporting the employment-guarantee idea was their desire to avoid 'displeasing madam'. Stalwarts like Pranab Mukherjee, or technocrats whose value to the party stemmed from their credibility with key constituencies—P. Chidambaram's rapport with business groups, for instance—could get away with voicing concerns. But even fairly senior Congress MPs had good reason to fear that dissent would harm their chances of ministerial office or access to party funds, or even that it might result in their deselection at the next election.

In their analysis of the judiciary's role in NREGA's origins, Lakin and Ravishankar claim that 'the position on employment programs coming out of the Supreme Court made it politically difficult to openly oppose NREGA'.[146] Yet, there is no reason to believe that Congress politicians, let alone those from other parties, felt constrained by Supreme Court orders, which in any case surely did not compel the newly elected government to initiate a guaranteed-employment programme. A more measured conclusion is supplied by MacAuslan, who argues that 'the Supreme Court's favourable opinion encouraged activists to increase the intensity and scope of their demands for improved government programmes'.[147] The Supreme Court's parameter-setting role is less significant than another implication of its engagement in the right to food case: the creation of an institutional framework, centred on the court-appointed commissioners, for continuous monitoring of government food and nutrition policy. This provided a natural link between civil society and the state,[148] a point emphasised in earlier studies of anti-corruption activism in India.[149] Through their ongoing engagement with the work of the food commissioners, civic activists working with and on behalf of poor rural people vastly increased their awareness, skills, confidence, and connections—in short their political capacity. This paid off in a variety of ways, as we have seen, during the drawn out process of creating NREGA, and would continue to do so during later battles to ensure full implementation.

An alternative perspective on the political dynamics underlying NREGA's creation is provided by Chopra, whose analysis is more nuanced and, ultimately, more satisfying. She argues that the boundaries separating different categories of policy actors in India are increasingly 'blurred'[150]—a position that applies as much to the artificial distinctions between social movements and NGOs as it does to those between progressive former bureaucrats and the civic activists with whom they joined forces to pass NREGA.[151] Chopra's mapping of policy-relevant actors has its drawbacks. Her model, for instance, does not accord a significant role to India's Supreme Court. But Chopra's analysis of the techniques adopted by civil society accurately captures the multiple roles that such actors have found themselves playing. These roles evolved in the process of pursuing a 'twin strategy' on NREGA—pushing for textual amendments and compromise language when operating inside institutional forums, while simultaneously resorting to a familiar but effective protest repertoire from beyond these circles. Even as they infiltrated the state's bureaucratic structures, right to food activists 'appeared to be standing in opposition to the state, pressurising the state to fulfill its commitment'.[152]

Chopra's analysis also helpfully extends into the period after passage of the Act. The intensive engagement of key actors in civil society with senior officials in India's civil service continued during the process of drafting NREGA's Operational Guidelines.[153] Continued civil society engagement was facilitated beyond that point through the appointment of activists (and others) to the Central Employment Guarantee Council (CEGC). The CEGC's substantive work was not directly consequential, but it did give a platform for activists to continue not only working to influence processes within the sprawling NREGA-linked bureaucracy, but also to engage in public debates over the nature of the programme—for instance, when corruption issues arose, or when the minimum wage was at stake, or in response to violence against NREGA auditors. As Chopra notes, the CEGC put 'non-state actors together on a common platform with the MoRD officials to help in the implementation and monitoring of the policy'.[154]

Where Chopra's analysis falters is in overstating the extent of institutional transformation. She argues, for instance, that parliament's consideration of the NREG Bill not only altered the legislation, which is true enough, but that it 'also reinvented the very parameters of the state',[155] a claim for which little evidence is supplied. Even more of a stretch is Chopra's assertion that the UPA-Left Coordination Committee was just as boundary-transgressing as the multiple roles played by the right to food activists, whose infiltration of the state (through NAC membership and other means) was so central to NREGA's adoption. Chopra maintains that UPA-Left coordination meetings 'saw Left leaders actively negotiating with the UPA leaders outside the formal parliamentary system but still within the confines of closed doors, signifying the internal deliberations of the state'.[156] The meaning of the term 'signifying' in this context is not obvious, nor is the logic underlying the claim that this relatively common form of political maneuvering could be seen as approximating, let alone mirroring, the workings of official government bodies. There is, after all, nothing particularly noteworthy about closed-door meetings between ministers and MPs from parties that support a government without participating in its Council of Ministers.

One crucial implication of the NREGA story that all of the interpretive accounts discussed in this chapter neglect to mention concerns the nature of India's public sphere. For all the partisan discord that characterises Indian politics, it is striking that the activists who sought the enactment of employment guarantee legislation were able to court, in quick succession, the Congress, the BJP, and the Left in order to achieve their goal. This was not a smooth process by any means. Gaining the ear of just the right interlocutors required an ability to understand the complex motives that animate politicians of different persuasions, and to support impassioned advocacy with the kinds of empirical evidence that can—under the right circumstances—help to blunt the force of political resistance. Beyond this, however, the receptivity of three such different partisan camps to the activists' message underscores the extent to which high politics in India increasingly relies on a shared political culture.

* * *

When parliament finally passed NREGA in August 2005, it did so unanimously. The occasion was celebratory. Rural Development Minister Raghuvansh Prasad Singh offered the house a rousing oration on the significance of this landmark legislation. He ended with a movement-like call: '*rozgar guarantee zindabad*' [long live employment guarantee]. The house, including those who had resisted the Act's more radical provisions, responded with what Dreze described as 'roaring applause'.[157] But Dreze also knew that the appearance of 'political unanimity' could be, and was, deceiving. Throughout the process of formulating and enacting NREGA, there had been a great deal of covert influence-peddling.[158] The emergence of 'a powerful "anti-NREGA" lobby', which was 'very vocal in the corporate-sponsored media', was in a sense a sign that rights-based activism in India had become a force to be reckoned with. But the near-success of this 'small lobby' in neutering the bill before it became law was also a 'telling symptom of the elitist nature of Indian democracy'.[159] That such powerful interests were 'organically linked' to the Finance Ministry and the Planning Commission, foreshadowed the implementation battles to come. Following NREGA's passage, Dreze did not expect 'a backlash against the Act'; he considered 'quiet sabotage' more likely.[160] All of this was consistent with the underlying political ethos from which NREGA was conceived. As Dreze put it, '[t]he process of mobilising for effective implementation of the Act also has much value in itself, as an opportunity for unorganised workers to organise'.[161]

We turn now to an analysis of the politics of implementing NREGA, including battles within and between the tiers of India's system of 'local government'— at the district, block, and village levels, where politics, even among administrative officials, is never far removed from the decision-making process.

3

ALL POLITICS IS 'LOCAL'?

NREGA IMPLEMENTATION
AND MULTILEVEL GOVERNANCE

This chapter examines the complex interplay between NREGA and the multiple levels of political representation that comprise India's system of *panchayati raj*, which includes elected councils at the village, block, and district levels. In analysing the political dimensions of NREGA implementation through these institutions, we assess the roles played by both politicians (whether or not they hold elective office at any given time) and administrators operating at each of these three levels. We examine both formal decision-making channels and the informal means through which influence is exerted by politicians, government administrators, and other actors.

The relationship between NREGA implementation and *panchayati raj* is reciprocal and iterative. Power dynamics within and between these institutions profoundly affect NREGA implementation, which in turn affects patterns of political activity. The relationship is also iterative in that political actors are continuously adapting to the new incentives created by changes to NREGA regulations, to shifts in the relative power of other actors, to pressures exerted by groups in civil society (and by society more broadly), and to increased awareness of the effects produced by different courses of action. We examine these dynamic interactions through three NREGA-related processes: (1) the increased power and resources of elected local councils, and the consolidation of power within these councils by their leaders; (2) the rationing of work opportunities, and the political logic behind the exclusion of certain groups; and (3) the struggles between village- and block-level actors over opportunities to steal funds from NREGA projects.

The analysis is drawn primarily from our field research findings in Rajasthan and Madhya Pradesh, the states that are the focus of the two subsequent chapters. But we also rely on evidence and observations from other states. While there is great variation across India both in terms of how NREGA has been implemented and the results achieved, the purpose here is to identify fairly common dynamics that have characterised the ground reality of programme functioning. Of particular interest is what these dynamics reveal about how various actors deploy their political resources—official positions, vertical connections, procedural knowledge, funds, and local support—in order to make NREGA serve their interests.

Increased Power of Elected Village Councils
(and of Leaders within these Councils)

Panchayati Raj Institutions—as distinct from traditional *panchayat* bodies, which lack formal legal authority—have existed in one form or another since the 1950s. While in some states and at some times *panchayats* were important centres of political influence, it was not until the 73rd Amendment to India's Constitituon came into force in 1993 that rural *panchayats* became a legally entrenched element of India's political system. (The 74th Amendment did the same thing for urban governance institutions.) The 73rd Amendment made it a requirement for state governments to constitute *panchayat* institutions and to hold regular elections. Although the constitution gave states latitude in designing their own structures, minimum standards for the administration of *panchayats* were also established.

There has been considerable variation in the vigour with which states have pressed ahead with democratic decentralisation. States such as Kerala and Madhya Pradesh made serious efforts to establish *panchayats* as viable institutions for development planning, whereas states such as Andhra Pradesh and Bihar have systematically disempowered *panchayats*, though in different ways.[1] There has also been substantial variation over time. Some of the pioneering experiments of the 1990s and early 2000s in Madhya Pradesh, for instance, were later scaled back or even reversed. The importance of different levels of the three-tier framework (village, block, and district) has also varied both between states and over time. In all states, elected councils in the middle tier of political representation—which corresponds to an administrative 'block'—have been kept weak, in contrast to elected councils at the district level above them and at the village level below. Bureaucrats therefore dominate at the block level. (As we shall see, this has important implications for the functioning of NREGA.) Moreover, village councils, or *gram panchayats*, often consist of a group of nearby settlements rather than a necessarily organic community of the sort implied by the term 'village'. In sparsely populated areas, the settlements that comprise a single *gram panchayat* can be a considerable distance from one another.

In most states, *gram panchayats* have had few resources to work with and little de facto authority over the allocation of whatever funds they received.[2] The huge infusion of NREGA funds, and the limited but important increase in planning discretion, was therefore the most important change to *panchayati raj* since the passage of the 73rd Amendment. Under NREGA, at least half of the funds allocated to works projects had to be devolved to elected local councils. In some states, this figure is closer to 90 per cent. Increased financial resources, somewhat enhanced autonomy from higher-levels of the political system, and an expanded range of administrative responsibilities have combined to enliven local politics considerably. For the first time in most states, almost all local groups (including the poor) see that local *panchayat* decisions can make a material difference in their lives.

The elites who usually head *gram panchayats* have long had to compete in local elections for the votes of poor villagers, who usually possess great numerical strength. They have been forced to compete even more energetically in recent years. This is partly because NREGA has inspired poor people to engage more with council politics. But two other recent trends have also contributed to the intensification of elite political competition. First, more local council seats have been won by poorer people. Some of these are seats 'reserved' for Dalits, Adivasis, and OBCs, but increasing numbers of 'open' seats (which can be contested by anyone) have been won by candidates from disadvantaged backgrounds. Second, the declining significance of caste hierarchies in many parts of rural India has made disadvantaged groups less deferential to elite castes.[3] This has increased pressure on the elites seeking their votes to deliver on their promises in tangible ways.

Local council politics is an arena in which the strong 'allergy' among government actors to transparency (having to reveal their decisions and actions, as well as the information on which these were based and the effects that they have had) and to downward accountability (having to answer to, and possibly be sanctioned by, people of lower social and economic status) is manifested most intensely and consistently. While local leaders cannot stop villagers from observing that substantial new resources have flowed from NREGA to local councils, and that the stakes in local politics have therefore been raised, they can deny ordinary people (such as NREGA workers) information that could be used to expose abuses of authority. Powerful actors at the local level—including the *sarpanch* (the directly elected local council head), the *panchayat* secretary (the local council's chief bureaucrat), and bureaucrats at the block level—have strong incentives to avoid acquainting poor villagers with the specific rights conferred upon them under NREGA.[4] They are, for instance, reluctant to advertise the demand-driven character of this programme, and the obligation under the Act that decisions on the nature and scope of works projects be taken in village-level mass meetings (*gram sabhas*), or that local residents are, theoretically, empowered to audit the use of the substantial new funds that NREGA has provided. It is thus not surprising that many poor villagers had not fully grasped that NREGA gave them the 'right' to work, to be compensated if their applications did not lead to employment within the stipulated fifteen-day timeframe, and to benefit from certain workplace requirements (for instance, that shaded rest areas, drinking water, and child-care facilities be provided).

As we have noted in earlier chapters, awareness of NREGA's provisions has been slow to develop. A study conducted during NREGA's first year in operation by the Society for Participatory Research in Asia (PRIA), a non-partisan CSO, found that a lack of awareness among the public was a severe problem.[5] Our surveys in Rajasthan and Madhya Pradesh (presented in Chapters 4 and 5), conducted two and a half years after the programme had been inaugurated, revealed similarly underwhelming levels of public awareness—even in two states ruled by governments that had sought to promote the programme for their own political ends. Three-and-a-half years after NREGA's introduction, people's knowledge of basic programme rules was still largely absent in Uttaranchal,[6] and also in the more developed coastal districts of Orissa, where the state government appears, perversely, to have implemented NREGA more energetically than in the deprived inland districts.[7] More recently, awareness has gradually increased, as evidence from Karnataka and Tamil Nadu indicates, though a survey conducted in mid-2013 showed that in some places awareness of NREGA and its rules was declining (likely the result of the UPA government's tepid support for the scheme in the latter stages of its tenure).[8]

Translating increased awareness of how NREGA procedures should work into effective collective action in support of people's rights, and into greater leverage for the poor in local politics, has been a painfully slow process.

The impact of the substantial new funding for *panchayats* on the intensity of local politics has been greatest in the majority of Indian states where, historically, local councils have been seriously under-funded. The change is particularly marked in places like Uttar Pradesh. But funding increases have also had a significant effect in states such as Kerala, where successive governments since the mid-1990s have devolved significant financial control. It is not necessarily the case, however, that increased interest from the poor in the affairs of better-funded councils has made council leaders more accountable to them. In fact, to better appreciate the nature of accountability relationships, we must consider another consequence of this injection of funds. The new political and administrative processes created by NREGA have also— unintentionally—triggered a centralisation of power within many, and probably most, local councils. We have observed this phenomenon in localities that we have studied in our field research, and have received informal reports of similar tendencies from other sources. This trend towards *sarpanch*-centric governance at the *gram panchayat* level is something that has been almost entirely unremarked upon in other studies. To understand what centralisation means in this context, and how it came about in the cases we have examined, let us consider the informal changes in power dynamics that NREGA has wrought in local arenas.

The elected leaders of local councils—or else their *panchayat* secretaries, where council leaders are timid or ineffective—have become more powerful in relation to their elected peers on the local council, and to local residents more generally. The processes that have produced this change will be discussed in Chapter 5, through case study examples from Madhya Pradesh, but their implications can be further examined here. In many parts of India, even within states where democratic decentralisation was taken seriously by the ruling party, much *gram panchayat* activity has typically been confined to decision-making on matters that required collective council action to ensure enforcement—such as identifying which families would receive means-tested subsidies paid by central or state government agencies, regularising pre-existing encroachments on village lands, or mobilising local residents to participate in forming water-users' associations that might (or might not) attract limited funds from central or state government-controlled development agencies. The *sarpanch*'s part in such decisions was of course crucial, but also fairly constrained. His or her role was typically that of first among equals. There were few resources under the direct control of the *sarpanch* that could be deployed to incentivise other council members to pursue a favoured course of action. Cultivating their support, not least through log-rolling, was a constant necessity—that is, when any activity was undertaken at all. Many *gram panchayats* in many parts of India have been characterised by chronic lethargy—an understandable state of affairs when neither funds nor powers had been granted to their leaders.

Naturally, the extent of a *sarpanch*'s authority depends to a considerable degree on his or her personal, social, or economic status. It also varies between states, depending on the funds and responsibilities state governments chose to devolve to local bodies and the requirements stipulated in the accompanying administrative and financial regulations. But the relative power of *sarpanches* in any given state or district also often depends on an important political variable that is difficult to pin down: the degree to which political competition at higher levels of the system creates incentives for potential patrons to court *sarpanches* as a way of building an electoral base. Where such competition is lively, a *sarpanch* who delivers political support to leaders further up the hierarchy may receive a particularly valuable payoff: instructions to the district and block-level bureaucrats who answer to these higher-level political patrons (state legislators, district councilors, party leaders) that the *sarpanch* in question be extended special privileges as a political client. Such privileges could mean the difference between getting a local project cleared and getting overruled or stonewalled indefinitely by a block-level bureaucrat. Skill at gaining access to (and using) such networks of influence has been a crucial means by which otherwise relatively powerless *sarpanches* have strengthened their positions vis-à-vis local political rivals, including other *panchayat* members. NREGA funds and projects are an important currency in which such largesse—from political patrons to their clients—is doled out.

The increase in funds that NREGA has provided to *panchayats* has, indirectly, conferred another new source of power on *sarpanches* in most states, in addition to those that they may already have enjoyed. The required administrative procedures that accompany NREGA funds are in theory overseen by the entire *panchayat*—and some elements of the implementation framework in fact require the *panchayat* to convene open village meetings (*gram sabhas*). But in practice the administrative mechanisms for implementing NREGA tend to fall under the control of the *sarpanch*. This is mainly because the degree of complexity requires fairly constant attention and oversight (which *sarpanches* are best placed to provide), coordination of various reporting formats (which tends towards centralisation by one individual), and intensive involvement by the council's main (in some cases only) administrative official, the village secretary, who reports to the *sarpanch*. For instance, under the various regulatory orders issued pursuant to NREGA, as well as related programme rules, *gram panchayats* are required to maintain numerous financial registers (estimates in different places range from seventeen to twenty-one). This is on top of their already onerous paperwork burden. As the primary custodians of NREGA accounts, local council leaders gain control over the official version of what has happened under the programme. Other councillors are disinclined to inspect the documents, or are prevented from doing so. The informational and agenda-setting advantages conferred by these roles place *sarpanches* in a strong position when it comes to making decisions about how to implement NREGA, including the best means of illegally diverting funds, a share of which usually makes its way to favoured colleagues on the *panchayat*.

These advantages are enhanced by the *sarpanch's* typical role as the locality's primary interlocutor with the bureaucratic actors who dominate at the block level, and on whom successful implementation of works projects relies. Frequent meetings with financial and technical officials at the block level are necessary to discuss NREGA business. Most *gram panchayat* members know only what council leaders tell them about these crucial meetings, though they may harbour suspicions about whose interests the *sarpanch* is advancing. The ability to control information, as well as the crucial decisions that information both reflects and shapes, enhances the influence—indeed, in many cases, the dominance—of the *sarpanch* within local politics. Moreover, because it is the job of elected councils at the district level to aggregate local NREGA works prioritisation documents into approved plans for the district (and block), political lobbying at these levels is also necessary. Journeys to block headquarters once or twice a week are not uncommon. Depending on distances, a monthly visit to district headquarters is also frequently called for. *Sarpanches* are often the only local councillor to participate in these interactions with higher-level officials. This is partly for sound technical reasons: because *sarpanches* oversee the maintenance of NREGA records, they are often the only people with a complete picture of what has happened at the local level. But other reasons, relating to the process through which illicit income is distributed, loom large as well. We will return to this issue later in this chapter, in the discussion of the dynamic relationship between different levels of the political system that NREGA has both affected and been affected by.

Because NREGA has increased the amount (and to some degree, the predictability) of funds available to local councils, *sarpanches* also tend to make more energetic efforts to manipulate local politics in ways that strengthen their influence over council affairs. Much more is at stake than before NREGA was enacted. One reason why *sarpanches* seek greater influence is to siphon funds. Illegally diverted funds can be put to a variety of purposes—increasing the *sarpanch's* personal wealth, of course, but also paying off block- and district-level bureaucrats whose acquiescence is required to ensure that works projects are sanctioned, inspection reports signed, and funds released; cultivating and cementing alliances among powerful political allies beyond their localities; and buying support among local faction leaders and others. The lines separating these various uses are often, in practice, rather blurred. For instance, when enhanced personal wealth takes the form of improvements to the *sarpanch's* lands—a form of 'public works' project that is not unknown in the annals of NREGA implementation—local political allies may be permitted to share in the bounty through access to the now more fertile grazing lands and more abundant water resources.

Whatever combination of motivations a *sarpanch* may have for using his or her position to divert funds illegally from NREGA projects, the ability to do so tends to further consolidate the *sarpanch's* power. This is not of course universally the case: some *sarpanches* corner such a large share of the programme's resources that an alliance of sorts emerges—between disgruntled workers (who have been denied work or wages) and alienated faction leaders (who feel entitled to a share of the proceeds of corruption). Typically, however, *sarpanches* use their new power to benefit diverse social groups within the locality, mainly because doing so is in their political interest. They want to remain broadly popular in order to get re-elected.

One institutional feature of *panchayati raj* that has limited this incentive is the system, which has prevailed in some states at certain times, of 'rotating reserved constituencies'.[9] Under a rotational system, the *sarpanch's* post within a *gram panchayat* is reserved for members of a particular community (or gender) for one electoral cycle, and then returned to the 'open' (non-reserved) category in the next cycle, at which point the leader's position in a nearby *gram panchayat* would then be reserved. After the requisite number of electoral cycles (which depends on the proportion of reserved seats), the *sarpanch's* position would again be reserved in the original village. Rotational reservation systems in effect impose term limits on *sarpanches*. This is true both for *sarpanches* from groups for whom reservations are legally mandated

(Dalits, Adivasis, OBCs, and women), because they tend not to be re-elected once the reservation period—usually a single term—has expired, as well as for *sarpanches* from non-reserved groups, who must cede office when the *panchayat* leadership is again returned to reserved status.

Despite these and other mitigating factors, the general trend towards the consolidation of council decision-making power in the hands of the *sarpanch* tends to undercut the capacity of other elected members to represent and to meet the needs of their constituents. The main change is that villagers (both poor and non-poor) must reach out not to all councillors but mainly to the council leader. In many localities, council leaders favour certain groups or areas within their bailiwicks—which often means that people from marginalised groups suffer.[10] Thus, the net effect of NREGA-induced revival of *panchayat* institutions is genereally not to make local councils more transparent and accountable to the poor. Better outcomes for poor people occur mainly when collective action has been catalysed.

In some ways, the provision of NREGA funding has enhanced the autonomy of *gram panchayats*. Several local council leaders said this when they boasted that they now controlled more money than their state legislators. As one put it, 'I can now do more than he can, and I no longer have to rely on him or others'.[11] But the increased resources available to councils may not have augmented their institutional substance. The centralisation of power within many *panchayats*—in the hands of their *sarpanches*—has diminished crucial capacities. The ability of *panchayats* to act as mechanisms for identifying common priorities, resolving conflicts, and lengthening the notoriously short time horizons of locally elected officials, has often been severely undermined.

Work Rationing, Patterns of Exclusion, and the Limited Role of 'Fixers'

NREGA promises jobs 'on demand'. But many, if not most, poor rural people have little or no experience of making direct demands on authority figures. They often live within local societies characterised by severely unequal power relations. Assertive behaviour by low-status people tends to be punished. State institutions are very often sufficiently remote, corrupt, and dysfunctional to offer few viable options for redress. In theory, the 73rd amendment brought representative governments closer to rural people. In practice, village councils—not to mention those at the block and district levels—have generally been dominated by powerful interests and members of elite communities. They have, moreover, possessed insufficient powers and resources to stimulate robust democratic politics at the village level.

Given this unpromising context, it is perhaps not surprising that the willingness, let alone ability, of non-elite people to operationalise their rights under NREGA is frequently in short supply. Indeed, much of the time, opportunities to undertake NREGA work are 'rationed' by powerful actors in local arenas—usually by the heads of elected local councils, acting in concert with fellow *panchayat* members and administrative officials. The withholding of job opportunities where they were most needed—where large numbers of BPL families lived—was documented from the programme's earliest years, even in West Bengal, where the ruling Communist Party of India-Marxist (CPI-M) was ostensibly championing NREGA's potential to alleviate the plight of agricultural labourers.[12] Rationing undermines three interrelated aims of NREGA, which is designed as an 'entitlement' programme. The first is material: that rural households seeking work have access to 100 days of wages annually. The second is instrumental: that those seeking work would not face an eligibility-screening process that would subject them to demands for bribes, to the whims of favouritism, or to the inefficiencies of state bureaucracies. The third aim is political: that poor villagers should see themselves (and be seen by others) not as passive 'beneficiaries' of government largesse, but as proactive claimers of rights.

The rationing of work opportunities under NREGA occurs in three ways. The first is for would-be applicants to be told by local officials, elected and administrative, that NREGA employment is currently unavailable, and will be for the foreseeable future. The reasons given for the lack of work tend to vary, but one that is frequently cited is that the planting and harvesting season is either underway or about to start—and thus there is (or shortly will be) high demand for agricultural labour. The implication—often not stated—was that there was no need for NREGA works because plenty of other employment opportunities were available, or that farmers were facing a shortage of agricultural workers, which the state should not exacerbate. There is no evidence that state governments in Rajasthan and Madhya Pradesh, where we conducted field research, imposed official moratoria on NREGA activities during planting or harvesting seasons as a matter of government policy, as some state governments have done. But there are, at a minimum, indications of a very strong informal tendency among local-level leaders in those two states, as elsewhere, to suspend NREGA work to avoid alienating land-owners who rely on agricultural labourers in those seasons and are reluctant to pay higher wages to attract workers who might be inclined to opt for NREGA employment instead.

In some cases, those who ask about or seek formally to apply for work are told that none is presently available because of bureaucratic delays or partisan discrimination imposed on the locality by officials further up the administrative and political hierarchies. This is often true, but can also serve as a convenient excuse, designed to conceal other reasons including the desire to shield private farmers who hire agricultural workers from labour shortages that drive up wages. There is evidence of nation-wide reductions in NREGA employment during the main planting and harvesting seasons, which vary greatly by crop and by region. One analysis of trends during 2010 found a large difference between the amount of NREGA work provided during months where high levels of agricultural employment tend to be experienced (July and August), and those in which less agricultural employment tends to be offered (May and June). While only between 80 and 110 million NREGA-project workdays per month were generated during the peak agricultural months, more than three times this number (between 300 and 330 million) were generated during the less-intensive agricultural months.

In theory, because NREGA work is supposed to be demand driven, the disparity reflected in these figures should reflect the preferences of workers seeking better-paying private-sector work during peak agricultural months, which in turn would reduce the number of workdays during those periods. In practice, however, because of the reluctance of local officials to accurately record applications for NREGA work (since they do not want documentation revealing a failure to supply work within fifteen days) we cannot know what proportion of a decline in NREGA workdays from month to month might be attributable to rationing. In fact, even some NREGA supporters have cited data on the decline in workdays during peak agricultural months to counter claims that the programme was causing farm labour shortages. Ironically, such a rebuttal was a tacit admission that one of NREGA's objectives—of increasing agricultural wages—was not being realised.[13]

Whatever the truth of the matter, in response to increasing complaints from workers and civil society groups about the use of de facto rationing to dampen upward pressure on wages, over time, *sarpanches* and administrators became more likely to cite reasons other than private-sector labour shortages for the non-availability of NREGA work. Though local officials were required by law to supply workers with a written reason as to why work was not supplied within the fifteen-day timeframe, applicants almost never received this. Indeed, the overwhelming tendency in many places has been for officials to refuse even to register people's applications for work in the first place, thus evading the need to provide official reasons why neither work was granted, nor an unemployment allowance paid. This plainly undermined the right to work, but two mitigating circumstances are worth stressing here. First, most poor households that suffered from rationing were able to perform at least some work under NREGA—so employment opportunities were usually curtailed, but not completely denied. Second, curtailments of the right to work that were visible in most localities, especially in *gram panchayats* where people's participation in village planning sessions (even as mute observers, as was frequently the case), supplied them with information about other works projects in the pipeline. Inequities (between identity-based groups or localities, for instance) were also visible, due to the public presence of NREGA worksites: those receiving employment could be seen and counted. These and other programme features heightened awareness among local people that something to which they had a legitimate claim—even if the idea of possessing a 'right' was not necessarily the conceptual framing—was being unfairly denied them. An observation sometimes made by activists seeking to organise local people was that, particularly when no NREGA work was available at all, people were more inclined to express discontent in some kind of collective fashion. This did not necessarily take the form of protest. Far more typical were small group visits by frustrated NREGA job-seekers to the homes of locally influential co-ethnics. Such signals of dissatisfaction do not necessarily go unnoticed in rural India, especially in villages where no local party-affiliated faction has achieved long-term political dominance.[14]

It is difficult to quantify the proportion of NREGA applicants who were denied work on the basis of official statistics. Workers who press forcefully to have their applications registered—receiving paper receipts as proof that they have done so—are routinely informed by *panchayat* officials that, as a result of such assertive behaviour, not only will their demands not be met, but that they will be excluded from NREGA work opportunities that may eventually arise. Such threats carried weight because local officials had, in most places, been able to demonstrate early in the NREGA implementation process that there was not, in practice, enough work to go around. De facto rationing was the norm to which people became socialised. Selective exclusion emerged as a credible means of convincing applicants to refrain from actively asserting their rights. It is worth noting that two analyses of all-India data found that 'on balance, the rationing process...generally favours the poor, not the non-poor'. In other words, 'overall it is the non-poor who are more likely to have unmet demand for work on MGNREGS'.[15] According to official statistics, since the programme was extended from the initial pilot districts to the entire country in 2008, almost all households that sought employment under NREGA obtained at least some work. The figures range from a low of 94 per cent in 2008–9 to a high of 99 per cent in 2010–11. But even the official data indicate that the average number of days worked was far less than the 100-day maximum guaranteed under the law.

Table 3.1: Average work days per household (per annum)

Year	No. of days worked
2008–9	47.95
2009–10	53.99
2010–11	46.79

Source: NREGA website: nrega.nic.in—DMU Reports.

Of course, not every household seeks the full 100 days, but many do and are turned away. Others, conditioned to expect local rationing rather than automatic entitlement, do not bother applying for the full 100 days. To better understand how the process operates at the local level, we must consider the political logic that drives the exclusion of would-be workers. This, it must be stressed, is distinct from the economic logic that might be employed by officials seeking merely to maximise their income. The two are not completely unrelated, in that illicit income can be used not merely to augment personal wealth, but also to advance political objectives, such as buying the support of patrons and consolidating a local faction.

There are several reasons why locally influential political figures systematically seek to limit NREGA employment to certain groups among the poor (or, in a smaller number of cases, to deny it entirely). They are motivated by electoral calculations, social prejudice, political mistrust, or quite often a combination of two, or even all three, of these considerations.

The key decision-maker is usually the elected head of the local council—sometimes along with some of the ward councillors. If the *sarpanch*'s ruling group considers a particular locality (*mohalla*, hamlet, village) implacably opposed to its continued rule, then residents of that locality may find themselves partly or entirely shut out of NREGA work. As with all forms of clientelism, past voting behaviour is used as a guide to future electoral loyalties. But defections, coaxed through offers of patronage (such as NREGA jobs or works projects designed to benefit residents in a particular locality), are always a possibility, making for a sometimes fluid political dynamic. Factional conflicts within local arenas often loom large here—and it is common to find members of elite groups leading rival, socially diverse factions. Calculations about past and potential future voting intentions are also made with reference to caste groups, local lineages, and other forms of politicised identity.

Local political leaders who determine the distribution of NREGA benefits sometimes approach caste differences less instrumentally, however—in which case social prejudice can be as powerful a motivation as political advantage. Where coalitions among caste groups are necessary to constitute an electoral majority—as is frequently the case in rural India—social prejudice tends to be a less visible predictor of how NREGA jobs are distributed. But when political calculations are, for whatever reason, sublimated, biases against certain social groups can be decisive. Typically, local decision makers motivated by social prejudice are from elite communities, and work to exclude members of lower castes, Adivasi groups, or religious minorities. In some cases, however, lower-caste groups are in power, and discriminate against upper-caste applicants who have made their distaste for working alongside people they consider their social inferiors clear.

The third motivation behind the denial of NREGA benefits to a particular local group is political mistrust. This refers to a concern on the part of key decision-makers that members of certain groups are more likely to complain about wage underpayments, spur agitations, ask uncomfortable questions about the conduct of works, seek information relating to project implementation, and insist on the convening of *gram sabhas* to undertake the required social audits. Those who have displayed such non-compliant behaviour, and those guilty merely by association, tend to have their access to employment opportunities under NREGA curtailed, sometimes drastically.

Local leaders recognise that retaining discretionary power over the selection of workers on NREGA-funded projects through the 'rationing' process outlined above can be used to augment their political leverage, increasing the number of transactions through which they can expand and deepen their clientelist networks. It can also, of course, be used as a means of maximizing the proportion of funds that can be siphoned off from the programme. This is because, as we have seen, rationing can be used to exclude workers who might be more inclined to demand full payment of their wages or insist on the full implementation of transparency provisions that could expose corruption. Even workers who might otherwise be likely to insist on being accorded all of their rights—assuming that they are aware of them—can over time become less demanding once it becomes evident that rationing can be used to exclude them from future work. Workers are keenly aware that the local patrons who help them to secure work from programme implementers in the first place—leaders from their caste, lineage, faction, or neighbourhood—tend not to look kindly on overly assertive behaviour from workers, not least because such leaders are often themselves implicated in the system of corruption.

Political middlemen linking local residents directly to administrative officials could, in theory, help to overcome some of the exclusion problems outlined above. Recent research has found that across most of India, local-level political entrepreneurs who travel back and forth between villages and government offices at higher levels—usually to block and district headquarters—have played an important role as intermediaries, helping villagers to gain access to government programmes or to obtain various official clearances. These entrepreneurs—which researchers call *naya netas* (new leaders) or small-time 'fixers'[16]—often come from beyond the ranks of traditionally dominant local communities whose power stems from their high social status or control of land. Some *naya netas* concentrate on assisting members of the poorer (usually lower-status) groups from which they come. We might therefore expect them to engage widely with NREGA, and to promote awareness among poor people who stand to gain from the programme.

Some of this is happening, but much less than might be expected. Our field surveys in Madhya Pradesh and Rajasthan found that poor villagers were interacting almost entirely with leaders and members of local councils rather than with political fixers. An explanation for this is suggested in one of the studies that initially called attention to the role played by fixers. Its analysis of eight varied Indian states found that when elected councils were endowed with authority and resources, the space for fixers to operate was quite limited. This was because the primary comparative advantage of a fixer is his or her connections to higher levels of the political and administrative hierarchies. When local councils become firmly integrated into such hierarchies, they become direct conduits to the higher-level decision-makers that fixers have traditionally supplied. Fixers, therefore, tended to have almost no engagement with government programmes administered through local councils. In states where such *panchayats* were strong and well resourced, ambitious young people tended not to become free-booting fixers. They instead sought election to local councils.[17] Demand for fixers has remained extremely robust, however, in the majority of states where *panchayats* are weak and poorly funded.

We saw earlier in this discussion that NREGA (a) is substantially implemented through *panchayat* institutions; (b) has provided local-level councils with abundant funds, in many states for the first time; and (c) has operated in ways that allow the elected heads of local councils to exercise a near monopoly on interactions with the block level. These three features of NREGA implementation have, in other words, created precisely the conditions that the literature on fixers has identified as limiting their ability to work as intermediaries between individual claimants and the bureaucrats who implement NREGA.

But there is a second dimension to the work of *naya netas* that is less often remarked upon—not their role as 'retail' agents who assist individuals in conducting business with government offices, but as 'wholesale' vote brokers to whom politicians sometimes turn to secure pledges of electoral support in exchange for promises of preferential treatment—or at least reduced marginalisation—for entire neighbourhoods.[18] These geographic areas are often coterminous with electoral polling stations and inhabited largely by members of a single caste or community, making possible the monitoring of electoral loyalties. Though Anirudh Krishna, who first employed the term *naya neta*, does not employ the retail-wholesale distinction, both roles are analysed in his study of districts along each side of the border separating the same two states that are the focus of this book's empirical investigations: Rajasthan and Madhya Pradesh.[19] Krishna's key limiting condition in explaining the role of *naya netas* was that they can effectively function as wholesale political brokers only when the locality on whose behalf they are negotiating possesses high stocks of social capital. It is this latent resource—dense local social networks embedded in norms of trust and reciprocity—that skilled *naya netas* can 'activate' in order to secure for such communities promises of preferential treatment from the political actors who, in theory, exercise influence over the administrative organs of government.

Local fixers were said to have played just such a role in a number of localities during the 2008 assembly election in Rajasthan.[20] They helped localities that received limited NREGA benefits during its early phases—from 2006–8—to bargain for better treatment in the next phase. According to knowledgeable informants, party operatives working for BJP candidates in assembly constituencies in Banswara and Jhalawar districts, both of which border Madhya Pradesh, engaged with local political brokers from Dalit and Adivasi communities—classic *naya netas*. In both constituencies, *naya netas* worked on behalf of hamlets where virtually no residents had received NREGA jobs during the two years the programme had been operating in the area at that point in time. In one case, the hamlet's long-time political leader—an elder of the *Bhil* community, of impeccable reputation but unschooled in recent development policies and procedures—represented a faction opposed to the *gram panchayat*'s reigning *sarpanch*. Because the hamlet was relatively socially homogeneous, the *naya neta* was able to credibly offer *en bloc* voting for the BJP candidate in the upcoming assembly election in exchange for a promise to pressure local NREGA implementers to ensure that jobs went to the hamlet's residents, many of which had stopped inquiring about NREGA employment, so dejected had they become. Part of the bargain was that the candidate would have to demonstrate his ability to fulfil his commitment by leaning on block authorities to bring jobs to the hamlet in the months before the election (which was held in late 2008). Because the BJP, the candidate's party, was at the time in control of the state government, this was theoretically within his power. However, no jobs appeared within the stipulated timeframe. The local *Bhil* community, through their broker, informed the candidate's operatives that they would not be voting for the BJP, which indeed lost the constituency and the state election.

Our key informant in this case admitted that the local community's reluctance to back the BJP candidate stemmed in part from a belief that Congress would form the next state government, in which case supporting a BJP legislator would indeed not have been a shrewd option. This is just one example, but the phenomenon of *naya netas* acting as wholesale vote brokers, with NREGA forming an increasingly important currency in their political exchanges, was a frequent part of the narrative among political observers in many parts of Rajasthan.

Forms of Corruption in NREGA Implementation

A diverse repertoire of mechanisms can and has been used to steal funds from NREGA. By outlining these here, we do not suggest that the programme is being thoroughly plundered. Indeed, many of these maneuvers have become exceedingly difficult because of the transparency and accountability provisions built into NREGA, as well as the measures introduced after it came into being. It is harder to divert funds from NREGA than from almost any of India's other nationwide anti-poverty programmes. This includes the Public Distribution System (PDS), through which subsidised foodgrains and other essential commodities are supplied on a means-tested basis through a network of 'fair price shops'; the Swarnajayanti Gram Swarozgar Yojana (which in 1999 incorporated the twenty-year-old Integrated Rural Development Programme, the Million Wells Scheme, and other initiatives); the Indira

Awas Yojana (which subsidises the upgradation of rural housing for the poor); and a variety of social-insurance schemes that fall under the National Social Assistance Programme (for the elderly, for widows and orphans, and for pregnant women).

The first, and perhaps most basic, form of corruption consists of the up-front costs associated with the early phases of obtaining NREGA work. For instance, just to obtain a job card—without which participation in works projects would not be possible—many people seeking employment under the programme have to pay an up-front bribe. This is usually payable to local council officials—the *sarpanch* or *panchayat* secretaries—or to an intermediary who procures the job cards on the worker's behalf. This malpractice does not directly involve actors at higher levels, though their awareness of its existence tends to increase the size of the tribute they demand from local officials. Another up-front cost associated with the programme's early days was the holding of local NREGA 'awareness building' campaigns. Fictitious civil society organisations, or organisations created overnight, were often contracted for this purpose, though in most cases few (or no) outreach activities were performed. The funds claimed were pocketed by officials who could easily falsify the required documentation.[21]

A second form of corruption takes place when worksite supervisors make entries on workers' job cards indicating fewer days (or hours) than they actually worked, thus reducing the amount owed to workers. This less-than-actual figure is reflected on the 'unofficial' muster rolls (employment registers) available at a given job site, and held in the files of the village *panchayat* office. The higher (actual) number of days is entered into the 'official' employment registers filed with higher authorities and subsequently entered into NREGA IT system. Copies of these official registers are also held in the village *panchayat* office. Depending on which type of actor seeks access to local financial records, a different set of accounts can be produced. The difference between the amount claimed through official submissions and the amount actually paid to workers on the basis of understated hours listed on unofficial employment registers, is pocketed by officials. Using this relatively straightforward method of theft became far more difficult following the introduction of rules requiring that the amounts listed on official forms submitted to the state government be paid directly to workers' bank accounts in 2008.

A third mechanism of corruption was for officials to obtain illicit income by including the names of people who performed no work in NREGA daily employment registers. Because each such entry requires the name of an individual who has been issued a job card, officials must obtain job cards for these 'ghost workers'. One source of such cards are people who do not want to work on NREGA projects—because they have migrated, have alternative sources of income, or find such work beneath their dignity. Such people sometimes have job cards issued in their names without their knowledge, and these are kept in the possession of local programme implementers who use them to derive income for the 'work' these ghost employees ostensibly performed. In other cases, particularly where fears of audits are strong, people who have no intention of working can be induced to fill in the forms necessary to receive a job card, knowing that it will be used to claim funds for work that they never performed. Those who 'lease out' their names and cards in this way may receive a share of the funds obtained from the local officials who engineer the fraud, or else their complicity may be compensated in the form of other benefits the officials are in a position to provide, such as preferential treatment on other government programmes. Some non-workers are coerced by local leaders into handing over their job cards and receive no additional compensation.

A variant of the pre-meditated ghost worker approach occurs when people who had not been selected for work at a given worksite appear anyway, providing bribes to supervisors to have their names added to the employment register. They then receive wages which exceed the cost of the bribes, whether or not these additional workers actually performed any labour.[22] This maneuver may not even involve local council leaders, representing instead a freelance appropriation of valid workers' wages by worksite supervisors, who sometimes also derive additional income for themselves by claiming funds from the government for the provision of required worksite amenities—such as staffed crèche facilities—without actually supplying them.

In theory, these forms of corruption—which range from collusive to coercive—need not entail theft from genuine workers' wages. But in practice, in places where a 'piece rate' system is in effect and block officials come to measure the amount of work performed (the length of road repaired, for instance), the addition of ghost worker names to the employment register has the effect of reducing the average work output attributed to each individual listed, thereby depriving genuine workers of the full wages they were due.

In at least a few places, when wage payments to workers are delayed (a frequent occurrence), the elected heads or members of local councils provide workers with prompt cash outlays amounting to a sizeable proportion of the wages due to them. (Indrajit Roy, who discovered this in Bihar and West Bengal, cites a figure of 80 per cent of the full amount earned.) When the full payments eventually reach workers' accounts, the councillor would insist on the full amount, claiming the additional 20 per cent as a kind of service charge or interest on a short-term loan.[23]

In some instances it has been possible for officials to divert funds from NREGA without directly reducing the wages of genuine workers. This requires the block-level officials who measure the extent of the work completed to fraudulently certify that the works were more extensive than they actually were. This allows additional ghost workers to be added to the employment registers—and their unearned wages to be divided among those complicit in this fraud—without reducing the recorded work output (and therefore wages) of genuine workers. This form of fraud can only be perpetrated, however, when block officials are sufficiently confident that no further auditing by either official actors or civil society groups will take place and potentially expose their misdeeds. This confidence is sometimes a reflection of the nature of the project, particularly when it involves mainly earthen works, such as low-tech irrigation channels or canal desilting. In such instances, if an audit revealed that project documents had overstated the amount of work performed, this could be blamed on subsequent weather-induced erosion by the certifying official. The other main source of confidence among block officials that no additional auditing will take place stems from an awareness of deep and abiding political protection by a particularly powerful patron.

Some local officials have made deals with contractors to implement projects—illegally, since contractors are banned under NREGA. For an agreed fee, the contractors, some of whom are themselves local elected officials, completed the projects using earth-moving and other forms of machinery (which are also banned). Local officials then made false entries on job cards and in the IT system showing that extensive labour was used on the project, so that the funds that they receive (ostensibly to pay the workers listed) exceeds the fee paid to contractors. Though the acquiescence of some job card holders required that they too receive a share of the profits, this method could earn local officials a substantial amount of illicit income. This practice was rare in the states where we did field research, but it has been more common in others.[24] Because the use of contractors and/or machines was fairly obvious, and the profit margins known to be considerable, additional payments would often have to be made to block-level officials to certify that the works had been completed with the use of labour alone.

Local leaders also routinely inflate the costs incurred in obtaining and transporting materials for NREGA projects. This form of fraud is often undertaken in collusion with private-sector vendors—local transport providers and building-supply merchants—who furnish false invoices, and promise to maintain their financial records in ways that will conceal the misdeeds of officials. This source of illicit income for local officials does not come directly from workers' wages because NREGA rules permit a maximum of 40 per cent of project budgets to be devoted to non-wage costs. Yet, had this form of fraud been effectively checked, in theory an even higher proportion of project costs could have been devoted to wage payments.

There have been numerous variants on these basic approaches to stealing funds from NREGA projects, most of which have been made much more difficult by the introduction of the requirement that wages be paid directly into workers' bank accounts. Such techniques have not always been rendered completely unviable, however. For instance, a corrupt official can sometimes get an accomplice to impersonate an account-holder (whether a genuine NREGA labourer or a ghost worker) at a bank branch or post office where payments are collected. This may involve the need for a side-payment (or other inducement) to the branch manager or postmaster. After bank account payments for NREGA wages had been made mandatory, workers who 'leased out' their job cards to officials (or were coerced into parting with them) had to participate more actively in executing this form of fraud by collecting the 'wages' from the bank before handing them over to the *sarpanch*'s representative. This also meant, in many cases, that the ghost worker could obtain a larger share of the illicit income, as they could see how much was being claimed in their name, whereas previously they had to take the word of the *sarpanch*, who had an incentive to understate wages being claimed against each job card.[25]

Other methods have also been devised to work around the bank account constraint. For instance, before the bank account requirement, workers were sometimes paid less than the minimum wage for their work, but the IT records showed that they received the higher, official wage. (In some parts of Madhya Pradesh, they were paid Rs. 50 or 70 per day when the official rate at that time was Rs. 100.) Local leaders then pocketed the difference. The introduction of bank accounts created an incentive for local leaders to maximise the amount of wages due to workers through the IT system, since they can only obtain a portion of those wages by persuading or forcing workers to part with some of their wages. However, local leaders were often hesitant to do this because their involvement in the extortion of wages becomes far more visible—both to the victimised workers, who become resentful and often more proactive and truculent, and to other local residents whose votes will decide the next local election.

Despite these ingenious adaptations, there is abundant anecdotal evidence to suggest that the introduction of the bank account requirement has led officials who seek to siphon NREGA funds to shift a good deal of their attention from workers' wages (which account for 60 per cent of NREGA budget) to the manipulation of documents relating to the acquisition of materials for works projects and the transport of such materials.

Power Dynamics between Local and Block Levels

Let us now look beyond the grassroots (or *gram panchayat* level of the local government pyramid) and consider the interactions between local leaders and actors at higher tiers of the system. Though NREGA has brought greater resources and authority to elected local councils, allowed *sarpanches* to consolidate power within these bodies, and provided ample opportunities for local officials to steal NREGA funds, in order to implement the programme they still have to contend with bureaucrats at the block (or subdistrict) level. The key actor here is the Block Development Officer (BDO), who coordinates the work of engineers and other officials from various line departments, such as public works, irrigation, forestry, and public health. Both individually and collectively, these officials act as 'veto players' in the process of implementing NREGA. Even before the programme's advent, block-level officials had long possessed considerable authority over public works projects, anti-poverty programmes, and other forms of government action. But the scale and structure of NREGA has invested their powers with far more significance. They approve projects, attest to their technical feasibility, measure and inspect works, certify completion, authorise the disbursal of funds, and verify compliance with a large range of additional requirements under NREGA and other relevant regulations. Most block officials see such authorisations as a source of leverage, and are unwilling to grant them without some form of compensation.

In theory, there should be systemic constraints on the ability of block-level bureaucrats to engage in such exploitation. Among the most important is that block-level bureaucrats should be answerable to (and subjected to oversight by) elected councils at the block level of the *panchayati raj* system.[26] Voters might be expected to pressure their block-level councilors to rein in corrupt officials holding up funding for works projects. However, in every Indian state, elected block-level councils are extremely weak.[27] Not only do block-level councils have few powers delegated to them—they are mainly responsible for various 'coordination' functions—they also have few resources under their direct control. This tier of the *panchayati raj* system is also weakened by the presence in block-level councils of politicians from other representative bodies, such as Members of the state's Legislative Assembly (MLAs) from the area. So, in practice, bureaucrats dominate at this middle-tier of the administrative and political system.

Compounding the innate institutional weakness of block-level councils is the assumption that NREGA's architects appear to have made about where the bulk of programme abuses were most likely to take place. The elaborate accountability safeguards built into NREGA, as well as the regulations framed pursuant to the Act, focus almost entirely on the local level. The rules are targeted mainly at the elected heads of local councils, *panchayat* secretaries (government functionaries), and to a lesser degree the 'mates' who supervise labourers on work sites. These actors were identified as the main potential villains, who would be responsible for most of the corruption in the system. Focusing transparency mechanisms at the level at which most citizens engage with public authorities makes good sense. The village level is where people were to seek employment, undertake work, and have their wages paid. It is where they would gain direct knowledge of malfeasance, which could then be put to use in a public forum for airing grievances and seeking disciplinary action against errant officials. It was in local arenas that ordinary people would be best positioned to engage in collective action to expose abuses in programme implementation. Moreover, to strike at the illegal activities of *gram panchayat* officials—elected and bureaucratic—would be to strike at the 'root' of corruption.

This assumption is flawed on a number of grounds. First of all, it is important to emphasise that the gross income that a *sarpanch* and his local accomplices might be able to skim from NREGA projects does not represent net profit. A range of legitimate (and not-so-legitimate) business expenses significantly cuts into the bottom line. They receive a modest government stipend each month to attend to NREGA duties, in addition to a similarly modest sum for their other responsibilities, but these do not begin to cover their costs. Most *sarpanches* must travel weekly to block-level offices for consultations with bureaucrats, so travel costs use up much of their allowances. Many also pay literates in their villages to assist in maintaining records. They must offer tea and snacks to large numbers of constituents who call at their homes and offices—a common estimate was 200 visitors per month. They must meet these costs from their own pockets. They are required to provide more lavish food and entertainment to visiting dignitaries (legislators and senior officials). And above all, they must recoup the high cost of past and future election campaigns, which at a minimum runs into tens of thousands of rupees.

Still, it is clear from the evidence from our field research in Madhya Pradesh and Rajasthan that local-level actors do indeed require close monitoring. Left unchecked, they would likely pilfer an even greater share of the resources that are intended for workers and for the infrastructure projects they are supposed to be building. But a key source of corruption in the system lies elsewhere—at the next level up in the system, the block, which has not been targeted by any transparency mechanisms. Given the considerable authorising powers of veto players in the block-level administration, the lack of safeguards at this level of NREGA implementation was a serious design flaw.

The result of this combination of institutions and incentives has been a state of more or less constant competition between local-level leaders and block-level officials for increased shares of the illicit income that can be derived from NREGA implementation. The relationship is characterised by collusion. But it is also one perceived by both sides as largely a zero-sum game in which trust is in short supply. We noted earlier in this chapter, in the discussion of how *sarpanches* have consolidated their power within local councils, that the *sarpanch* is usually the only local-level representative involved directly in consultations with block-level officials over NREGA implementation issues. One reason for this, as people familiar with NREGA administration have observed, is that a substantial portion of the discussions at block headquarters involves negotiating the illicit payments that block-level officials will receive for various approvals—and, by extension, for allowing local leaders to engage in the irregularities through which they obtain corrupt income of their own. It is logical that both sides would want to limit the number of individuals present at such negotiations. All those concerned want to avoid potential incrimination, which becomes more likely when additional persons witness the planning.

Just as importantly, however, block-level officials want to reduce the chances that information will leak about how much they are being paid for their services—and for acquiescing to corruption by local leaders. This is a particular consideration when a *gram panchayat* is—for one reason or another—given a favourable (lower than normal) rate by block officials. Should such information become more widely known, block officials would face pressure to grant the same rate to other *panchayats*. If, on the other hand, the payments charged to local leaders are higher than the norm, block officials would be equally disinclined to have that revealed, for fear of alerting their superiors, who might demand increased tribute in turn. *Sarpanches*, too, have an interest in maintaining secrecy in order to consolidate their role as 'gate-keepers' between local and block levels, but also to allow them to overstate the amounts they are paying to block- and district-level officials to their *gram panchayat* colleagues. Doing so allows *sarpanches* to increase their share of the illicit income.

Several aspects of the rent-sharing dynamic make life extremely difficult for local council leaders. The first is the difficulty of ensuring that agreements with block-level bureaucrats are adhered to. What might have appeared to a *sarpanch* as an all-inclusive agreement with a BDO—covering all necessary clearances and certifications for a given project or a specified time period—sometimes proves insufficient to prevent other block-level officials from demanding additional payments for specific services. Junior engineers who ask for bribes from local leaders for such minor but important tasks as the periodic measurement of works sometimes claim to have no knowledge of any prior agreement with the BDO, or complain that the BDO is keeping all the funds for himself. Newly transferred engineers and accountants are particularly well-placed to advance such claims. When the cost of delayed certification or sign-off is high to a local leader—whether in terms of his local reputation or because it will have a cascade effect that undercuts the viability of later phases of the project—he has little choice but to pay.

Local leaders are limited in their ability to appeal effectively against such predations by junior officials. The BDO with whom a *sarpanch* thought he had an agreement may plead that he is powerless to police those who ostensibly work under his direction. Excuses of this type are all too plausible given the complex administrative hierarchy in India's development bureaucracies, which is often less than straightforward. While an engineer, accountant, or other relatively junior official may be assigned to work under a BDO, he may also report to his departmental superiors, in a chain of command that reaches up to ministry headquarters in the state capital. Such an official may, moreover, perceive that his future career prospects are better advanced by seeking the favour and protection of a senior official at the district level (or higher) with which he has a family or community connection. The ability of a BDO to rein in junior officials under such circumstances may in fact be limited—or the BDO may merely claim, disingenuously, that it is limited when faced with complaints from local council leaders of having been subjected to an unauthorised 'shake down'. It is a matter of intense local speculation as to whether or not such demands for additional bribes were in fact orchestrated by the BDO, who is presumed to receive a cut of such payments.

Another source of grief for local leaders who seek to implement NREGA works on the basis of limited skimming and a relatively stable set of expectations, arises when BDOs renege openly on illicit revenue-sharing agreements. This can happen, for instance, when externally imposed scarcities become widely known—for instance, a temporary fiscal cut back announced by the state government. A BDO may attempt to use such a situation to his or her advantage by persuading a local leader that renegotiating their arrangement has become necessary. BDOs also sometimes fabricate 'news' of changed circumstances inside the state administration to increase their bargaining leverage—a change that is not at all difficult to imagine. A typical excuse is that the BDO is facing pressure from his superiors to increase the amount of funds payable up the hierarchy— possibly at the behest of political patrons anticipating campaign expenses for a forthcoming election. Typically, a BDO might mention that if he could not find additional funds to satisfy his bosses, he might be transferred to another locality. The not-so-subtle implication was that, in such an event, the *sarpanch* in question would have to begin from scratch with a new BDO, who would neither honour prior agreements nor refund advance payments made to secure future administrative authorisations.

Some elected local councillors—particularly those with strong personalities and political skills—have been able to manage this complex relationship and the uncertainties that come with it. But even they find the effort involved in decoding the intentions of their block-level counterparts, and in collecting information to verify their claims and those of other actors, extremely costly. Many less formidable local leaders, who are far more common, have become deeply disillusioned, to the point where efforts to implement NREGA have ground to a halt. In Madhya Pradesh, a knowledgeable civil society activist has seen a few reduced to tears.[28] These stresses have even persuaded some local council leaders that they should retire from politics.

Not all local councils suffer the same frequency and intensity of predatory and duplicitous behaviour from block-level officials. The variation is largely the result of two main factors. The first is the ability, which varies considerably, of local leaders to make use of connections, often through political parties, to politicians and bureaucrats operating at higher levels of the system, particularly the district and state levels. Such actors may have good reason to restrain block-level officials. An approach to a state legislator, and/or occasionally to the elected head of the district *panchayat* can prove useful in some cases, but if these people belong to a party that is not in power at the state level, these connections are (in most states) of little help. A legislator from an opposition party may lodge complaints and appeal for more generous treatment of party colleagues at the village level, but he is unlikely to have much impact. Indeed, in some parts of Madhya Pradesh where legislators from the opposition Congress Party held office, the ruling BJP took a certain pleasure in disregarding their protests and continuing to squeeze village-level leaders for illicit payments. Even when complaints arose from a Congress minister in the national government whose traditional base included these areas, nothing much changed.[29] The BJP saw this as a means of undermining his profile in the region by graphically demonstrating the diminution of his external influence.

Only members of the ruling party at the state level can have much hope of triggering meaningful pressure from party allies on bureaucrats at district and block levels. But even this may not help much because many state legislators are jealous of the powers and funds that have been devolved onto local councils, and are thus reluctant to help council leaders. Though this often proves, in retrospect, to have been politically unwise, as they will need support from local council leaders at the next state election, many legislators blindly persist in the practice.

The second weapon deployed by local leaders in response to duplicitous behaviour from block-level officials is to resort to dissimulation and concealment. In the early days of NREGA, they used these tactics to cheat workers of their wages (partly to obtain funds for kickbacks), and to hide that from block-level officials. This was less easy than it used to be in the pre-NREGA era, as the combination of job cards and the IT system created impediments. But after 2008, when payments to workers through bank accounts became mandatory, it became increasingly difficult to siphon off workers' wages in this way. So, in most localities, leaders have resorted to concealing and inflating the costs incurred in purchasing and transporting materials—activities that remain unaffected by the advent of bank accounts for NREGA workers. In several states in recent years, however, bureaucrats at block and even district levels—who see that materials offer the main hope for profiteering—have centralised their procurement.[30] That deprives many local council leaders of funds from this vital source of illicit income. Block-level officials of course assume that local leaders are engaging in dissimulation and concealment. They therefore inspect local record books, and when they find (or claim that they find) irregularities, they often threaten disciplinary action unless additional bribes are forthcoming. They also tend to presume that local leaders inflate the costs for materials, and factor that into their calculations before making demands for kickbacks. To further increase their bargaining leverage, block-level officials feign a lack of awareness that having to pay workers' wages through bank accounts has made it extremely difficult for local council leaders to divert funds.

Three features of NREGA place local leaders at a serious disadvantage in their dealings with block-level bureaucrats. First, the latter are responsible for works measurements which determine the amount of funds that can be committed to local projects. Second, concealment is of no use in combating demands from block-level officials for kickbacks at flat rates, such as 10 per cent or 20 per cent, when a sum is released from the block level to local councils—a malpractice which has diminished since the Indian government took steps in early 2009 to combat it. Finally, the Act gives local leaders few protections against bullying intrusions by block-level officials. It is local leaders who must face the ire of applicants for employment when works projects have not been sanctioned.

Finally, it is worth noting that our interviews at the local level and extensive discussions with people who have studied NREGA in various parts of India both indicate that discrepancies found in account books sometimes occur because local leaders do not understand the details of the Act and the complex procedures that it entails, or because they lack the time and skill to maintain all of the records. But because block-level officials assume that all discrepancies are the result of calculated corruption, they interpret any honest mistakes as a tactic designed to reduce the share of corrupt income to which they are entitled. Their subsequent demands for restitution can seriously exacerbate tensions. In a variation on this theme, block-level officials who encounter a local leader who is quite honest, and thus irritatingly reluctant to pay bribes, may concoct cases against him for excessive corruption in order to force him to deliver illicit payments, and to remind others that fair-dealing is risky behaviour when it comes to NREGA implementation.

* * *

The continuous tug-of-war between local councils and block-level officials for control over NREGA implementation (and the corrupt income that it could generate) sometimes involved one or another side seeking to increase its leverage by drawing in political and bureaucratic actors at higher levels of the system. The effects—on the relative shares of the spoils—were not always predictable, and the impact on NREGA's intended beneficiaries became exceedingly difficult to determine. Moreover, changes emanating from much further up the political food chain—in state capitals or even New Delhi—sometimes produce major changes in the rules of the game. The requirement that wages be paid through workers' bank accounts was a shift that was downright transformative, but others also had some impact.

In early 2009, for instance, the MoRD took steps to ensure that funds released for the first phases of new works projects were disbursed directly from district accounts to village *panchayats*, bypassing the block-level offices. This made it impossible for block-level officials to obtain the 10–20 per cent kickback they typically demanded before agreeing to release these start-up funds. Even so, some block-level officials have sought—sometimes successfully—to persuade financial officers to delay the release of funds from higher-level accounts to local councils until local leaders provide them with their cut. Where this tactic has proven ineffective, block officials have demonstrated great determination in recouping this 'loss'—through higher charges on other 'services' provided to local councils or through other means.

In 2010, the Government of India again revised rules concerning the roles and responsibilities of various actors in the process of certifying NREGA works. This was in part aimed at breaking the monopoly that block-level officials enjoyed, and which was increasingly known to be causing corruption, delays, and inefficiencies in programme implementation. The new rules gave state governments the option of engaging qualified persons from outside government to undertake measurement activities. Only a few state governments introduced this change. Those that did not were motivated primarily by the desire to continue protecting the development bureaucracies through which ruling-party legislators derived a share of their illicit earnings.

In the next two chapters, we will see not only how NREGA beneficiaries experienced the programme in two states, but also how efforts by state governments to tailor NREGA to their own circumstances—including the political interests of leading decision-makers—have occasionally affected the cat-and-mouse game between *gram panchayat* and block-level actors. Our analysis of how politics manifests itself in the relationship between India's multiple levels of governance continues in Chapter 7, which examines the extent to which malpractices evident within local implementation have shaped, and been shaped by, heated debate over NREGA's future at the apex of India's political system.

4

STATE POLITICS AND NREGA I

RAJASTHAN

As we saw in Chapter 2—on NREGA's structure and origins—Rajasthan has played a particularly important role in the development of the entire approach underlying the Act. Movement groups in Rajasthan pioneered the social audit method, and in the late 1990s and early 2000s pressed successfully for a state-level Right to Information Act in Rajasthan as well as crucial legislative amendments to the state's Panchayati Raj Act. In addition to NREGA, these groups were subsequently central to the passage of the national Right to Information Act 2005 and other key pieces of legislation during the UPA government's two terms in office. This history was bound to affect the way that NREGA was pursued in the state.

Predicting the impact of this legacy, however, has proven rather difficult. On the one hand, Rajasthan's impressive performance in implementing many aspects of NREGA—the large number of employment days created, for instance, or the comparatively high rate of women's participation—is a quintessential case of path dependence. Rajasthan has a long history of operating 'famine relief' works to create jobs. This goes back to the colonial era, as it does elsewhere. But unlike many other states, Rajasthan's attachment to drought-relief works remained notably strong in the decades following independence. During the twenty years preceding NREGA's passage, household food insecurity worsened for the poorest Rajasthanis.[1] Official declarations of drought by a succession of chief ministers triggered additional state and fed-

91

eral funding on a more or less permanent 'emergency' basis for programmes that hired wage labourers on public works projects. Even in the immediate pre-NREGA era—during, for instance, almost the entirety of Chief Minister Ashok Gehlot's first term (1998–2003)—much of Rajasthan faced drought or near-drought conditions. The state's awareness of which locations faced acute famine vulnerability was heightened during the 1990s thanks to sustained empirical research, focused policy advocacy, and effective popular mobilisation by social activists from within and beyond Rajasthan.[2]

Given this history, it is no surprise that the state's rural development machinery was geared up to implement employment-creation programmes on a much wider scale when the opportunity arose. Many factors that account for patterns of NREGA implementation in Rajasthan, such as migration, are discussed later in this chapter (migration is examined in relation to poverty dynamics in Chapter 6 as well). For the present, let us note that not only does Rajasthan have vast experience with employment-creation programmes; it had over the fifteen years preceding NREGA's passage continuously sought, largely under pressure from civil society, to improve the state's ability to target beneficiaries, design appropriate works programmes, eliminate administrative inefficiencies, and address leakages stemming from corruption.

While path dependency was clearly at work in certain aspects of Rajasthan's NREGA performance, on other matters politics played a larger, though sometimes ambiguous, role. For example, because Mazdoor Kisan Shakti Sangathan (MKSS) activists who were widely associated with NREGA's passage enjoyed a personal rapport with Sonia Gandhi, they had far greater clout to press for model implementation of the programme. But that same association meant that these and other activists were more easily cast as partisan by the BJP government in Rajasthan during the first two-and-a-half years of the programme's operation. Their political sympathies laid bare, activists became easy targets for fierce (and collective) political resistance at the most local levels of political organisation—arenas over which BJP politicians in Jaipur claimed, to some degree truthfully, to have little control.[3]

Congress supplanted the BJP as Rajasthan's governing party following state assembly elections in 2008. Even here the effects on NREGA were less than clear, as we will see throughout this chapter. Much of the time, the government of Congress Chief Minister Ashok Gehlot worked with Rajasthan's formidable array of social movements. This was mostly at the state and district levels, with inconsistent backing (at best) at the block level and below.

Indeed, one thing that marked Rajasthan out among India's many NREGA-implementing state governments was the array of district-level governance experiments that were undertaken there. These included initiatives in Jalore, Rajsamand, and Sirohi districts, which are briefly analysed later in this chapter. That these governance experiments often failed to work as planned at block level and below is further confirmation of the alienation between the district level and above, on the one hand, and the block level and below on the other.

Context and Background

In terms of area, Rajasthan is India's largest state, but ranks eighth in terms of population (seventy million) due to the low population density found in the Thar Desert and its semi-arid periphery. There are both optimistic and pessimistic versions of Rajasthan's recent economic history. Economist Arvind Pangariya notes that at the beginning of the 1980s, when India took its first cautious steps to liberalise parts of its economy, the only state with a lower per capita income than Rajasthan was Bihar. After low-to-moderate growth in the 1980s, when Rajasthan performed below the all-India average but better than in the past, the state began to catch up with India's accelerated growth trend of the late 1990s. Since the turn of the 2000s, Rajasthan has become one of the leaders in terms of per capita economic growth, albeit starting from a relatively low base. From 2003 to 2009, Rajasthan's annual per capita GDP growth averaged 9.4 per cent. This tied it for second place with Orissa, another dark horse in the new millennium growth sweepstakes. Haryana, at 10 per cent, took first place. These statistics challenge the dominant image of Rajasthan as a land-locked desert state, lacking in economic dynamism. But even more striking is the state's ability to translate modest income levels into a relatively low rate of poverty. As Pangariya puts it, '[w]hereas the state's per-capita income has been well below the national average throughout the post-Independence era, the poverty ratio at 22.1 per cent in 2004–5 was well below the national average of 27.5 per cent', and even better than the 'far richer states of Tamil Nadu, Maharashtra and Karnataka'.[4]

The pessimistic account of Rajasthan's economic scenario points to the state's dismal scores on a variety of developmental measures that assess human well-being, as opposed to income poverty, which optimists generally prefer to cite. While the state's capital of Jaipur has over the past two decades experienced unprecedented economic growth and an unmistakable physical transformation, the rest of Rajasthan has not fared as well. The Government of India's Human Poverty Index for rural areas placed Rajasthan twenty-eighth out of thirty-two states.[5] This was despite a huge improvement in the rate of rural literacy, which almost doubled from 30 per cent to 56 per cent between 1991 and 2001. Moreover, Rajasthan's per capita income of Rs. 8,609—below the national average of Rs. 10,441[6]—has indirectly harmed progress on other economic measures of importance to poor people, such as access to essential services (health and sanitation) or even the ability to travel easily to and from one's place of residence. The state's level of infrastructural development is four-fifths of the national average, and its road connectivity is the second worst among India's states: just 38 per cent of villages with populations below 1,000 residents are linked to roads.[7] Rural Rajasthan's average annual job growth in 1993–4 and 1999–2000, at 1.3 per cent, was on par with the all-India rate of 1.4 per cent. Income inequality in Rajasthan, however, was lower than the national average—a Gini coefficient of 0.477, versus 0.536 for India as a whole.

Rajasthan, like many other Indian states, consists of a number of political units that existed prior to Indian independence in 1947. The former 'princely states', which varied greatly in size and prestige, were amalgamated in a multi-stage process to create 'Rajputana', a constituent state of the Indian union. It was later renamed Rajasthan. There were also important variations between the princely states that came to constitute Rajasthan in terms of land tenure systems, modes of taxation, judicial institutions, and other aspects of governance. The leading princely states were Jaipur, Jodhpur, Udaipur, Bikaner, and Kota. These remain Rajasthan's key geographic and administrative centres. The state is in the Hindi belt, though a variety of local dialects exist, such as Marwari which is spoken in the region centred on Jodhpur. Differences from 'British India' also meant that the princely states experienced an alternative form of nationalist movement, one less united and less powerful than that which prevailed in British India. Even so, following independence, all the way through the integration of the princely states into the Indian Union, and during the reorganisation of states along linguistic lines in the late 1950s, the Congress Party emerged as the key political force in Rajasthan. Gerrymandering had something to do with this, but so did the fertile soil into which the trans-actional politics of clientelism were implanted. This required the creation of political relationships based on 'diffuse reciprocity', a reality to which the people of a 'declining feudal order' could readily adapt.[8]

Elections in Rajasthan have long been dominated by the Congress Party and the BJP, or the BJP's organisational and ideological predecessors, the Jana Sangh and the Hindu Mahasabha. Almost every government since independence has been led by one of these two parties, with the Congress more or less monopolising power at the state level for the first twenty-five years. This did not happen without controversy—notably, there was a constitutional crisis which centred on the alleged use of the (centrally appointed) governor's office to keep the Congress Party in office following the fractured verdict delivered by Rajasthan's voters in the 1967 state assembly election. Because Rajasthan experienced coalition governance relatively early on (and has been experimenting with it ever since), the state's political class understood how to operate such a mechanism long before other north Indian states. Rajasthan developed a political culture in which contacts across party lines were not only tolerated but also considered normal—possibly even desirable. It was in this mode that one of Rajasthan's most revered (and wily) Chief Ministers, Bhairon Singh Shekhawat, operated for most of his political career.[9]

Other aspects of Rajasthan's political culture can also usefully be considered when assessing the political dynamics underlying NREGA's implementation. One example concerns the configuration of identities around which parties seek to build electoral coalitions. In a classic account of Rajasthan's political sociology, Mathur and Narain argued that a singular social order is evident in Rajasthan, one distinct in its structure and modes of behaviour from those prevailing in most other parts of India.[10] It centres on the Rajput caste. Rather than rural social mobility occurring through the efforts of lower-status *jatis* to emulate the worldview and practices of Brahmins, Mathur and Narain maintain, that in Rajasthan, group status aspirations were enacted through the adoption of Rajput characteristics by groups further down the status hierarchy. This tendency could be expressed in a number of ways, but typically took the form of a group sending its sons into the police or military services, or by buying additional land on which a new branch of the family could flourish. These were seen as surer routes to respectability than sanskritisation or brahmanisation, which anthropologists studying politicised social mobility have emphasised elsewhere in India.[11] The distinctiveness of what Narain and Mathur called 'Kshatriyanisation' in Rajasthan also influenced how Hindu nationalism has been received in the state. Efforts to politicise religious identities are mediated through region-specific symbols, none more important than the Rajput caste itself.[12] While this has lent enhanced leverage to some particularly objectionable events—such as support for *sati* from a Rajput-led group of politicians in the 1980s—in general, Rajasthan's form of politicised Hinduism has been less violent and institution-destroying than it has been elsewhere in north and west India.

Precursors and offshoots of the Congress Party and the BJP have emerged from time to time, and in some cases have joined in coalition governments, as have smaller parties, especially the various incarnations of the Janata Dal and the Communist Party of India. The Swatantra Party, which championed free enterprise policies and the need for a check on Prime Minister Nehru from the 'secular right', achieved notable success in Rajasthan during the 1960s, with various royals winning election to the state legislature and the national parliament. The salience of Rajasthan's princely lineages in electoral politics has declined in recent decades, although the BJP's Vadundhara Raje Scindia hails from a princely family in Madhya Pradesh and married into another from Rajasthan. Still, the proliferation of parties witnessed in other parts of India—such as Uttar Pradesh in the north and Tamil Nadu in the south—has not taken place in Rajasthan.

Nor have any explicitly regional or caste-based parties emerged in a significant way in Rajasthan. This is largely a reflection of the comparatively slow pace of lower-caste political assertion in Rajasthan and the persistence of traditional social relations in much of the state.[13] While factional rivalries are strongly present in local politics, they tend not to reflect high levels of party identification or ideological attachment. Instead, party labels are typically grafted onto pre-existing factions, whose leaders seek access to resources and influence, and generally display little long-term loyalty to any particular party.[14] Occasionally, lower-caste parties that have performed well in other states—such as the Dalit-oriented Bahujan Samaj Party (BSP)—have made some electoral inroads in Rajasthan.[15]

Rajasthan's state bureaucracy has become increasingly politicised over the past two decades. The upper echelons of the civil service, which once prided itself on its ability to serve governments ruled by any party with impartiality, tends now to be divided into coteries associated with either the Congress Party or the BJP. Even so, the ability of elected politicians to exert pressure on civil servants to take manifestly illegal actions is far less in evidence than in many other Indian states. Corruption among officials, usually in collusion with senior politicians, is routine—particularly with respect to procurement contracts, transfers and postings of subordinate officers, and the forcible acquisition of land by the state for industrial installations, infrastructure projects, and housing and commercial real estate development. However, the systematic intimidation, verbal abuse, and harassment of senior civil servants by elected officials found in some other states is rare in Rajasthan.

Rajasthan's elected local government bodies—the *panchayats* that operate at district level and below—have been the subject of many hopeful reforms over the decades. The foundation stone for what was to be constitutionally enshrined as the country's foundational level of governance thirty-six years later was laid in 1957, when Prime Minister Nehru visited Nagaur in the Shekhawati region of Rajasthan to launch India's first *panchayati raj* bodies. Nehru's choice of Nagaur had more to do with political friendships and electoral considerations (and its proximity to Delhi, no doubt) than it did with any particular receptivity of Nagaur to institutions of local self-government. Indeed, Nagaur seems an unlikely selection for a number of reasons. It is a place where, even when Nehru was visiting, something like feudal social, political, and economic relations continued to exist—not just in practical terms, but in outward form as well. A land of princes, nobles, codes of valour, and *corvée* labour.

Since the coming into force of the 73rd and 74th Amendments to the Indian Constitution in 1993, the *panchayat* system has been the focus of considerable reform in Rajasthan. A large number of NGOs have taken part in awareness-raising programmes and efforts to train newly elected councilors—particularly women—in the skills necessary to function effectively in their new positions.[16] Amendments to the state's local government legislation in 2000 introduced reforms that prefigured many of the innovations that were to be disseminated across India five years later when the Right to Information Act and NREGA were passed in New Delhi. These included a requirement that local government institutions make available to the public—upon request, or in some cases *suo moto*—all documentation related to public expenditure and development initiatives within their jurisdictions, and that village assemblies (*gram sabhas*) be empowered to conduct 'social audits' of all village council (*gram panchayat*) decisions relating to the selection of beneficiaries of welfare programmes, the purchase of materials for public works, and the execution of centrally sponsored employment schemes.

As in Madhya Pradesh, Rajasthan's 2003 state legislative elections resulted in the ejection of a relatively *panchayat*-friendly Congress government and the installation of a BJP administration that, for much of its time in office, actively sought to undermine the functioning of local institutions and activists attempting to make them work in the interests of poor people. These were the state political environments into which NREGA was received.

Findings from a Survey in Two Districts

As in Madhya Pradesh, a survey was conducted in Rajasthan in late 2008 and early 2009 to examine perceptions among NREGA workers and non-workers of the functioning of the Act. Of particular concern was the extent to which workers were aware of their rights under the Act, and the extent to which the access to information and social audit provisions were being used by NREGA workers. Before turning to the findings, however, it is useful to gain some appreciation of what earlier studies uncovered concerning NREGA implementation in Rajasthan.

The 'NREGA Survey 2008' showed Rajasthan to be a stand-out performer in most aspects of implementation.[17] In terms of complying with the legislative and regulatory provisions relating to worksite facilities, Rajasthan was way ahead of most other states: 95 per cent of sample worksites provided drinking water, compared with only 52 per cent in the five other states in north India that were surveyed (Bihar, Chhattisgarh, Jharkhand, Madhya Pradesh, and Uttar Pradesh). Similarly, 60 per cent of Rajasthan's worksites had the required first-aid kit compared to 20 per cent for the other states. Childcare facilities were found in 17 per cent of Rajasthan's worksites; none were found in the sample for the five other states.

In Rajasthan, according to one study, 'contractors have virtually disappeared from NREGA'.[18] This contrasted with the situation in parts of western Orissa where 'contractor raj' held sway. In earlier employment programmes, Orissa had allowed labour contractors to serve as worksite supervisors. A study team that surveyed thirty worksites found that in roughly half of them, contractors were directly involved in operating NREGA projects. Though NREGA prohibits the use of contractors, where the cadre of worksite supervisors is composed of private contractors, it is not surprising that it would take time to counteract this 'quiet sabotage' of NREGA's 'transparency safeguards'.[19] This subversion in Orissa was abetted by certain design features of NREGA's online Management Information System (MIS), which allowed for 'adjustments' to be made by data entry operators. This made verification of the data almost impossible, even if one were able to gain access to the necessary records. As the study's author put it: 'In this opaque environment, contractors have a field day'.[20]

Women in Rajasthan participated in NREGA projects in huge numbers. During the three years beginning 2006–7, Rajasthan's average rate of 68 per cent of total NREGA employment days having been worked by women was more than one-and-a half times greater than the all-India figure of 43 per cent. During 2008–9, Rajasthan was the only state outside South India (and, oddly, Tripura) to exceed the national average. Both in terms of the aggregate figure and in terms of the state-level data, these are big increases over women's rates of engagement on pre-NREGA employment programmes. The share of total person days of employment accounted for by women workers under the *Sampoorna Gramin Rozgar Yojana* (SGRY) in Rajasthan during 2005–6—the last year before NREGA came into effect—was just 42 per cent.

But because NREGA is national in scope, variations between states in levels of women's participation suggest an important role for state-specific factors. A 2009 study of the gender dimensions of NREGA implementation in four states (Bihar, Jharkhand, Rajasthan, and Himachal Pradesh) concluded that state-level policies and initiatives were crucial.[21] In Rajasthan, particular emphasis was given to the state's training and placement programme for female 'mates', or worksite supervisors. Indeed, 'the female "mate" system, introduced in Rajasthan, encourages women's participation, as women workers find it more comfortable to work with a female mate.' Moreover, 'women rarely have any complaints of harassment and gender-related discrimination against female mate[s] which was a regular phenomenon in the case of male mate[s]'.[22] Another factor contributing to higher female NREGA participation rates in Rajasthan is the pattern of male outmigration. Men seeking work outside the state, many in the nation's capital or in the neighbouring state of Gujarat, is nothing new in Rajasthan. The state is sliced in two by the Delhi-Ahmedabad Highway, down which many able-bodied men seeking work have travelled, particularly since the onset of economic liberalisation in the mid-1980s. The lack of dynamism in much of Rajasthan's rural economy has exerted strong 'push' factors, but there are also strong 'pull' factors in neighbouring states too, such as the construction sector in Gujarat and Delhi.

In general, there is a continuing tension between, on the one hand, seeing women's NREGA participation in Rajasthan as a sign of their increasing empowerment, and on the other, a tendency to regard their intensive engagement in NREGA work as a reflection of the unpromising conditions faced by women in the state. In 2006, the first year in which NREGA was implemented, Rajasthan scored below the national average on both the Gender Development Index (0.577 versus 0.633) and the Gender Empowerment Measure (0.387 versus 0.451).[23] It seems likely that women's participation in NREGA would have been even higher had the scheme's rules been designed differently. NREGA's allocation of work on the basis of household quotas has been a particular bone of contention for gender-equality advocates. Using individuals as the unit of analysis, it is widely felt, would enhance women's intra-household bargaining power.

The survey for the present study was conducted among NREGA workers in thirty-two *gram panchayats* within Rajasthan. Because *gram panchayats* are a key NREGA implementation vehicle (as we learned in Chapter 3), they are the primary unit of analysis. The *gram panchayats* in which the survey was undertaken were located in two districts, Udaipur and Sirohi, located in the southwest portion of Rajasthan. The districts were not selected to provide a microcosm of the state. No two districts could capture the huge variation that exists among Rajasthan's regions, whether in terms of economic development, political history, social composition, or any other variable. The survey sought to capture differences between respondents' perceptions that might be traceable to district-level factors, particularly the character of district-level administrative and political leadership, which was examined qualitatively through interviews. We also examined block-level factors that could potentially explain variation in the responses received from NREGA workers surveyed.

In choosing Sirohi and Udaipur, we were in part attempting to avoid focusing the present study on either extremely challenged districts, such as Karauli and Dungarpur, or particularly privileged districts, such as Rajsamand and Ajmer, the two districts where MKSS is primarily based. Sirohi and Udaipur were districts that, when we began the field research in 2008, were depicted in news reports, preliminary government data, and anecdotal evidence from journalists and civil servants as being—in terms of NREGA implementation—somewhere in the middle of the curve. These were districts that faced challenges—Adivasis lacking documentary evidence of their continuous residence, for instance—but were not 'hopeless', a term readily (and accurately) applied by senior bureaucrats to certain districts. MKSS's influence could certainly be felt in some locations in Sirohi and Udaipur. But as we will see, that became part of the study design—the purpose being to determine whether groups affiliated with the state-wide network seeking robust implementation of both NREGA and RTIA could leverage their affiliation with this formation to foster change in their primary operational locations.

In each district, three blocks were examined. One block in each district was chosen because of the existence of a reasonably prominent local organisation seeking to mobilise people to demand full NREGA implementation, including rights provisions for workers. In the other two blocks in each district, the role of movements was far less in evidence (bearing in mind that some kind of NGO activity, broadly defined, can be found pretty much anywhere in Rajasthan). Thus, the survey sought to discover (among other things) whether people experienced NREGA differently in 'movement endowed' blocks compared to 'movement deprived' blocks. The 120 workers (each from a separate household) that were surveyed in each block were spread across fifteen *gram panchayats*.

In Sirohi district, locations in three blocks were surveyed: Pindwara, Sirohi town, and Abu Road. While Pindwara and Sirohi town were notable for the absence of organised activism directly related to NREGA, Abu Road was home to an NGO with deep local roots, strong connections to state-wide activist networks, and a commitment to realising NREGA's potential. An effort to construct a parallel set of cases in Udaipur district led to the selection of Girwa, Gogunda, and Kotra blocks. Girwa and Gogunda were (in relative terms) 'movement deprived' blocks, whereas Kotra could boast a strong activist-NGO presence. It was hypothesised that Abu Road (Sirohi) and Kotra (Udaipur) would stand out in their respective districts as places where workers were more aware of their rights under NREGA, and more likely to seek to exercise them.

This was partially borne out by the survey results. For instance, it turned out that people in the movement-endowed blocks were far less likely to make the initial application for a job card themselves, relying almost entirely on the *panchayat* authorities to do so on their behalf. In Kotra (Udaipur), despite the presence of an active movement, only 5 per cent of workers applied on their own; 95 per cent had their cards issued through an application made by the *panchayat*. In Udaipur's movement-deprived blocks, on the other hand, more than half of respondents (56 per cent) had applied for cards on their own. A similar discrepancy, though of a smaller order, was found in Sirohi district.

NREGA's administrative process begins to be affected by the presence of an activist movement at the next step—the issuing of 'receipts', which labourers could use to prove that they had submitted their work applications. Obtaining a simple receipt should not, in theory, require the intercession of any group or association. As we learned in Chapter 3, however, local officials routinely avoid issuing receipts. Receipts indicate the date on which workers sought employment, and therefore the date after which an unemployment allowance—payable by the state rather than the central government—should begin accruing. In the heavily movement-affected blocks in the Rajasthan sample, there was roughly four times the level of awareness of the existence (if not the full mechanics) of NREGA's unemployment-allowance provision as there was in movement-deprived blocks. In the end, not a single worker reported having received any form of 'unemployment compensation' at any time, even after having to wait a year or more for work.

On this issue the presence of an activist movement makes a difference, increasing the chances that work applicants receive application receipts. Whereas only 3–5 per cent of workers in the blocks lacking a significant movement group received receipts, activists in Kotra and Abu Road pressed successfully for receipts to be issued to workers on a regular basis. More than three-quarters of workers in Kotra received receipts verifying that they had applied for work under NREGA with the appropriate authorities. In Abu Road, 70 per cent received receipts. Interviews in Abu Road revealed that this symbolically important victory for this small but persistent local people's organisation was the result of a planned campaign. In mid-2008, a local NGO, working with people engaged in its development projects and Adivasi rights advocacy, used its clout to advance a collective demand that NREGA work applicants receive receipts without delay and free of charge from the *panchayat* office. There was, by early 2009, some speculation in the area as to whether the movement's leadership took a strategic decision to refrain from engaging people in making initial work applications: if the applications were handled by the *panchayat* authorities, perhaps the organisation would be better positioned to agitate for the issuance of receipts against these applications *en masse*.

It is impossible to know whether, on aggregate, corruption is better or worse in one jurisdiction than another. This is not only because of the inherently furtive nature of corruption, which makes credible data elusive. Even perception-based surveys are weak. For instance, there is the problem of definitions in a context in which the public-versus-private distinction is not as entrenched as it is in others. Moreover, specific experiential measurements of corruption do not necessarily serve as indicators of overall corruption levels. Indeed, there are so many different varieties of corruption that each source should, ideally, be measured separately. A thorough disaggregation might reveal that a locality distributes its opportunities for corruption among the various mechanisms available in different ways to neighbouring jurisdictions.

With these caveats in mind, it remains striking that in Rajasthan the blocks with active movements seemed to have significantly less difficulty obtaining a job card without paying a bribe. In Kotra, Udaipur district's movement-endowed block, just 5 per cent of respondents had to pay a bribe to obtain a job card. The rate of bribe-paying was more than three times as high in the blocks in Udaipur district that did not benefit from the active engagement of a people's organisation. The story is similar in Sirohi district: in movement-endowed Abu Road, only 7.5 per cent of respondents were forced to pay to obtain a job card, whereas in the district's movement-deprived blocks there was a much higher rate of bribe-paying, with a third of respondents reporting that they had to pay.

Interviews confirmed that the causal mechanism behind this correlation was likely the concerted effort of the local movement—which was growing to include local lawyers, farmers, traders, and Dalit groups—to bring the issue of corruption to the forefront of local politics. While corruption was common knowledge in the Abu Road area, it had never been an explicit point of contestation. A lawyer based in the district's headquarters explained this puzzling situation by pointing out that a huge proportion of the area's otherwise law-abiding residents had over the years been forced by circumstances to engage in corrupt transactions from time to time. Among the poor, economic survival often means having to make regular payments to avoid being charged with encroachment on 'forest' or revenue land by officials. Street vendors, rickshaw pullers, and many others operating in both the formal and informal economies must pay off officials in order to ply their trades.[24] Corruption has in many cases been institutionalised into fixed percentages for each type of transaction. Having become, in effect, complicit in corruption, illegal squatters and vulnerable workers might regard participation in a campaign to expose corruption as risky. Doing so could easily lead to retaliation by officials. Because many of the poor are on exceptionally weak legal ground with respect to homestead and livelihood security, they face proportionally higher costs if engaged in activism. Our interviews confirmed, over and over again, that these vulnerabilities rapidly deplete people's appetite for confronting local corruption.[25]

The Sirohi-based movement organisation, however, has worked assiduously to highlight the centrality of corruption in all aspects of NREGA implementation. Its activists have particularly heightened awareness about NREGA's transparency and accountability provisions, while also building a sense of solidarity that fosters greater trust among their co-agitators. As one put it, 'if false charges are brought against anyone, all will come to demand the case is thrown out'.[26] The time spent appearing in court to defend oneself against such claims can be considerable, and the legal fees are beyond the means of most people. Countering this routine but effective means of silencing people requires a strong mutual support organisation.

In terms of workers' rights, the picture is mixed, both across locations and across issues. Respondents operating amidst strong currents of movement activism were no more likely to know about NREGA's right to work orientation, or that each household was entitled to 100 days of minimum-wage employment. This contrasted sharply with what we found in Madhya Pradesh (see Chapter 5). On the other hand, with respect to other rights-related issues—for instance, the right to maintain possession of one's job card—the 'movement effect' could be seen in just one district. In Sirohi, 90 per cent of workers in the movement-endowed block of Abu Road held their own cards, compared to just under two-thirds of workers in the other two blocks surveyed in this district. But in Udaipur district there was no difference between movement-endowed and movement-deprived blocks, both showing roughly 70 per cent of workers maintaining job cards in their possession. The situation was even less clear-cut with respect to worker awareness of the requirement that officials place their employment information—including when they applied for work, how many days they worked, and the amounts paid—into NREGA online MIS. On this question there was almost uniformly low awareness (10 per cent), regardless of which district was surveyed or whether a movement organisation was active in the block.

The survey data also revealed a disparity between Rajasthan's movement-endowed and movement-deprived blocks on whether labourers had encountered problems in undertaking NREGA work. Workers in blocks where activism was reasonably widespread were more likely to report having encountered problems than in other blocks. Around 80 per cent of the former group reported problems, compared with only two-thirds of the latter. The typical explanation given by workers in interviews was that the movement made them aware of issues that they otherwise had not considered, such as the requirement that shaded rest areas be provided. Causality could plausibly run in the opposite direction, of course: it is possible that activism took hold where it did because of a keener awareness among people in some blocks, and it was this that then drew them to movements. However, conditions in the area, the results of other survey questions, and the chronologies recounted by workers and organisers in the area make this possibility seem, at best, very remote.[27]

As for the main problem faced by NREGA workers, a clear contrast emerges between movement and non-movement blocks. In movement-endowed blocks, the biggest difficulty was getting enough work, whereas in movement-deprived blocks, it was getting paid too low a wage. This question was asked irrespective of people's perceptions of why they were receiving such low rates. For instance, it did not matter whether the wage reduction was due to corruption by programme administrators, an unfair Schedule of Rates established by authorities, a minimum wage that was set too low, or some combination of these and other factors. The question was also independent of whether or not respondents knew about (or were actually receiving) the minimum wage, which was asked about separately by survey enumerators.

About half of workers (48 per cent) in movement-endowed blocks considered not getting enough work their biggest problem, while only about 6 per cent of those in movement-deprived blocks thought so. Supporting evidence for this is found in the data on whether respondents had to wait for work. Twice as many workers in movement-endowed blocks reported having to wait for work when compared with their counterparts in non-endowed blocks. And whereas only 10 per cent of people working in an environment characterised by protest and activism found the wage rate to be a major problem, about 40 per cent felt this way in places where there was no strong movement presence. These results must be treated with caution, but they nevertheless appear consistent with the narratives provided by respondents in places where activism and awareness-raising were taking place. In such localities, the potential for (as opposed to the exercise of) collective action among workers, supported by an organisation, appeared to have deterred officials from seizing wages to the extent predicted. Outright agitations took place at only a limited number of worksites, but strategic use of protest action appears to have had a significant impact.

The less-visible dimension to this narrative is the difficulty that workers in movement-endowed blocks experienced in securing sufficient employment. Interviews revealed that many workers in these areas felt discriminated against by the local officials who determined job allocations. While many different types of discrimination were discussed in interviews—including biases based on applicants' known party-identification or their caste, religious, or other ethnic identity—the type of discrimination that stood out was bias against anyone associated in any way with a local people's movement. This kind of 'blackballing' of applicants was the same whether he or she had joined in collective grievances on NREGA-related matters or had merely participated in the local NGO's non-NREGA-related programmes. Many such workers expressed great frustration at having been passed over for additional employment because they had complained about underpayment of wages or non-transparency in the operation of NREGA works.

A key issue for NREGA workers is whether they receive payment for each round of employment they undertake—an issue independent of the nominal wage rate received. The receipt of regularly paid wages is usually a good indicator of the workers' collective capacity to influence the actions of programme administrators. In Sirohi district, 98 per cent of workers received regular payment in the block where an assertive movement group was capable of sustaining pressure on elected representatives and bureaucratic officials. In the two blocks where such a movement was not in evidence, only 71 per cent of workers reported that they always or almost always received wages.

When it comes to the receipt of the minimum wage rate, however, a clear pattern emerges: workers in areas with a strong movement presence are more likely—considerably more likely in certain cases—to have been paid the full rate. Just 3 per cent of workers in Udaipur's movement-deprived blocks reported receiving at least the minimum wage for a typical work period. In movement-endowed Kotra, however, 24 per cent of workers said they were regularly paid at least minimum wage. In other words, they were eight times as likely to report receiving the minimum wage as workers lacking a movement to support their cause. The movement effect was also present in Sirohi district: 35 per cent of workers in Abu Road Block were paid at least minimum wage, whereas in movement-deprived blocks in the same district, less than half this proportion (16 per cent of workers) made a similar claim.

Furthering this comparison requires close assessment of survey data that illuminates the local political dynamics underlying NREGA implementation. One such data point is the question of 'who offered' employment to the respondent. The most striking finding here was the difference across the two states of Rajasthan and Madhya Pradesh. In Rajasthan, the overwhelming response was that it was the 'mate', or worksite supervisor, who was responsible—in practice, if not formally—for responding to applications with specific employment offers, including dates, worksite locations, and so forth. (In a smaller proportion of cases, the *rozgar sahayak*, or NREGA assistant, held this responsibility.) In Madhya Pradesh, however, it was much more likely to have been the *sarpanch* or the village secretary: in the movement-endowed district of Madhya Pradesh, around 80 per cent of respondents gave this answer; in the movement-deprived district, 97 per cent said it was one of these two local officials who offered employment. In both districts in Madhya Pradesh, more than 60 per cent of respondents had work offered to them by the village secretary. Moreover, a significant proportion of people (around one-quarter of respondents) said that either the *sarpanch* or village secretary 'looked after' NREGA works, whereas 100 per cent of the respondents in Rajasthan identified the mate as the holder of this function. This difference is likely to have affected the ceaseless contestation between elected village leaders and block-level administrators for greater control over NREGA and the illicit income that comes with overseeing its implementation—a dynamic outlined in some detail in Chapter 3.

The other relevant discrepancy in the 'who offered' finding was between the districts studied in Rajasthan. In Sirohi, a movement's presence in a block reduced the likelihood that *sarpanches* would be the officials who issued NREGA employment offers; in Udaipur, a movement's presence increased the chances that it would be the *sarpanch* (rather than the secretary) who would handle this function. In short, very local factors often play a crucial role in shaping the institutional terrain on which movement-led resistance against unlawful NREGA implementation gets unleashed—for example, the depth of support behind a *sarpanch*; the degree of political polarisation in a *gram panchayat*; or a village secretary's 'upward' connections to block, or even district, headquarters.

Another political dimension to NREGA implementation at the local level in Rajasthan comes through in the survey results: the focus in movement-endowed locations on making elected political leaders the targets of activism. Unlike state employees, who at worst could be transferred to a new location or department, *sarpanches* can be ousted by the electorate. A *sarpanch* should therefore be responsive to collective expressions of discontent, particularly when these are directed at his or her management of a high-profile development programme such as NREGA. In blocks lacking NREGA-related movement activism, roughly half of our respondents said the office-holder most willing to listen to their complaints and suggestions was the *sarpanch* (the other options were village secretary, *rozgar sahayak*, and 'no one'). But in the movement-endowed block surveyed in Sirohi, this figure climbed to 70 per cent. For the movement-endowed block in Udaipur, it was 85 per cent. These figures are consistent with the accounts given by social activists in these areas, who emphasise that the electoral potential of grassroots movements—not, for the most part, as candidate-producing organisations themselves, but as a site of collective action—gives them greater access to elected leaders than to any other category of elite. In the areas where movements are active—in both Rajasthan and Madhya Pradesh—the *sarpanch* is far more likely to be identified as the most important decision-making actor for implementing NREGA. Around three-quarters of workers in movement-endowed blocks identified the *sarpanch* as the most important decision-maker. Elsewhere in the same districts it was a bit more than half. Whether this was a pre-existing feature of the local political landscape, or it emerged through the efforts of civic actors who mobilised people to defend their rights, is very difficult to tell. In light of all the other evidence, however, it is hard to believe that the movement did not contribute to some of this heightened awareness of where power lies in local development administration.

The quality of the public works created under NREGA has been acknowledged as a crucial indicator of NREGA's overall popular legitimacy. Whatever other benefits it produces, if the works created are substandard, either in design or execution, or located inappropriately, the entire image of NREGA is tarnished. The survey data show that projects initiated at the village level (by the *sarpanch* and village secretary) are of better perceived quality than those initiated by government bureaucrats at the block level or above. Interestingly, this pattern holds regardless of whether a block is movement-endowed or not. Where the movement effect does matter, is on the location of NREGA projects. Workers in movement-endowed blocks were far less likely to report that projects disproportionately benefited the *sarpanch*'s own village or hamlet within a multi-settlement *gram panchayat*. In Sirohi district, only 45 per cent of people in the movement-endowed block said the *sarpanch* favoured his or her own neighbourhood. Where movement activism was absent, allegations of *sarpanch* bias almost doubled—rising to 81 per cent. NREGA workers in Rajasthan's movement-endowed areas were roughly one-fifth as likely as those in movement-deprived areas to have witnessed the illegal use of contractors.

It is through *panchayat* institutions that political practice and NREGA implementation were, by design, meant to combine. The institution that was supposed to act as the linchpin of such an interaction was the *gram sabha*, a meeting that all villagers are entitled to attend. *Gram sabhas* are charged with complementing the 'periodic accountability' represented by elections with a more 'continuous accountability' process, where actions are tracked against commitments, distribution assessed for equity, and administrative processes policed for instances of bias and capture. More broadly, the *gram sabha* was intended to help transform the politics of patronage into the politics of performance—that is, to move from clientelist politics to programmatic politics.[28] That this shift would take years if not decades was foreseen by some of NREGA's less wide-eyed advocates. But establishing universal participation could not wait.

Our survey results on the early use of NREGA's participatory auditing methods in Rajasthan showed that they were rarely, if ever, used. This was depressing from the perspective of accountability, but analytically speaking, not hugely surprising. The results in fact conform to the broad pattern emerging from most Indian states—of half-hearted implementation of provisions lauded as among NREGA's most distinctive. Only 38 per cent of respondents in Rajasthan's movement-deprived blocks reported their *gram sabhas* meeting regularly to discuss NREGA's operation. Moreover, the question used here did not call on the respondent to assess the quality of *gram sabha* deliberations and decision-making where *gram sabhas* had been held. At the same time, 38 per cent would be considered a high figure by international standards, and even the standards of several other Indian states.

In Sirohi's movement-endowed block (Abu Road), almost half of respondents were from villages where *gram sabhas* had discussed NREGA. Even where *gram sabhas* were held, only around one-quarter of respondents attended a *gram sabha*. Worker participation in *gram sabhas* was greater in the movement-endowed block of Sirohi district (38 per cent) than it was in its movement-deprived blocks (27 per cent). The reverse held true in Udaipur district, where the lack of sustained activism nevertheless increased the likelihood of participating in a *gram sabha*. There are several plausible explanations for this pattern. One commonly voiced in Udaipur was that people associated with grassroots movements were systematically denied entry to *gram sabhas* by local officials, who refused to publicise meeting time and place information. Sometimes direct physical intimidation was used to scare off dissidents. By packing meetings with supporters, the local ruling faction could approve, without proper scrutiny, bogus accounting statements and other project records.

That the 'movement effect' on NREGA implementation was felt more acutely in Sirohi than in Udaipur is supported by two further survey results. Workers in Sirohi's movement-endowed areas were twice as likely to have spoken at a *gram sabha* as those from movement-deprived areas. But what were the results of those interventions? Did participation in a deliberative body improve *gram panchayat*-level NREGA implementation for workers, or at least place their issues onto the *panchayat's* agenda? In Sirohi's movement-endowed areas, 38 per cent of respondents said yes; in movement-deprived areas, only 27 per cent did. This pattern was repeated in Madhya Pradesh. However, no such discrepancy between movement and non-movement blocks was found in Udaipur. The content of NREGA-related *gram sabha* discussions varied, depending on whether or not a movement group was present. The movement-endowed blocks of Sirohi and Udaipur, and the movement-endowed district studied in Madhya Pradesh, were each about twice as likely to have mentioned 'work availability' as the primary NREGA issue discussed in the *gram sabha*.

One reason why people have not been able to make much of an impact in local deliberative bodies is the thinness of people's organisations even in movement-endowed areas. In none of the sample blocks did more than 30 per cent of respondents report having participated in preparatory meetings prior to a *gram sabha*. People in areas with a strong movement presence were three to four times more likely to have participated in a *gram sabha* than those from non-movement areas. If there was any doubt as to whether the two phenomena were causally linked, this was removed by the response to the question of whether an outside group had organised or catalysed the calling of such a pre- or post-*gram sabha* meeting. In Rajasthan's movement-endowed areas, roughly three-quarters of respondents said that an outside group had been involved, compared with only 5 per cent in movement-deprived areas. (For comparable districts in Madhya Pradesh, the figures are two-thirds and zero.) This is the clearest indicator of the role that activist formations, where they exist, have carved out for themselves as facilitators of engagement through institutional spaces created by NREGA's underlying structure.

Perhaps the best indicator of how far most workers in Rajasthan are from enjoying the procedural safeguards built into NREGA, are measures of basic awareness of programme functioning. A large majority—often as high as 90 per cent—answered 'don't know' when asked what the role of various NREGA officials was. Almost no respondents, whether from movement-endowed or movement-deprived areas, had heard of someone suggesting to local leaders or officials ways that NREGA's functioning might be improved.

The Movement for NREGA Implementation in Rajasthan

Yet there were, at the state level and below, various activist groups working to improve NREGA implementation in Rajasthan. If something like a NREGA movement existed, it was capacious and sometimes contradictory, but composed of individuals and organisations that, in one form or another, had either sought action against officials deemed to be violating NREGA guidelines, or proposed policy or institutional changes to enhance the scheme's functioning.

In outlining the emergence of NREGA in Chapter 2, we introduced the MKSS—its genesis, its prior experiments with people's hearings, and its emphasis on using government-held information to discover and document abuses in anti-poverty programmes. This process unfolded over an extended period of time, from the end of the 1980s onwards.

The passage of NREGA (alongside the RTIA) in 2005 placed MKSS and its wide circle of allies in an excellent position to shape the regulations that would govern the Act's implementation. In developing these guidelines, a vast array of civil society organisations in Rajasthan (and beyond) were consulted—from trade unions to associations of Adivasis, from social work NGOs to human rights defenders. The ensuing discussions on the new regulatory environment's implications for Rajasthan strengthened the civic coalition committed to making NREGA work in the state. The result was the creation of the *Rozgar Evum Suchana Ka Adhikar Abhiyan* (RESKAA), or the Right to Employment and Information Campaign, which had existed in a less formal guise, and with a much less specific focus, for a number of years. RESKAA was composed of a range of activist groups, and drew on the support of even more. Among these were organisations of various forms, sizes, and political orientations. The civic groups from the two blocks we identify as 'movement endowed' both contributed to the state-wide campaign to improve NREGA implementation. While both were affiliated with RESKAA, each possessed an organisational identity prior to this association and enjoyed autonomy of action vis-à-vis the *Abhiyan*. Both pursued diverse activities on the basis of demands arising from their affiliated grassroots organisations, from which—ultimately—they derived their legitimacy.

SCJ (a pseudonymous acronym), an activist group working in Abu Road block, is an organisation with many faces. It is a development NGO operating programmes to aid the poor, including livelihood-assistance and service-delivery programmes. The SCJ's two key organisers are long-time veterans of movement politics and deeply connected to social-activist networks. But in addition to being a registered NGO, SCJ possesses a strong streak of grassroots activism which gives the wider formation an additional edge. Supporting demands for fair, equitable, and promptly paid wages, SCJ has also positioned itself as a quasi-union of agricultural and construction workers. Such hybrid people's organisations are a distinguishing feature of India's contemporary civic landscape.[29] SCJ's ability to connect to, and benefit from, closer association with wider organisational networks such as RESKAA heightened its local clout as well. In February 2007, a social audit was conducted in Abu Road with the assistance of other RESKAA members, while the SCJ supported the state-wide coalition's work in a number of ways—including by helping to prepare the RESKAA-led 2009 social audit in Bhilwara district.

Shanti (another organisational pseudonym) is an NGO active in a number of blocks in Udaipur district, including Kotra. There are many places where *Shanti* has little or no organisational presence, though its network of contacts, supporters, and 'stringers'—people who will reliably collect information and attend programmes—stretches across much of the district. Like SCJ, *Shanti* is a janus-faced organisation, a self-described 'independent people's organisation', which conveys the group's commitment to participating as a catalyst in transforming politics from below—that is, on the basis of grievances prioritised and pursued actively by members of socially excluded and economically exploited groups. *Shanti's* work is mainly in rural areas.

Demanding accountability in government rural development programmes is a critical component of *Shanti's* work. In other respects, the organisation functions much like a particular species of development NGO—a resource, documentation, and training institution that supports other groups, particularly those working at the grassroots, such as Adivasi associations, small agricultural cooperatives, women's rights collectives, and so on. Because many people's organisations have focused on non-payment and under-payment of wages by public- and private-sector employers, *Shanti* has been thrust into the role of a trade-union support centre, providing legal and accounting expertise while also seeking to exert political pressure on local implementers.

In January 2007, less than a year after NREGA came into force, Kotra was among the blocks in Udaipur where a social audit took place. In one *panchayat* of a nearby block, the *sarpanch* and the secretary were 'sent to jail', according to one informant. How long they stayed in jail could not be definitively ascertained. In Kotra, nothing quite so dramatic occurred, but the social audit process specified which information would need to be available for workers to verify whether programme administrators had (illegally) claimed resources in their names. This, alongside the process of identifying irregularities in the procurement of building materials and discrepancies regarding worksite location, raised considerable awareness among local people about how corruption occurred.

Our capacity to gauge the effectiveness of SCJ's mobilisational work in Abu Road, or *Shanti's* in Kotra, is limited by our inability to control for other variables between the movement-endowed and movement-deprived blocks in their respective districts. Abu Road is distinguished from the other sample blocks in Sirohi by having a grassroots organisation active on worker rights, but differs in another crucial respect as well: 98 per cent of its respondents were Scheduled Tribes (STs), compared with only 17 per cent in Sirohi's movement-deprived blocks. The same caveat extends to Udaipur district: STs accounted for 100 per cent of respondents in movement-endowed Kotra, while STs accounted for just 42 per cent of the sample in Udaipur's two movement-deprived blocks. The 'better' results in Abu Road and Kotra could indeed have been largely the byproduct of social homogeneity. However, there is good reason to believe that skilful political entrepreneurship, to revisit an issue raised in Chapter 3, was crucial to 'activating' the social capital possessed by the localities in those blocks.[30]

A second caveat relates to issues of comparability with respect to the activism practiced in Kotra and Abu Road, and the work of activists from other locations, particularly the heartland of MKSS's 'catchment area'. In these latter areas, by the mid-2000s intensive activist engagement with local officials reached a point where disagreements mainly concerned methods for fulfilling

NREGA's transparency provisions and what would constitute an acceptable social audit. By contrast, worker activism in Sirohi and Udaipur—even where a people's organisation had increased assertiveness among marginalised people—was clearly at a less advanced stage. To speak of 'stages' is not to imply a linear (let alone necessary) progression towards better outcomes. Rather, it highlights the extent to which our analysis inevitably rests on challenging comparisons. What these NGO-cum-movement groups have accomplished is remarkable. But they are not attempting interventions of the same scope or intensity, nor can the results be considered as credible in terms of sustainability as those pursued over two decades by MKSS and its close affiliates in central Rajasthan.

In the first five years following NREGA's passage, RESKAA embraced the need for Jaipur-based lobbying, whether in small meetings with legislators or in sizeable demonstrations on the streets of the state capital. Lobbying has also been on display in district and block headquarters across Rajasthan. RESKAA's district-level advocacy has produced a range of impacts, some of which will be discussed below in our analysis of efforts by creative district officials to improve NREGA functioning through locally tested innovations.

By far the most significant manifestation of the *Abhiyan's* energies during NREGA's first two and a half years was the series of social audits that its members, aided by supporters from other parts of India, helped to facilitate. The principles underlying the preparation for and conduct of these exercises became very influential, even on grassroots organisations that chose not to affiliate directly with RESKAA. NREGA's operational guidelines summarise the social audit concept by calling it 'a continuous process of public vigilance'. One of the first social audit experiments took place in Dungarpur district in mid-2006, the same year the programme began operating, with a follow up process the following year. The purpose of the first Dungarpur social audit was to gain a snapshot of an entire district—one known for its relative social and economic 'backwardness'. This was a 'hard case'—a place where stark inequalities might make the exploitation of NREGA workers seem inevitable. Coming just a few months after the Act was promulgated, the first Dungarpur social audit would provide a useful baseline of how the right to work was operating in practice.

The audit team took its initial cue from the *Abhiyan's* leadership, but included many local volunteers as well as supporters from elsewhere in Rajasthan, and, to a lesser extent, from other states. The team acted with the support of district officials, who instructed their departments to assist the process. This level of cooperation, however passive-aggressive in practice, does not occur without the permission—indeed, active direction—of officials in Jaipur. Roughly thirty-five teams of citizen-auditors, having received basic training in social auditing procedures, fanned out across the district to inquire about NREGA activities in virtually every *gram panchayat* in Dungarpur. The cooperation they received varied considerably from one locality to the next. By dint of perseverance as much as numbers, what resembled a social-science survey team managed to obtain sufficient information to take the process forward.

After conducting structured interviews and collecting data in a prescribed format, the audit team obtained access to information that would, eventually, permit local people to verify claims contained within each work project's statement of accounts. District officials assisted in the collection and consolidation of the information requested, as directed by superiors in Jaipur. A less charitable view of this practice was that the state government wanted—through its eyes and ears in the districts—to learn of any embarrassing details first, before they were discovered elsewhere. The usual rumours flew that ministers in the BJP-led state government were ordering officials to target Congress-controlled councils, and that the activists were determined to focus on a selection of BJP-led *panchayats* where corruption was common knowledge. To insulate themselves against charges of political bias, the social audit team worked in *gram panchayats* ruled by both Congress and the BJP.

Working under the authority granted by their line ministries in the state capital, and at the direction of the District Collector, district officials participated in most substantive aspects of the audit, such as the recording of specific charges alongside testimonial evidence. Some even agreed to seek answers from *panchayat* officers and technical specialists operating in the lower reaches of the state's bureaucracy. District clerks collated the reports submitted by the auditing team. These highlighted discrepancies within accounting statements, including blatant violations of directives issued by the MoRD in Delhi and by relevant state government departments. There were also discrepancies between entries made in relevant financial documents—including measurement books, muster rolls, and supplier-payment registers—and the testimony provided by workers and others involved with NREGA projects.

Pooling this dispersed information about *prima facie* cases of corruption in NREGA also made it possible to discern district-wide patterns—for instance, variations in the primary mechanisms used to extract illegal rents. The investigations conducted in Dungarpur concluded that NREGA was working tolerably well, all things considered. The transparency and accountability provisions even appeared to be having some effect: one report found that the 'fudging of muster rolls is rare in Rajasthan'.[31] If so, it represented a major improvement over the routinised muster-roll padding that took place before Rajasthan's right to information movement emerged in the late 1990s.

Some critics of the social audit process claimed that NREGA implementation in Dungarpur had experienced a greater degree of malfeasance than the team's audit report suggested. A government official who toured extensively in Dungarpur reported that in some parts of the district building contractors and earth-moving machinery were brought in by local officials, despite being specifically proscribed in the Act and completely contrary to NREGA's objective of creating—indeed, guaranteeing—employment.[32] As we saw in Chapter 3, this is a relatively efficient means of deriving illicit income: the machinery performs tasks at a fraction of the cost that could be claimed from the state as wages for labourers undertaking the same work. This corruption technique was viable, however, only if workers could be relied upon not to complain publicly if their names were used to pad falsified muster rolls—a condition which explains officials' eagerness to deny NREGA employment to workers who pose uncomfortable questions about the programme.

Another observer, who was not part of the Dungarpur social audit but conducted a separate assessment of NREGA implementation in the district in 2009, found that in some parts of Dungarpur, child labour was being used on NREGA worksites.[33] To those familiar with the lamentable reputation of Rajasthan's mining industry, this is not surprising. Child labour is rife, often in the most hazardous jobs within already-hazardous industries. The study found that on some job cards, ages were falsified; in other cases, younger siblings worked in place of their elders who could then be put to work on private lands. Family members in their prime could, in any case, more reliably fulfil the demanding piece-rates of private farmers who hire labourers for 'sowing and reaping' operations. Some local NREGA implementers were actually said to prefer child workers to adults because they were less likely to be assertive.[34] Not only are children, who are keenly aware of their inferior status, less inclined to organise resistance; their parents, who are complicit in illegality by permitting their children to work on the family's job card, are similarly reluctant to raise objections when wages are not fully paid or accounts are not accurately rendered to the village assembly. NREGA worksite visits that were part of our field research in Rajasthan uncovered numerous cases of children (mainly girls) working.

In a subsequent social audit in Banswara district, scheduled for December 2007, RESKAA experimented with a slightly different approach. In this case, the process began with a close investigation of just one block, though members of the collective had information about alleged irregularities in every one of Banswara's blocks. There was a strong sense from the outset that this pilot block would be a stepping stone to a more thorough sweep of the district by volunteer-auditors, aided by veterans of the *jan sunwai* method.[35] Things did not turn out that way. The state government, which had facilitated—or at least not obstructed—the Dungarpur exercise, had decided that it no longer supported, even rhetorically, the social-audit model that RESKAA sought to institutionalise. The government claimed it was opting for a local *gram sabha*-focused approach to conducting social audits that did not involve groups from outside the locality.[36] This was, in a sense, RESKAA's ultimate long-term goal too. But in the absence of concrete evidence that the formal institutional approach might become a reality any time soon, the activists remained committed to playing a catalytic role, in association with local groups and locally influential individuals.

It was not only politicians affiliated with the ruling BJP who complained about the Banswara social audit, primarily on the basis that it was being spearheaded by 'outside' groups. There was considerable resistance from local bureaucrats and elected officials as well, and this 'quickly snowballed into vituperative opposition from all political parties and interest groups'.[37] In the end, when an extended public protest did not produce the programme records requested (in accordance with the procedures set forth in the Act), teams of citizen-auditors decided to embark on an educational *yatra* (or message-oriented procession that can last days or weeks and which uses music, street theatre, and/or other forms of popular entertainment to engage local publics) throughout the district. Though unsuccessful by conventional measures, the attempt at a social audit had nevertheless revealed the administration's hostility to the idea of implementing NREGA's transparency and accountability provisions.

Two months later, in early 2008, just as NREGA was completing its second year in operation, another social audit was organised for Jhalawar district. Taking place on the heels of the Banswara episode, where officials had successfully short-circuited the social audit process, the activists planning for Jhalawar were determined to set a new precedent. It was also the district in which Chief Minister Vasundhara Raje's constituency was located. Taking on the state in this sensitive location was a high-risk decision by RESKAA's leadership, and a signal that Banswara had not robbed the movement of its resolve. In contrast to earlier social audits, including Banswara, opposition to the Jhalawar social audit appeared meticulously organised. A rallying together occurred among vested interests whose perquisites might be challenged if NREGA project records were subjected to sustained and genuine scrutiny. Village leaders throughout the district were resisting what they considered an attack on the foundations of local social power. To heighten popular outrage against the audit team's arrival, locally influential people asserted that the 'attack' on the district was being orchestrated 'from Delhi'—possibly even 'from 10 Janpath' (Sonia Gandhi's address in the nation's capital). Typically, the nexus of influential voices included the village secretary, elected *panchayat* members, large landowners, building contractors, prominent merchants, and people (including *naya netas*) with access to government decision makers outside the locality.

A preliminary audit-cum-study of three blocks in Jhalawar district—conducted six months earlier, in mid-2007—had given the district a fairly clean bill of health. A sample of muster rolls was selected at random in the Bakani block office, and the workers listed were able to verify the accuracy of the work dates and payment information contained in the records. As one account of this process put it, 'there was no evidence of "fake names" having been entered into the muster rolls'.[38] On the other hand, it also showed that workers were regularly being paid less than the statutory minimum wage. As the lead investigators put it, 'at the Block office in Bakani ... we did not find a single muster roll showing full payment of minimum wages'.[39] That labourers were being denied their full wages is not inconsistent with a finding that muster rolls were relatively free of padding. Indeed, as we saw in the partial catalogue of corruption techniques discussed in Chapter 3, directly siphoning the wages of workers is the most obvious alternative when using bogus names to derive illicit income becomes prohibitively costly.

This raises a key question that has been the subject of earlier research: why do some local works-programme implementers shave the wages of workers to enrich themselves, rather than paying workers their due while colluding with officials to derive income from 'over-measuring' works? Jenkins argued in a 2004 comparative study of anti-corruption movements in Rajasthan and Maharashtra that a crucial determinant in whether the 'zero-sum' (worker-harming) form of corruption prevailed over the 'positive-sum' (non-worker-harming) variety is whether a movement group has emerged to combine constructive work with mobilisational politics.[40] While the quantitative material for the present study was not sufficient to address this issue directly, interviews with both direct participants in and knowledgeable observers of the process of reporting on works projects, indirectly confirmed the central premise: that the existence of a countervailing movement inclined local leaders to use different techniques to steal public resources, and that these were less skewed towards the direct theft of workers' wages.

One method of extracting illegal income from works projects that became prominent after NREGA was rolled out nationwide was through kickbacks from subsidies for upgrades to the private lands of SCs and STs. The amendment to NREGA rules that allowed for works to include such improvements on private lands was justified by claiming that, three years into the implementation process, a shortage of viable projects was impeding the bureaucracy's ability to respond expeditiously to applications for work. Reports from other states subsequently indicated that abuse of this provision had become a widespread means of extracting illicit income from NREGA.[41] In both Udaipur and Sirohi districts, interviews indicated that officials and landholders colluded to relieve the state government of significant sums of money. It was possible in many cases for officials to do so while still paying workers their full wage. Even if the works recorded in project records were not fully completed because necessary funds were skimmed by project administrators, landowners receiving subsidised improvements rarely complained—and if they did, they were made to regret it by any local officials they sought to implicate. Regardless of how one interprets these variations in how illicit income is obtained, during 2006–7 Rajasthan's NREGA projects paid the lowest average wage of any state. This was the flip side of Rajasthan's positive record on increasing access—including to Adivasis, women, and others. The high NREGA take-up rates in Rajasthan, despite comparatively low wages, likely reflected the lack of alternative employment in the state.

In the end, the Jhalawar social audit, despite much preparation, did not turn out as planned. The volunteer auditors were on the receiving end of intimidation and violence—a sure sign that they had strayed onto serious evidence of malfeasance. More than 400 activists staged a *dharna* to protest the failure of officials in Manohar Thana block to release the documents required to conduct a full investigation of expenditure on NREGA works. The president of the association of *sarpanches* from Manohar Thana wrote to the block's NREGA programme officer indicating that 'no information would be provided' to the community organisation working with RESKAA to facilitate the social audit.[42] As with the Banswara social audit, *sarpanches* had closed ranks—supported by senior politicians from the district and their administrative accomplices—to thwart the audit.

By October 2009, the relationship between state government authorities and the core RESKAA leadership had matured to the point where it was possible to put some of their ideas to the test. Not coincidentally, the BJP government of Chief Minister Vasundhara Raje Scindia had been replaced (in late 2008) by the Congress government of Ashok Gehlot, which had every incentive to make Congress Party President Sonia Gandhi's signature programme work well in the state that inspired it. The proving ground would be Bhilwara, a heavily Adivasi district in southern Rajasthan—a place where, as we saw in Chapter 3, NREGA implementation had already become a matter of attempted influence-peddling by political 'fixers' of various stripes. The importance of this social audit to NREGA's future drew in civic groups from beyond the movement sector—including mainstream development-oriented NGOs—and such impartial institutions as the office of the Comptroller and Auditor General (CAG) of India. According to the organisers, the process of preparing for and conducting the Bhilwara social audit demonstrated the potential for collaboration between civil society and government agencies.[43] It also involved senior state government officials: the social audit director (a position that RESKAA had lobbied the state government to create), NREGA commissioner, and Rajasthan's minister of rural development. Even the minister of rural development and *panchayati raj* of the Government of India— Bhilwara was his parliamentary constituency—participated in the release of the audit's results.

RESKAA's leadership knew that such a high-profile investigation, conducted with the assistance of groups from beyond the area, would generate suspicion. Doubts had even been expressed by people who were positively disposed towards NREGA, the social audit method, and RESKAA itself. RESKAA acknowledged that the notion of the 'social audit' was at risk of becoming a 'buzzword', and that, so far, 'the experience with social audit has been mixed'. Some earlier so-called social audits had 'even been used by implementing agencies and vested interests as a means of certifying substandard work by only paying lip service' to the idea of accountability. So, even as it organised the Bhilwara social audit, RESKAA reiterated that, ultimately, it was the government's 'responsibility to ensure that social audits are carried out in all *panchayats* every six months'. Further, the state government—through the district administration—was responsible for ensuring that information was provided 'in a form that people can comprehend, with sufficient time to analyse the information'; for providing a secure and accessible space 'where people can receive this information and provide their reactions/responses/ feedback without fear'; and for taking action in response to 'the statements of the people' who participate in the social audits. Whatever role civil society might be able to play as a catalyst, RESKAA's message was clear: the state must not be permitted to abdicate primary responsibility for carrying out the functions assigned to it under NREGA.[44]

In the end, the process of carrying out the Bhilwara social audit faced little of the coordinated state resistance that characterised the Banswara and Jhalawar exercises. The findings, however, were cause for concern. Village walls, where NREGA-related expenditure information was supposed to be posted, were often bare or painted with outdated figures. There were widespread reports of wages not being paid; of job cards being withheld from workers; of favouritism in the allocation of job opportunities; of missing or clearly fabricated muster rolls; of bank accounts being manipulated by post-office officials; and of poor-quality construction. Even worse, the social-audit process turned up evidence that construction contractors and mechanised equipment had been used in several localities. None of these abuses was surprising,[45] but the scale on which they were committed was a disappointment. On the other hand, RESKAA activists were pleased to observe the willingness of the district administration, including the Collector himself, to order First Information Reports (FIRs) against errant programme administrators.

Parties, Elections, and the Politics of NREGA

NREGA was formulated and passed by a Congress-led government in New Delhi. But regardless of which party conceived NREGA or shepherded it through the legislative process, voters apportion 'credit' and 'blame' largely on the basis of their experiences of programme functioning. Only a small part of this assessment involves evaluating actions taken by the Government of India. Because state governments are so crucial to NREGA implementation, state-level ruling parties are likely to obtain most of the credit (or blame) for the scheme's operation. State governments make many of the key decisions—particularly with respect to wages and how these are determined—that affect the level and distribution of benefits. On the other hand, it is at the local level that crucial decisions—such as who is offered work—are made. Because party affiliation at the *gram panchayat* level is often fluid at best, there are few explicit indications of how the 'local' component of a voter's assessment is weighted.

Despite these caveats, NREGA clearly had at least some indirect electoral effects in Rajasthan. A survey conducted prior to India's 2009 parliamentary election found that, in Rajasthan, people who benefited from NREGA—as workers or in some other capacity (for instance, through use of or access to durable assets produced under NREGA)—were more likely to vote for Congress candidates than those who had not benefited. Among survey respondents who had heard of NREGA, 71 per cent reported having benefited from the scheme. Of these beneficiaries, 55 per cent voted for Congress candidates. The remaining 45 per cent was divided among other parties, with the largest share (34 per cent) being BJP voters. Among respondents who had not benefited from NREGA, however, just 43 per cent had voted for Congress's parliamentary candidates.[46] While these survey results provide a general indication of a 'pro-Congress NREGA effect', they are ambiguous. For instance, it may be that Congress-leaning voters were disproportionately selected as workers on NREGA projects in the months leading up to the polling—which, theoretically, would have been possible after Congress took power in Rajasthan in late 2008.

How the political credit and blame associated with NREGA's implementation would be apportioned between Rajasthan's two main parties was not something that party leaders were willing to leave entirely to chance. During the reign of BJP Chief Minister Vasundhara Raje Scindia, the state government sought to associate NREGA jobs with the state-level ruling party, by folding it into a state government-branded initiative called the Rajasthan Grameen Yojana (or Rajasthan Village Programme). Congress leaders complained bitterly about what they considered politically biased mislabelling—a hijacking of a centrally sponsored initiative. Congress's criticisms rang hollow, as Congress-led state governments had long used similar tactics. During the late 1990s and early 2000s, for instance, Madhya Pradesh's Congress Chief Minister, Digvijay Singh, repackaged centrally sponsored employment-creation schemes under a new label—the Rajiv Gandhi Watershed Mission—that was not only associated with the state government, but with an erstwhile Congress leader. Following the Rajasthan BJP's state-level rebranding of NREGA, however, Congress leaders in Rajasthan sought aggressively to create awareness of which party had advocated for (and funded) the scheme. The president of the Congress Party organisation in Rajasthan, incensed that the BJP had attempted, in his words, to 'steal' credit for NREGA, launched a publicity campaign throughout the state to correct what he regarded as a manifest injustice. As one analysis put it, '[h]e brought the credit back to the Congress by letting people know it [NREGA] was a Congress programme.'[47]

Voter perceptions of corruption in NREGA drove other, arguably partisan, efforts as well. Between January 2009—soon after the new Congress-led government took power—and August 2010, the Rajasthan police displayed uncharacteristic vigour in pursuing charges of *panchayat*-level corruption throughout the state, investigating more than 350 cases.[48] This was a highly significant move. In Rajasthan, as in most other states, the police are controlled by the state's ruling party. They answer to the chief minister directly, for matters of his choosing, or through district administrators (chief ministerial appointees) in other instances. It is, moreover, very rare for state police officials in India to conduct *suo moto* investigations of rural elected self-government institutions, such is the fear of political backlash.

The anti-corruption investigations launched in the early days of Chief Minister Gehlot's government—during the first half of 2009—revealed a large proportion of cases involving either allegations of NREGA abuses, or *prima facie* evidence of such abuses having occurred. Senior figures in the ruling party cited these investigations as evidence that Congress was getting tough on *panchayat*-level corruption—something Gehlot, a self-styled Gandhian, was eager to be associated with. Officials insisted that preserving NREGA's image nationally was a crucial motivation for the crackdown.[49] Certain geographic pockets of the state received the brunt of police zeal. Fifty (or 14 per cent) of the cases were in Nagaur, a district that contained less than 5 per cent of the state's population. Nagaur was, however, home to many of Gehlot's political opponents from the BJP, as well as rivals from within the Congress Party. Unleashing Anti-Corruption Bureau investigators against local governments in the CM's home district of Jodhpur did not convince skeptics that the state government's anti-graft campaign was an even-handed attempt to detect and prosecute criminal abuses wherever they might be found. Investigations in Jodhpur were seen as lacklustre, and in any case mainly confined to locations where Gehlot's men were out of power at the time.[50]

The corruption investigations in Nagaur, by contrast, were unusually thorough and persistent, and turned up very few culprits from the faction in district politics that supported Gehlot.[51] But even if every case investigated contained a *bona fide* example of corruption, with documentary proof to match, the question would always remain: what about those localities, and therefore local ruling factions, that were not subjected to investigation? Why were they spared? In a context where corruption is more or less assumed in every *panchayat*, the issue of selectivity in the government's pursuit of corruption was bound to be an issue.

Continuous Reform: Attempts at Innovation

In the process of implementing something as wide-ranging as NREGA, the scope for innovation is massive. In addition to minor adjustments within the existing NREGA framework—for instance, two changes to the Schedule of Rates during 2006–8—the Rajasthan government made several efforts to reform the way in which it administered NREGA. These were largely driven by pressure from movement activists. The degree of state responsiveness varied over time, and was at least partly a function of which party was in power at the state level. In general, the Congress government (installed following state assembly elections in December 2008) proved more likely to engage in discussions with social movement actors and to translate reform proposals into changed structures and practices. There were also variations in the types of reforms that state-government actors were willing to pursue.

A reform with significant potential was initiated in September 2009, when the Rajasthan government agreed to establish a Directorate of Social Audit. It was only the second state—after Andhra Pradesh—to do so. The purpose was to create a permanent structure within the state administration, staffed by officials who would be responsible for ensuring that social audits took place according to the specifications provided in NREGA Operational Guidelines. As we have seen, audits took place only sporadically during the three years prior to the creation of the new directorate. It was obvious to most people involved in NREGA implementation in Rajasthan that a coordinating body was needed to ensure a more systematic approach. The directorate's officials were to work with administrative offices at the state and district level—as well as with NGOs—to develop procedures and guidelines for the conduct of social audits. A budget for supporting the activities that go into conducting a social audit was also to be supplied.

One reason why the Rajasthan government was amenable to creating a social audit directorate was the positive example set by the Government of Andhra Pradesh.[52] Modeling the Rajasthan approach, in theory, on a structure and programme developed elsewhere, provided a comfort level to Rajasthan's political and administrative leadership that would have been lacking if the only instigators of the reform were social activists, no matter how eminent. However, these same activists had been instrumental in devising the very same administrative structures and procedures around which the Andhra Pradesh system was built. It was an MKSS activist—working 'on loan' to the Andhra Pradesh government—who played a crucial cross-pollinating role. Having seen the results produced in Andhra Pradesh, Rajasthan's government—Congress-led, as in Andhra Pradesh—was ready to risk the consequences.[53]

Potential improvements suggested themselves from the earliest stages of what might be thought of as the typical NREGA project cycle. For instance, in two blocks of Bikaner district, a joint effort between government engineers and prominent NGOs sought to improve the design of works projects and the procedures for determining which projects would most directly address local needs. There have been similar experiments relating to how accounts are submitted to IT processing centres (Barmer district) and how wages are paid to workers (Karauli district).

Indeed, the district level has come to occupy an important niche in NREGA innovation. This is partly because of the uniquely wide-ranging authority of the District Collector (DC)—the state government's representative in the district—particularly when the DC is not at odds with the other key district-level administrator, the CEO of the Zilla Parishad, who, as the title suggests, answers to the elected district council. Because NREGA implementation cuts across departmental boundaries, systematically changing procedures requires the Collector's direct backing.

The district level is often portrayed as far less significant than either the block or *gram panchayat* levels, whether administratively, or in terms of the influence exerted by political leaders. There is considerable truth to this, in the sense not only that the Act charges local officials with selecting and implementing projects, but also because it is beyond the capacity of district officials to keep track of (let alone exercise close superintendence over) the large number of works underway in any given district. Both de jure and de facto, therefore, the local level is of paramount importance. But this assessment should not be extended to the point of entirely discounting the consequential nature of NREGA politics at the district level. NREGA's Operational Guidelines accord a prominent role to the elected district council: 'The shelf of projects for a village will be recommended by the *gram sabha* and approved by the *zilla panchayat*'. This provides a powerful veto point for district-level party and faction leaders. Obtaining clearance from district council members usually comes at a cost. Members do not generally concern themselves with most of the projects in their districts. They have neither the time nor the inclination to do so. Interventions take place on a district councilor's pet projects, or when clients operating at lower levels of the political hierarchy complain that local rivals are seeking approval for projects that will harm the client's interests. An Udaipur-based journalist with a major Hindi daily newspaper described several such cases that took place in Udaipur district during 2006–8. In each case, an out-of-power village faction leader sought assistance from his district-level patron. The objective was to delay or scrap NREGA projects promoted by their local rivals.[54]

One particularly promising district-level experiment took place in 2008 in Jalore, in western Rajasthan. The initiative dealt with seemingly mundane questions of 'worksite management', which turned out to be highly consequential for worker well-being. Worksite management can include issues relating to transparency (whether job cards and muster rolls are available for inspection) or technical oversight (whether the works created are structurally sound and/or functionally operational). There are also a range of questions concerning the conditions under which labourers work, and many of these are addressed in NREGA and its operational guidelines. For instance: in the far-flung locations where works take place, what is the most efficient method for ensuring that provision is made for childcare, drinking water, and shaded rest areas (all of which are required under the Act)?

One crucial place where issues of transparency, technical oversight, and worker conditions converge, is in the system used to measure work outputs. The main excuse given by NREGA administrators for failing to pay workers the statutory daily minimum wage is that workers did not perform the quantity of labour that constitutes—under NREGA guidelines—a day's work. The quotas used for workers have long been a source of contention between workers and activists, on the one hand, and project implementers on the other. That workers are not paid solely on an hourly basis is itself, to some, a violation of the state's conception of the minimum wage, as articulated in statute and jurisprudence.[55] As with many aspects of NREGA, a state government is permitted significant leeway in determining its mode of implementation. NREGA allows payment to be calculated on the basis of either 'daily' or 'piece' rates. With respect to the latter, the Act stipulates that the Schedule of Rates must be structured to ensure that seven hours of work would be sufficient to accomplish the assigned tasks. Rajasthan uses the piece-rate system. When constructing a check dam, unpaved road, or water tank, the amount of earth or other building material that must be moved to meet the daily work quota, and therefore to obtain the minimum wage, depends on factors such as the nature (size and weight) of the materials, the distance that they must be carried to reach the construction site, and the gradient of the surface across which they must be hauled. The method of calculating these factors is a constant source of tension.

In addition to the question of competing methodologies for measuring work output, and how these are, or should be, applied in particular cases, there is the perennial issue of incentives. The prevailing NREGA system measures the collective output of the entire work group and divides it in equal parts among all workers. If, for instance, the Schedule of Rates says that a group of fifty workers is supposed to move 500 cubic feet of earth from point A to point B to qualify for the minimum daily wage rate, based on a quota of 10 cubic feet per worker, but in the end only 250 cubic feet is shifted during the day, then the entire group receives credit for only half the required work quota. This means that each individual will receive only half the daily wage.

Clearly, when measurement and payment are determined at the group level of aggregation, but the daily minimum wage is supposed to be the right of each individual, an incentive problem will arise. Workers who perform below the average are subsidised by those who outperform them—a system that is workable, and may even be desirable, if building solidarity and protecting the infirm are considerations. But where there are workers whose performance is close to zero because their political connections allow them to be listed as workers without having to work (or in some cases even turn up), but nevertheless count as sharers in the collectively determined payment pool, then the predictable result is resentment on the part of those performing the lion's share of the labour. The latter may agitate for a fairer system, or in some cases just 'go slow', as the payoff from enhanced effort is so small.

The Jalore district administration attempted to address the incentive problem through an administrative procedure that would shift the unit of performance from a large group to a small group model. Prodded by movement activists, this effort was led by a Collector who expressed a strong commitment to addressing obstacles that prevented payment of the minimum wage. The Collector also clearly recognised the reputational benefits of being seen as a policy innovator. The key feature of his district-level reform effort was to permit workers to self-form into groups of five. Groups would be collectively measured, with the resulting wages shared equally among workers within each five-person group. Under such an arrangement, workers would naturally seek as teammates the most productive workers. Shirkers, whose reputations are generally well known, would be isolated to their own groups, reducing the incidence of free-riding.

Executing this innovation was easier said than done, however. Adopting a small group system required new forms to be devised, and training to be organised for workers and mates on how to form groups, how to measure their work, and how to enter the information generated through these processes into the existing administrative formats, both hardcopy and online. A considerable buzz surrounded Jalore's experiment with group measurement, not least because of the slick and widely disseminated PowerPoint presentation the Collector had produced to communicate the results of the initiative throughout, but especially beyond, the district.

The results were, in the end, less impressive than the district administration may have led some to believe. A survey team that examined NREGA implementation in two blocks found not only that 'trained' mates were unaware of the procedures for operating the group measurement system; they were, on the whole, remarkably unfamiliar with basic NREGA principles, such as what the minimum wage was, how people should apply for work, or the existence of an unemployment allowance.[56] (The training of female mates, on the other hand, was said to have produced excellent results.) Group formation had not taken place at some worksites, and even more worryingly, the field report from the study stated that '[g]roup measurement was not happening at any of the worksites that we visited'. The team found from oral testimonies that in some cases group measurement had been used, but that it was discontinued because the differential wages paid between groups had stoked conflict, including a 'fight'. Paying differential wages to reward individual work (and to counter exploitation at the hands of free-riders) was of course the primary objective of the group measurement approach. Its erasure in the name of equity, by mates unable to resist local pressure, was not altogether unexpected. Even so, the investigators were not convinced that an observed increase in wages in Jalore—from around Rs 45–50 to Rs 65–70 during the second half of 2007—had much to do with this administrative experiment.

Similar innovations were developed in other districts. In Rajsamand, in central Rajasthan, the Collector who held office during 2008, agreed to experiment with two different procedures that might result in both reduced rates of theft from workers' wages and increased productivity. The first was a version of the small group approach that had been introduced in Jalore. Rajsamand is the MKSS's home district, and the movement's leadership was sufficiently established to work directly with the Collector and other bureaucratic actors to design new forms. This shared practical goal spurred a period of collaboration. The new form included a section where the measurement for each individual worker could be recorded (whether depicted as a share of a large or a small group). It would be retained by the worker and could serve as a receipt in support of a demand to be paid. Workers often laboured for weeks without being aware of the daily amount that had been registered against their names. The new form would address this problem and also include places to record the days worked and payments received, as well as a line for the work-site supervisor's signature. This latter innovation would aid citizen-led auditing by providing a receipt. This was, in a sense, a more precise and compact job card, one that would be kept in the possession of the worker rather than the *panchayat* or work supervisor.

Soon after the Collector's transfer, however, the impetus for this initiative began to wane within the district bureaucracy. This did not come as a surprise to the MKSS workers, who were all-too-well acquainted with the vagaries of officialdom. On an afternoon in January 2009, a group of MKSS activists was called to a worksite not far from Tilonia, where the MKSS's sister organisation is based. Upon arrival at the worksite, the activists asked for the muster roll and measurement sheets and found that the small group measurement forms were being used only haphazardly. There was information penciled in for some weeks but not for others. In addition, it was clear that the purpose of the small group forms—to incentivise productivity by rewarding productive workers, and to deter shirkers by reducing opportunities for free-riding—had been lost on the mate. Where the small group forms were used, each group had been paid exactly the same amount.[57]

Another set of experiments took place in Churu district, which was reported to be the first district outside Goa capable of delivering worker payments within fifteen days. The state government planned to deposit wages directly into personally named bank accounts, which, by September 2008, project implementing agencies were by law supposed to establish for each worker employed under NREGA. The Collector of Churu was, like his counterpart in Jalore, eager to project an image of competence and integrity to politicians operating at the state level. This again cuts against the conventional wisdom that, given the pervasiveness of corruption, politicians clearly reward illicit 'fundraising' over performance. Despite the obvious need for elected officials to have bureaucratic accomplices for whatever illegal rent-seeking they engage in, 'all politicians', as one observer stated, 'will eventually require some capable and honest officers'.[58] In Churu, the district administration's innovation was to merge the process of establishing bank accounts with the system of compiling rosters of workers by holding a series of registration/documentation 'camps' in locations throughout the district. This created administrative efficiencies, undercutting the common complaint that NREGA imposed too many burdensome bureaucratic requirements on besieged local *panchayats*.

Another example was a mid-2010 initiative in Bhilwara, in which the district administration established a single, one-stop 'helpline' for people to call with concerns and questions related to NREGA and its implementation. Through a dedicated telephone number, members of the public could submit complaints about irregularities, seek information concerning process issues, or pose queries concerning an individual's own work/payment entitlement. This initiative was conceived as a pilot project, with potentially state-wide applicability. The idea was to reduce a huge disincentive faced by people considering whether to engage with the state: the lack of clarity as to the primary state interlocutor. This problem is magnified for programmes, such as NREGA, that cut across such a large number of administrative entities, functional areas, and levels of government. Who in the government to telephone (or whether to telephone at all) is not obvious, particularly to people residing in remote locations. The helpline's impact was difficult to gauge: whatever the number of phone queries, and no matter what proportion receive a rating of 'addressed/resolved' (the bureaucracy's scoring methodology being a matter of some debate), the numbers will look paltry compared to the estimated need for external intervention to compel compliance with programme norms by local political figures who violate legal and regulatory provisions with seeming impunity. Even so, the idea was considered promising enough that the Government of Rajasthan's NREGA commissioner eventually agreed to develop a strategy to have the entire state covered by such a system within three months.[59]

* * *

One reason why Rajasthan saw innovation at the district level, was that civil society actors worked with district officials as part of their advocacy work. The movement was at times distant from the Rajasthan government's political leadership, including when its leading figures were publicly challenging the country's prime minister (who, like Chief Minister Gehlot, was from the Congress Party) over the applicability of the national minimum wage to NREGA. During these periods of relative alienation from the state government, movement activists worked with district-level officials to maintain a degree of continuous engagement with the state. These were some of the same activist groups that were instrumental in securing passage of Rajasthan's original Right to Information Act, and amendments to Rajasthan's Panchayati Raj Act—both of which took place in 2000.

Interestingly, senior figures in Gehlot's government, like their BJP counterparts, often blamed poor NREGA performance on their relative lack of influence below the district level, where the vagaries of 'local politics' held sway. There is a more convincing explanation for the intensity of the backlash from *sarpanches* against civil society-led social auditing of NREGA performance. Not only did they (like government actors at all levels) suffer from an acute 'allergy' to transparency and downward accountability; local elites also knew from prior experience how effective these particular activists could be in documenting *prima facie* cases of official misconduct.

But a range of other non-party political formations emerged in response to NREGA as well. And, to some degree, Rajasthan's experience of NREGA to date has revealed differences in the worldviews of different civil society actors. As Sahoo has argued, struggle-based organisations in Rajasthan have tended to be involved in mobilising demands for full NREGA implementation, whereas service-delivery NGOs have tended to focus on technical issues.[60] For the most part, this was true in the areas where we conducted fieldwork. But in many instances, the roles were not so clearly defined. For instance, we witnessed sharp criticisms of the Rajasthan government's handling of NREGA by an allegedly more establishment-oriented NGO—the same one, as it happens, that was studied by Sahoo. Such groups are usually thought to be far more coopted. We also found that the same movement-oriented group that Sahoo examined was also involved in funded projects related to NREGA implementation. In short, the lines separating different types of actors continue to blur.

Finally, it is worth noting that two crucial features of the party structure in rural Rajasthan are important to the processes and outcomes detailed in this chapter. The first is the extent to which local party organisations are weak and rely on local faction leaders to build statewide networks of electoral support. The second is the relative ease with which local faction leaders are willing and able to switch their support between the state's two main parties, the BJP and Congress. This makes it very difficult for state-level party leaders to subject their local affiliates to scrutiny and exposure by activist groups seeking to enhance local government accountability.

5

STATE POLITICS AND NREGA II

MADHYA PRADESH

Madhya Pradesh shares a border with Rajasthan, and is similar in many respects. There are also significant differences—in cultural traditions, economic conditions, and political trajectories. It is thus not surprising to see significant divergences in how NREGA has evolved in these two states. As in Rajasthan, NREGA has achieved a great deal in Madhya Pradesh, despite the ambiguities and limitations that are in large part the subject of this chapter. In what follows, we argue that the pattern of similarities and differences found across Rajasthan and Madhya Pradesh is best explained through the lens of politics, which has profoundly influenced both the conceptual approach to NREGA and how the programme has unfolded in practice.

Two differences between Rajasthan and Madhya Pradesh should be noted at the outset, as both have been important to the implementation of NREGA. First, unlike its neighbour, Madhya Pradesh has not faced the constant threat of severe drought over the last four decades, so its experience with drought-relief works has not been as extensive as in Rajasthan.[1] Madhya Pradesh is certainly no stranger to droughts: it suffered them in four out of five years around the millennium, with deeply damaging consequences, as we witnessed first-hand in rural areas during that period. The reasonably effective state government of the day responded with works programmes, an energetic water-capturing initiative, and much else. But such programmes are not as deeply rooted in the state government's DNA as they are in Rajasthan.

The second difference is bound up with the first. Partly because drought was a less persistent threat in Madhya Pradesh, voluntary organisations that engage in policy advocacy on drought and related issues have not developed the same degree of state engagement (or social capital across the public-private divide) as their counterparts in Rajasthan. Effective civil society organisations have emerged in Madhya Pradesh, and many have gone on to engage with the state government on numerous occasions—including one organisation that strongly influenced a constructive decision about the design of NREGA. But they have not had the kind of continuous interactions with officialdom—partly collaborative and partly adversarial—that Rajasthan has witnessed. Rajasthan's experience in this respect is a distinct rarity. Only Kerala (at times) and Maharashtra (through the cooperative sector), and perhaps one or two other states, have seen similar levels of state-movement cooperation.

As a result, in Madhya Pradesh we do not find what we described in the chapter on Rajasthan as a continuous reform process that takes place through an intermittent quasi-alliance between social activists and state officials. Instead, we find a diversity of non-trivial but less constant and less momentous interactions between civil society organisations and government actors. Two examples will illustrate the diversity and the main types of civic associations found in Madhya Pradesh.

The movement group with the broadest popular following is a Gandhian organisation called Ekta Parishad, which campaigns energetically, and sometimes agitates, for landless and land-poor people. The existence of Ekta Parishad's mass base—reckoned to include at least 250,000 people—persuaded the Congress government that ruled the state between 1993 and 2003 to enter into a political arrangement with the group. The chief minister agreed to certain policy changes that Ekta Parishad had demanded, in exchange for promised support of his party, or at least his government, at the 2003 state election. Congress Chief Minister Digvijay Singh seldom engaged closely with civil society organisations from within the state. But for Ekta Parishad, a movement with a mass following, an exception was made.[2] After the BJP took power following the 2003 election, Ekta Parishad was largely frozen out by the state government. (The BJP was re-elected in late 2008.) Ekta Parishad nevertheless continued with its efforts to mobilise poor people. The main activities, however, concerned land issues and forest rights. Ekta Parishad scarcely engaged with NREGA; its leaders viewed the programme, and efforts to monitor its functioning, as a distraction from the group's core work.[3]

The most important civil society organisation for this discussion is Samarthan, which operates very differently from Ekta Parishad. Samarthan has long adopted a quietly diplomatic, non-confrontational approach to whatever party is in power in Bhopal—in the manner of the formidable national-level organisation, PRIA (Participatory Research in Asia), which is Samarthan's institutional partner. In recent years, both Congress and BJP governments have been at best inconsistent, and often aloof, towards civil society in Madhya Pradesh. This is in stark contrast to Rajasthan. Yet subtle diplomacy, unfailing courtesy, and a well-earned reputation for careful research, have enabled Samarthan to inject constructive ideas into policymaking, at least occasionally. A good example was a 2005 discussion, led by Samarthan, between civic groups and the senior bureaucrat responsible for designing the state's NREGA implementation plan. As we will see in greater detail below, the official was persuaded that projects designed and implemented by elected local councils would be more transparent than those run by line ministries. The state government decided to channel 90 per cent of NREGA funds—not the recommended 50 per cent—through such councils (*gram panchayats*).

That episode depicts civil society at the zenith of its influence over NREGA in Madhya Pradesh. At most other times, bureaucrats and politicians were far less willing to listen to such voices. There is no counterpart in Madhya Pradesh to the 'state-movement symbiosis' in Rajasthan, however unstable. Indeed, apart from Ekta Parishad, civil society activities in Madhya Pradesh do not display sufficient coherence or popular participation to justify describing them as a 'movement'. Yet that one encounter with a single senior official in 2005 helped civil society organisations to substantially alter the character of NREGA in the state. Because elected local councils are more responsive to citizen pressure than line ministries are, the devolution of funds in Madhya Pradesh ultimately enhanced both operational transparency and the likelihood of the programme becoming genuinely 'demand driven' throughout the state.

In short, unlike in Rajasthan, civic groups in Madhya Pradesh almost never managed the feat of exercising substantial and ongoing influence over the design of policy implementation methods while simultaneously retaining the autonomy to challenge key government decisions. This crucial difference requires us to structure the discussion of Madhya Pradesh a little differently from the chapter on Rajasthan. Civil society's engagement with NREGA is examined in a section of this chapter on implementing the programme in the absence of a state-wide movement. That section is more concise than its counterpart in the preceding chapter because civil society's impact in Madhya Pradesh was less potent than in Rajasthan. There is no section on continuous reform emerging from interactions between civil society and government because very little of that occurred in Madhya Pradesh. However, the concluding section of this chapter—on parties, elections, and the politics of NREGA—is more extensive than its counterpart in the Rajasthan chapter, because NREGA in Madhya Pradesh has been more strongly influenced by political actors operating outside civil society.

Alongside these contrasts, one key similarity between Rajasthan and Madhya Pradesh stands out: bureaucrats in both states have suffered less bullying and abuse by politicians than their counterparts have in some other north Indian states—including Haryana, Uttar Pradesh, and Bihar. Decades of mistreatment in those states has severely eroded the morale and autonomy of the civil service and its capacity to implement programmes intended to foster development, poverty reduction, and social justice. The bureaucracies in Madhya Pradesh and Rajasthan have not entirely escaped such damage, but it has been comparatively modest.[4] Administrative structures in each state can make a programme like NREGA work tolerably well in a good proportion of their districts.

'Tolerably'—a word that suggests limitations and ambiguities. We find plenty of these, and in an analysis of state-level NREGA implementation, one is striking. In Madhya Pradesh, bureaucrats—and, as we shall see, elected leaders of local councils—have a strong aversion to downward accountability to ordinary (and especially poor) people. As a result, they have done little to acquaint potential workers on NREGA projects with key details of the programme. Our surveys and interviews at the grassroots in both states revealed that the vast majority of poor villagers were unaware that they had the right to demand work, that an IT system existed to track wage payments and detect corruption, and that they were entitled to compensation if they did not receive work within fifteen days of applying.

Two minor strands in the Madhya Pradesh story suggest part of the explanation for this dismally low level of awareness. First, the performance on NREGA awareness-raising is in marked contrast to the handling of the highly successful Education Guarantee Scheme by the state government under Digvijay Singh in the 1990s. The Education Guarantee Scheme, a homegrown initiative, guaranteed and delivered basic schools to all villages that staked a valid claim. It was relentlessly promoted by the state administration. In the case of NREGA, however, the Madhya Pradesh government neglected to mount an energetic publicity campaign to inform poor people of their rights under the programme.[5] This was a conscious decision rather than an oversight. Second, the state government, uniquely in India, issued job cards to almost every rural household. It appeared a cost-free means of conveying the impression that the government was compassionate. But by taking the initiative in distributing cards, the state government made NREGA appear as yet another programme offering benefits to be bestowed by bureaucrats on citizens with the requisite connections or cash. The fact that potential workers did not need to proactively demand job cards contributed to a lack of popular awareness that people were 'entitled' to employment. The mass distribution of job cards subtly undermined the intention of making NREGA truly demand-driven. It also undercut the idea of encouraging downward accountability at the local level. In many localities, NREGA job cards were handed out by leaders of local councils engaged in complex clientelist calculations; a top-down ethos inevitably gained currency in and around the programme.

A group of well-informed scholars and civil society activists who assessed this programme in numerous states stressed in interviews that the most fundamental problem afflicting NREGA during its first seven years was the acute allergy of government actors to transparency and downward accountability.[6] Indeed, they regard this chronic syndrome as the key besetting sin of the Indian state. From our evidence, this observation holds true in most of Madhya Pradesh and much of Rajasthan, although the problem is mitigated in certain areas of the latter state through the impressive efforts of civil society organisations.

One last introductory point deserves emphasis, since it emerged vividly from our fieldwork in Madhya Pradesh. NREGA's architects created formidable transparency mechanisms to combat malfeasance. Indeed, no large-scale social-protection programme in a low-income country has such extensive transparency and accountability provisions. But as we saw in Chapter 3, in the stylised depiction of relationships found in India's multilevel system of governance, these mechanisms are targeted almost entirely at local actors. They do little to directly affect the actions of people at higher levels, including the next level up—the immensely important sub-district, or 'block', level. Officials at the block level exercise significant powers under NREGA—to approve, inspect, measure, certify, and release funds for works projects. These powers have not been accompanied by corresponding transparency mechanisms to shed light on the actions of these officials.

Context and Background

Geographically, Madhya Pradesh is India's second largest state. Only Rajasthan is bigger. Madhya Pradesh's population of 60.35 million, according to the

2001 census, is the seventh highest among India's states.[7] Madhya Pradesh is also one of the least economically developed. Developmental deficits are especially acute in rural areas, which NREGA targets. When India's Planning Commission devised a Human Development Index for the rural areas of thirty-two states in 1991, Madhya Pradesh came last (Rajasthan was twenty-ninth).[8] A Human Poverty Index for rural areas of the same states placed it twenty-fourth (Rajasthan was twenty-eighth).[9] Thanks to a massive literacy campaign and the state's Education Guarantee Scheme, Madhya Pradesh increased its literacy rate from 35.87 per cent in 1991 to 58.10 per cent in 2001(Rajasthan achieved good results too). But literacy in the state still fell just short of the all-India rate in 2001 of 59.21 per cent (Rajasthan's literacy rate was 30.37 per cent in 1991, and 55.92 per cent in 2001).[10]

Income inequality (both rural and urban) in Madhya Pradesh is slightly lower than the national figure—a Gini coefficient of 0.513 against 0.536 for India (Rajasthan's is still lower at 0.477). But annual per capita income in Madhya Pradesh, at Rs. 6,368, is much lower than the Indian average of Rs. 10,441 (and Rajasthan's figure of Rs. 8,609).[11] The development of infrastructure lags behind the national average, with an index of 74.1 against 100.0 for India (and 83.9 in Rajasthan).[12] Madhya Pradesh came last among Indian states for road connectivity, with only 22 per cent of villages with fewer than 1,000 residents linked to main roads.[13] (It was far behind the second-worst, Rajasthan, which had 38 per cent of such villages connected.) Most tellingly for a study of NREGA, despite significant growth in the state's overall economy in the late 1990s, Madhya Pradesh witnessed an annual increase of only 1.4 per cent in rural employment between 1993–1994 and 1999–2000—identical to the Rajasthan figure and barely above the very low all-India rate of 1.3 per cent.[14]

Madhya Pradesh is in some respects an unusually difficult state to govern. It probably contains more internal variations than any Indian state. This is a legacy of the creation of Madhya Pradesh, which is sometimes called the 'remnant state'—or, less kindly, the 'dustbin state'—because it was assembled from Hindi-speaking areas sliced out of other states when boundaries were redrawn along linguistic lines in 1956. The various sub-regions thrust together in the new Madhya Pradesh had previously maintained only tenuous links to one another. For a century and a half, these now unified territories had been governed—in very diverse ways—by rajas, big and ordinary, or else directly by the British. Madhya Pradesh's regions had different political and administrative traditions. The sheer number of these different governance traditions, and the sheer size of the new state, made Madhya Pradesh perhaps the least well-integrated state in the country—a problem that persists to this day.

Madhya Pradesh has long witnessed bipolar party competition. The Congress Party and the BJP, the only serious contenders for power, have alternated in power twice since 1992. The BJP has governed there since 2003, shortly before NREGA was introduced. It has not developed a coherent, regional version of Hindu nationalism of the kind which (as we saw in the previous chapter) has emerged across much of Rajasthan, where it built upon traditions in the caste system described as 'Kshatriyanisation'. The more marked internal variations within Madhya Pradesh have made that impossible. Hindu extremists have worked assiduously to spread their message, especially in predominantly Adivasi ('tribal') areas of the state. This has involved social programmes and other forms of outreach. But voters across the state, including in mainly tribal areas, have supported the BJP not because they find Hindu chauvinism attractive, but for more mundane reasons: disappointment with the ruling Congress in 2003,[15] and appreciation for the performance of the BJP government in 2008.

The failure of Hindu extremism to take root in Madhya Pradesh is evident from several recent episodes. At the state elections in 2003 and 2008, the BJP carefully downplayed its Hindu nationalist agenda as party leaders knew it lacked mass appeal.[16] In 2001, when Congress was in power, an incendiary Hindu bigot entered Madhya Pradesh to whip up anti-Muslim hysteria. His speeches had triggered communal polarisation and violence elsewhere in India. Soon after he arrived, Chief Minister Digvijay Singh had him arrested in a district far from the state capital. The extremist refused to provide bail, on the assumption that mass protests outside the jail would force the government to free him. After three days, when only desultory demonstrations materialised, he quietly agreed to leave the state if released, and did just that. Hindu nationalism has yet to inspire fervour among the people of Madhya Pradesh.

In Madhya Pradesh, as in many other states, neither the BJP nor Congress possesses enough organisational strength to effectively penetrate below the district level into rural areas across most of the state.[17] Partly as a result, the great majority of villagers do not identify strongly with either party, to the extent that local politics in Madhya Pradesh are less tinged by partisan passions than in many other Indian states.[18] Since 2005, it has only been the BJP that has implemented NREGA in Madhya Pradesh.

As in Rajasthan, both of Madhya Pradesh's main political parties have tended, until recent years, to depend heavily on the distribution of patronage (goods, services, funds, and favours) through patron-client networks. Under this form of clientelism, in various regions of the state, powerful political 'barons' have presided over networks of clients, many of which, in turn, operate as patrons over subordinate networks. Because both parties are organisationally weak, and because a popular political awakening has long saddled all state governments with demand overload, clientelism has been an inadequate device to getting ruling parties re-elected for many years.

In recent years, the insufficiency of clientelism has driven senior politicians to adopt two inter-connected approaches to governance: 'post-clientelist' initiatives, and an increasing dependence on the bureaucracy (rather than weak party organisations) to implement those initiatives. Post-clientelist initiatives are mainly government programmes that are largely or entirely insulated from politicians who seek to transform state resources into patronage for distribution through clientelist networks. Post-clientelist initiatives have not replaced clientelism, since that would trigger resistance from potent political 'barons'. Instead, they supplement it—they are 'add-ons' to clientelist systems which continue to operate. In Indian states where post-clientelist initiatives have developed considerable substance, they have become visible counterpoints to patronage distribution. Madhya Pradesh is one such state. Indeed, it outstrips nearly all other states—possibly including Rajasthan—in this respect.

Madhya Pradesh's ability to adapt to these changing realities had much to do with the adroit, imaginative leadership of Congress leader Digvijay Singh, who served as chief minister between 1993 and 2003. Singh did more to develop post-clientelist approaches than any other state-level politician in that era.[19] He governed in a period of fiscal stringency (which eased after 2003 due to a surge in state and central government revenues). This trimmed the potential size of Singh's post-clientelist initiatives. None could entail a huge outlay of funds. The most innovative were designed with politics in mind—the aim being to generate a tangible impact among large, identifiable segments of voters. They included the strengthening of *panchayati raj*, an effective literacy campaign (akin to a similar drive in Rajasthan, which explains the extraordinary rise in literacy in these two states), and above all, the Education Guarantee Scheme.

That last programme enabled elected local councils to hire local residents with some education to serve as para-professional teachers in primary schools in villages with no nearby school. Half the villages in the state created such schools. A total of 1.16 million students (many of whom would otherwise have had no education) attended them. Their examination results were slightly better than those in conventional government schools. This stemmed from the fact that local councils had been empowered to suspend the salaries of 'no show' teachers, a major affliction of India's state-run schools.[20] This legacy, from which BJP governments in Madhya Pradesh have departed only partially since taking power in 2003, is relevant here because NREGA—a demand-driven programme, at least on paper—is intended to be a post-clientelist initiative.

The second recent trend noted above, which is also a response to the weakness of party organisations in Madhya Pradesh, is an increased dependence on the bureaucracy as the main instrument for implementing government programmes. Following independence in 1947, clientelism became the predominant mode of governance in India. In the late 1960s, a popular political awakening placed massive demands on governments at both the state and national levels, and from a direction to which they were not necessarily used to responding—below. By the late 1970s, this demand overload combined with political decay within the Congress organisation—caused in part by Indira Gandhi's assault on her own party, whose rising leaders she perceived as a threat to her power—to make clientelism an inadequate means of ensuring re-election.

The decreasing reliability of clientelist networks as a means of delivering favourable electoral results, and the organisational weakness of both the Congress and the BJP in Madhya Pradesh,[21] persuaded senior politicians to rely increasingly on bureaucrats and official programmes, rather than on party structures that supervise patron-client networks, to reach rural voters.[22] Such politicians have been encouraged and enabled to do so by the comparatively healthy condition of the bureaucracy in these two states. This is in stark contrast to, as noted above, some other north Indian states.

NREGA depends in part on the bureaucracy, but also on *panchayats* (elected councils at lower levels) and especially at the local (*gram panchayat*) level. Between 1993 and 2003, the Madhya Pradesh government did more than most other states to strengthen these institutions, or at least those at the district and local levels. Like all state governments across India, it provided little power to the intermediate-level 'block' (or sub-district) councils,[23] which is why, in this book's discussions of block-level politics, bureaucrats rather than elected politicians loom so large. Elected representatives at the block level have almost no practical influence over programme implementation (or much else, for that matter), and as chief minister, Digvijay Singh conferred a range of new powers on district and local *panchayats*. He considered this a logical response to Madhya Pradesh's challenging internal diversity, and believed that democratic decentralisation would improve development outcomes and enhance his party's popularity. In 2001, Singh was forced by legislators to reduce the powers of district-level *panchayats*, but despite that, the state's local *panchayats* remained comparatively robust.[24]

The BJP government that took office in December 2003 was less sympathetic than its Congress predecessor to democratic decentralisation. In some respects, the BJP government has undermined *panchayat* institutions in Madhya Pradesh. It removed the power of district councils to transfer lower-level bureaucrats. The ability to arrange a bureaucrat's transfer—from a post that offers few opportunities to take bribes, to one that offers many such opportunities—is an important source of political influence (and of illicit income). By handing this power back to the state government, this decision in effect weakened democratic processes at the local level.

The BJP state government also reduced the number of committees within local councils from eight to two. It promised to frame new rules for the remaining two, but has failed to do so. As a result, in most localities, committees of the locally elected council have not been formed. The state government also failed to frame new voting procedures for *gram sabhas*—the local mass meetings that the Congress government under Digvijay Singh saw as central to democratic decentralisation. In theory, *gram sabhas* are forums in which local residents can question elected council members and participate in certain key decisions. They could hardly fulfil a fraction of this promise during the Congress administration that promoted them, and under the BJP government that has shown no interest in developing them, *gram sabhas* have been reduced to little more than organisational shells. This state of affairs has important implications for how we understand the institutional politics of NREGA, since *gram sabhas* are intended to play key roles in local decisions about priorities under the programme and in ensuring transparency and downward accountability at the grassroots level.[25]

Findings From a Survey in Two Districts

Let us turn now to the findings from our survey in Madhya Pradesh. The survey was conducted in thirty-two village council (*gram panchayat*) jurisdictions. Survey enumerators used a questionnaire to seek information from people who had worked on NREGA projects, so that the sample consisted overwhelmingly of the poor. Half of the respondents were women, half were men. The surveys were complemented by numerous interviews that we conducted with knowledgeable informants in these various villages, and in block and district headquarters. Those interviews revealed that district- and block-level leadership was indeed important (see the discussion of 'worst' and 'best' case districts below).

The thirty-two *gram panchayats* were distributed equally between two districts—Shivpuri, in the northern sub-region of the state, and Barwani, in the far southwest. Thus there were sixteen *gram panchayats* surveyed in each district.[26] No two districts can supply a microcosm of a state as internally variegated as Madhya Pradesh. On the other hand, neither of these two districts is especially atypical. Shivpuri and Barwani vary somewhat on a number of measures, but are sufficiently similar to enable us to gain insights into what is driving both commonalities and variations in district-level administrative and political dynamics.

As in Rajasthan, in both districts in Madhya Pradesh, the survey was conducted within three blocks (sub-districts). In Rajasthan, certain 'movement endowed' blocks were deliberately chosen—places where groups affiliated with the state-wide right to work campaign were working to monitor and promote improvements in NREGA implementation. Other blocks were 'movement deprived'. In Madhya Pradesh, no equivalent state-wide 'movement' to engage government actors has emerged. To aid comparison with the Rajasthan case, however, we included a district (Barwani), where substantial efforts by a civil society organisation had occurred, and compared it with one (Shivpuri) where local activism of this sort had not arisen. It was hypothesised that poor villagers in this organisationally-endowed district would be more aware of their rights under NREGA, and more likely to exercise them. As in Rajasthan, the findings of the survey lent some credence to the hypothesis, although ambiguities also arose.

Two early questions in the survey—about how many people had applied for job cards, and how many had to pay bribes in order to obtain them—proved to be revealing in Rajasthan. But since it was the policy of the Madhya Pradesh government to send job cards to all local residents, these questions had less importance there. Only 12.5 per cent and 22.5 per cent of respondents in the two Madhya Pradesh districts said that they had applied, as against 42.5 per cent and 55.8 per cent in the Rajasthan districts. It is worth noting, however, that in both states significant numbers of people said that they had paid bribes in order to obtain their cards—in Madhya Pradesh from their local council, through which cards were distributed, rather than from agents of the state government. In the two Madhya Pradesh districts, 25 per cent (Barwani) and 17.5 per cent (Shivpuri) of respondents stated that they paid bribes to obtain a job card. These figures were somewhat lower than those for Rajasthan (32.5 per cent and 17.5 per cent), but the amounts paid in Madhya Pradesh were a little higher.

That bribes had to be paid by 25 per cent of job card-seekers in Barwani District, the home of a creative and committed civil society organisation that bears certain resemblances to Rajasthan's MKSS, highlights the potential for NREGA-related corruption. Our interviews in Barwani suggested that, in at least some parts of the district, demands for bribes fuelled poor people's resentment of the privileged, and heightened their awareness of corruption in the programme. By contrast, in Shivpuri district, where civil society groups scarcely operate and there is nothing like an MKSS-style campaigning organisation, survey respondents who paid bribes to officials implementing NREGA told us in interviews that they regarded this as standard practice. On this issue, they saw nothing especially new or different about NREGA.

We then asked about the next step in the process—how many people had been given receipts when they sought job cards (as the law requires). Here, as in Rajasthan, the findings were dismal. All respondents who applied in organisationally-endowed Barwani District, and 96.3 per cent in Shivpuri District, failed to obtain receipts. It should be added, however, that significantly more potential workers in the Madhya Pradesh districts kept possession of their job cards, and were not required to hand them over to local council leaders or the 'mates' who manage project worksites. Keeping possession of one's own job card impedes efforts by local council leaders to make corrupt use of them. In these two districts, 88.3 per cent and 92.5 per cent of workers, respectively, held their own cards. These figures are matched in Rajasthan only in the part of Sirohi District that was movement-endowed.

Responses to questions about workers' awareness of key aspects of NREGA reveal a mixed picture, as they did in Rajasthan. In Madhya Pradesh, respondents were only half as likely as their counterparts in Rajasthan to be aware of the 100-day guarantee. When asked whether NREGA gave them the right to work, 48.3 per cent of respondents in organisationally-endowed Barwani District were aware of this, compared with just 34.2 per cent in Shivpuri. Unlike in Rajasthan, there was also a sizeable disparity in the degree of awareness of this entitlement depending on the district: in the district that did not have a strong activist presence (Shivpuri), 31 per cent were aware; in organisationally-endowed Barwani, the figure rose to 48 per cent. Rajasthan and Madhya Pradesh were on roughly equal ground concerning workers' awareness of the minimum wage—60.8 per cent of workers in Barwani District (where civil society activists have been at work) stated that they knew it, and even more in Shivpuri District (61.7 per cent). As in Rajasthan, the 'movement effect' in Madhya Pradesh was unpredictable—revealing itself as influential on some worker rights and welfare issues, but not on others.

Our survey found that relatively high proportions of the sample had encountered problems working under NREGA. In Barwani, 58 per cent of workers surveyed (65 per cent in Shivpuri) had experienced difficulties— denial of sustained employment, irregular or delayed wage payments, demands for bribes, and so forth. In Shivpuri, 14.2 per cent of workers had been denied wages for some or all of the work they performed. In movement-endowed Barwani the figure was just 4.2 per cent. Solid majorities of workers in both districts believed that they had been paid the minimum wage, but when we asked what they had been paid, it emerged that many—especially in Shivpuri— had received less than the minimum wage, suggesting that they had not known what the minimum wage actually was.

Despite the presence of civic activists, 46.7 per cent of job applicants in Barwani waited more than 60 days to obtain work. In movement-deprived Shivpuri, the figure was somewhat lower, at 38.3 per cent. Very few applicants (8.3 per cent in Barwani and 3.3 per cent in Shivpuri) knew they were entitled to unemployment compensation payments if employment was not provided within fifteen days. But not a single respondent reported having received an unemployment allowance. Interviews in Barwani, however, indicated that a very small number of people who were supported by the civil society organisation there had obtained compensation—indeed, it was reportedly the first district in India where this had occurred.[27]

Only 7.5 per cent of respondents in each Madhya Pradesh district knew that NREGA work was supposed to occur within five kilometres of their homes, but since all respondents reported obtaining work within that range, this was not a significant issue. Here, as in Rajasthan, very few workers were aware of a key transparency mechanism, the requirement that details of their interactions with NREGA be recorded in the programme's dedicated IT system. Only 11.7 per cent of respondents in Barwani District and 13.3 per cent in Shivpuri knew that an MIS existed for this purpose, and still fewer understood that the MIS data should match the information on their job cards. Given this lack of awareness and low literacy rates among workers, it therefore appears that this transparency mechanism was largely regarded as something for others to use.

In Rajasthan, women participated in NREGA at an average rate of 68 per cent over the first three years of the programme, which is more than one-and-a-half times the national figure of 43 per cent. Several things contributed to this outcome. Some were common to all Indian states—most crucially, perhaps, the requirement that women and men receive equal wages. Our interviews with poor women in Madhya Pradesh indicate that this was a very welcomed incentive, which persuaded many women to seek work, but also that this was not a universal phenomenon. Less was done there than in Rajasthan to provide child-care facilities at work sites for women with young children. Only 12.5 per cent of survey respondents in one Madhya Pradesh district said that such facilities were available, and the figure was 9.2 per cent in the other. The figures for the two Rajasthan districts where the survey took place were much higher in one and somewhat higher in the other (57.5 per cent and 17.5 per cent, respectively). Officials in the state government in Madhya Pradesh acknowledged in interviews that greater efforts could have been made on this front. This partly explains the lower participation rate among women in NREGA work in the state.

Some readers who are deeply sceptical of NREGA—about both the concept and how it has been operationalised—might interpret the survey results as evidence that the programme did not work well. But in assessing their significance, we need to bear two important points in mind. First, in Madhya Pradesh (and Rajasthan) our survey data, and abundant evidence from other sources, much of it from other states, indicate that very large numbers of poor and 'near poor' people—the latter including people who would be considered extremely poor in many other countries—obtained work under NREGA and received wages that made a vital material difference in their lives. The overwhelming majority of respondents (86.7 per cent in Barwani and 95 per cent in Shivpuri) stated that the wages were a significant help to their families.

Our additional interviews with poor villagers and knowledgeable informants in these and other districts indicated that NREGA earnings were usually used for constructive, often critically important purposes. Obtaining more and better quality food emerged very prominently in these discussions. People said repeatedly that, thanks to NREGA, they were able to provide more than just one meagre meal per day for their families. Civil society activists working with poor people in Madhya Pradesh reinforced this point by noting that under a state government programme introduced in May 2008, the poor could obtain a kilo of wheat for Rs. 3.5. This meant that just one day's work on a NREGA project, if paid at the minimum wage, enabled a worker to feed a family for fifteen to twenty days.[28]

Our interviews with poor villagers also revealed that food was a priority item under the 'home expenditure' category (two-thirds of respondents in Barwani and 81.7 per cent in Shivpuri mentioned this to enumerators). This is crucial, since a study by a New Delhi-based organisation found severe malnourishment among children in Barwani and other districts in the state to be 'shocking'.[29] A small minority of NREGA workers were also able to invest some of their earnings in things such as seeds and fertilisers for small plots of land and livestock. This enhanced their productive capacity and earning power.[30] These gains are far from trivial.

Second, the disappointments that poor people experienced during programme implementation possessed constructive potential. The programme's design is sufficiently transparent to enable local residents to understand the various abuses to which they are being subjected. Awareness helped NREGA applicants to move from being repeatedly disappointed to being politically discontented—and therefore more likely to operate proactively in the public sphere. This process of political transformation resembled the trajectory that NREGA's architects foresaw and intended: a gradual process of enhancing the political capacity and influence of some of India's poorest and most marginalised people.[31] Other non-rights-based government programmes have had much less (or in many cases, no) impact of this kind. So despite the many ambiguous and negative findings that emerge from our survey evidence, our stakeholder interviews seem to suggest substantial 'citizenship assertion'. By citizenship assertion, we mean something larger than just demanding new rights or the full recognition of rights acknowledged earlier. Here we refer to demands by citizens to participate directly in state institutions that are designed to hold officials accountable for their performance in delivering improvements to specific aspects of people's well-being.

Implementing NREGA in the Absence of a State-Wide 'Movement'

In the previous chapter, we explained that interactions between the Rajasthan government and what can justifiably be called a state-wide 'movement' strongly influenced NREGA implementation in that state. As noted above, the only organisation in Madhya Pradesh that approximates the kind of dual movement/NGO entity found in Rajasthan,[32] the Gandhian organisation Ekta Parishad, has scarcely engaged with NREGA. So here—as in nearly all other Indian states—NREGA has been implemented without the partnership or constructive criticism of a social movement. In the absence of such a movement, two important realities came powerfully to the fore: (i) the state government and official actors had great freedom to act independently of social forces when implementing NREGA; and (ii) political dynamics in which civil society organisations play modest roles at best—and often no role at all—strongly influenced NREGA implementation at state, district, sub-district, and local levels. Those topics are discussed in the next and concluding sections of this chapter.

In Madhya Pradesh, civil society organisations, especially in rural areas, are far less robust than in Rajasthan and somewhat less strong than in most other Indian states. In most districts of this comparatively under-developed state, voluntary organisations have little substance outside urban areas. Grassroots, bottom-up civil society organisations have some strength at, and just above, the village level. But in many districts, they are only tenuously—if at all—connected to district-level organisations, which tend to be based in urban centres.

Over the past two decades, however, many district-level civic associations in Madhya Pradesh have coalesced into state-wide networks. This was largely the result of sustained efforts by one particularly effective civil society organisation, Samarthan, which operates out of the state capital. Samarthan has long concentrated on informing poor and socially excluded groups, enabling them to operate effectively in the public sphere and strengthening their engagement with elected councils (*panchayats*). Samarthan also interacts quietly and diplomatically with state-level policymakers. Samarthan, in fact, played a key role in one crucial episode—persuading officials that *panchayats* should receive 90 per cent of NREGA funds, not just the 50 per cent the law required. Samarthan has also undertaken analyses for the state and national governments of the operation of NREGA, the Right to Information Act, and other legislation. Samarthan works intensively in two of the state's forty-eight districts, in the manner of its national-level partner PRIA, one of India's most formidable civil society organisations. In the other forty-six districts of Madhya Pradesh, Samarthan works through a network of civic associations it has helped to create. In some districts, this has produced organisations that have pushed for significant change,[33] but often little local initiative is in evidence. Samarthan's influence is far more visible in the two districts where it works intensively.

Because the BJP has held power in Madhya Pradesh since NREGA was introduced,[34] we might expect civil society organisations associated with the Hindu nationalist movement to become involved in the programme's operation. Social welfare organisations associated with the *sangh parivar* have a

history of working among deprived communities as an entry point for ideological persuasion.[35] In this case, however, such organisations have instead
concentrated mainly on their traditional concerns—social polarisation along
religious lines and acquainting ordinary people with Hindu nationalist ideology. In some districts, these organisations have won government contracts to
conduct social audits and/or to foster popular awareness of the details of
NREGA. They have been ineffective on both fronts—raising suspicions that
they used most of the funds to pursue other activities.

In a small number of districts in Madhya Pradesh, civil society organisations
have played a significant role in mobilising poor people. One especially
impressive example is the Jagrut Adivasi Dalit Sangathan (JADS), or the
Adivasi and Dalit Awakening Organisation, in Barwani district. JADS operates mainly among Adivasis (tribals), who account for two-thirds of Barwani's
population. The organisation's approach contains elements exhibited by the
more formidable MKSS in Rajasthan. JADS concentrates on making information available to the rural poor, building their political capacity to make
demands, and pressing officials to implement laws (including but not limited
to NREGA). The group has made considerable headway on these issues in a
number of localities.[36]

JADS has sufficient substance to persuade bureaucrats in the district to
tread carefully in their dealings with the organisation, and with the woman
who built it up, Madhuri Behn. But no Rajasthan-style state-civil society collaboration has developed in Barwani. Officials in Barwani District are mightily irritated over the activities of the organisation. The less diplomatic voices
among them say that JADS is trying to drag the district into the 'red belt'—
the area of central India where Maoist insurgents confront the authorities.[37]
That accusation is wildly inaccurate. JADS' work makes it less, not more, likely
that poor villagers will turn to insurrection. Dreze's analysis of NREGA's
impact across India cites JADS as an example of how the Act can catalyse
activism. In Barwani district, 'NREGA had been actively used as a means of
public mobilisation' thanks to the work of JADS,[38] almost doubling the levels
of NREGA employment to eighty-five days a year for each applicant household, compared to forty-three statewide.[39] Dreze also asserted that 'the
Sangathan's organisational work' generated 'high awareness levels among
NREGA workers and their confidence in the power of collective action'—a
considerable feat.[40]

NREGA implementation in rural Madhya Pradesh began in September
2006, about the same time as it started in most other states, after a period of

administrative preparation. NREGA was initially introduced in 18 districts of Madhya Pradesh. These were among the 200 districts targeted in the first phase. Thirteen more districts followed in 2007–8, and all 48 of the state's districts were included by 2008–9, when the programme went nationwide.

Like many (but not all) other state governments, Madhya Pradesh approached NREGA implementation enthusiastically. The state government demonstrated solid commitment to making the programme work. Senior politicians inserted capable civil servants into key supervisory roles at the state level, gave them substantial authority, and encouraged them to ensure that the programme worked well across most of the state. The main exceptions to this were four or five of the state's 48 districts—the 'worst case' districts, discussed below—where politicians at the state level sought to extract significant illicit funds from NREGA. The state has not adopted the aggressive strategy that was used to pursue the state's Education Guarantee Scheme before 2003. For that scheme, the state government provided district administrators with detailed instructions on how to publicise the programme among poor people and then to deliver swiftly on requests from below. It also informed bureaucrats at lower levels that the then chief minister insisted that their support for this scheme would form part of their annual performance evaluation. Here, as in nearly all states,[41] the 'promotion' of NREGA has mainly entailed the distribution of printed guidelines to bureaucrats.[42]

But Madhya Pradesh's approach to NREGA has differed from nearly all other states in two key respects. It decided to channel not just the recommended 50 per cent, but fully 90 per cent of NREGA funds through *gram panchayats*, and it sought to issue job cards to every rural household. An understanding of the political context may help to explain these divergences. The BJP has held power in Madhya Pradesh since NREGA was inaugurated (it retained power at a state election in late 2008, and again in 2013). This has ensured policy continuity. It was by no means certain that the BJP government would implement NREGA energetically. The BJP is the main rival (at both state and national levels) of the Congress Party, and the programme was the brain child of a Congress-led coalition government at the national level. It was well known among politically knowledgeable people, and to a significant degree among ordinary folk, that it had emerged from a committee chaired by the Congress Party's president, Sonia Gandhi. NREGA's architects carefully avoided attaching a label to the scheme that would associate it with the Nehru/Gandhi 'dynasty', as had been done with several other initiatives,[43] because they wanted it to be embraced by all state governments as a non-partisan measure.[44]

BJP leaders in Madhya Pradesh might have feared that robust NREGA implementation would serve mainly to enhance the popularity of their Congress Party rivals in New Delhi. After much deliberation, however, they decided to pursue NREGA vigorously. They saw that it offered very substantial funds, and could make a potent impact. It addressed a genuine need among the rural poor, who loom large in this under-developed state, not least because they vote in large numbers. And if they responded half-heartedly (as, for example, the BJP government in Karnataka did), their Congress opponents within the state would berate them for callously neglecting impoverished villagers. They reckoned that if they made a success of the scheme, voters would give them and not their adversaries in New Delhi much or most of the credit. This was not the only state government headed by opponents of Congress to take this view. Indeed, in 2006, a review by the Congress Party concluded that its adversaries, who were implementing NREGA at the state level, were doing it better than Congress state governments.[45]

By deciding to channel not 50 but 90 per cent of NREGA funds to local councils, Madhya Pradesh's senior officials rejected the reasoning that prevailed in most other states.[46] Most other governments preferred to channel as much funding as possible through line ministries, which were controlled by their own ministers, and to avoid going through *panchayats*, many of which were controlled by opposition parties. Party leaders in most states believed that NREGA's political payoff would be greater if 'their' ministers managed the flow of resources. In Madhya Pradesh, however, the party's leadership maintained that NREGA's political payoff for the ruling party would be greater if *panchayats* received most of the resources. Three main reasons were cited. First, implementation would be more transparent if *panchayats* and not line ministries managed it—and transparency was crucial to the perceived popular success of this programme. Second, ruling-party leaders knew that projects initiated by line ministries are very often 'supply driven', reflecting the organisational priorities (and personal interests) of ministry officials. This would undercut the 'demand driven' nature of NREGA.[47] Third, because NREGA projects are supposed to address urgent local needs, *panchayats* are (at least in theory) much better positioned to identify which works might translate into political support. BJP leaders also knew that partisan sentiments at the local level were less intense in Madhya Pradesh than in most other states, and so it was less problematic that local councils led by opposition parties would share the political credit.[48]

The idea of disbursing 90 per cent of NREGA funds to *panchayats* emerged from a process in which a senior civil servant rather than a politician played the pivotal role. Politicians had to endorse it, but in Madhya Pradesh—whose bureaucracy has largely escaped the severe damage done by bullying politicians in some other north Indian states[49]—it was possible for a bureaucrat to perform this function. At an early and decisive stage in NREGA's existence, this experienced civil servant was placed in charge of implementing its provisions. He had the sophistication in policy matters to design a strategy that conformed to the Act's requirements and to anticipate many of the issues that would arise as implementation proceeded. He had a famously gruff, forceful manner that made him difficult to deal with, but which also ensured that directives from his office usually produced results at lower levels in the administrative system. However, this official was open to reasoned argument, which proved crucial when the question of how to disburse NREGA funds arose. Civil society leaders, with Samarthan playing a key role, asked for a meeting to make the case for devolving a greater proportion of funds to the councils. Samarthan's reputation for dispassionate argument based on solid research, and for impressive constructive work in support of local councils, helped to open the door.[50]

The interview was granted, and the civil society leaders argued—quietly and at length—that if funds were transferred to line ministries, they would be managed with almost no transparency. By contrast, a great deal more transparency would attend the management of funds by local-level *panchayats* for three main reasons. First, their actions are far more visible to ordinary (and poor) people at the grassroots than are the actions taken at higher levels by line ministry personnel. Second, *panchayat* leaders (unlike line ministry bureaucrats) depend on local residents for election to office, making them susceptible to local constituent pressure. Finally, NREGA's transparency mechanisms target the local *panchayat* level rather than government employees at higher levels. These arguments have been borne out by subsequent experience. Line ministries have released very little information about NREGA projects they have implemented. The costs of those projects on which information has been made available have often been twice as high as similar projects undertaken by local *panchayats*. This has inspired suspicion that more funds have been diverted by line ministries than by local *panchayats*.[51]

After making inquiries of his own, the civil servant was persuaded by the arguments advanced by civic advocates who participated in this meeting. He then convinced senior politicians that devolving a greater share of funds to elected local councils made good sense, both developmentally and politically.[52] Civil society organisations in Madhya Pradesh are not as formidable as their counterparts in many other states. But they have enough experience—and crucially, sufficient constructive arguments and diplomatic skills—to prevail when bureaucrats receive them with open minds.

However, we should not assume from this episode that the Madhya Pradesh government worked closely with the state's more constructive civil society organisations when it began implementing NREGA. In reality, it did little of that. Most politicians in the ruling BJP view civil society organisations that seek to promote participatory development with some suspicion. All but one of those organisations have carefully remained politically neutral as the BJP and the Congress Party have vied for power.[53] But their broadly liberal outlook inspires scepticism among BJP leaders,[54] who prefer to work with Hindu nationalist voluntary associations which focus far more on social polarisation than on participation or development.

The importance of this becomes clearer when we consider the contrast with Rajasthan. The BJP governed there from the introduction of NREGA in 2006 until it lost a state election in December 2008. While it held power, it was at least as unsympathetic towards constructive, non-partisan civil society organisations as was its counterpart in Madhya Pradesh. However, when the Congress Party took office in Rajasthan in late 2008, the new government reached out to those organisations that had long sought to promote participation (and access to information) by ordinary villagers, including the poor. In Madhya Pradesh, no such change of government occurred. The BJP retained power in the state at the election of December 2008, and remained aloof from constructive civil society organisations.

But the Madhya Pradesh story involves more than the proclivities of the BJP. All governments in that state—whether headed by the Congress Party or the BJP—have typically been hesitant to engage with civil society organisations that stress open, participatory governance. This is rather curious because Chief Minister Digvijay Singh shared their enthusiasm for open participatory governance during his decade in power, from 1993 to 2003. But while he drew civil society leaders from outside the state into policy advisory committees, his government did little to embrace constructive civic associations within Madhya Pradesh (apart from one, Ekta Parishad, mainly because it was unique among such organisations in having a mass following). In one important instance, a serious personality clash developed between one of Singh's senior aides and a civil society organisation that worked imaginatively to promote basic education. That episode had a chilling effect on relations between the Congress state government and civil society.[55] But, on the whole, Madhya

Pradesh has not experienced the kind of intense, if often troubled, relationship between the authorities and constructive civic groups that Rajasthan witnessed after December 2008, and then again after December 2013, when the BJP returned to power.

One important implication of this lack of state-movement engagement in Madhya Pradesh became apparent once NREGA implementation activities began to intensify. A notable example concerned the system for awarding contracts to conduct awareness campaigns and social audits. In some districts, contracts were awarded to Hindu nationalist organisations that have little interest in using NREGA to enhance the political capacity of poor villagers through participatory processes. These organisations often used the funds from contracts to popularise Hindu nationalist themes.

But in most districts, officials implemented procedures in a politically neutral, mechanical manner. They allotted contracts to whichever organisation's bid was lowest, irrespective of their experience in conducting social audits. In many districts, this meant that contracts went to fly-by-night 'organisations' created solely to capture the funds that contracts offered. Several of these were headed by owners of photography studios who learned of NREGA when they were hired by officials to produce job cards bearing the pictures of labourers applying for employment. They submitted bids that grossly underestimated the costs required to spread awareness of NREGA and to conduct genuine social audits. These contractors merely went through the motions of completing these crucial tasks, which partly explains the widespread lack of awareness found in our survey results, as well as the lack of dynamism in the conduct of social audits. This system for awarding contracts poses a dilemma for civic groups with a track record of promoting participatory development. If they seek sums that are, realistically, needed for minimally effective social audits, they will be denied contracts because others have entered lower bids. The alternative is to submit extremely low bids and then to supplement inadequate government funds with their own resources so that meaningful social audits occur. But since all of these organisations have very limited funds, they have only been able to subsidise government grants in a tiny number of districts.

The state government's decision to issue job cards to every household made Madhya Pradesh unique among Indian states. It was mainly inspired by a desire to demonstrate to villagers (who are also of course voters) that the state government was concerned for their welfare. The results were ambiguous. Madhya Pradesh issued more job cards (11.2 million) in the first year than any other state, accounting for 39.8 per cent of all cards issued across the country, despite only making up 5.9 per cent of India's population. This was partly a reflection of the fact that Madhya Pradesh's districts were overrepresented among those included in the programme's two-year pilot phase. But even in NREGA's third year (2008–9), by which time all of India's districts were covered, Madhya Pradesh still accounted for 38.3 per cent of all job cards. The state government actually issued more cards than the number of rural households listed in official statistics. In 2008–9, it distributed job cards to 122 per cent of Madhya Pradesh's rural households, against a national average of 64.2 per cent.[56]

Providing job cards in this way somewhat undermined the rights-based nature of NREGA—the crucially important idea that poor villagers were entitled to ask for and receive job cards. More people obtained cards as a result of this decision, but the manner of their delivery meant that less was done here to stimulate demand from below. By initiating the process itself, the state government had, in a sense, made rural dwellers passive recipients of government largesse. On the other hand, the mass distribution of cards alerted a vast number of rural dwellers to NREGA's existence, which partly explains why the percentage of households who obtained work in the first two years of the programme (when it operated in poorer districts) was above the national average.[57] Our village-level surveys indicate that most poor villagers undertook work only when it was offered to them by local leaders.

Official figures therefore overstate somewhat the degree of genuine demand. In the case of Madhya Pradesh, it is more accurate to say that most households 'obtained' work rather than successfully 'demanded' it. Two things should be stressed by way of mitigation, however. First, as a result of the mass distribution of job cards, poor people in Madhya Pradesh avoided (illegal) exclusion from NREGA, which was common in other states among villagers who did not possess BPL cards.[58] Second, our interviews with villagers indicated that at least a significant minority of those who initially received work without demanding it came to understand, once they started working, that NREGA gave them the right to demand it.

The mass distribution of job cards also meant that cards were issued to many people who were not poor. Many cards went to people who would never use them—including for example, Kamal Nath, a Congress minister in the cabinet in New Delhi.[59] Many (perhaps most) job cards were sent not directly to villagers but to the addresses of their local councils. This allowed *sarpanches* and/or *panchayat* secretaries to steal NREGA resources by making false entries in programme records to indicate work that was never performed.

(Some non-poor recipients of job cards 'leased' them out to officials for this purpose, obtaining a share of the illegally derived income in return.) The prevalence of such methods provides another part of the explanation for the high percentages of rural households obtaining work. There were, however, variations in the degree to which corruption afflicted NREGA in different parts of the state—differences that were reflected in the existence of 'worst case', 'best case', and 'ambiguous' districts. Because these distinctions resulted from the political calculations and actions of powerful actors, we turn now to an analysis of the influence of politics on the implementation of NREGA in Madhya Pradesh.

Parties, Elections, and the Politics of NREGA

Politics—that is, the interplay of institutions, interests, actors, and ideas in the pursuit of power—strongly influenced the implementation and the impact of NREGA in Madhya Pradesh. This was true at all levels: state, district, sub-district, and local. There were important differences between the various levels—in political dynamics and in the influence wielded by key actors. The latter can be depicted schematically as follows.

Table 5.1: Degrees of Influence on NREGA Implementation (by actor and level)

	Elected politicians	Bureaucrats
State level	Strong	Moderate
District level	Moderate	Strong
Block level	Virtually none	Dominant
Local level	Strong	Moderate

At the state level, ministers make most of the key decisions about the implementation of NREGA, but in Madhya Pradesh (unlike some other north Indian states) civil servants are consulted and given considerable autonomy, so the latter exercise moderate and sometimes significant influence. The episode discussed above, in which a senior civil servant persuaded ministers to channel not 50 but 90 per cent of NREGA funds through elected local councils, is an example of such influence. This occurred at the design stage, before the commencement of programme implementation, after which state-level civil servants had somewhat less influence.

At the district level, numerous elected politicians are active: the members and heads of elected district councils (*zilla panchayats*), district 'ministers-in-charge', state legislators, and MPs. Their influence is limited. Elected *Zilla Panchayat* members have had little leverage since those councils were substantially disempowered in 2001, under a Congress government. Ministers-in-charge are sometimes able to affect decision-making at the margins, but usually leave the day-to-day running of NREGA projects to district-level bureaucrats. State legislators and MPs occasionally involve themselves in NREGA implementation matters, usually in response to pleas from political clients further down the hierarchy. But in most districts, MLAs and MPs have other priorities. This leaves key bureaucrats (who are identified in the discussion below) with an unusually large degree of influence.

At the block level, elected councils exist, but (as in all Indian states) they have very little power. State legislators tend to intervene only in cases of egregious trespass on the interests of particularly important constituents, and even then, their main source of leverage—the ability to lobby for the transfer of bureaucrats—is of limited effectiveness. This leaves key bureaucrats (identified below) in a position to dominate most sub-districts. Their freedom of action is considerable, partly because they are not directly targeted by the transparency mechanisms built into NREGA.

At the local (*gram panchayat*) level, the elected heads of local councils (*sarpanches*) are usually extremely influential. Indeed, as we saw in Chapter 3, the introduction of NREGA has helped to centralise power in their hands—at the expense of other elected members of local councils, and of local residents. Local bureaucrats (*panchayat* secretaries and NREGA programme assistants) usually have less power than *sarpanches*—except in places where the latter lack confidence, skills, connections, or strong personalities. So at this level, elected politicians tend to predominate.

Let us now examine the impact of political dynamics at and between these various levels in Madhya Pradesh. Civil society organisations wield far less influence here than in Rajasthan, so this discussion of Madhya Pradesh—unlike that in the preceding chapter—gives more attention to other political actors. The analysis that follows proceeds from state to district levels, but political dynamics at (and between) lower levels of the political hierarchy (notably the local and block levels) have, as indicted in Chapter 3, a crucial impact on NREGA's functioning.

At the state level, the BJP government in Madhya Pradesh (in power from 2003 to the time of writing), like its BJP counterpart in Rajasthan (2003–2008 and 2013 to the present), implemented NREGA energetically, despite the omissions and disappointments described above. Like their counterparts in Rajasthan, senior BJP leaders in Madhya Pradesh feared that voters would give much of the credit for benefits obtained under NREGA to the Congress-led government in New Delhi that introduced it. But BJP leaders in Madhya Pradesh also calculated that a serious (and visible) effort to make the pro-gramme work could deliver significant political dividends. This was particu-larly true for an under-developed state such as Madhya Pradesh, where work opportunities for poor villagers were scarce for much of the year, and where there was a great need for the modest but targeted infrastructure projects that would be constructed under NREGA. Like the senior Congress politicians who had governed the state for a decade before they took power in 2003, BJP leaders in Madhya Pradesh believed (for the most part) that effective imple-mentation of NREGA was 'good politics'.

They were largely correct in their calculations. The BJP was re-elected with a reduced but reliable majority of 144 seats in an assembly of 230 at the state election in December 2008, and it did reasonably well at the national parlia-mentary election in May 2009, winning sixteen of twenty-nine seats. An opinion poll conducted in mid-2013 found that only 16 per cent of voters in Madhya Pradesh agreed with the accusations voiced by the state's Congress opposition, that the state government was unduly 'taking credit for funds given by the Centre for Centrally administered schemes', such as NREGA.[60]

The defeat of the BJP in Rajasthan at the 2008 state election occurred, not because voters gave Congress the credit for NREGA and other poverty-reduction programmes, but for other reasons. Most notable was the chief minister's inept leadership, which affected not only relations between various communities, but development programmes as well. In Madhya Pradesh, other factors were more important contributors to the party's successes at both of these elections. Since the government in Madhya Pradesh did not change in 2008, as it did in Rajasthan, the state government did not engage in the kind of post-election effort, which occurred in Rajasthan, to uncover cor-rupt actions that took place before 2008—some of which involved manipula-tions of NREGA.

There are three strands to the explanation of how NREGA and other anti-poverty initiatives affected voting behaviour in Madhya Pradesh in the 2008 assembly elections and 2009 parliamentary elections. First, it is apparent from reliable opinion polls conducted well before the 2009 national election that voters in some states gave most of the credit for NREGA to their state govern-ment, while in others they credited the central government in New Delhi. But despite these variations, the advantage which one or the other government gained as a result was not large enough to determine an election outcome.[61] That view gained further credence from polls conducted during the 2009 parliamentary election campaign, which showed that in every Indian state except Jharkhand (where the state government was in severe disarray), both state governments and the central government had positive approval ratings from voters. This is explained in part by the surge in revenues after 2003, which gave governments in New Delhi and in all states far more money to spend on popular development programmes such as NREGA. The ratings for our two states were as follows:

Table 5.2: Public Approval for Central and State Governments, 2009[62]

	Central Gov't	State Gov't
Rajasthan	66.9%	66.3%
Madhya Pradesh	74.6%	82.3%

Second, polling data at both of these elections indicated that governments that had undertaken effective development programmes tended to be popular. BJP leaders in Madhya Pradesh had good reason to suspect that this would be the case since they had unseated the ruling Congress Party at the 2003 state election by strongly emphasising development issues.[63] They were thus correct in calculating that the enthusiastic pursuit of NREGA would earn them popular support—not only because it gave poor people opportunities to earn urgently needed wages, but also because the public works that it generated would indicate the government's interest in development.

Third, some voters responded positively to NREGA and other programmes created to address poverty. This finding emerges from an assessment of national voting patterns. The all-India evidence collected during the 2009 national election indicated that no party had more than a minimal advantage among voters who had heard about NREGA and similar programmes. But the ruling Congress Party and its allies, which had pursued these programmes, gained a modest advantage among voters who had benefited from them.

This advantage may have been 'modest', but it was not trivial. Yogendra Yadav has indicated that in close contests for seats in parliament, small differences could decide outcomes—and a small but significant number of races were close.[64] It may appear curious to deploy data showing that the Congress Party gained from pursuing anti-poverty programmes in a discussion of why BJP leaders in Madhya Pradesh were politically shrewd in implementing such programmes. But since a strong association with such programmes pays electoral dividends, and since (as noted above) state governments share in those dividends, it made good political sense for this state government to do so.

Table 5.3: Voting Preferences of Programme Beneficiaries & Non-beneficiaries

	NREGA	Pension	Mid-day Meal	Health Insurance	Loan Waiver
Congress voters					
Benefited	33.2%	31.6%	27.9%	32.8%	30.0%
Not benefited	25.4%	27.4%	30.7%	28.2%	28.9%
BJP voters					
Benefited	16.2%	11.7%	19.3%	14.4%	17.2%
Not benefited	20.4%	19.2%	17.8%	20.8%	19.0%

* NB: The total shares of the vote in the 2009 national election were 29.67 per cent for Congress and 19.29 per cent for the BJP.[65]

There was one other way in which senior politicians in the state government gained an advantage from NREGA. In a very small number of districts, they siphoned off large amounts from the programme's plentiful funds and added them to the party coffers—turning these into 'worst case' districts (see below). Corruption among politicians works differently in the Madhya Pradesh BJP than in other parties, notably Congress. It is highly centralised, and most of the illicit income generated goes to the party rather than to individuals. (The same is true of the BJP in most other states, though there are exceptions—notably Karnataka).[66] A perceptive legislator who belonged to neither major party put it like this: 'In Congress, minor politicians look to senior leaders and say "They loot, we all loot". In the BJP, lowly politicians say "Only they loot—for the party".'[67]

Let us now consider the impact of political dynamics at the district level. Across most of Madhya Pradesh, BJP leaders did not seek to milk NREGA for party 'fund raising', and in a handful of districts, they worked hard to ensure that it operated extremely well. But in a very small number of districts—including one in which we did intensive research—they diverted a large proportion of programme funds, and the amounts of money passing to individual districts under NREGA were substantial enough to guarantee that significant resources could be obtained by this means. As a result of these varied approaches, we find that the state contains 'best case', 'ambiguous' and 'worst case' districts. The key point is that these three categories did not arise by accident. They are the product of conscious political decisions which require further explanation.

There are forty-eight districts in Madhya Pradesh. Of these, four or five qualify as worst case districts, in that NREGA implementation has been very poor and has been badly afflicted by widespread and systematic corruption. A somewhat larger number—perhaps seven—can be described as best case districts, insofar as the programme has worked quite well there and suffered no more than the generally accepted levels of petty corruption. The great majority of districts stand in the middle ground between these two extreme categories—they are ambiguous cases. Our enquiries in other Indian states indicate that similar patterns exist in many of them, although some are more encouraging than Madhya Pradesh, others less so. What happens within each type of district? How do political calculations, actions, and power dynamics, explain these variations?

Worst case districts require planning (at the state level), the assiduous management of malfeasance (mainly from the district level), and sustained pressure (from state and district levels) on actors at the sub-district or 'block' level to pass abundant illicit funds from NREGA projects (and other programmes) up through the administrative hierarchy. Block-level officials obtain the money by squeezing *sarpanches* and council secretaries at the local level. Actors who are involved at block, district, and state levels are permitted to retain some of these ill-gotten gains, but a substantial portion flows to senior politicians at the state level.

Districts are carefully selected to become 'worst cases' for a number of reasons. First, senior politicians from the state's ruling party may perceive a particular district to lack visibility, such that if they encourage flagrant malpractices there, they are likely to go largely unnoticed. Low visibility may derive from several characteristics: the district's geographical location (in a remote area, badly served by road and rail links); poor media coverage (due to a lack of interest); the weakness of civil society organisations (which may attempt to publicise misdeeds there); and low levels of political capacity among poor people (so that villagers tend to be quiescent, incapable of actions that might call outside attention to events there). Second, a state's ruling party may perceive a district as lying outside its core support base, so that if gross malfeasance alienates voters, it will do little to undermine the party's overall strength. This includes districts where the chance of attracting substantial new supporters is considered extremely remote. Third, legislators from the ruling party may be more interested in sharing in the profits siphoned from NREGA works than in building their popularity by ensuring that programme benefits reach the rural poor. These politicians may believe that money rather than their performance will win them re-election, and/or that the district is so under-developed that voters will support them even if little development occurs. (BJP legislators in Madhya Pradesh are under more pressure from their party bosses to be disciplined, so this feature is less evident there than in most other states.) Fourth, senior civil servants in the district may be unusually dishonest and/or susceptible to demands that they loot NREGA resources— indeed, the state government may have inserted them there for precisely this reason. Fifth, constructive civil society organisations have often done little or nothing in the district to promote awareness of NREGA's demand-driven character, or to enhance the political capacity of poorer people to discourage the brazen theft of programme funds.

As with worst cases districts, best case districts also result from conscious action—by politicians at the state level and by civil servants at the district level. There are, again, usually several strands to the explanation of how best case districts come into being. First, senior politicians at the state level may regard certain districts as highly visible so that they may become obvious to the media or showpieces for visitors. High visibility may derive from their location (because they are close to and easily accessible from major urban centres), from good media coverage, from the presence within them of civil society organisations (which are capable of publicising events that occur there), and from greater political capacity (so that villagers may themselves be capable of actions that attract the attention of outsiders). Second, the state-level ruling party may see certain districts as part of its core political base. To cultivate and maintain its popularity in such places, senior leaders frequently seek to ensure that NREGA is especially well managed there. Third, one or more of the district's state legislators from the ruling party may take a similar view and use their leverage to ensure that the programme is well funded and run. Fourth, senior civil servants in the district may be unusually honest and effective—either because the state government has carefully inserted them there, or due to the luck of the draw. Fifth, constructive civil society organisations may have made successful efforts to promote awareness of NREGA's demand-driven character and to enhance the political capacity of poorer people to engage with it.

In short, the number of 'worst case' districts in Madhya Pradesh was kept relatively low because state-level politicians believed that if NREGA was at least reasonably effective in a large majority of districts, it would ease poverty, produce welcome developmental outcomes, and enhance the ruling party's image and popularity. The funds allocated through NREGA are so substantial that carefully orchestrated theft from a few worst case districts nevertheless significantly boosted its efforts at illicit fundraising.

Bureaucrats at the district level play a key role in determining whether a district falls into the 'worst' or 'best' case categories, or somewhere in between. The holders of three posts are of particular importance. The first is the chief administrative official of the district (the Deputy Commissioner, or 'Collector', as s/he is routinely called in Madhya Pradesh). The second is the Chief Executive Officer (CEO) of the elected district council (*zilla panchayat*) who oversees the *panchayat* system at district, block, and local levels, and (theoretically) the development programmes implemented through *panchayats*. The third is the district Project Officer for NREGA. Those last two posts are held by the same person in some districts, including some that qualify as worst cases. The first two officials are career civil servants, while the third post is sometimes filled by a person hired on a fixed-term contract. The Project Officers manage (and in some cases 'completely control')[68] the work of other officials at district and block levels who have been specially hired, also on a contract basis, to administer NREGA projects.

Collectors are usually the predominant influence in determining how NREGA functions in any district. In 'worst case' districts, their actions are closely coordinated with those of the *zilla panchayat* CEO (with corrupt intent), and the NREGA project officer is induced to acquiesce (or else that post is also held by the *zilla panchayat* CEO). Close coordination is also evident in 'best case' districts, but in these districts officials seek jointly to minimise corruption. In 'ambiguous' districts, less coordination tends to occur, and the Collector and CEO may pursue somewhat different aims.

Given their importance, a crude typology of Collectors is worth noting, since it will indicate the range of possibilities that we encounter: honest and proactive; honest and passive; corrupt and passive; and corrupt and proactive. The terms 'proactive' and 'passive' refer only to their approaches to NREGA, to which most Collectors tend to be somewhat passive in their dealings.

A single district may of course experience different types of Collectors over time, as officials are transferred in and out. This occasionally triggers marked changes. For example, one district that we studied had been administered, within a short period, by an honest and proactive Collector, who was replaced by one who was corrupt and proactive. The honest and proactive official lasted only a few months before being transferred—mainly for that very reason. (Under the BJP government that transferred him, decisions on transfers, right down to the block level, were taken at the highest levels of the state government.) The corrupt and proactive Collector swiftly became firmly entrenched and was expected to remain in the post for a considerable time—largely because he had close ties with, and provided abundant illicit funds to, senior politicians in the state government. He turned the district into a 'worst case'. (To reiterate: this sort of arrangement is extremely unusual in Madhya Pradesh where the vast majority of districts are 'ambiguous' cases, and where 'best cases' outnumber 'worst cases'.)

This classification of course oversimplifies what is a complex reality, not least because it does not include other key actors at the district level—notably the *zilla panchayat* CEO and NREGA project officer (roles often performed by a single official). The most important way in which they (and Collectors) are 'proactive' is in their dealings with officials at the block level. District officials who are honest put pressure on block-level subordinates to restrain their demands upon local *panchayat sarpanches* and secretaries for bribes. Those who are corrupt apply pressure to maximise bribes, and then extract hefty percentages from the block level. So these district-level officials also powerfully influence the operation of NREGA within their districts.

In 'worst case' districts, substantial funds have been stolen from NREGA projects. The main initiators are block-level bureaucrats who are discussed below. In 'best case' districts, NREGA is not totally pristine, but the problem of corruption is quite modest. *Sarpanches* and *panchayat* secretaries at the local level face few demands from block-level officials for kickbacks from NREGA funds, and they sometimes find it possible to defy such demands without suffering serious delays or other problems as a result. Local *panchayats*, or more often their *sarpanches*, are free to decide which projects they wish to pursue under NREGA (sometimes in consultation with mass meetings of villagers), and their decisions are not countermanded by block-level officials. Their plans are readily incorporated into the block plan or list of projects which are often ignored in 'worst case' and 'ambiguous' districts. Delays may occur in payments to *panchayats* and to NREGA workers, in technical advice from the block level on complex projects, or in measurements by block-level officials of the work completed. But for the most part, these are the result not of attempts by block-level officials to extract 'speed money' from the local level, but of bottlenecks and inefficiencies in the system, or a shortage of personnel at the block level.[69]

* * *

Madhya Pradesh, like Rajasthan, was the site of better-than-average performance on many aspects of NREGA implementation during the programme's first five or six years in operation. The leadership of both state governments saw the political and developmental potential inherent in NREGA, and undertook relatively vigorous actions to ensure that the programme was relatively well managed. These were different in each state: Madhya Pradesh emphasised enrolment through active (some might say overactive) job card distribution and a radical devolution of funds to *panchayat* institutions; Rajasthan stressed innovations in programme management and (not always successful) efforts to stimulate the process of conducting social audits.

What is particularly striking is the extent to which two key structural differences between Madhya Pradesh and Rajasthan did not appear to make much difference in terms of NREGA's performance, whether measured in terms of the administrative data supplied by government entities or the results of our surveys among workers. The first difference between the states was the pattern of party rule: in Madhya Pradesh, the same party (the BJP) was in power throughout the period studied, whereas in Rajasthan, a change of government (from the BJP to Congress) took place at the end of 2008, two-and-a-half years into the programme's implementation. Even with Congress in power in Rajasthan and the BJP governing in Madhya Pradesh, a similar pattern was evident with respect to underlying political dynamics between the state and district levels, and between the local and block levels. The political leadership of each state adopted a strategy of permitting NREGA to be systematically looted in certain ('worst-case') districts, while ensuring that programme performance in others was sufficiently impressive for them to be showcased as 'best case' districts. Moreover, in both states and regardless of which party was in power, the same tug of war continued between local and block-level officials over how to share illicit rents from NREGA works. Neither the distinct ideologies of the ruling parties in the two states, nor the fact that Rajasthan (unlike Madhya Pradesh) was governed by the same party that ruled in New Delhi, altered the nature of the political calculations behind the key actors responsible for overseeing NREGA's implementation.

The second key difference between the states was the existence of a substantial state-wide movement in Rajasthan devoted to demanding transparency and accountability in the operation of NREGA, and the lack of such a movement in Madhya Pradesh. While this affected the degree to which (and the ways in which) civil society actors worked with state officials, and their ability to coordinate grassroots activism in response to programme failures, in a broad sense, the results across the two states have not been dissimilar. More important has been the role of more localised forms of civic engagement, which this study has examined across districts in Madhya Pradesh and across blocks within districts in Rajasthan. A powerful theme in both states has been the extent to which efforts by activists to raise people's awareness of their rights under NREGA, and to organise them to demand better implementation, was aided by prior and ongoing developmental activities undertaken by civic groups working in particular localities. This finding contradicts a claim, often asserted but rarely documented, that civil society formations which engage in 'constructive work'—accepting institutional funding to run health, education, or livelihood programmes—tend in the process to become less 'political', and to acquiesce more readily in the face of powerful actors who abuse their positions of influence.

It is not possible to generalise from the small number of local groups we have examined across these two states, but combined with the evidence we have collected from elsewhere in India, these findings at least call into question what has become a convenient narrative concerning the 'NGO-isation' of civic activism in India.[70] Engagement in what might be seen as conventional development activities need not compromise the assertiveness of civic actors. Indeed, as we will see in Chapter 7, on the national policy debates in which NREGA has figured, some of the most active participants in seeking to redefine development—towards a focus on the empowerment of poor and marginalised people—have been actors closely associated with relatively mainstream development institutions.

6

NREGA'S IMPACT ON THE MATERIAL
WELL-BEING AND POLITICAL CAPACITY
OF POOR PEOPLE

NREGA's promise of employment to all rural households was designed primarily to promote the economic well-being of poor people by delivering material benefits in the form of wages and community assets. NREGA's governance arrangements, on the other hand, were designed to enhance the political effectiveness of poor people by endowing them with specific rights and creating opportunities for them to hold government officials to account. In the process of implementing NREGA, these two objectives have become inextricably linked—most obviously in the link between political effectiveness and economic well-being. Indeed, it was widely anticipated by NREGA's architects that people endowed with new entitlements would engage in collective action to ensure that these entitlements were delivered.

This chapter, however, focuses on a different, somewhat unexpected, phenomenon: the process by which NREGA's material impacts have contributed to enhanced political capacity among poor people. This second-order effect has been relatively neglected in discussions of NREGA, but it has important implications for our understanding of the politics of anti-poverty initiatives.

What follows is not just a summary of evidence on material changes wrought by NREGA, which others have ably provided.[1] Instead, the analysis focuses on the implications of material changes for various political dynamics. As in earlier chapters, the terms 'politics' and 'political dynamics' refer to more than power relations within formal government institutions. They also refer to informal politics—to interactions between castes, factions, groups, and individuals within villages; to interactions between and even within households; and to informal interactions between actors in state institutions (bureaucrats and politicians) and people who stand outside those institutions. When tangible material changes occur, they affect power relations between various groups or individuals. And when there are changes to political perceptions, and to the dynamics within political processes, this may expand the opportunities for poor people to make further material gains. We distinguish between the non-material effects that arise from increased income through NREGA (such as reduced dependence on powerful local actors), and the non-income-related positive impacts generated by participating in NREGA, such as increased solidarity among poor but ethnically heterogeneous people.

Who Gains from NREGA?

As discussed in Chapter 3, a research team that conducted field work in Andhra Pradesh, Maharashtra, and Rajasthan has argued that non-poor villagers (those who fall above the officially designated poverty line) have secured much of the new employment created under NREGA, and that they may be crowding out genuinely poor people.[2] Our evidence, and that of a World Bank study,[3] indicates that considerable participation in NREGA projects by the non-poor has indeed taken place, but that the result of this trend has not necessarily been detrimental to the interests of the poor.

Let us begin with the indications that 'non-poor' people are working, or appear to be working, on NREGA projects. There is no doubt that the names of non-poor people are often listed, without their knowledge, as having worked on job sites. The wages due to these non-workers are pocketed by officials. (In other cases, the non-poor allow local leaders to credit them with work that they do not perform, with their undeserved wages being shared—the distribution of the shares varies—with programme implementers.) However, our interviews in Madhya Pradesh, Rajasthan, Karnataka, and Andhra Pradesh have revealed that at least some people with household incomes above the poverty line still feel poor enough to find manual labour at NREGA wages an attractive hedge against economic insecurity. That is, after all, their right under the Act—and it in no way contradicts the intention of NREGA, which is as much to prevent poverty as to alleviate it.

Sainath has examined this phenomenon of non-poor workers, and found that people from 'most' households of the traditionally dominant Reddy caste across much of one district in Andhra Pradesh were taking part in NREGA projects. They did so because poor economic returns on their rain-fed lands had made them feel poor enough to take this step. Sainath actually understates the enormity of the socially, politically, and economically pre-eminent Reddys deciding to engage in NREGA work when he says that it entailed 'a big shift in attitudes'. In fact, it represented a breathtaking reorientation of their self-perception. One Reddy elder revealed how acute the issue of status was when he said that he refused to take NREGA work because 'I own nine acres'. The very idea of labouring on a public works project was 'insulting'. Sainath later discovered that the man's son was among the labourers on an NREGA site.[4]

Some other 'non-poor' people have pursued NREGA work in response to economic shocks in their families such as injuries, illnesses, or deaths among wage-earners.[5] One study in Tamil Nadu found that when a downturn in the garment industry—stemming from adverse market conditions in the global economy—threw many villagers who had previously received good wages out of work, they turned to NREGA works as a partial alternative.[6] Other people, especially women in households with gross incomes just above the (very low) poverty line, performed NREGA labour to supplement household incomes.

These examples of the 'non poor' participating in NREGA works are a far cry from the stories of 'elite capture' often peddled by those who see NREGA as a 'leaky' programme that should be replaced by a strictly targeted approach to addressing the needs of the most destitute. In fact, the participation of people above the official poverty line helpfully reinforces the idea of NREGA as a 'social protection' programme—a safety net to be used by anyone in times of crisis or uncertainty. Self-targeting implies self-assessment by each household of its degree of economic vulnerability. That this will result in a proportion of 'non-poor' people undertaking work through NREGA is mainly a reflection of the inadequacy of income-based definitions of poverty and the lack of economic alternatives facing many households.

There may in fact be other advantages—from a systemic perspective, as opposed to one that takes household decision-making as the sole analytical focus—to having a broader pool of NREGA beneficiaries. When people outside the ranks of the chronically poor take part in welfare programmes, it can lend the schemes respectability. This can remove the stigma that might deter genuinely needy people from availing of benefits that might assist them, and to which they are doubtless entitled. In addition, the political base of support for NREGA, and programmes like it, is expanded when they benefit groups beyond those at the bottom of the income hierarchy. One reason why Social

Security—the primary old-age pension scheme in the United States—retains such a high degree of political legitimacy, is that its beneficiaries include not just the poor, but all Americans that have been in formal employment and their dependents. NREGA beneficiaries are not, moreover, recipients of unconditional transfer payments. They must, in theory and usually in practice, work for their wages—something that makes any attempt to trim the programme far more politically unpopular than is the case for other entitlement programmes that do not include a work requirement.

No reliable figures are available on the extent to which, over wide areas, participation by the non-poor in NREGA projects has crowded out genuinely poor people. In theory, NREGA's demand-driven model should not involve any crowding out at all. Work opportunities under NREGA should be a 'non-rivalrous' good. Even in the context of de facto rationing, however, the substantial over-representation of the SCs and STs among NREGA workers suggests that any crowding out problem that does exist is not acute. India's poorest and most vulnerable people have benefited from the programme disproportionately.

Table 6.1: Percentages of Total Person-days Worked (all-India)

	Scheduled Castes	Scheduled Tribes
Person-days, 2006–8	25–31% of total	24–36% of total
Person-days, 2008–12*	28.8%	21.3%
Proportion of total population	*16.2%*	*8.2%*

* Sources: Desai, Sonalde, Prem Vashishtha and Omkar Joshi, *Mahatma Gandhi National Rural Employment Guarantee Act A Catalyst for Rural Transformation* (New Delhi: National Council for Applied Economic Research, 2015); and NREGA website, nrega.nic.in, DMU Reports. The figures for 2012 cover only part of that year.

Further evidence that the poorest have benefited disproportionately emerges from a study in three states which found that most NREGA workers had not, until they began receiving NREGA wages, been able to purchase enough food to feed their families adequately.[7] Another study found that 81 per cent of NREGA workers in six states lived in non-permanent houses; 72 per cent had no electricity in their homes; and 61 per cent were illiterate[8] (as opposed to 24 per cent of the population as a whole). These and other findings strongly suggest that crowding out of the poor by the non-poor is not a severe problem—except perhaps in Maharashtra, the only state where participation rates among SCs and STs are below their respective proportions of the population.[9] The research team that raised concerns about the participation of the non-poor did explain that 'the more deprived were more likely [than other groups] to participate' in NREGA work, but that they were also 'likely to participate for shorter spells'.[10]

One further feature of the programme is important to note in this context. Twelve per cent of NREGA works have taken place on privately owned lands. These lands are owned overwhelmingly by poor people.[11] (Because they possess land at all, the owners are almost by definition not the poorest of the poor, but that distinction is not at issue here.) The improvements made on these privately owned lands have had a significant material impact on the households that reside there. One study from Madhya Pradesh found that households whose lands had been improved through NREGA works had increased their cultivated area by 15 per cent, and increased the period that their food stocks would feed their families from six to nine months.[12]

Sainath has vividly illustrated NREGA's impact on the poorest rural dwellers. He asked a villager in his 70s why he was participating in the 'body sapping work that a hungry malnourished people do, in sizzling temperatures'. The man's reply: 'Why work at 70? You may as well ask why eat at 70... We returned to work as the rise in food prices has destroyed poor people these last few years'. When Sainath asked another worker what would happen if NREGA wage was halved to Rs. 50 per day, the answer again took the form of a question: 'How will we survive? We need this wage'.[13]

Similar trends emerge in the remaining sections of this chapter, as we consider NREGA's impact on wage rates for unskilled labour, and NREGA workers' use of wages; on economically induced migration; on women's economic activity; and on the erosion of many poor people's bonds of dependence on elites. For the present, let us emphasise again that the material gains experienced by NREGA workers also enable poor people to make political gains. When they obtain economic benefits from NREGA, their capacity to operate in the public sphere is usually enhanced, and their bargaining power with potential employers, social elites, political actors, and bureaucratic decision makers, is strengthened.

Wage Rates and Workers' Use of Wages

In the years following the passage of NREGA, a lively debate developed among economists about its impact on rural labour markets and wage rates for unskilled rural workers. There was disagreement on, for example, whether NREGA's chief impact was to draw previously inactive people into the workforce or to create labour shortages during planting and harvesting seasons by attracting active workers to NREGA projects. Some analysts attributed labour shortages more to a rise in demand from land owners who turned to more labour-intensive methods than to reductions in the supply of available agricultural labourers.[14] A valuable distillation of recent research noted that 70 per cent of NREGA works occurred during the lean season when demand for agricultural labour was slack. Thus, 'the impact of MGNREGA was additive, expanding the labour market by attracting new labour to the workforce'.[15] Others disputed this finding. As discussed in Chapter 3, there were also disagreements over whether NREGA wages were too high or not high enough.

We do not seek to resolve these debates. But further evidence is worth noting here, since it indicates that in many rural areas, poor people have benefited from rising wage rates for unskilled labour, which are partly explained by NREGA. This finding emerged from our field research in both rural Madhya Pradesh and Rajasthan. A more wide-ranging investigation of 249 districts from across nineteen states found that NREGA had caused overall increases in agricultural wage rates, and, crucially, that the effect was greatest in areas where workers' wages had previously been lowest.[16] This suggests that the poorest have been the greatest beneficiaries.[17] The same message emerges from a study of 214 districts in nineteen states, showing that increases in agricultural wages since the introduction of NREGA affected unskilled but not skilled workers.[18] Consider also the complaint in 2010 by land owners in six districts of Karnataka, which stated that because NREGA offered comparatively attractive wage rates, there were 'no takers' for employment opportunities on private farms.[19] When one of us gave a public lecture on the politics of NREGA in Hyderabad that same year, representatives of landowning interests present in the audience echoed this feeling. On the other hand, the Governor of the Reserve Bank of India stated in 2014 that NREGA had contributed only about 10 per cent of the increase in rural wages, the rest having resulted from high government-paid rates for agricultural produce.[20]

How do poor people use increased wages from NREGA once they receive them? This question is important in assessing the material impact of NREGA. Earnings from the programme mattered greatly to the workers and their families whom we encountered during field research in Madhya Pradesh and Rajasthan. In the former state, when asked if wages were a 'big help', 86.7 per cent of poor respondents in one district and 95 per cent in the other said 'yes'. They, and others across India, put wages to a variety of uses. Expenditures on food were a major factor. A longitudinal study in Andhra Pradesh that straddled periods before and after the introduction of NREGA reported that wages 'had a significant and positive impact on consumption expenditure, [and] intake of energy and protein'.[21] Similar findings emerged from three other studies,[22] and from our field research in rural Madhya Pradesh and Rajasthan. We were repeatedly told that NREGA wages enabled poor families to increase the quantity and quality of food purchased.

Before NREGA was introduced, many poor families found it difficult to provide even one meal per day. Once NREGA was up and running, things changed significantly. Through the Public Distribution System (PDS), the Indian government provides subsidised food to BPL families. These subsidies are supplemented by many state governments, which further reduce the price at which specified quantities of locally important foodgrains are sold at so-called 'ration shops'. These mechanisms work imperfectly at the best of times, but our field studies indicate that in most places, most NREGA workers can take advantage of them to supplement purchases made through private market channels. In Madhya Pradesh, for example, a single day's wages from NREGA work can enable a poor family to provide two adequate meals per day (as opposed to just one previously) for roughly two weeks. This additional income helped these families to escape a well-known vicious circle, whereby low wages lead to poor nutrition, which causes low productivity and vulnerability to illness, and thus leads to a further reduction in earning power.

Increased spending on food is, of course, only part of the story of how NREGA wages impact the material well-being of poor (and nearly poor) households. One study found that while overall household consumption expenditure for NREGA workers went up by about 10 per cent in any given year, outlays on non-food items grew by 23 per cent. Another analysis yielded similar findings.[23] Some of those expenditures were on education, clothing, healthcare, and improvements to housing. As we explain later in this chapter, some NREGA wages have also been used by poor people to expand their own small enterprises;[24] to increase productivity on small plots of land; or to rent and then cultivate additional plots.[25] Another study conducted in 200 districts (with 300 NREGA beneficiaries surveyed per district) found that more than half of workers' households had used NREGA wages to purchase livestock, which were used to improve household nutrition, improve agricultural productivity, and to enhance income through husbandry practices.[26] Each of these uses generates additional earnings, so that they have multiplier effects.

A significant number of poor households also manage to save portions of their earnings from work on NREGA projects. In one locality, the average balance in bank accounts created to receive NREGA wages was Rs. 300.[27] Our interviews with workers in both Rajasthan and Madhya Pradesh indicated that this figure was not inordinately high. Such savings and earnings from the programme have given workers' households greater protection against shocks such as injuries and illnesses.[28] And the use of bank accounts opens up opportunities for poor people to access government pensions as well as health and life insurance schemes.[29]

NREGA's Impact on Migration

Another material benefit that the architects of NREGA hoped to generate was reduced levels of 'distress migration', which occurs when poor, unskilled labourers feel compelled to travel well beyond their home regions in order to find work and avoid destitution. Migrating—whether it takes the form of commuting to urban centres or long-distance travel—is expensive. One typical commuter in Karnataka found that it consumed half of his earnings.[30] Most long-distance migrants face squalid conditions and threats of exploitation in the places to which they relocate. People who own or rent small plots of land are unable to tend their own fields properly (or at all) when they have to migrate for work.[31] When a poor villager migrates, the family is either divided or it migrates as well. Either decision is disruptive, and if the family moves, any hopes that children have of basic education often evaporate.[32] It is no surprise, therefore, that a research team in Andhra Pradesh found that as migration declined, school attendance by children from poor households increased.[33] A decline in distress migration by entire families reduces levels of child labour, since children in migrating families are sometimes put to work alongside adults. (Indeed, and crucially, adults' NREGA wages have reduced child labour even in families that have never contemplated migrating.)[34]

Seasonal migration, often for extended periods, also undermines the already minimal political influence of the poor—which is one dimension of their poverty. If they reside elsewhere, their influence at local elections declines.[35] And between elections, they cannot add to the numerical strength of the village poor, which sometimes matters when local elites are forced to compete for support—an increasingly important trend in countries like India, where democratic institutions exist at the grassroots.[36] As one perceptive Congress Party leader shrewdly argued, migration also denies poor villagers opportunities to enhance their political capacity—their political awareness, confidence, skills, and connections—by participating, even from the margins, in local politics.[37] Given all of this, the reduction in distress migration which NREGA had produced, represents a far from trivial gain in efforts to reduce multiple dimensions of poverty.

There is considerable evidence to suggest that the programme has indeed had this effect in many areas of India.[38] However, it appears to have done much less to curb migration (or in some cases, commuting from villages) by poor male labourers. Men seek higher incomes in urban centres, while female or elderly members of their households take on NREGA work to supplement family income. This phenomenon might be termed 'opportunity migration'. Our interviews in Madhya Pradesh and Rajasthan, and with male workers in Karnataka who commuted daily by rail into Mysore City from fairly remote villages to do relatively well paid construction work amid the building boom there, confirmed what has also been found in extensive studies in a number of states by the International Water Management Institute.[39] That opportunity migration has not been impaired is in some ways encouraging because combining the comparatively high wages from such work with NREGA wages earned by relatives who stay behind, increases a household's chances of raising itself out of severe poverty. In short, NREGA offsets some of the costs of migration mentioned above, including lost opportunities for political advancement.

As for 'distress migration', numerous sources indicate that NREGA has had some (and often a significant) beneficial impact.[40] A 2006 study by the Institute of Applied Manpower Research found that migration from villages where significant NREGA works were undertaken continued in just 25 per cent of the localities surveyed. This suggests that NREGA was having a substantial positive impact, even at an early stage of its existence.[41] A 60 per cent reduction in migration was reported in a study of one Madhya Pradesh district in 2008.[42] Surveys conducted in Jharkand, Himachal Pradesh, Madhya Pradesh, and Chhattisgarh in 2008 also found migration to have declined significantly.[43] A 2010 analysis of a block in Chhattisgarh's Bastar District found an 85 per cent reduction in the number of migrants (from 4500 to 500).[44] In 2010, research on migration from rural Rajasthan to urban centres and to other states found similar results.[45] Our early 2009 survey in Barwani District of Madhya Pradesh found that distress migration by males from very poor households had all but ceased after NREGA came into force, and a knowledgeable observer of the poorer western districts of that state said that such migration there was 'well down'.[46]

A 2010 report by a firm that provides research for Indian and foreign corporations and investors found poor workers returning to their villages, or not migrating in the first place.[47] When NREGA was temporarily suspended in northeastern Karnataka in 2010, there was a surge in migration to Bangalore (and presumably to Hyderabad) for work.[48] One study in Andhra Pradesh found that distress migration levels in sample villages had declined 'from about 27 per cent to 7 per cent',[49] and a further analysis in two districts of that state noted clear reductions.[50] A sharp decline in the migration of agricultural workers from Uttar Pradesh and Bihar[51] to Punjab occurred despite offers of more attractive wages, accommodation, and conditions in 2009, and the pattern was similar in mid-2010—a result widely attributed to the availability of alternative work under NREGA.[52] A similar dynamic was seen in Himachal Pradesh, where fruit producers had to attract enough migrant labourers by significantly increasing daily wages to a level far above what they had paid before the introduction of NREGA, and by providing waterproof tents and high-quality meals.

Not all of the evidence is positive. As early as 2007, the head of PRIA's network of civil society organisations argued that delayed payment of NREGA wages—a widespread problem discussed elsewhere in this book—was driving many poor workers to resume distress migration.[53] That view was later corroborated by a number of reliable analysts.[54] Sainath found that migration by entire families continued from Bolangir and Kalahandi districts of Orissa—among the least developed in India—to the brick kilns of Andhra Pradesh, where working conditions remain appalling. He pointed out that the 100 days of work per household per year under NREGA struggles to compete with the 180–200 days per year available in the kilns for each family member (including children).[55] It must be stressed, however, that references to those Orissa districts do not provide a fair test of NREGA because the state government had largely failed to implement the programme there, due in part to administrative incapacity, even though Orissa's need is greater than almost anywhere else in the country.[56]

There are, as always, variations from region to region, among groups, and over time, but the overall trend is both strong and encouraging.[57]

Material (and Political) Impacts of NREGA on Women

One aim of NREGA was to encourage women from poor households to undertake work. Indeed, the Act mandates that women perform at least 30 per cent of the labour under the programme. That target has been greatly surpassed, as the table below indicates.

Table 6.2: Percentages of NREGA Person-days Worked by Women (all-India)

2006–7	40%
2007–8	43%
2008–9	48%
2009–10	48%
2010–11	48%
2011–12*	47%[58]

Provisional figures.

Women's share of work on NREGA projects exceeded their share of all other types of casual labour,[59] and their share of all forms of work for which records were kept.[60] Between 2006 and 2012, 53 trillion rupees were spent on wages for women under the programme.[61] This was true even though the 'rationing' of work opportunities has tended to favour men.[62] Other research findings 'suggest (that NREGA triggered) an upward movement of (all types of) unskilled wages for women.'[63]

That NREGA could be an effective means of empowering women was understood by those who had designed the programme. Assessments of NREGA's precursor programmes, particularly Maharashtra's EGS, had demonstrated the profound impact it had on women's sense of autonomy and its contribution to the idea—and to some degree reality—of gender equality. For instance, Devaki Jain's interviews with women EGS workers in Maharashtra in the 1980s revealed that 'having once tasted the value of bringing home a money wage from their own labour, they had developed a sense of confidence and also release from the authority of the family and had started to gain the confidence to take up other types of work in the area'.[64] Research on the EGS conducted two decades later by Aruna Bagchee found that gender pay equality under the scheme helped to explain 'why the EGS was so popular among women labourers'.[65]

There are several worthwhile reasons to focus NREGA work opportunities on poor rural women. Male household members often find it possible to obtain casual labour outside NREGA, so targeting women is often the best way to enable poor families to supplement their income. As noted above, men from such households often migrate to other regions or to urban areas, sometimes for long periods, to find work. When other family members do not accompany them, opportunities for women back home to work on NREGA projects can provide a family with crucial sustenance until male household members return with wages earned elsewhere. Before NREGA, those opportunities were severely limited. Jean Dreze cites a 2008 survey which found that only 30 per cent of female workers in the programme had earned any wages before enrolling under NREGA.[66] When entire families migrate, opportunities for women under NREGA in the places to which they travel can supplement incomes for extremely poor households. But wherever women find work under NREGA, it is seen to be—and actually is—a welcome alternative to degrading or ill-paid work, or often no work at all.

Both of those terms—'degrading' and 'ill-paid'—are worth noting. Even close to home, where power dynamics between employers and women employees were often grossly unequal, women engaged in non-NREGA work run a very real risk of abuse or sexual exploitation at the hands of unscrupulous employers.[67] Even when this does not occur, they face suspicion from male members of their households, and local residents more generally, which can create tension and even strife. A major attraction of NREGA for women (and their male relatives) is the widespread belief among both that 'government' work was respectable and safe.[68] 'Government' was thus penetrating into local arenas in ways that offered decency and, despite the hard manual labour that was often required, a certain respectability.

NREGA also offered poor households a hedge against destitution, as the work was—at least in theory—not 'ill-paid'. The National Sample Survey found that NREGA had reduced pay differentials between men and women, compared to other public works programmes.[69] Other analyses 'suggest [that NREGA triggered] an upward movement of [all types of] unskilled wages for women'.[70] And in many cases, the alternative to NREGA work was no work at all. A study in ten districts of six states found that 70 per cent of poor women respondents had received no cash income over the previous three months from a non-NREGA source. Half of them said that without NREGA they would have been long-term unemployed.[71]

The impact of women's earnings on incomes in the poorest households, a notoriously difficult group to reach, has been substantial—a fundamentally important point. A survey of 600 women workers across Chhattisgarh found that households with incomes below Rs. 8,000—'the poorest of the poor'—declined from 94 per cent of respondents to 57 per cent.[72] NREGA wages were especially crucial for female-headed households, in which women's earnings represented the main or only income. A survey in six states found that '67 per cent of the women [household heads] stated that MGNREGA had helped them avoid hunger and 46 per cent said that it had helped them avoid illness'.[73]

Children also benefit from the economic gains that women workers derive from participating in NREGA projects. In both their home areas and elsewhere, women who earned NREGA wages often obviated the need to send children out to work, increasing the chance of school attendance. Women employed under the programme in or near their home villages become less inclined to accompany men from the household who migrate, so that they need not have their own social networks disrupted, nor uproot their children from schools. And a decline in male migration, which NREGA has produced, means that fewer families face the severe disruption that migration inevitably entails. A study conducted by the Institute of Development Studies (Jaipur) found that 68 per cent of female NREGA workers across multiple districts spent at least some of their earnings on the education and welfare of their children—especially girls, who otherwise often get left out.[74]

Many women who work on NREGA projects gain greater autonomy and self-esteem, and are empowered as actors both within households and in the wider public sphere. One multi-state study found that women workers tend to collect their wages themselves: in Andhra Pradesh, the wages of only four per cent were paid to their male partners; and in Rajasthan, over 90 per cent of women received wages themselves. Similar findings emerged from other states, including two (Chhattisgarh and Bihar) where this outcome was unexpected.[75] Another multi-state study found that within households, women wage earners strongly influenced how wages were spent—81 per cent in a district of Tamil Nadu, and 96 per cent in a district of Chhattisgarh.[76] A study by a team from the Administrative Staff College of India (ASCI) found that NREGA wages gave women greater leverage in their efforts to persuade their husbands to abandon factional violence in the Rayalaseema region of Andhra Pradesh.[77] One research team even found that in Himachal Pradesh, households in which women had taken NREGA work experienced a decline in domestic conflict.[78]

NREGA work—which takes poor women outside the household and into the public sphere, in many cases for the first time—emboldens them over time to assert themselves in at least modest ways. In Tamil Nadu, Indira Armugam found that women workers increasingly demanded breakfast and lunch at project sites, as well as other rights provided for under NREGA.[79] Journeys to branches of banks or post offices to collect wages[80] also drew poor women out of their dwellings and into the public sphere, and enhanced their confidence and political capacity as actors in that wider arena.[81] That change has one extremely important consequence, which only becomes apparent from studies of democratic decentralisation. Women usually serve as the gatekeepers between the household and providers of health services. When they become better able to operate in the public sphere, the uptake on vital health services (ante- and post-natal care, inoculations, child health screenings, etc.) increases significantly, so that illnesses are prevented and lives are saved.[82] NREGA has facilitated this kind of change.

Eroding Bonds of Dependence

There is an additional effect of NREGA implementation that has largely been overlooked by analysts of the programme's performance. This is the impact that participation in NREGA works has on the bonds of dependence that poor, often low-status people have on members of more prosperous, higher-status groups. The nature of this dependence takes many forms, some of them economic—for instance, the sources of financial credit to which poor people have access, or their ability to engage in private labour markets, interact with officials who distribute government subsidies, or rent cultivable land. But by their very nature, status distinctions also involve significant psychological and cultural dimensions. Thus, the process by which subordinated groups break free of dependence entails both reducing their material reliance on better-off groups and overturning the cultural norms that validate their continued subordination.

No single government programme, no matter how well designed and administered, can adequately address these interlinked sources of dependence. However, NREGA has done far more to advance this agenda than has generally been recognised. This is a strange and serious omission. Bonds of dependence have long forced impoverished people to submit to prosperous, landowning elites and castes. This has denied poor villagers opportunities, liberties, dignity, and the chance to develop their political capacities. Dependence has locked them into 'poverty'. Even before NREGA, this had begun to change, but the material impact of the programme, and some of its cultural effects, have accelerated the process in many parts of rural India.

When poor NREGA workers use wages to enhance the productivity of their own (very often small) landholdings, the effect on bonds of dependence can be even more pronounced. Mihir Shah has stressed the point, which is seldom recognised, that a 'very high proportion of agricultural labour households' own at least some land: 50 per cent of such households in Rajasthan and Madhya Pradesh; 60 per cent in Orissa and Uttar Pradesh and 70 per cent in Chhattisgarh and Jharkand. Shah has seen 'hundreds of examples' of NREGA wages helping to increase productivity on those plots, an outcome that renders poor workers less dependent on prosperous members of local society.[83] In a related development, Indira Armugam found that poor villagers from disadvantaged groups in Tamil Nadu often used NREGA wages to rent land—the only option available, since higher castes often will not sell land to Dalits—and to make small investments to make them more productive.[84]

NREGA wages have also enabled poor people to escape two kinds of exploitation. In the first, landowners lock poor workers into agreements to work for an entire season at very low fixed rates of payment. The alternative employment offered under NREGA has made such invidious contracts more difficult to arrange because it gives very poor labourers greater bargaining power.[85] Much more dramatically, NREGA has helped free some people from the very poorest stratum from bonded labour. This practice has been repeatedly banned by Indian governments—since, and indeed before, independence—but it persists in some places. It arises when a poor person obtains a loan in exchange for a promise that he or she, or a family member, will work for the lender without pay until the sum is paid off. In most cases, due to compound interest, rigged accounting, or exploitative pricing for 'living expenses' supplied by the debt-holder, the arrears can never be fully paid, leaving the bonded labourer, or his or her descendants, trapped in perpetuity. The ASCI study cited above found that NREGA wages earned by relatives of bonded labourers were used in Andhra Pradesh to pay off such debts.[86]

Anthropological research in many parts of rural India has for decades generated compelling evidence that changes in material conditions can trigger change in social systems, and thus in local power structures. The declining influence of caste hierarchies over villagers' thinking and actions has been the result of a complex array of changes, but it is widely accepted that occupational diversification—and the spread of education which facilitated that diversification—played major roles. They contributed to the substantial disintegration of the old *jajmani* system that had largely confined members of various castes to their traditional occupations—the least remunerative and respectable of which rendered poorer groups dependent on local elites. As the material underpinnings of that system started to crumble, the old hierarchies began to wane.[87] In many localities, NREGA has contributed to the further erosion of such bonds of dependence, with similar results. As we have seen, intra-household forms of dependence are also under challenge: women workers, who have performed nearly half of the labour under NREGA, acquire greater financial autonomy and enhance their capacity to operate in the public sphere.

Even before NREGA was introduced, many people who belonged to groups that occupied the lower rungs on the traditional caste ladder had largely ceased to accept the legitimacy of those hierarchies.[88] But since many such people remained materially dependent upon local elites, they were generally prevented from giving much overt expression to these views. Adivasis (Scheduled Tribes)—another severely disadvantaged group that stands largely outside established caste hierarchies—have also become more impatient with their low status and with the exploitation that they have suffered. Despite occasionally successful efforts to mobilise Adivasis behind assertive campaigns for political recognition, in general their dependence on traditionally high-status groups has limited their capacity to live in dignity and to voice demands. NREGA has eroded these bonds of dependence by altering economic relationships between elites and the poor, and by providing members of impoverished groups with a degree of economic security. NREGA has also contributed to changes in social interactions and power dynamics at the grassroots. This contribution has been relatively modest in some places, but far more significant in places where social movements have been able to facilitate collective action.

An especially vivid indication of the process by which bonds of dependence can be eroded, emerges from an assessment of the impact of NREGA in the three main regions of the pre-2014 undivided Andhra Pradesh. This study was undertaken by the same ASCI research team mentioned earlier. Among the areas studied was the Rayalaseema region of the state, which has been notorious over many decades for widespread, persistently violent conflict between political factions that have organised private armies to advance their claims to local supremacy. These factions are headed by members of the prosperous landowning Reddy caste, but the armed combatants who mainly commit the violent acts have come primarily from lower-caste Hindu and, to some extent, Muslim groups that have been dependent on Reddys for their economic well-being and for whatever degree of social standing they have been able to attain.

In the process of conducting the research, the ASCI team encountered a group of severely disadvantaged Muslims who, at the bidding of Reddy leaders, had long worked as foot soldiers in violent faction fights. Some clashes had been lethal—three people had been killed in 2001. The degree of physical intimidation is harder to measure, but the area is known for the chronic insecurity suffered by its residents. The pattern of repeated bursts of violence and threats, punctuated by frequent retaliation, caused long-term damage to lower-caste and Muslim members of that faction's armed group: twelve foot soldiers were jailed after the 2001 episode, and legal costs forced many of their families to sell off some of their already meagre landholdings. Recurring violence prevailed in the region even though many members of the rival factions that they had attacked were from the same impoverished, relatively low-status caste.[89]

In the course of conducting interviews with members of these private armies, however, the ASCI researchers discovered (to their surprise) that a fair number of the foot soldiers had recently begun refusing to take part in factional battles. They were defying the orders of the socially and economically dominant Reddy faction leaders. To explain this remarkable turnabout, the interviewees cited three recent changes—all of which, it turned out, were linked to their engagement with NREGA. First, on NREGA work sites, they found themselves toiling alongside their fellow caste members—people who had long been on the opposite side of these violent encounters. In the process, foot soldiers from across the factional divide learned that they had a great deal in common with their erstwhile adversaries—far too much, in fact, to justify continuing efforts to maim and murder one another. Second, and more importantly, the foot soldiers found that the wages they earned from NREGA work enabled them to purchase better quality 'inputs'—seeds, fertilisers, pesticides, livestock, and agricultural implements—to use in cultivating their small plots of land. The productivity of their lands increased—in one case by 40 per cent.[90] A study of 200 districts across India in 2006–7, with 300 NREGA beneficiaries per district, found that more than half of the poor households surveyed had used NREGA wages to purchase livestock.[91] These advances—particularly the ability to diversify their livelihoods—provided them with a substantially enhanced degree of financial autonomy from the prosperous Reddy landowners who had long paid—and virtually compelled—them to attack the very caste fellows with whom they now found themselves working. Finally, NREGA wages that poor women earned bolstered their influence within these households, lending weight to their pleas to husbands to abandon factional violence.

Taken together, these developments persuaded and enabled many of these low-status foot soldiers to refuse to work as the hired muscle for Reddy-dominated factions. As a result, their villages gradually became far more peaceful than they had been for decades. Village festivals, which had been suspended since the late 1990s because of factional strife, were revived amid this new tranquility.[92] A senior police officer who had been involved in tackling the violence in Rayalaseema confirmed that changes such as this—complemented by more assiduous policing—had driven reductions in the scope, frequency, duration, and intensity of factional violence, in some cases quelling such clashes altogether.[93]

While cases such as this demonstrate the potential for work on NREGA sites to break down factional divisions within a disadvantaged and formerly dependent caste, there is also evidence that barriers between different castes are eroded when they labour alongside one another on NREGA work sites. In a number of places, the barriers breached are between traditionally upper castes and low-status groups.[94] When people from elite and disadvantaged communities work together on NREGA sites, it can contribute to a decline in the power of caste hierarchies. This process can unfold in a number of different ways. For instance, the culturally sanctioned—and, in the minds of the more traditional, divinely ordained—association of certain communities with certain types of work is disrupted when NREGA employment involves members of higher-status groups in activities they would otherwise abjure and supervisory roles for low-status groups that have traditionally been denied them. This weakens the authority and mystique of status hierarchies. Alternatively, the employment of members of high- and low-caste groups on the same NREGA site can generate accommodations across caste lines—processes which have acquired considerable momentum across much of India.[95]

Further evidence that NREGA is contributing significantly to the erosion of dependence of poor, lower-status people on formerly dominant landowning groups has emerged from other parts of India as well. Villagers in Chamarajanagar District of Karnataka made this point about NREGA wages that they or their wives could earn.[96] Researchers who have worked in western Tamil Nadu have also noted this trend,[97] and Indrajit Roy found something similar in his research in Bihar. One landless labourer told him that even though they could earn more money by migrating to Punjab for work, they preferred to stay at home because NREGA had made it possible for them to 'desist from working the *jamindar's* [landlord's] land even if we stay in the village'—a choice that both reflected and hastened the erosion of status-based dependence. Another low-caste worker stated that:

> Before this program, we were...subservient to the *jamindar*, and to the 'high' caste. With the NREGS, we can live in the village without having to adhere to the village rules, of working the *jamindar's* land. By seeing us in the village, with-

out us begging him for work, he understands that we are human beings too, capable of a dignified life.

Emboldened by this display of assertiveness, another labourer added, 'His [the landlord's] economy be damned'.[98]

NREGA has had a similar impact elsewhere. Sainath found that in parts of Andhra Pradesh, '[b]ecause the labourers have the option of Rs. 100 a day (NREGA) work here', a change could be discerned not only in relative economic leverage, but in the tenor of social relations as well: 'Now when landowners call Dalits (Scheduled Castes) and Adivasis (Scheduled Tribes) to work, they are relatively more respectful'.[99] In a similar vein, Indira Armugam's field research in Tamil Nadu revealed that NREGA wages had broken confining, monopolistic ties between landowners and very poor labourers, who were able to choose whom to work for—a substantial, liberating change. Partly in response to this shift in power dynamics, local politicians from elite backgrounds became more solicitous of the poor. This had more overtly political implications as well. Once poor people began to use the institutional mechanisms for securing their rights that NREGA made available to them, and once they began to realise some modest material gains from NREGA work, local politicians from elite backgrounds who wanted their votes had to 'come down and engage' with the poor. They also had to deliver tangible benefits; mere promises no longer sufficed.[100]

In other words, in places such as this—and there are many—NREGA is facilitating the emergence of new relations of both status and power. It is a largely unremarked-upon implication of the trend (noted earlier in this chapter) of participation by non-poor families in NREGA projects. Those members of the pre-eminent Reddy caste in Andhra Pradesh who felt the need to take NREGA work were not only demonstrating the economic vulnerability of households that fall outside the official (income-based) definition of poverty; their actions were also removing some of the stigma of manual labour that has characterised relations between upper and lower castes. In the process, they were—perhaps unwittingly—challenging received notions of ascribed status. That these impecunious Reddys were in some cases employed on NREGA works devoted to making improvements on Dalit-owned lands, merely intensified these counter-cultural effects.

The widespread problem of delayed payments for NREGA work outlined above and elsewhere in this book has prevented some poor people from extracting themselves from these and other types of exploitation.[101] Others have found themselves thrust into the hands of moneylenders[102] and exploitative contractors, who are legally banned from NREGA works, but when used anyway generally pay promptly.[103] But many poor people have also made remarkable gains on this front.

* * *

This discussion of the diversity of material benefits generated by NREGA supports the conclusion that, while unevenly distributed and available only under certain propitious circumstances, these gains can be substantial. Moreover, they can have important, though often overlooked, effects on the autonomy of the mainly poor people who participate in the programme. Such people are able to resist some of the more invidious 'contractual' relationships in which they have often found themselves—relationships that have very real political implications. By providing a viable fall-back option, and a means of livelihood-diversification, NREGA has increased the leverage of people whose choices were (and still are) highly constrained.

Somewhat paradoxically, even the participation of the non-poor in NREGA works can have positive effects: it broadens the constituency that favours continuing and indeed expanding the programme; enhances the respectability of NREGA work; undercuts traditional claims of social superiority among higher-status groups; and creates shared interests among poor and near-poor residents in local politics. Similar effects on autonomy and leverage are found within households when NREGA work is undertaken (and wages earned) by women, who also find themselves far more likely to participate in the public sphere, including in political activity.

Indeed, it is no stretch to say that the material improvements wrought by participation in NREGA works contribute substantially to enhancing the political capacity of poor people. It is important to note that this process is distinct from the gains derived from participation in the social audit processes through which the programme's architects primarily expected citizen empowerment to take place. In addition to the improved bargaining position that labourers obtain through the option of NREGA work, they enhance their political *awareness* in a number of ways, not least through observing at close hand the rivalries that exist among elite groups—rivalries that often compel elites to compete for the support of less well-off people in local electoral contests. Moreover, because of the reduced need to migrate in search of work— whether for long or relatively short periods—poorer people who participate in NREGA are in a position to develop the *skills* that come with continued exposure to, and practice of, politics at the local level: when to make demands;

which officials to approach for assistance; how to play elites off against one another; and so forth. Heightened political *confidence*, similarly, emerges through a variety of channels, including the process of demanding delayed or unpaid wages, engaging with officials responsible for implementing NREGA works, and winning even small battles over working conditions (which their increased awareness has shown poor people they are entitled to). Finally, and perhaps most importantly, the material benefits of NREGA have allowed many poor people to forge *connections* that enhance their political capacity. Moving from the depths of destitution to the comparatively more secure ranks of the merely poor—a feat that NREGA has helped many households to accomplish—can buy people the time needed to attend meetings among fellow workers and to cultivate relationships with potentially powerful patrons. Above all, by reducing (if not completely obliterating) the economic dependence of poor people on powerful groups, the possibility of forging alliances on the basis of relative choice, rather than direct compulsion, begins to emerge. Thus, their political awareness, skills, confidence, and connections are improved. In short, their political capacity has been enhanced.

None of these processes takes place quickly, or without continued struggle among all members of any oppressed group. And it certainly does not occur everywhere. In some localities, districts, regions, or even entire states, very few of these second-order effects are in evidence. But their mere existence—in some places, at some times, for some individuals and groups—holds out the promise that these transformative possibilities could be extended to others. Enhancing the autonomy and political capacity of poor people is something that state action can accelerate. NREGA is but one example of how this might work.

7

NREGA, NATIONAL POLITICS,
AND POLICY EVOLUTION

We have argued throughout this book that politics has infused both the enactment and the subsequent implementation of NREGA. This is in large part because of the orientations of NREGA's architects, who saw both the legislation and the state-level employment programmes to which it gave rise as fundamentally political in nature. NREGA's design was forged through political engagement that began decades earlier, and was executed through a complex web of institutions, into which politics of almost every conceivable type would find expression. Most of all, NREGA was envisioned as part of a strategy of political mobilisation—a means of continuously encouraging what some activists have called a process of 'democratic struggle'.[1]

Among the objectives of NREGA's architects was the intention to develop the political capacities of poor and marginalised people. This was expected to take place over time, through an extended process of interaction with the state agencies responsible for delivering on the Act's promise of guaranteed work, at the minimum wage, within a stipulated timeframe, and under certain regulated conditions. Prolonged engagement would, it was hoped, foster awareness among often voiceless people about the workings of government. Doing so, in turn, might induce workers to recognise that not only were they bearers of certain social and economic rights, which it was the state's duty to fulfil, but that they were also the bearers of certain political responsibilities, particularly the obligation—if NREGA's vision of citizen-led accountability was to be realised—to engage with a set of purpose-built governance mechanisms. These mechanisms were designed to leverage the possibilities of continuous citizen participation in local decision-making. This is, to put it mildly, a demanding form of citizenship, and one that reflects a powerful strain of political activism in post-independence India. NREGA's institutional arrangements and procedural requirements were explicitly designed to provide workers the opportunity to pursue democratic claim-making—notably by insisting that officials be held accountable (whether in terms of answerability or sanctionability) to people at the local level.

As we saw in Chapter 2, the coalition of activists, bureaucrats, and party leaders that helped to bring NREGA into being understood that the striking disparity between the state's enormous ambitions and its ability to deliver would, over time, breed disillusionment. NREGA's designers knew, from long experience of engaging with workers on employment programmes (and the officials who administer them), that a wide array of abuses would inevitably occur during implementation, and that these would be all-too-readily apparent to members of the public. This was partly because of the Act's transparency provisions, but also because of the impressive level of resources and authority devolved to local elected councils under the Act. As the preceding chapters have shown, NREGA bestowed upon local officials more decision-making power than they had enjoyed previously. For instance, this included the power to determine which works projects would take place, how much work would be made available, when, and to whom wages would be paid (and, de facto, how much). The model of change on which the NREGA experiment rested posits that even where localised corruption takes place in response to decentralisation, this quickly becomes apparent to workers who, by definition, live in close proximity to the officials skimming from their wages. Local corruption networks become particularly apparent to NREGA workers when elected *panchayat* heads become engaged, as they so frequently are, in more or less perpetual conflict with block-level bureaucrats over their respective shares of illicit programme spoils—a process detailed in Chapter 3.

While NREGA (including its procedures) was designed to cultivate discontent among workers at the grassroots, in the hope of sowing seeds of collective action that might translate grievances into concrete demands for both case-specific accountability and reform to governance functions beyond NREGA, in practice it was not only rural job-seekers who became disgruntled. During its first five years in operation, NREGA spurred discontent among many actors engaged in national-level policy debates. These included politicians from across the political spectrum, leaders of social movements, development practitioners, policy analysts, civil servants, representatives of sectoral interest groups, media commentators, and indeed NREGA's architects themselves. Often the debates concerned how to reform (or whether to abolish) NREGA, but just as frequently, NREGA was invoked to make a larger point—or advance a broader agenda—regarding matters such as poverty and its definition, corruption and how best to combat it, the nature and role of the state in the economy (in India and in general), labour market dynamics, and the fiscal health of the central and state governments. In this chapter, we discuss some of the ways in which NREGA (both in concept and operation) figured in these discussions, as well as examples of how arguments deployed in these debates influenced reforms to NREGA. As with the local- and state-level processes discussed in Chapters 3, 4, and 5, politics of various types—partisan, ideological, and personal—is never far from the surface.

This chapter's central contention is that NREGA's size, scope, and continuous process of institutional reform have—both directly and indirectly—influenced a wide range of crucial national policy debates in India, from public finance to internal security to rural development, and that NREGA's operation (including its political viability) has, in turn, been affected by the tenor and substance of many of these debates. This set of mutual effects runs parallel to, and interacts with, those identified in other parts of this volume: changes to local political dynamics (Chapter 3); to the political calculus of state-level leaders (Chapters 4 and 5); and to social status and relations (Chapter 6). These are all channels through which NREGA exerts important, though often invisible, political effects.

As with the debates over amendments to the NREG Bill (discussed in Chapter 2), those that emerged during the Act's implementation have centred on corruption, including the best means of combatting it, and the potential costs associated with the programme. But several issues beyond corruption and cost have also been on the political radar. These include the programme's distributional implications and the impact on broader macroeconomic variables. All of these will be touched upon—some in more depth than others—in this chapter. But the discussion will concentrate on three key issues: (1) corruption and governance; (2) wages and works; and (3) India's development paradigm. Some related issues, such as what India's counterinsurgency strategy should be, enter the analysis only briefly to illustrate a particular point, but the variety of such cameos, taken together, hints at the range of political debates into which NREGA has seeped. Where relevant, changes to the regulations governing NREGA's implementation are discussed to underline the iterative (and gradual) nature of policy revision. NREGA, like most laws (including others passed during the UPA's term in office, such as the SEZ Act, 2005) led to a high degree of regulatory revision.[2]

After discussing each of these three issues in turn, including policy revisions in their respective domains, the chapter concludes with an examination of the major rethink on NREGA that took place following the Congress-led UPA government's re-election in 2009. UPA-2, as the second term came to be known, witnessed less steadfast commitment to NREGA than it had enjoyed during UPA-1. Despite promising to create a revamped NREGA 2.0, built around the lofty but hard-to-operationalise idea of 'convergence'—where NREGA works are integrated with other rural development objectives and programmes—the UPA-2 government engaged with NREGA erratically, both in terms of substance and rhetoric.

Corruption and Governance

Discussions about corruption in India, and the modes of governance that either enable or impede it, have been closely intertwined with debates over NREGA. This connection dates back to NREGA's inception. As we saw in Chapter 2, critics of the original proposals for employment-guarantee legislation frequently cited the potential for 'leakages'. Ironically, the programme's architects—activists who had sought to use transparency to expose abuses in existing programmes—understood better than perhaps any other participants in the debate exactly how precursor employment-generation schemes had been looted. They were not at all surprised when NREGA-related corruption, defined broadly as the abuse of public power for private gain, became an almost constant topic of political debate after NREGA began operating in early 2006. The complaints were a direct extension of objections raised during the parliamentary process. Indeed, the lens of corruption dominated political discussion of NREGA, in the process distorting public perceptions of the programme. As Dreze put it, 'if one were to go by many of the media reports, one would get the impression that programmes like ... NREGA ... are little more than hotbeds of corruption and waste'.[3] The more complicated picture—which of course includes plenty of corruption and waste, but also much else besides—tends to fall by the wayside in heated television-studio debates.

Controversies over corruption usually erupted into political debate with greatest vigour whenever official reports on programme performance were issued. By far the most likely triggers for such disputes were the periodic reports of the Comptroller and Auditor General (CAG) of India. The 2008 CAG report on NREGA, based on a survey of the programme in 513 *gram panchayats*, identified numerous problems. These included the failure of most *panchayats* to hold social audits regularly; the persistent shortage of dedicated NREGA 'programme officers' and other key staff (such as *gram rozgar sevaks*, or village-level employment secretaries); the widespread underpayment of wages (and non-payment of unemployment allowances); and the incomplete distribution of job cards in roughly 15 per cent of the localities the CAG team surveyed.

NREGA's critics, and much of the media (in English, Hindi, and other languages), jumped on these and other findings as evidence that NREGA was failing. The programme was, in fact, failing to meet many targets, including, in most places, the requirement that a third of the work be performed by women. But corruption was not preventing NREGA from having a salutary impact on the wages of many rural households during difficult economic times. This did not stop corruption from being the public issue most closely associated with NREGA—the master variable underlying almost every aspect of underperformance, according to people determined to see the worst in a scheme they never liked in the first place. Speeches in parliament called for investigations into official abuses; opposition parties in various states complained of politicised implementation. More striking was the extreme view of some critics that NREGA was irredeemable.

More sober commentators, however, recognised that the CAG report was far less damning than the chorus of complaint seemed to indicate. An unsigned editorial in the left-leaning but hardly uncritical *Economic and Political Weekly* (*EPW*) observed that the CAG's 'findings are being sensationalised', particularly by the scheme's most implacable opponents, who seemed to see every glass as half-empty, and worse, incapable of being refilled. For instance, should not the CAG's finding that job cards had been effectively distributed in 85 per cent of the localities surveyed (the flip side of the 15 per cent figure mentioned earlier) be seen as an impressive feat? The *EPW* editorial also argued that NREGA's critics had become unreasonably exercised over the CAG's finding that just 3.2 per cent of registered households had received (the maximum of) 100 days of paid employment. This low figure stemmed from the high number of job cards issued, including to households that would not seek the full 100 days of work available under NREGA—or in some cases, any employment at all. This group saw the job card as an insurance policy of sorts.

The *EPW* advised die-hard NREGA critics to acknowledge that prompt payment of wages in 60 per cent of the *gram panchayats* surveyed by the CAG was a huge improvement over the 'prolonged delays ... under earlier public works schemes such as the national food for work programme'. NREGA's critics should 'acknowledge and learn from these achievements as much as from the failures'. Rather than 'consistently attack[ing] the programme for being an example of waste and "sops"', they might recognise that the 'history of public works in the subcontinent suggests that expecting corruption to disappear overnight is unrealistic'. It would be preferable to press both the central and state governments to 'invest more' in the 'strict enforcement of the transparency safeguards under NREGA', which experience had already shown 'can go a long way in preventing corruption'.[4]

NREGA's architects, particularly those who had pressed vigorously for the inclusion of citizen-led accountability mechanisms in the original legislation, were highly critical of implementation lapses, but remained deeply committed to making the programme function more effectively. Dreze called the first set of NREGA works during 2006–7 'an unprecedented achievement in the history of social security in India, or for that matter anywhere in the developing world',[5] while still acknowledging that 'major leakages' undermined the programme's effects.

The legislation's 'transparency safeguards' made NREGA 'something of a test case of the possibility of eradicating corruption from development programmes'.[6] Ensuring the effective use of the Act's social audit provisions would be an uphill climb in much of the country, as 'vested interests still have an upper hand in many states' when it comes to controlling the administrative machinery through which NREGA is implemented.

Media interest in NREGA-linked corruption tended to peak whenever a social audit resulted in violence, with the amount of reporting related to the scale on which such abuses were perpetrated. In May 2008, activists in Jharkhand, which achieved statehood in 2000 when it broke away from Bihar, set about collecting from government offices NREGA records that they would need to conduct the comprehensive social audit they had been planning in conjunction with local groups. These were mainly paper documents, which would be systematically compared to the electronic data trail compiled by the NREGA secretariat's management information system (MIS). The activists' efforts, immediately visible in a village context, made them targets for local officials who preferred that files relating to the works projects they administered remain inaccessible.

One particularly prominent victim of reactionary violence was an activist named Lalit Mehta. He had been working with Dreze on one of the latter's many research and advocacy projects. The method involved helping to organise a public accounting for public works undertaken in Jharkhand's Palumu district. Mehta was murdered, a crime which was interpreted by local people as 'intimidation' and a warning 'not to conduct an audit' that had been scheduled for ten days later.[7] The vulnerability of would-be social auditors, who are best classified as human rights defenders, became a point of intense discussion among people concerned with NREGA's fate. For some, the death was a sign that India—or possibly just 'traditional' rural India—was not ready for this level of real-time democratic scrutiny. For others, it merely confirmed that more resources, and better legal and security protections, were desperately needed to empower local catalysts for political change.[8]

Indeed, one of the main NREGA issues social activists were taking up was accountability. There were many manifestations of this, including in states such as Rajasthan, which, as we saw in Chapter 4, engaged in several experiments to improve NREGA governance. Prompted by a variety of pressures, the central government sometimes took decisions that ran counter to the state government's seeming receptivity to civil society engagement in improving programme performance. For instance, an administrative order issued by the Ministry of Rural Development (MoRD) in New Delhi stated that *gram sabhas* were the only bodies authorised to conduct statutorily-mandated social audits. This meant, in effect, that *panchayat* officials would be even more insulated from demands by activist groups for access to programme records. This became a point of serious contention in public debates in Rajasthan and elsewhere because it had become clear to most observers in the state, through the succession of NREGA social audits that had been conducted there (discussed in Chapter 4), that the only time serious, systematic investigations took place was when RESKAA and its affiliated civic organisations took the initiative.

Despite impressive feats of accountability-seeking among activists in many parts of India, it is fair to say that citizen-activists capable of organising social audits—and overcoming the resistance to holding them—have been in short supply. It seems unlikely that more than 25–30 per cent of *gram panchayats* have gone through all the motions of conducting a social audit, and even that figure seems optimistic to some observers. On the other hand, the existence of the social-audit provisions has helped to drive the creation of a growing pool of experienced investigators-for-hire. This was not the vision sold to NREGA doubters when the Bill was making its way through parliament in 2004 and

2005. In the original concept, local people would emerge as citizen auditors. But local constraints are formidable, so the emergence of a cadre of individuals and groups that have developed various techniques associated with investigating abuses of NREGA is welcome. Some social auditors, in fact, have become more or less full time corruption investigators.

The limited and largely unsuccessful efforts by central authorities to expose and punish large-scale corruption under NREGA—with some notable exceptions—reflects the political constraints under which the central government must act. In theory, the authorities in Delhi could suspend funding disbursements to districts that are credibly suspected to have witnessed widespread and systematic theft of public resources. This is specified in the Act, but as per bureaucratic rules, this requires a finding that local mechanisms to check corruption—such as social audits—have either not been used, or have been compromised by the actors orchestrating the abuses. The Central Employment Guarantee Council (CEGC) has occasionally contracted researchers to examine NREGA's functioning in states where activist- and NGO-connected CEGC members knew corruption to be rife. One particular target was Uttar Pradesh, which had gained a (deserved) reputation for poor performance. During 2010, one researcher uncovered large-scale corruption in a number of locations, including in the parliamentary constituency of Congress Party heir-apparent Rahul Gandhi.[9] Disciplinary action was recommended as a result of follow-up investigations by Uttar Pradesh's civil service. But no action was initiated by the MoRD in New Delhi. As the CEGC investigator pointed out, the central government is reluctant to use the suspension-of-funds as a weapon, since doing so automatically 'becomes a political decision': 'a blockade of funds impacts people directly and that could lead to an agitation'.[10]

There is also of course the inherently political tension that arises when the state and central governments are ruled by different parties, as they were in the case of Uttar Pradesh during that period. When officials in the MoRD (overseen by a minister from the Congress-led government in Delhi) found the Gujarat government to have systematically violated NREGA programme rules, supporters of Gujarat Chief Minister Narendra Modi, then widely expected to be the BJP's standard-bearer in forthcoming national elections, complained that the charges were motivated by politics.[11] Attempting to avoid appearing partisan can, in fact, prevent the central government from taking action that is both reasonable and necessary—with the result that accountability suffers. In the case of Uttar Pradesh, the problems afflicting NREGA were considered dire enough that independent (court-sanctioned) investigations were initiated—a sign that the political process had broken down. The 'irregularities' in a Congress-branded scheme operating in a Samajwadi Party-ruled state were reported with much glee in the right-wing press.[12]

The process of implementing NREGA had two somewhat contradictory influences on corruption debates. On the one hand, there was a kind of demonstration effect for the methods (particularly social audits) and principles (especially transparency) built into the legislation. Social audits were an important tool for exposing and deterring corruption in many places, mainly when supported by a committed state government (as in Andhra Pradesh for some years) or a network of civil society organisations (as in Rajasthan for a time). On the other hand, the NREGA experience of corruption highlighted the need for specialised institutions to carry out investigations and to see them through to actual prosecutions (a point we touch on shortly).

NREGA has been examined in great detail by all types of organisations. Many reasonable objections to the programme's design and performance have been put forward. But a subset of particularly vehement critics have levelled ill-informed charges that, through sheer repetition, have begun to emerge as a kind of conventional wisdom in policy circles. These need to be addressed.[13] Some commentators have claimed that significant NREGA funds have been stolen. We saw an example of this in the 'finding' by Parsuram Rai that 70 per cent of the programme's funds in Madhya Pradesh were being illegally diverted. After interviewing many of the same villagers whom he met, we found that Rai worked in the tiny minority of districts in that state which are considered 'worst cases' and then (knowingly or not) exaggerated estimates of corruption by scaling his figures up to produce misleading state-wide statistics.

NREGA critics who have made grossly exaggerated claims about the nature and extent of corruption in the programme have tended to ignore a second salient fact: the existence of a process of virtually continuous reform to NREGA. Led by civil society organisations, with backing from various quarters, the results of this process have over time made it more difficult to divert funds from NREGA works than from almost any other government initiative in India. Most of the methods of stealing from NREGA that existed in 2006, when the Act's associated regulations were promulgated in their original form, have been curtailed. By far the most significant NREGA policy revision driven by concerns about corruption was the introduction, late in the UPA government's first term, of a new rule that would affect all implementation authorities, from the state government secretariat to the *gram panchayat* office. From mid-2008, each NREGA labourer's wages had to be paid into an individual bank or postal savings account held in the name of the worker concerned. This was a direct and major assault on the nexus of political and administrative middlemen who pervade rural development bureaucracies throughout India. This radical reform, whatever one's view of its effectiveness to date, was driven in large part by accusations of corruption in NREGA projects, and by an understanding among activists that it was necessary to close the audit loop by instituting mandatory bank transfers, which always produce receipts. The complaints of corruption that drove this process came from local civil society groups empowered by the Act's transparency and social-audit provisions—something NREGA's architects counted as a victory.

Introducing the mandatory bank account payment system required intensive inter-ministerial consultation. The result was a complex, and not always internally coherent, set of regulatory changes. The process of devising the policy revisions took place under the overall guidance of the MoRD, but with the engagement of numerous public-sector entities, including the postal authorities: the national post office network was supposed to scale-up its system for establishing and servicing accounts to meet the expected demand that the new rules would generate. In each state, detailed administrative rules were drawn up to operationalise the system of direct-deposit payments. These specified which kinds of banking institutions could be used and imposed requirements on postal officers as well as government payment agencies. Consultations took place within and outside the bureaucracy, with the NAC's activist contingent helping to straddle the state-civil society divide and UPA MPs leading outreach to their respective parties. What made this particular policy revision significant was that, for probably the first time in a scheme of this nature, the payment agency was to be distinct and separate from the implementing agency.[14]

The result made falsifying muster rolls a less attractive prospect because deposits in bank accounts could be tracked. However, as Bhatti points out, even with this reform 'corruption opportunities remained'.[15] Two of the three types of corruption identified by Bhatti are familiar to those who have engaged with the comparative literature on the politics of corruption. Comparative frameworks often invoke a distinction between 'collusive' corruption, based on secret agreements between public officials and their accomplices, and on the other hand, what is sometimes called 'extortionate' (or compulsory) corruption, which involves the payment of gatekeeper fees to an official who holds all or most of the bargaining leverage. But there is a third variety, 'deception'-related corruption, in which workers' accounts are 'manipulated' without their knowledge. It is deception-related corruption that has been mainly disrupted by this and other reforms to NREGA's operational protocols, though this has had spillover effects on the other two forms of corruption also.

After 2009, when the bank payment system began operating, it became far more difficult for programme administrators at the village and block levels to steal from workers' wages—on which 60 per cent (and in some states, more) of NREGA funds are spent.[16] In 2009, a young man who had recently secured a job in the programme at the sub-district level in Rajasthan told our field research colleagues that before bank accounts were introduced, he had been able to pocket Rs. 600,000 per year, but that he could only make Rs. 100,000 annually thereafter. The introduction of bank accounts has discouraged many would-be profiteers, who thus gravitated towards other, more lucrative opportunities for 'partnership with the public sector', notably infrastructure contracts and real estate development rights.

Thefts from workers' wages were not totally eradicated by the direct deposit payment system. But when thefts do occur, they are almost always visible to NREGA labourers—who are compelled by various forms of social, economic, and political pressure to relinquish portions of their earnings after withdrawing them from their accounts. This process triggers two changes that worry local councilors who oversee (or at least overlook) the theft of workers' wages in this fashion. First, it damages the perpetrators' reputations, and thus their chances of re-election. Second, it sows discontent among labourers, which enhances their political awareness and makes them far less pliable as constituents. As a result of these dynamics, and of the increasing risk of discovery, a much smaller proportion of workers' wages was diverted. The main remaining mechanism for looting NREGA funds involved officials submitting falsified invoices showing inflated prices for the purchase and/or the transport of materials (such as sand and cement) for public works. The officials illegally retain the surplus reimbursements for their personal use, typically in collusion with suppliers. Changes to NREGA's online tracking system introduced in 2010–11 made this and other manoeuvres more difficult as well. Even when the chances of punishments actually being meted out are low, the consequences for a bureaucrat's record (and chances for better, more lucrative postings) are in some cases enough to deter certain corrupt acts.

As usual, the architects of NREGA understood (and indeed welcomed) the discontent then being sown through the debate over the Act's original anti-corruption mechanisms, which were clearly insufficient—particularly at the block level, as discussed in Chapter 3. What made the debates over NREGA's functioning so productive in terms of policy revisions was that the advocates of the policy under scrutiny—those with the most invested in its success—were among the loudest voices criticising not only aspects of the scheme's performance, but elements of the legislation itself, which these same critics had helped to draft. Dreze—who, as we have seen, was centrally involved in the conception, formulation, and execution of NREGA—stated that the original 'grievance redressal provisions under NREGA ... [were] very weak'.[17] The reporting relationships were underspecified and the penalties (and procedures for determining and implementing them) were vague, all of which was 'making it possible for government officials and *gram panchayat* functionaries to get away with gross violations of the Act on a routine basis'.[18] But Dreze expected to keep 'battling' for full implementation as part of a gradualist model of change. The first rounds of NREGA implementation had created more conducive conditions for improved governance because they had 'at least led to a major refocusing of administrative energies, financial resources and political attention towards the concerns of rural workers', making it 'a small but significant step towards the realisation of the right to work'.[19]

In addition to national-level policy adjustments to improve governance discussed here, smaller experiments in states and districts were examined in Chapters 4 and 5, on Rajasthan and Madhya Pradesh, respectively. We have personally witnessed many such efforts by committed officials—alert, energetic people who sought out information about problems in the implementation process,[20] and took action to put things right.[21] This is worth bearing in mind when we consider another set of grossly overstated criticisms of the programme.

Debates over corruption under NREGA—over whether it was unavoidable, measures to curb it, and reasons why they may or may not be effective—directly influenced the larger governance agenda that the UPA government pursued in its second term (a subject discussed in the penultimate section of this chapter). This included plans for a Lok Pal Bill, which were developed from skeletal concept notes into legislative language by civil society representatives within the NAC, working with civil service colleagues with deep knowledge of the legal processes that govern the work of investigative and prosecutorial agencies. It was in the NAC, for instance, that a general Grievance Redressal Bill (GRB) was devised. The GRB's detailed time-bound provisions imposed general requirements, applicable to officials throughout government, rather than provisions specifically to govern NREGA. Nevertheless, debates over NREGA's performance influenced how key decision-makers perceived the need for new governance legislation, including not just the GRB, but also the Jan Lok Pal Bill, the Judicial Standards and Accountability Bill, and many others—some of which became laws.

The highly contentious and drawn-out process through which the Lok Pal Bill was formulated ended up placing the NAC's civil society members into conflict with other civic activists, particularly the leaders of the India Against Corruption (IAC) movement. The IAC's two main leaders, Anna Hazare and Arvind Kejriwal, pushed for a stronger Bill than even the NAC's civil society members were comfortable advocating. The rising profile of the IAC movement had been fuelled by outrage over several high-profile corruption scandals. These included kickbacks related to the construction of facilities for the 2010 Commonwealth Games in Delhi; the awarding of non-competitive coal exploration and mining concessions to a number of large industrial houses; and irregularities in the allocation of parts of the 2G wireless spectrum to politically well-connected (and well-resourced) telecommunications companies in the private sector. Even so, the experiences of corruption in NREGA projects, which had shaped so much of the public discussion—through media analyses of various CAG reports, for instance—played a role here as well. It was notable that the UPA government's initial draft for a Jan Lok Pal Bill included provisions for citizen engagement of the sort that had been pioneered by NREGA, and which were the subject of much subsequent public debate. In late 2012, a large section of the IAC movement came together to form the nucleus of the Aam Aadmi Party (AAP) under the leadership of Kejriwal, Hazare having chosen to follow a more Gandhian, non-party political approach to effecting social change.[22] AAP maintains a deep commitment to evolving participatory mechanisms, including provisions for enhanced transparency, that NREGA (and the debates about its implementation) helped to make mainstream.

Discussions over corruption in NREGA projects were closely intertwined with debates over the role of decentralised governance structures. In theory, the Act greatly augmented both the authority and resources conferred upon Panchayati Raj Institutions (PRIs). PRIs in some states had so badly atrophied after decades of neglect that they could not cope with their new responsibilities and demands. Because NREGA's architects sought to preserve the programme's decentralised governance structure, problems with ensuring local control over decision making prompted a number of policy revisions. The process of bringing about these changes pitted state governments against not only the PRIs within their jurisdictions (local government being a state subject under India's federal constitution), but against the Government of India as well. Despite having no formal control over the operation of the states' NREGA-compliant employment programmes, the central government was able to influence implementation through its constant adjustments to programme rules. The MoRD was particularly insistent when it came to issues of decentralisation. For example, in July 2010, a key NREGA official in New Delhi was empowered to take a harder line with state governments that evaded regulations that required them to ensure that labour-budget decisions for NREGA works were taken at the *panchayat* level.[23] Block-level bureaucrats had taken over much of NREGA planning process, and the MoRD threatened to withhold NREGA funds from state governments unless they made sure that *panchayats* were sufficiently empowered to fulfil this duty.

Wages and Works

The second domain of political discussion in which NREGA played a significant role concerned the broad area of employment, including wages (what determines their level, modes of payment, and so forth) and the rural public works projects undertaken through the programme.

Upon assuming office in 2004, the Congress-led UPA government's top priority was creating jobs to absorb new labour market entrants whose aspirations the previous government had been unable to meet. The BJP-led National Democratic Alliance (NDA) government had been ousted in 2004 despite an impressive growth performance during its time in office. Even while the NREG Bill was being debated in 2005, it was invoked by UPA ministers and senior civil servants as an example of the government's commitment to robustly addressing the problem of 'jobless growth' in the Indian economy. Rural areas—precisely where jobs were needed to prevent people who were 'exiting' agriculture from migrating to India's already overwhelmed cities—were particularly afflicted by this syndrome. Unemployment among households reliant on agricultural labour for their livelihoods had reached 15.3 per cent in 2004–5. This had increased sharply from 9.5 per cent in 1993–4,[24] despite the expansion of the Indian economy during the intervening decade. A combination of population increases and reductions in the proportion of self-employed people meant that during most of the 1990s, employment in rural areas was created at only half the rate at which new entrants to the rural labour market were appearing.[25] In a speech in London in early 2005 (well before NREGA's final passage),

Finance Minister P. Chidambaram, the cabinet's chief NREGA sceptic at the time, specifically mentioned the contribution that NREGA could make to alleviating unemployment and underemployment. The remarks were delivered not at a conference on poverty reduction or social development—venues where NREGA would in later years be a subject of frequent discussion—but to a largely private-sector audience at the Guildhall in the City of London.[26]

Whatever the central government's larger intentions, there was considerable variation between states in how they implemented NREGA. Among these were differences in the methodologies used to decide which types of works projects would be undertaken, effective wage levels, and the information systems used to monitor progress. The issue of wages was such a staple of public discussion on NREGA because it rested at the intersection of crucial questions about the programme's identity. As we saw in the previous section, theft of wages was (in the early years, before bank accounts) a major element of the corruption that afflicted the programme, and wage levels were seen to have an impact not only on the programme's overall budgetary cost, but also on the wider rural economy, and indeed on such macroeconomic variables as food price inflation.

The level and applicability of minimum wage provisions in the operation of NREGA-compliant job schemes were subjects not only of policy debate, but of public protest as well. For instance, there were debates over the applicability of the central minimum wage. Did it indeed have to prevail if local minimum wages were lower, and did the state wage have to prevail if it was higher? The Government of India's logic was that it had a fiduciary responsibility to taxpayers to sanction payment at the least costly rate permissible by law in each jurisdiction. Opponents, including from within the NAC, staunchly opposed this position. Some Rajasthan-based activists in the NAC, and others associated with them who had been involved in the struggle to fulfil the employment guarantee, had been advocating the payment of a minimum wage since the time of Sanjit Roy v. Rajasthan in the early 1980s, and even before then. They were probably the least likely group of people in a country of more than a billion to capitulate on the issue of minimum wages. They certainly would not acquiesce without a spirited fight.

The protests that took place over the minimum wage during 2010 (and to a limited degree thereafter) were also deeply political. They were built around pre-existing (non-party) political formations,[27] and were linked to a wider agenda of social justice. (Sen and Dreze, whose work on this subject is discussed in the next section of this chapter, have pointed to such linkages as a defining feature of the rights-based approach to poverty reduction exemplified by NREGA.) Focusing on the issue of minimum wages was a natural decision for the Rajasthan-based network of right to work activists known as RESKAA, whose advocacy around NREGA was discussed in Chapter 4. The group's work conducting social audits—and in the process, showcasing the potential of CSO-facilitated audits—produced impressive results. They exposed both local corruption and the hypocrisy of state-level officials. But the group had also never abandoned its pressure-group role, through which it undertook both traditional lobbying and protest movement functions. The former was aimed at influencing senior officials responsible for framing the formal rules, procedures, and institutional mechanisms through which NREGA was operationalised, while the latter focused on ensuring full realisation of the governance rights granted under NREGA.

In autumn 2010, as the commitment of both the central and state governments showed signs of waning, RESKAA took the lead in organising a Mazdoor Haq Yatra (Worker's Rights March). Among the protestors' demands was that any increase in the minimum wage, as was then being planned, be matched by a commensurate increase in NREGA wages. State governments are given latitude in adjusting the minimum wage upward, but not downward. In theory, any increase should apply automatically to wages under NREGA projects. In practice, however, evasion of this stipulation had become common in many states.

One key to the success of the Yatra was the movement's discipline in specifying a small number of key demands that were of common interest.[28] This excluded certain single-issue groups from the movement, but it also meant that those groups that did participate were fully committed—they would not peel away as 'their issues' were targeted with small concessions. Regardless, backing for the Yatra went far beyond RESKAA and its immediate circle of supporters. The Yatra's success stemmed as much from the commonality of purpose among the participating organisations—itself, as suggested above, a reflection of sound political strategy—as from the perceived righteousness of the cause.

In early 2011—after much debate, and pressure from Sonia Gandhi, the NAC, and the CEGC—the Prime Minister's Office and the cabinet agreed to raise the minimum wage and to link it to the consumer price index.[29] The debate of 2010–11 had shifted considerably since 2004–5, with fiscally conservative voices coming to the fore.[30] Wage level issues were still alive in 2013 (when Aruna Roy departed the NAC over the issue of minimum wages), and in 2014 as the country's general election grew nearer.[31]

Alterations to minimum wages were usually effected through a government notification that required no parliamentary intervention. And as doing so required no changes to NREGA Guidelines—the evolving regulatory rule book—technically, much of the senior civil service could avoid explicitly signing-off on these changes. This is another manifestation of the Indian state's 'allergy' (or structural aversion) to substantive transparency and individual accountability. In some cases, wage revisions were intended primarily to reflect informal practices that had arisen in various state jurisdictions. A March 2012 wage revision notification[32] posted rates for thirty-four states and union territories, and in the process identified the explicitly bifurcated wage regimes in effect in two states: Himachal Pradesh and the Andaman and Nicobar Islands. In the Andaman and Nicobar Islands, NREGA workers in Andaman received Rs. 178 per day, compared to Rs. 189 in Nicobar. And in Himachal Pradesh's 'scheduled' (Adivasi-concentrated) areas, the daily wage rate was Rs. 157, as opposed to Rs. 126 in the rest of the state (the so-called non-scheduled areas). Whatever their merits, such two-tier systems have major downsides. They sow confusion in the minds of workers and their advocates as to which wage rate prevails, and workers from different areas can become alienated from one another, their divisions working to the advantage of powerful elements within and outside the Indian state who seek to limit their gains. Through the central government's publication of this state-by-state wage schedule, however, it was possible for activists to learn definitively that bifurcated wage systems did not exist in most Indian states—a useful piece of information when confronted by officials who react to protests by invoking policies and provisions that either do not exist or do not say what officials claim on their behalf.

Another way in which this notification helped to formalise aspects of the policy about which there had been widespread uncertainty, was to explicitly link the future application of the wage policy to already agreed procedures. For instance, the notification devoted the second of its three paragraphs to specifying how its contents would be made consistent with, and assist in giving effect to, an order that had been issued by Karnataka's High Court regarding the formula to be used in determining wage increases.[33] The methodology spells out each step in the process of calculating the wage ultimately arrived at for Karnataka—Rs. 155 per day, a figure that put it near the middle of the all-India distribution. Increasing the specificity of the procedural information provided workers and workers' rights advocates with a better basis for asserting demands for implementation and indeed for adjustments to variables contained within the formula—a method that can make it easier for the state to concede to demands because their fiscal implications are less readily apparent in political debate.

The UPA government's approach to wages under NREGA—both in terms of levels and how they were distributed—tended to be ad hoc and driven by short-term financial, political, and administrative compulsions. At one point, for example, the MoRD reversed its earlier insistence on the use of bank accounts to pay workers, acknowledging that the rural banking network lacked the capacity to deliver fully. In other instances, a lack of clarity on fairly fundamental elements of NREGA's structure continued to plague implementation for excessively long periods. In September 2011, for example, an all-India NREGA workers' advocacy coalition felt moved to mention in its newsletter that it was 'of particular importance' that the incoming minister of rural development had issued a 'clarification' to the effect 'that NREGA work cannot be suspended in the agricultural season'.[34] More than five years into the scheme's operation, this particular implementation 'battle' should have been won—or if not won in practice, at least settled as a matter of official policy. Many thought it had been: the Act states unambiguously that the supply of works projects and the allocation of workdays are to be determined by the demand for employment among rural workers, not commands from labour-purchasing land-owners to officials who control the flow of NREGA projects and funds.

Another wage-related issue concerned the impact of NREGA on rural and agricultural wage rates, and the relationship between wages and overall incomes. This is, of course, a topic that cannot be separated from the issue of prevailing minimum wages. We mainly address this question in Chapter 8, where we provide an overall assessment of NREGA, viewed through the lens of political ideas, interests, and institutions, rather than the narrow cost-benefit calculations used by the programme's most obdurate critics. But let us note here that farmers and those speaking on their behalf—including many Congress Party legislators—became active in the debate over how best to manage tensions between wage payers and earners amidst the debate over NREGA and its ostensibly wage-inflating effects. Their general thrust was for informal procedures to be put in place to limit NREGA works during peak 'reaping and sowing' seasons. Through this means, agricultural interests, in some cases represented by political actors whose appeals for support are primarily caste-based, became important actors in this distributional dilemma. Lakin and Ravishankar argue that, during 2004–5, farming interests did not enter into the debate over the potential impact of the NREG Bill on wages paid to agricultural workers in the private sector.[35] They cite the seminal work of Varshney, who has claimed that in the first several decades after independence, farming groups in India tended to focus on state-procurement prices and subsidised agricultural inputs, such as fertiliser, water, electricity, pesticides, and seeds. Rural wage rates were, in effect, left to market forces (shaped by highly unequal social relations) to resolve. Subsidy and price issues, not management of labour, have been the 'main bone of contention between the state and farmers'.[36] NREGA may, however, have begun to shift this pattern of interest-group demand-making.

Also of great concern to the farming interests just discussed were the works completed under NREGA—'playing with mud', as they were derisively described by Surjit Bhalla, one of the programme's fiercest critics. Issues included everything from the local appropriateness of particular NREGA works to the mechanisms used in various types of projects to yield corrupt income (a theme running through seemingly every NREGA-related public debate). The controversies in this area were politically salient enough to elicit criticism from national media commentators, influential NGO actors, academic researchers, and international analysts. The debates were relatively one-sided, for NREGA's supporters were, as we saw in Chapter 4, actually among the loudest complainers in localities where CSO-facilitated social audits revealed shoddy (or non-existent) works, or evidence that local priority-setting exercises had not been conducted, despite what might have been stated in reporting documents submitted by local officials. Indeed, NREGA's true believers had predicted the eruption of many of these problems, but traced them to a different source: insufficient decentralisation—an issue, as we saw in the previous section, that the central government sought to address.

Official rules governing the selection, costing, location, construction, and use of NREGA works have been subjected to a number of revisions, encompassing both minor changes that are effected through bureaucratic notifications, and others that require a more demanding process. In January 2009, near the end of UPA-I, the MoRD issued draft Guidelines for Implementation of Works on Individual Land under NREGA.[37] The updated guidelines stated that, while Schedule I, Para (iv) of NREGA allowed works projects to include providing 'irrigation facilit[ies] to land owned by households belonging to the Scheduled Castes and Scheduled Tribes or to land of beneficiaries of land reforms or that of the beneficiaries under the Indira Awas Yojana' programme, using NREGA projects to upgrade the lands of housing subsidy recipients had not worked particularly well. The new guidelines also noted that subsequent amendments, most effected through edict-like government notifications, generally included an expansion of those covered under this provision. One such modification, dated 6 March 2007, allowed for the 'provision of irrigation facilities, horticulture plantation and land development facilities on land owned by households belonging to the Scheduled Castes and the Scheduled Tribes or to Below Poverty Line families or to beneficiaries of land reforms or to the beneficiaries under the Indira Awas Yojana of the Government of India'. Such additions vastly extended the potential scope of NREGA works. On 24 July 2009, the list of beneficiary categories was amended to include 'small farmers or marginal farmers as defined in the Agriculture Debt Waiver and Debt Relief Scheme, 2008'. This is a broad cross-section of rural people, most of them the working poor rather than simply unemployed, but many non-poor people were also among them. Some economists thought it possible that the public-private partnership model could increase the long-term productivity of infrastructural improvements conducted under NREGA: if the works were taking place on private lands, the owner would have a strong incentive to ensure that they were conducted properly.[38]

Either way, state governments had to be told what the constraints were on the operation of NREGA works on 'individual' land. In addition to the regular requirements (use of machinery prohibited, a 60:40 labour-to-material ratio), additional conditions were imposed. First, it would be the responsibility of 'the beneficiary household' whose land received improvements to maintain over time the works carried out with NREGA funds. Second, individual land project beneficiaries would have to be job card holders, and a maximum of Rs. 150,000 could be allocated to improvements for each. Since there are often multiple job card holders in any given house, this formulation effectively increased the amount of funds devoted to such projects. Anyone in a position to handle such a large works project was likely not the type of beneficiary originally envisaged. It was notable to those who closely followed this process that an effort was being made to avoid defining maximum benefits in terms of the size or value of a particular land parcel. Third, the notification indicates that all categories of beneficiary (that is, not discriminating against or in favour of the original categories) should receive equal treatment. Finally, the document calls for the competent authority to 'maintain [a] balance of work on individual land and works on common property resources'.[39] Since threshold levels to operationalise this commitment are not specified, it was difficult to enforce. Even so, administrative procedures have been established for realising the policy changes. Annexes III-VII of the guidelines are forms which MoRD officials expected state governments to fill in periodically. Annex III, for instance, explains the cost-breakdown (and method for arriving at it) for each category of allowable expense under 'horticulture plantation' projects. Annex IV consists primarily of a template for reporting how and when assets on individual lands are registered. As with most other aspects of NREGA, these instructions were complied with at different rates, using different approaches—sometimes resulting in sharply contrasting implementation methods and results across states, districts, blocks, and even adjacent *gram panchayats*.

In 2012, An 'Empowered Committee' was established by the CEGC 'to scrutinise and discuss Anticipated Labour Demand of States for 2012–13'. Among its other responsibilities, the Empowered Committee sought to tackle issues with the quality and suitability of physical assets, which some members considered to be NREGA's Achilles' Heel. The general practice among NREGA implementors with corrupt intentions was to delay the conduct of substantive, physical audits of NREGA works projects. To do this, local authorities would put off for as long as possible those actions—such as drawing down funds—that are supposed to trigger the routine internal auditing process (which is not to be confused with the monitoring conducted by agencies like the CAG, discussed earlier in this chapter). They also did this by systematically withholding information that would 'capture data on closure/completion/partial completion/abandonment of works in the [central Rural Development] Ministry's MIS'.[40] This was one of the reasons why '[t]he work completion rate is low' in Bihar (and presumably other states as well).[41] The Committee told state government officials that 'completion certificates need to be issued on priority'. The Committee was well aware of the main reason for continued delay: officials seeking to avoid accountability for the quality of the works. When enough time has elapsed it becomes exceedingly difficult to hold anyone accountable for certain earthen works, no matter how useful they may once have been. The presumed wear and tear of weather imposes its own statute of limitations.

India's Development Paradigm

The third area of public debate in which NREGA figured prominently is even broader still. It centres on the question of what constitutes an appropriate development paradigm for India. This has long been the subject of contentious, wide-ranging debate, which nevertheless tends to revolve around two key issues: the relative priority to be given to economic growth or poverty reduction (or other objectives); and the role of the state in shaping the nation's economic—and often political—destiny. NREGA has been a mainstay of these debates, usually in a supporting rather than starring role, since it amounts to less than one per cent of GDP. Yet, because of its symbolic value, in political debates, NREGA has punched well above its economic weight.

One place where this dynamic played out was in the debates that emerged between two of India's most visible academic economists: Amartya Sen and Jagdish Bhagwati, each working with a long-time research collaborator—Jean Dreze and Arvind Panagariya, respectively. Each of these duos released a book in the first half of 2013. This coincidence, combined with the authors' public visibility, generated considerable media interest. Perhaps inevitably, the two books were held up as competing economic visions for India as national attention turned towards the 2014 general election. While, as we have seen, NREGA was a constant talking point in public policy discussions, the noisy confrontation between Bhagwati and Sen in 2013 was a turning point: from then on, debates concerning NREGA would be hostage to the unforgiving dualism of the states-versus-markets debate.

Both Bhagwati and Panagariya have been making the case for less intervention in the Indian economy for decades. In their book *Why Growth Matters: How Economic Growth in India Reduced Poverty and the Lessons for Other Developing Countries*,[42] they sought to debunk a series of 'myths', mainly about market-oriented policies and their effects in India, and to outline a comprehensive agenda to cure India's economic ills. Their prescriptions largely involved reducing the state's role in economic decision-making. This, they maintained, would stimulate faster growth, which they considered by far the best antidote to poverty insofar as it creates economic opportunities for the poor while providing tax revenue to fund public services and social protection programmes. At several points, they invoke 'lessons' from NREGA to illustrate one or another of their arguments. Apart from one substantive section, these are relatively fleeting references, and generally cast NREGA in an unflattering light. In at least one place, praise for NREGA was placed in the service of a highly dubious conclusion. Bhagwati and Panagariya dismiss concerns about growing disparities between Indian states in their rates of industrialisation and personal income growth, claiming that NREGA employment, funded by revenue from fast-growing states, cushioned poor people living in the states that were being left behind.[43] While social programmes can indeed mitigate the effects of inter-state inequality, invoking NREGA to justify complacency with worsening regional economic imbalances is at odds with the spirit in which it was enacted.

Bhagwati and Panagariya rightly claim that NREGA funding has been the direct result of buoyant tax revenues since 2003–4.[44] This is a fact that no one engaged in public policy discussions in India disputes (we note this phenomenon ourselves in Chapter 1). Unfortunately, Bhagwati and Panagariya do not consider a question that arises logically from this information: if NREGA was most strenuously implemented during the high-growth period of 2003–10, what does this say about its allegedly perverse, growth-retarding effects? And, by the same token, why did reducing NREGA's size during 2010–14 not boost economic growth during this lower-growth phase? No doubt, Bhagwati and Panagariya, if so inclined, could provide a range of explanations for this disconnect, including time-lag effects or the proposition that growth would have been even (marginally) higher in both the high-growth and lower-growth periods had NREGA never existed at all. Such subtleties were not offered, however.

One of the most confounding passages in Bhagwati and Panagariya's vision of a new Indian development paradigm has to do with targeting. They cite NREGA in support of their proposals for extensive means-testing (targeting) on virtually all social protection programmes.[45] This argument is quite astonishing because NREGA is not means-tested. It is, as we have seen, self-targeting—open to any rural household that wishes to participate, but in practice an option attractive only to the genuinely poor. NREGA was designed that way precisely because of the concern that a means-tested scheme would place too much power in the hands of those testing the means of programme 'applicants'. The kinds of means-tested mechanisms that Bhagwati and Panagariya call for would—as neoliberal economists, of all people, should know—inevitably place that power in the hands of political actors, and thereby risk abuses that NREGA, in part, avoids. It is unclear whether Bhagwati and Panagariya are aware that NREGA is not means-tested, or whether they have chosen to pretend that it is in order to associate their proposals with NREGA's well-earned reputation for the low rate at which errors of exclusion were experienced.

Bhagwati and Panagariya devote most of a chapter to damning NREGA with faint praise.[46] They grant that it has successfully reached many poor people, while building a considerable amount of physical infrastructure and boosting rural incomes in some very desperate locations. They make clear, however, that NREGA's positive effects only look rosy when compared with doing nothing. In comparison with the alternative programmes that they favour—cash transfers and health vouchers, for instance—NREGA, they claim, looks downright shabby. They argue that this state of affairs is largely due to 'leakages' in NREGA, which could be avoided through a system of transfers directly to recipient bank accounts. Bizarrely, the authors do not seem to find it terribly important that since 2009, NREGA has used bank transfers to transmit wages to workers. Had they engaged more fully with this aspect of the NREGA case, Bhagwati and Panagariya would have understood at least some of the ways in which corruption can still flourish under such a system. They claim that a cash transfer scheme would have 'almost no disadvantages', failing to mention either the problems under NREGA or the very high likelihood that under their preferred dispensation, corruption would arise in the process by which recipients seek to have their BPL status conferred (and periodically confirmed).

Jean Dreze and Amartya Sen, coauthors of *An Uncertain Glory: India and Its Contradictions*,[47] are associated with what is usually considered the opposite perspective—that more forceful government action is needed in a range of policy domains to ensure that the fruits of economic growth are distributed more evenly. Sen is one of the originators of the 'capabilities' approach to development. Dreze, as we have seen at many points in the present book, is a prolific researcher, a committed activist, and a member of the National Advisory Council (NAC) under the UPA-1 government.[48] Dreze and Sen argue, among other things, that increased funding for publicly provided education, nutrition, and health is vital not only as a matter of basic human necessity, but also as a means of producing a workforce that can push India's economy onto a more robust and sustainable growth trajectory.

Because these pairs of authors have been cast as leaders of opposing ideological camps, it is easy to overlook how much common ground there is between their positions. Both agree that neither the market nor the state can be the sole instrument for improving economic outcomes, whether these outcomes concern primarily the productive economy (for instance, the level or sectoral composition of output and exchange), or basic measures of human well-being (such as infant and maternal nutrition and mortality). Dreze and Sen acknowledge that without private-sector-led growth, sustained poverty reduction is unlikely to occur. Bhagwati and Panagariya concede that poverty cannot be tackled by growth alone, and that an effective state is crucial to every country's development prospects. In many countries, where the intensity of ideological battles allows no admission of common ground, forging this degree of consensus would be cause for celebration. But in India, the result was not to explore points of convergence, but rather a series of sharp attacks and counterattacks that mixed the personal and the political. As the debate boiled over, attempts by government officials—Montek Singh Ahluwalia, P. Chidambaram, Kaushik Basu—to highlight commonalities between Bhagwati and Sen ended up exacerbating what had already become an extremely bitter slanging match, played out in front of India's news media.

Whatever their points of agreement, the authors of these two books disagreed profoundly on how to interpret India's economic performance. This is true whether the period covered is 5, 10, 20, or even 40 years. Whether examining industrial output or living standards, the two books relentlessly (and, of course, selectively) deploy official statistics and the findings of researchers to bolster their respective claims. Underlying many of their disagreements is a lack of consensus on what should be measured, the relevant comparative standard, the degree of disaggregation required, the appropriate timeframe, and much else. So while Bhagwati and Panagariya applaud India's success in reducing the poverty rate over the past two decades, Dreze and Sen provide data to show that such claims reflect the lifting of many people's incomes to a level just above the pitifully low threshold that divides the poor from the merely near-poor. Where Bhagwati and Panagariya welcome the proliferation of private healthcare services, Dreze and Sen invoke historical evidence to claim that no country has been able to sustain improved health outcomes without a strong system of basic public provision. Bhagwati and Panagariya point to India outpacing sub-Saharan Africa on many human development measures; Dreze and Sen point out India's underperformance when compared to its neighbours in South Asia, particularly Bangladesh.

The two books' starkly contrasting assessments of NREGA—the passage of which in 2005 was in no small measure the work of Dreze and his colleagues on the NAC—reflects these differing conceptions of the politics of development. Whereas Bhagwati and Panagariya see NREGA as a symbol of waste—both in direct corruption and in opportunity costs, even where implemented relatively cleanly—Dreze and Sen insist that a fair assessment of NREGA must include its (allegedly positive) effects on the capacity of poor people to mobilise for continued change.

In one sense, the key difference between these highly influential works of public advocacy is the unit of analysis around which each set of co-authors has built their model of social and economic transformation. This, as much as the degree of faith or mistrust in the current condition of the Indian state, seems to be at the root of their disagreement. While Bhagwati and Panagariya have adopted the language of empowerment, this mainly refers to individual hold-ers of economic assets and the transactional choices they are permitted to make. Hence their advocacy of school vouchers and means-tested public fund-ing of private health insurance. Dreze and Sen, on the other hand, are focused on various collectivities, whether defined by locality (e.g. displaced communi-ties), ethnic identity (e.g. Dalits), or economic niche (e.g. agricultural work-ers). Their preoccupation with economic inequality is about not merely the injustice it represents, but, just as importantly, its adverse effects on social cohesion and the capacity of marginalised people to act collectively.

Perhaps the most important substantive divergence concerns how the two books regard the state. This is more than a question of whether the state should have a larger or smaller role in stimulating growth or combating pov-erty. At issue is whether the state—any state, but particularly India's—should be regarded as immutable in character. While Bhagwati and Panagariya are subtle enough to distinguish between different public institutions, and to disaggregate the various functions governments might want to perform, they nevertheless take the nature of the state as a given: it is inherently corrupt, inhabited by self-serving officials, and a drain on society. This, according to Bhagwati and Panagariya, is an insurmountable problem for any 'approach that assigns a prominent role to the government' in service delivery.[49] Reform-ing the state is worthwhile, mainly insofar as it involves requiring it 'to com-pete with private sector providers on equal terms'.[50] Dreze and Sen, by contrast, see many more possibilities for making the Indian state more effec-tive. Indeed, as they put it, '[o]ne of the biggest obstacles to restoring accountability is the pessimistic impression that nothing can change in this respect'.[51] Their approach seeks to fundamentally re-engineer, through the creation of more participatory forms of governance, the relationship between citizens and the public institutions constituted to act on their behalf—a pro-cess that, they concede, will also require shifts in 'behavioural norms and practices'.[52] Even commentators who share Bhagwati and Panagariya's unease with programmes such as NREGA, demonstrate far greater awareness of the need to make the Indian state a more capable entity. Arvind Subramanian, for instance, has been highly critical of what he calls 'redistribution through rights and entitlements'.[53] Though he considers this approach—epitomised by NREGA and the more recently passed National Food Security Act—'self-defeating', Subramanian nevertheless recognises that what India must learn from China's success is not the importance of market forces, a lesson it has already imbibed, but the need to enhance the state's capacity to perform a wide range of functions.[54]

Beyond the Sen-versus-Bhagwati debate, much of the critique directed at NREGA rails against the perceived opportunity cost. This argument—which highlights the other uses to which NREGA funds could have been put—has an obvious appeal. The alternative scenarios set forth by opportunity-cost critics sometimes rely on unduly optimistic assumptions about both the likelihood of such policies being adopted, given political realities, and the possibility that they will not be subverted by many of the same actors who, everyone admits, are a constant menace to NREGA. Besides, even critics who have found fault with NREGA, holding it up as the antithesis of the market-centric future they have envisioned, have been willing to acknowledge certain benefits from the programme, including those that may have been, in a sense, unintended. Some economists, for instance, argued that programmes like NREGA that did not see a decline in demand during periods of economic downturn—indeed, they usually saw a surge of interest among job-seekers—were a valuable counter-cyclical mechanism for an economy such as India's, where the formal sector reached only so far. Even as far back as 2005, when NREGA was about to be enacted, politically engaged economists in India had argued that the crisis in the country's rural economy was driven by a lack of aggregate demand in rural areas, which increasing purchasing power among people near the bottom of the economic pyramid could ameliorate, if not solve.[55] During the economic downturn that began in 2008–9, NREGA was referred to by some economists as an 'automatic demand stabiliser'. Dreze notes that even some of the economists who dismissed NREGA when it was first proposed, on the grounds that they thought it would be fiscally ruinous, later came to see some of its macroeconomic benefits—including 'guarded support' beginning in 2008, 'when the worldwide financial crisis led to a broad-based call for higher government expenditure as a means of "pump-priming" the economy'.[56]

Debates over an appropriate development paradigm for India during this period usually involved claims that government initiatives were needed to create economic opportunities in places where the state's penetration was weakest. Much of the hand-wringing over Maoist-inspired 'Naxalite' violence in central India focused on the developmental deficits in the regions where the insurgency was most active, including the indignities and abuses visited upon Adivasi communities there. NREGA entered these discussions precisely because it was seen as a way of both fighting material deprivation and cementing ties between the state and people in troubled regions. By engaging citizens in registration paperwork, workday tallying and bank-account processing, NREGA could serve as a useful means of bringing rural people who live in the shadow economy into something like the formal sector.[57] One study found that when NREGA was implemented capably in Maoist-dominated localities, levels of violence declined. NREGA was a central component of the strategy to expand India's counterinsurgency efforts beyond an almost exclusively security and law enforcement model to one in which specific forms of development outreach—those that facilitated participation—were prioritised by the state. It is noteworthy that similar strategies have been used in peace-consolidation/state-building contexts, such as Afghanistan, where the national solidarity programme was built around essentially the same principles.

NREGA, Convergence, and the UPA-2 Reform Agenda

As we have seen from this necessarily brief glimpse into three areas of public debate with strong links to NREGA, for almost the entire period since it came into force in early 2006, cabinet ministers and senior bureaucrats in the Government of India (and in those states that have sought to make something of the programme) have been engaged in an ongoing process of revising NREGA's structure and rules. A particularly active reformist period immediately followed the UPA government's re-election in 2009, which was nearly as unpredicted as the UPA's initial victory in 2004. For example, MoRD officials involved in overseeing NREGA implementation interacted intensively with development practitioners from other countries and international institutions, discussing NREGA's successes and the challenges of delivering more fully on its promise.

Throughout its second term in office, the UPA government faced additional pressures for reform. These stemmed in large part from the changed composition of the ruling coalition. In 2008, the left parties collectively withdrew the support they had been extending to the UPA government since 2004. This meant fewer natural allies—especially when it came to wage issues—for the activist contingent within the UPA. Indeed, it was to counter the influence of the activists who had reached Congress Party President Sonia Gandhi that NREGA's sharpest critics resorted to a kind of political subterfuge to emasculate the programme. Rather than water down any of the key commitments under the Act, the MoRD announced its intention of expanding the programme by working to promote complementarities between NREGA and other government schemes. The MoRD called the new plans, initially announced in August 2009, 'NREGA 2.0'. The intention was to increase convergence with programmes run by departments outside the

MoRD. The minister of rural development understood 'the importance of expanding the programme by converging it with other ministries'—their programmes, procedures, funding cycles, personnel and so forth.

Each of the three issue areas discussed in this chapter—corruption and governance; wages and work; and India's development paradigm—were reflected in NREGA 2.0. Regarding wages and work, for instance, a key aspect of the convergence agenda was a more flexible attitude to labour contractors. This was justified as a way of ensuring that better, more durable rural assets were built. Efforts would also be made to connect NREGA to initiatives in forestry, minor irrigation works beyond low-tech improvement projects, and the creation of drainage infrastructure for rural roads. An issue-specific collection of revised procedural norms was effected via a set of policy changes known as NREGA Audit of Scheme Rules, 2011. On 1 September 2011, senior officials in the MoRD circulated a document entitled 'Reforms in NREGA Implementation'. The paper identified '[n]ine major challenges facing NREGA implementation, and diagnostics or solutions for each of them'. The MoRD, as had been its practice over the previous two decades, sought comments from the public, particularly CSOs working in the field. The focus was on making the 'demand-driven' nature of the programme operate in practice, and on improving the payment process. Local activists were invited to write in, and an email address was provided for the minister's personal secretary. At least twenty specific proposals were received, according to the ministry.

As part of the convergence effort, thirty new construction activities were added to the list of works permitted under NREGA.[58] Newly installed Rural Development Minister C.P. Joshi announced that the idea of convergence would be central to the UPA's approach to NREGA during its second term in office. This was to involve, among other things, constructing 250,000 *panchayat* administrative centres. Building 'mini-secretariats' with NREGA funds was supposed to 'ensure the effectiveness of Indian panchayats'. In November 2009, the ministry passed an order that included a new item among the list of approved NREGA works projects: the construction of citizen service centres called 'Rajiv Gandhi Sewa Kendras'.[59] This was widely viewed as a clumsy attempt to further link NREGA to the Gandhi name, and to the Congress more generally—what one disaffected civil servant called 'political convergence'.[60] Activists began to voice a range of concerns about the direction being taken by UPA-2. Jean Dreze called convergence 'dangerous'—a dilution of the energy that could go into fixing basic problems with the scheme's implementation, such as assuring that the minimum wage was paid. A showy makeover would inevitably draw a much wider array of government stakeholders into discussions, and thereby delay action on key problems such as the failure to institutionalise (or provide government support to) the social audit process in most states. The idea of permitting NREGA funds to go to private-sector contractors was considered a particularly egregious betrayal of the programme's original conception. Dreze was dead set against proposals to reduce the proportion of NREGA funds devoted to unskilled labour carried out on *kuccha* works.[61] The minister did not react well to criticism, possibly because much of it was voiced by activists from his home state of Rajasthan. When, in 2010, a journalist asked him about his differences with activists, Joshi 'began striking the palm of his right hand against his left fist'. He reiterated that he was 'a minister', and that the Congress Party had decided to pursue convergence. His voice 'filled with rage', as Joshi asked, 'Do I have to go by the mandate of my party or by Jean Dreze?'[62] In 2011, shortly before leaving his post, the minister, backed by other Congress leaders, helped to ensure the departure of both Dreze and Aruna Roy from the Central Employment Guarantee Council.[63]

Governance issues were mostly addressed in the UPA-2 reforms through a largely quixotic attempt to improve bureaucratic coordination. Because we have focused in this book on two relatively well performing states, it is helpful to consider how the central government sought to engage Bihar, a state that at the time had perhaps the worst reputation for governance in India, though Bihar Chief Minister Nitish Kumar had struggled mightily to turn things around. The Empowered Committee mentioned earlier in this chapter noted that, '[d]ue to non-appointment of Members, the [State Employment Guarantee] Council has not been operationalised' in Bihar.[64] Encapsulating the fraught relationship between national and provincial levels, Bihar's MIS and the online platform maintained by the central ministry were found to be incompatible, and '[t]hus the State needs to explore possible convergence of the data generated' by these two systems.[65] The Empowered Committee urged Bihar's officials to take the lead on upgrading this crucial element of NREGA's accountability infrastructure to ensure the creation of more durable rural assets to support agricultural productivity. The reforms, Bihar's officials were told, 'must be carried out in a campaign mode', meaning that officials would need to be given wide, cross-departmental latitude to carry out specific objectives. The campaign mode of governance for poverty-reduction was very closely associated with one of the two states that are the focus of this book: Madhya Pradesh. The Rajiv Gandhi Watershed Mission was a prime example of this model, the intention of which is to cut through regulations that prevent any one official from taking substantive action sufficient to dispose of a particular case. However, the only concrete commitment extracted by the Empowered Committee was that the Bihar government would designate a 'nodal officer' to ensure 'timely resolution of VIP references and complaints received on implementation of MGNREGA'.[66]

By mid-2012, NREGA online system possessed a number of admirable new features. First it provided a portal for programme implementation agencies to conduct their quite distinct business transactions. A list of tabs across the top of the website referenced different categories of user-district councils, local officials, and workers themselves. It was possible to search by either district or block, with pull-down menus indicating specific projects under construction. Anyone could thus arrive at the list of works in one block of Gujarat; then click on Muster Roll No. 52393; and using the Work Code associated with it, see which category of project was being undertaken. This system had great potential to promote accountability.

Still, it was missing crucial components. Despite the move towards electronic muster rolls, as of late 2012, data on work and wages in Orissa, Rajasthan, and other states were still largely entered into the IT system at the block level. This long journey from paper to pixel opened a wide array of opportunities for manipulation. In some of Gujarat's districts, data was apparently entered at the *gram panchayat* level, but in others, it was entered at the block level.[67] In Bihar, the state government entered little more than half of the data (58 per cent) it was required to supply to NREGA online portal in accordance with MoRD rules.[68] Moreover, some systems operated online, others offline. Those that had moved furthest ahead with implementation were being 'requested [by the MoRD in New Delhi] to host teams from other states' for cross-learning exchanges.[69] This is just one example of a complex process of state-level adaptation, which involved state governments responding to the demands of various interests and gauging the capacity of their own administrative machineries. It is a common pattern of policy implementation in India.

How to execute the convergence agenda triggered the greatest divergence of opinion. The technocrats wanted NREGA works to be tied to specific targets, processes, and labour-market models. By contrast, the more politically-minded Sharad Pawar—minister of agriculture and chair of the Group of Ministers (GoM) responsible for addressing conditions of drought—pressed hard for an increase in the number of days of NREGA work—from 100 to 150—in drought-affected districts. Under reforms introduced in 2012, an additional fifty days of employment was supposed to be made available for Adivasis seeking work under NREGA.[70] This trend led fiscal hawks to worry about the cost implications of such a change. Some claimed that expanding NREGA in this way would crowd out other programme priorities. Another concern, voiced privately, was that it would be hard, if not impossible, for the Congress Party or its coalition allies—only one of which actually ran a state government—to reap political dividends from any such expansion of the programme's coverage. Some Congress leaders argued that such a 'giveaway' would reinforce the image of a desperate government resorting to populist gestures.

The effects of NREGA 2.0 reforms—whether grouped under the term convergence or any other analytical construct—were hardly impressive. This was partly the result of a distinct lack of enthusiasm for reform among the key central government ministries involved, particularly the Ministry of Finance. The lack of sustained efforts to encourage social audits was particularly notable. After the initial spurt of reform activity in the first eighteen months of UPA-2, the government was engulfed in a succession of damaging controversies. Thereafter, official efforts to improve the functioning of the programme were haphazard, and commitments were not matched by follow-up action. Committee reports recommending policy revisions resulted in very few concrete changes to operating procedures. Even the examples of 'successful' convergence publicised by the MoRD—such as a horticulture development programme in Andhra Pradesh—were highly questionable in terms of the targeting of benefits.[71] It was the government's focus on such reforms as the expansion of permissible works, at the expense of ensuring that minimum wages were paid, that ultimately led to fairly widespread disillusionment with the UPA-2 government among the most ardent believers in NREGA's potential. When, in May 2013, Aruna Roy announced her decision not to seek another term on the NAC, she used the occasion to criticise the government for refusing to abide by a Karnataka High Court judgment requiring the payment of minimum wages to NREGA workers. In a letter to NAC chair Sonia Gandhi, Roy stated that her efforts to push for better implementation of NREGA would thenceforth need to 'continue outside the NAC'.[72]

Still, the dream of convergence was being pursued all the way up through the 2014 general election. Rural Development Minister Jairam Ramesh said that '2014–15 should be celebrated as Convergence Year for MNREGA', and called on 'officials to bring MNREGA workers under the Rashtriya Swasthya Bima Yojana', or National Health Insurance Programme.[73]

The late UPA-2 period saw the airing of several governance and accountability reform ideas. In 2013, for instance, regulations were proposed that would have involved chartered accountants in auditing the US $6 billion spent annually on NREGA.[74] 'One of the most important decisions' that Ramesh says he took during this period—in 2012—was 'to allow cash payments' to NREGA workers, because '[i]n many parts of India there are no bank accounts or post offices', and often 'no connectivity'. It was not clear whether the government regretted its reform of three years earlier, which required wages to be paid exclusively through worker bank accounts, but Ramesh portrayed this decision as evidence of his ministry's willingness to respond to implementation realities. He even suggested an alternative form of accountability to replace the electronic paper trail of the banking system: every cash payment would thenceforth be video-recorded in front of a group of at least five people.[75]

* * *

Debates over NREGA often seem to have a predictable quality to them. All sides insist they are empowering the poor. There is a sense at times that the tactics deployed on all sides are designed more to create a general impression rather than to convince on their own merits. Dreze claims that NREGA's most implacable foes sometimes use methods that Noam Chomsky called 'propaganda techniques in democratic societies'. NREGA supporters, Dreze says, were constantly subjected to 'flak'—to 'a barrage of attacks', often lacking in logical consistency but large in number. The focus of these attacks were 'ideas that challenge the interests of established power'.[76] Chomsky's definition of flak involves personal attacks on conceptual innovators—something Dreze says happened when a leading opponent of the programme called pro-NREGA activists 'ignorant' and 'brazen', not to mention 'liars'.[77] The disagreements between the pro- and anti-NREGA camps, Dreze asserts, were not only personal; they remained exceedingly raw for a considerable time after the events he describes took place. Jairam Ramesh's backing for NREGA, as a NAC member and thereafter, earned him the label of 'turncoat' in a section of the business press, an insult he took to heart, apparently. The other half of 'flakking', Dreze notes, was to use dubious statistics. And on this count, even the few pieces of data cited in press analysis of the CAG report on NREGA provide a glimpse.

By mid-2013, when the Bhagwati vs. Sen debate outlined above was in full swing and the 2014 general election was in sight, NREGA was increasingly discussed not on its own merits, but as a symbolic representation of a package of rights-based legislation, and thus of a particular approach to addressing the multi-dimensional nature of poverty. Discussions of NREGA were especially evident in the debates that accompanied the UPA government's final round of governance reforms—including the Judicial Standards and Accountability Bill, the Grievance Redressal Bill, and others. The one that most closely resembled NREGA, however—one that could without difficulty be classified as enshrining an additional governance right—was the National Food Security Bill 2011, which after a drawn-out final stage of debate and amendment, eventually emerged as the National Food Security Act of 2013. Arguments about the overall approach and specific provisions of the Bill were increasingly couched in terms of the larger 'rights agenda' pursued by the UPA government. One set of critics complained that it was a continuation of the 'dole' mentality of bureaucrats and activists who were either unable or unwilling to grasp the genuinely empowering effects of economic growth. By allegedly breeding a 'culture of dependency' among poor and marginalised people, the UPA's rights-based laws were said to be undercutting individual initiative, as well as diverting resources away from the kinds of investments that could help to transform the rural economy.

What added to the sense of NREGA being a political platform as much as a welfare initiative, was the lobbying that accompanied the frequent revisions to programme regulations. The potential importance of even small rule changes—whether regarding worksite management or funding formulas—made it essential for CSOs to track and influence the many reform proposals working their way through the state and central bureaucracies at any given time. Activists also had to make NREGA workers and other stakeholders aware of regulatory changes that were ultimately adopted.

One legitimate reason why coverage of corruption under NREGA received such prominence in India's business press, was that the programme was perceived as (indirectly) crucial to ensuring the political sustainability of economic reform itself. Corruption in NREGA is tiny compared to the massive sums that arise from urban land deals or kickbacks from industrialists, especially (but not only) in the extractive industries. But the abuses that afflict schemes such as NREGA may be more consequential because such programmes are supposed to compensate, however inadequately, the 'losers' from economic reform.[78] Endemic corruption thus undermines an essential part of the political strategy for forestalling effective demands for a return to a statist development model. Moreover, the widespread abuse that plagues social welfare programs is precisely the kind of corruption for which the market has no real antidote. Where excessive business regulation provides officials with the ability to abuse their positions of discretion to obtain illicit income, de-regulation remains a possible remedy. But only the most ardent neoliberals hold out much hope for exclusively market-based solutions to counteracting liberalisation's adverse effects on vulnerable communities.

8

IMPLICATIONS

This chapter draws together the findings presented in the course of the book thus far in order to advance a series of arguments concerning the relationship between politics and NREGA. These arguments are of three main types, distinguished according to the breadth of their implications. The first, most narrow-gauged set of arguments engages with existing analyses of NREGA that characterise its significance or evaluate its performance. The second set links our analysis of how NREGA has been implemented in practice—including the marked variations between jurisdictions and over time—to broader debates in the study of Indian politics and political economy. Third, we put forward arguments intended to address longstanding issues of theoretical concern that reach beyond the Indian case—particularly issues that arise in the comparative study of development politics.

The book's six main claims—introduced originally in Chapter 1—are divided among the three categories outlined above: two claims related to evaluating NREGA; two directed at debates regarding India's political economy; and two addressed to the comparative and theoretical literature on development politics. Where appropriate, we briefly illustrate the connections between these claims. We conclude the chapter, and the volume, with a brief epilogue, which situates NREGA amidst India's 2014 general election campaign and its outcome.

Assessing NREGA's Performance and Significance

Our first category consists of a pair of claims that respond to the fairly widespread tendency among policy analysts and media commentators to characterise NREGA as a well-meaning failure—a doomed experiment that became, over time, the poster-child for liberal paternalism run amok. In response, we argue that:

1. *The process of implementing NREGA, for all its faults, has improved the well-being of tens of millions of poor and marginalised people.*

The evidence surveyed in this book, including both large-N studies and our own mainly qualitative field research, confirm the positive impact of the programme. Despite its uneven coverage, and at times halting implementation, NREGA has provided a vital lifeline to people living with persistent economic insecurity. This is not the view of all observers, naturally. Surjit Bhalla describes the UPA government's anti-poverty programmes and rights-based initiatives—of which NREGA is the largest—as 'policies meant to help the poor but which ended up hurting them massively instead'.[1] It is deeply perverse to argue that NREGA damaged the poor. It is a claim that has been repeated widely and demands a response. Evidence provided in Chapter 6 demonstrates that poor and marginalised groups have gained disproportionately from this programme. The data presented below gives some idea of the progress achieved, which a knee-jerk dismissal of NREGA obscures.

Table 8.1: Percentage of Total Person-days Worked (all-India)

	Scheduled Castes	*Scheduled Tribes*
Person-days, 2006–8	25–31%	24–36%
Person-days, 2008–12	28.8%	21.3%
Share of population	16.2%	8.2%

Sources: NREGA website, nrega.nic.in, DMU Reports.

Our findings on NREGA's pro-poor impact are also consistent with the positive impact that UPA policies in general had on rural India during that government's time in power. One authoritative study, directed by a formidable research team,[2] surveyed 41,554 households across India in 2011–12—the very same households they had surveyed in 2004–5. Their objective was to determine whether economic growth in recent years had been 'inclusive'. Inclusion was a key objective of UPA policies, which sought to ensure, first, that rural dwellers were not left behind as urban centres boomed, and second, that poor people (in both rural and urban areas) made significant gains. The study found that between 2005 and 2012, real average household incomes in rural areas had increased by 5 per cent annually—almost twice the increase of 2.6 per cent experienced in towns and cities over the same period. When the researchers adjusted their calculations to reflect household size, the growth of rural incomes was even more impressive: an annual average of 7.2 per cent.

Government policies—in which NREGA loomed very large—had clearly helped to make growth more 'inclusive' in rural-urban terms. To examine income group variations, investigators separated survey respondents into six social groups. While per capita household incomes among high-caste Hindus (the most prosperous group) increased by 4.6 per cent per annum, significantly larger gains were made by all other social categories, all of which were economically inferior. Castes from the OBC category saw their per capita income increase by 7.3 per cent. For Dalits, the increase was 7.8 per cent; for Adivasis, 5.7 per cent; and for Muslims, 5.4 per cent.[3] These last three groups include many of the poorest people in rural India, a group that is overrepresented among agricultural labourers, who saw their wages triple between 2004–5 and 2011–12.[4] These and other findings are consistent with the positive picture that emerges from our reading of what NREGA was able to achieve during more or less the same period—the period during which, it should be noted, NREGA was most energetically implemented. The poorest gained disproportionately from the programme.

A further issue of genuine concern is the degree to which NREGA has benefited the 'non-poor'. It has been carefully investigated by a research team led by Raghav Gaiha. Their evidence, like ours, indicates that many people who might be considered 'non-poor' have benefited under the programme—although there are significant variations from state to state. But they explicitly resist facile claims that in this respect NREGA has been 'an unmitigated failure'.[5] Bhalla, after a crude calculation, writes ludicrously that 82.35 per cent of the programme's funds went to the non-poor.[6]

Much (but not all) of the explanation for the resources that have flowed to the 'non-poor' is provided by the ability of local leaders to skim wages through the use of bogus muster rolls. There is, however, a second and major part of the explanation which makes us somewhat less concerned than Gaiha and his colleagues about gains for the 'non-poor'. Many people who might be seen as 'non-poor' were in reality poor enough to need NREGA wages, and so chose to work alongside others who are regarded as 'poor'. A meticulous investigation in Andhra Pradesh by a team from the Administrative Staff College of India (noted above) found that numerous members of the locally-dominant

Reddy caste, who are conventionally considered to be among the 'non-poor', faced sufficiently serious deprivation to seek work under the programme. They were 'non-poor' in name, but not in reality. And in exercising their right to work and labouring alongside people from disadvantaged castes on NREGA work sites, invidious social barriers between these different groups were eroded.[7] Our field work in Rajasthan and Madhya Pradesh yielded similar findings, as have field investigations in Tamil Nadu and Karnataka.

Bhalla's claim that those programmes 'ended up hurting them [the poor] massively' is based primarily on the claim that fiscal profligacy (and particularly the injection of cash into the countryside) fuelled inflation, depressed the value of wages, and choked growth by crowding out private investment. His economic worldview does not allow for the possibility that NREGA might have had other impacts. In fact, far from creating a dole culture, NREGA was designed to overcome passivity by making poor villagers proactive participants in the public sphere—often for the first time. Our evidence plainly indicates that it has succeeded—not entirely, but to a considerable extent, given the extremely challenging circumstances that confront poor rural people.

Some critics of NREGA argue that it is too expensive. Those claims need to be assessed in the context of the funds that have been available to central and state governments in recent years. Table 8.2 provides data from India's central bank on gross revenues since 2002–3. They reveal a surge in revenues before, and especially since, NREGA began operating in 2006.

Table 8.2: Gross Revenues of Central and State Governments
(in billions of rupees)

	Central government	State governments
2002–3	2,162.66	2,577.07
2003–4	2,543.48	2,899.61
2004–5	3,049.58	3,291.53
2005–6	3,674.74	3,824.58
2006–7	4,735.12	4,561.84
2007–8	5,931.47	5,218.44
2008–9	6,052.99	5,483.18
2009–10	6,245.28	5,628.97
2010–11	7,868.88	7,358.20
2011–12	9,324.40	8,620.01

Source: Reserve Bank of India, 'Direct and Indirect Tax Revenues of Central and State Governments', 2013, Table 116. Available at: http://dbie.rbi.org/DBIE/dbie.rbi?site=publications.

These figures need to be adjusted for inflation, but they plainly show that state and central governments have had vastly more money to spend in recent years than they did twelve years earlier. In the period since NREGA's inception in 2006, those revenues have increased more rapidly than have the costs of the programme. Nor has the decline in economic growth rates since 2011 been matched by a corresponding decline in revenues. They have continued to increase. Even in the financial year 2013–14, when GDP growth stood at 4.7 per cent (a steep fall from a high of 10.3 per cent four years earlier),[8] revenues still increased by over 20 per cent. With such abundant—and growing—resources in hand, why should NREGA be deemed unaffordable?

Finally, let us briefly consider NREGA's impact beyond India, which demonstrates that the political dimensions—for good or ill, depending on the eye of the beholder—are considered central to its appeal. Many donor governments, international organisations, and development NGOs have been intrigued by NREGA from its earliest days. The World Bank—which is generally suspicious of large-scale intrusions into the operation of markets—went from early skepticism about NREGA (particularly its cost and the potential for leakage, precisely the worries of India's finance ministry when the NREG Bill was being debated in 2004–5);[9] to veiled criticism in the Bank's 2009 *World Development Report* (*WDR*), which suggested that it had distorted rural labour markets by 'crowding out private employers' and 'constraining the process of labor reallocation out of agriculture and into more productive sectors';[10] to a relatively balanced, if non-committal, assessment of the programme in *WDR 2013*;[11] all the way to robust advocacy for programmes such as NREGA in *WDR 2014*, in which it was appreciated not only for the financial 'safety net' it provides, but also the ways in which the programme's rights-based orientation 'promotes dignity' among marginalised people, including rural women.[12] By 2015, the NREGA model was being invoked by the UN as the kind of social protection initiative that, if suitably reformed and adapted to diverse national contexts, could be a central pillar for advancing gender equality. The 2015–16 edition of UN Women's flagship publication, *Progress of the World's Women*, noted the shortcomings of NREGA (particularly the household-based entitlement of 100 days of employment), but was impressed enough that it included within its conclusions a recommendation that such rights-based programmes, which underpin a broader 'right to work', be instituted as a means of improving women's income, enhancing their engagement with the public sphere, and promoting their participation in both the labour market and the formal financial sector.[13]

As early as 2007, NREGA had caught the attention of the International Labour Organisation (ILO), which encouraged governments in other developing countries to adopt similar programmes. Several have considered this, two of which are worth noting in particular. An official delegation from China visited New Delhi in 2012 to compare notes on various development programmes. The only Indian initiative about which the visitors wanted to learn was NREGA. Detailed discussions ensued and the Chinese took extensive notes, though they eventually explained that they had no interest in its rights-based and demand-driven features.[14] If such a programme is introduced in China—which at the time of writing had not yet happened—it would be 'top-down' in character, involving the bestowal of government largesse upon largely passive recipients. So that encounter does not qualify as an example of NREGA's wider impact—although it is the Chinese and not the Indian officials who bear the responsibility for that.

However, a second episode is more encouraging. In South Africa, it is estimated that more than half of people between the ages of 18 and 35 have never been employed, and the most severe poverty there is in rural areas. To tackle this problem, in 2007, a researcher and civil society leader who was advising key government ministries began considering the adoption of a programme similar to NREGA. Elected local councils in South Africa are weak as a result of serious flaws in the design of the country's newly decentralised system,[15] so another means of stimulating grassroots participation had to be found. The solution was to draw civil society organisations that promote collective action by local communities into a fledgling programme to organise local residents to select and then oversee works projects. Early pilot initiatives showed promise, and senior government figures then endorsed what is now called the Community Work Programme.

There were, however, teething problems that generated scepticism within the South African government. In 2012, one of us was invited to discuss details of our research on NREGA with representatives of the Presidency and Treasury, and to give a public lecture on some of the key findings. At the lecture, the head of the powerful Congress of South African Trade Unions—which forms a core part of the African National Congress-led ruling alliance—made a rousing call for such a programme. His presence ensured that this was televised. Thereafter, the government committed itself more fully to this initiative. It hoped to expand it so that the programme could play a major role in government efforts to provide work, eventually, for as many as six million people—although at the end of 2013, only 195,000 were employed under the scheme.[16] This is the most telling example to date of NREGA's direct impact outside India.

In summary, despite disappointments and ambiguities, NREGA has had a substantial constructive impact upon the material well being of poor people, the opportunities available to them, and their political capacity, which is an important dimension of their 'poverty'. Because it is self-targeting, it does not exclude the large number of poor people who have been prevented from obtaining 'below poverty line' cards. It has disproportionately benefited the poorest rural dwellers—a remarkable achievement since most other poverty programmes fail to do so.

This brings us to our second key claim, which like the first, addresses what we see as a major shortcoming in much of the existing analysis of NREGA's performance and its significance as a milestone in the development of India's welfare state.

2. *NREGA's political aims and implications must be recognised in order to appreciate its significance as a development initiative.*

The most vehement and ideologically-driven criticisms levelled at NREGA are largely based on a misunderstanding of the political intentions of its architects as well as both its short- and longer-term political implications. A more accurate assessment of its performance and larger significance as a human development intervention requires an understanding of NREGA's essentially political nature. As one close observer of the UPA's flagship welfare programmes put it, 'the politics of entitlement becomes important not just as legislative rights which can be enforced and justiciable, but as a participative political process'.[17] NREGA is part of an activist political agenda, rooted in a particular model of political change—one based on a commitment to progressive legal reform coupled with a pursuit of what NREGA's architects and main exponents have called 'democratic struggle'.[18] NREGA must, therefore, be viewed as a deeply 'politically embedded' initiative—one whose political implications are sufficiently far-reaching to qualify it as an 'audacious reform', to use Grindle's term.[19] NREGA's political dimension is real, and not a product of academic over-interpretation. The Government of India's own 2010 'Report to the People' on NREGA's first four years in operation identified impacts 'beyond wage employment' that had allowed NREGA to 'promote multiplier effects'. Among these were 'social capital formation', improvements to local 'democratic process', and enhanced capacity among 'the most vulnerable people' to 'articulate needs and negotiate their rights'.[20] As we have argued throughout this book, NREGA's architects expected the procedurally demanding nature of the programme to severely challenge and expose the limitations of the local Indian state. By incentivising a form of continuous democratic struggle, however, NREGA channeled discontent in ways that enhanced the political awareness, skills, confidence, and connections of people who engaged with the programme.

NREGA created not just a framework and a set of processes through which people could voice their demands and obtain a measure of accountability; it also created new opportunities for labour organisers, such as the New Trade Union Initiative (NTUI).[21] The NTUI and like-minded organisations seek to make inroads among informal sector workers, notably agricultural workers, who face huge barriers to even the most rudimentary forms of collective action.[22] Local manifestations of this impulse could be seen in many parts of India. A fledgling union of rural workers in Gujarat called the Grameen Mazdoor Sabha (GMS) decided soon after NREGA was passed that it would prioritise efforts to organise NREGA workers by channeling their demands to key implementation authorities in Dang, Panchmahal, Narmada, and Sabarkantha districts. In 2008, GMS helped workers to become aware of their rights, to demand access to project documents, and to file court cases against local authorities that were not distributing job cards or providing work within fifteen days. In 2010, a rural workers union in Karnataka called the Grameen Coolie Karmikara Sangathana (GCKS) helped to organise an extended protest outside the *zilla panchayat* of Raichur district. Their demands were for the payment of wages that were, in some cases, months overdue. Eventually, the elected *zilla panchayat* members negotiated with the group to cover past wages, though demands for disciplinary action against officials who failed to discharge their responsibilities under NREGA were not acted upon. A memorandum submitted by the GCKS to the minister of rural development in September 2010 highlighted the widespread violations undertaken by the Raichur district administration. In 2011, this group and others took part in a protest, held in the state capital of Bangalore, which demanded accountability for the state government's lacklustre implementation of NREGA, including its failure to pay the minimum wage or to check corruption. The ombudsmen appointed at the district level were seen to be ineffectively monitoring the programme.[23]

Existing analyses of NREGA have criticised it for fostering welfare dependency, with adverse medium- and long-term effects on the poor. Others have echoed that view by stating that NREGA was 'only a subsidy'.[24] Such comments are ignorant and misleading, suggesting (inaccurately) that there is great passivity among programme beneficiaries. In fact, NREGA is nothing like the 'dole' or a 'handout'.[25] NREGA workers perform hard manual labour, often on difficult terrain and in sweltering heat. They are not supine idlers who wait for government assistance to come their way. Commentators who describe NREGA in those terms also demonstrate their limited understanding of 'poverty'. They tend to operate with a narrowly economistic definition of 'poverty'—as a severe shortage of incomes and assets. They tend to see economic growth as the main or only means of reducing poverty. Some of them go further and pour scorn on attempts to make growth more 'inclusive' by pursuing redistribution.[26] A broader definition of poverty makes more sense—a definition that recognises that poverty also entails a severe shortage of freedoms, opportunities, and capabilities. By enhancing the 'political capacity' of poor people, NREGA has addressed a key dimension of their poverty, while simultaneously increasing their incomes.

NREGA gave all rural households the right to proactively demand work. That has actually happened a great deal of the time. Once they began performing labour under the programme, women workers moved into the public sphere, where NREGA projects were being undertaken. Women accounted for a large minority of person-days worked—usually well above the 30 per cent minimum stipulated in the Act. Many women who previously had seldom left their homes have taken up NREGA employment, and in the process have found themselves—for the first time in their lives—taking part in public activities unaccompanied by male relatives.

NREGA also sought to give poor villagers a voice in setting priorities and in social audits of the programme through village-level mass meetings (*gram sabhas*). It is clear from studies of democratic decentralisation across the developing world that it is very difficult to make such processes work well. Local leaders are reluctant to share information and expose themselves to cross-examination at such meetings.[27] But the administrators of NREGA in New Delhi made strenuous efforts to make this happen, and despite disappointments, such meetings actually occurred far more often than the dismal international norm. Thus, some headway was made in catalysing this type of engagement among the rural poor.

NREGA's architects on the NAC knew that *gram sabhas*, social audits, and other transparency mechanisms built into the programme would encounter problems. But by making the process transparent—and by requiring that at least half of the programme's funds pass to local councils, whose actions are far more transparent than the workings of line ministries—they ensured that irregularities in implementation and attempts to steal from workers' wages would be more visible to poor villagers. The architects of NREGA hoped this would inspire discontent among the poor and encourage them to forge more connections to other workers and to allies among the non-poor.

The desire to create institutions that could fuel and channel discontent, in the interest of holding public officials to account, was arguably the dominant theme behind NREGA's complex administrative architecture. The Act's architects were under no illusion that these flawed institutional forms—the result of many political compromises at the drafting stage—would perform these oversight roles perfectly. But smaller, contingent advantages could be obtained nonetheless, including opportunities for critical voices. The Central Employment Guarantee Council (CEGC), for instance, was for most of NREGA's existence, prevented from playing the macro-monitoring role assigned to it, not least because of interference by the ruling party, which sought—especially in UPA-2—to close ranks against erstwhile social-activist allies whose criticism had become a major irritant. The short-circuiting of the CEGC—convening meetings irregularly, not issuing reports in a timely fashion, withholding information from members—is not surprising to those who have seen earlier institutional experiments meet a similar fate. Where the CEGC did make a difference, however, is at a broader level of accountability—the process of seeking 'answerability', a reasoned account by public officials for their actions (and inactions). Non-governmental members of the CEGC gained the legitimacy conferred by association with a statutory body. CEGC membership was never going to endow great stature, but it did permit sympathetic members of the government or of parliament to include CEGC members in informal meetings in ways that prevented less-sympathetic (or outright hostile) officials from excluding outsiders. Media outlets seeking comment on aspects of government policy (including revisions to existing policy) often turned to CEGC members. CEGC members also obtained access to information. Much of the documentation—such as expenditure data at various levels of aggregation—would in theory have been available to any member of the public under the RTIA, but there would have been (greater) delays in obtaining it. By getting routine access to at least some privileged information (in more or less real time) about policy development matters—such as internal reports on the performance of post offices in paying wages according to revised NREGA rules—those non-governmental members of the CEGC who sought to closely scrutinise NREGA implementation could ask more penetrating questions, and highlight discrepancies between officials' statements and other government data.[28]

The reduction in person-days worked under NREGA beginning around 2010 was seized upon by the programme's critics as evidence that NREGA's failings have put off would-be labourers. A more sophisticated understanding of the political dynamics at work yields a more nuanced and accurate interpretation of this troubling phenomenon. By way of illustration, consider the following figures from Rajasthan, one of India's generally higher-performing states, drawn from an analysis by Deepta Chopra:[29]

Table 8.3: Decline in Person-days of Employment in Rajasthan Under NREGA

Year	Person-days worked
2008–9	482,955,000
2009–10	449,809,000
2010–11	259,518,753
2011–12	212,055,139
2012–13	220,303,090

Over 200 million person-days in one state in a single year is still an impressive figure, but this downward trend is worrying nonetheless. Why did it take place? Some commentators would have us believe that demand from rural households had declined because they have experienced so many problems with the programme.[30] If their argument is correct, it follows that NREGA should be wound down—which is what some of these critics desire. However, there is solid evidence to demonstrate that they are wrong—that, in fact, demand for employment remains high. Something else has likely triggered the decline in NREGA person-days worked.

One of the key factors explaining the decline is deeply rooted in politics: the increasing unwillingness among bureaucrats and elected *panchayat* leaders at the local and block (sub-district) levels to implement the programme. They have reduced the number of local works projects, and thus the number of employment opportunities. Their reluctance is the result of several interlinked factors. First, as we have noted, powerful political actors at the local and sub-district levels have come to understand that the direct and indirect costs of siphoning funds from workers' wages, which constitute the bulk of NREGA spending, have become prohibitively high. The programme's transparency mechanisms, especially following the introduction of new safeguards, pose

serious dangers that corrupt officials will be found out and held accountable—
if not on the first attempt, then on the second or third. This is an important
part of the explanation for the decline in employment days created under
NREGA over recent years.[31]

These new safeguards emerged in conjunction with the introduction of the
Electronic Fund Management System (EFMS) in 2011. In theory, EFMS
withdrawals from *panchayat* bank accounts would automatically occur during
the processing of NREGA projects. Electronic submission of muster rolls, and
of sanctions for works commissioned or completed, triggered payments
directly to the accounts of workers and of suppliers and transporters of materials. This payment architecture makes it more difficult, though not impossible,
for *panchayat* leaders to earn illicit income by processing false invoices for the
purchase and transport of materials. In one respect, such a system has the
effect of increasing the leverage of vendors: having received funds into their
accounts, they are in a position to negotiate a larger share of whatever corrup-
tion-related rents might be available. In practice, officials' faith in e-govern-
ance collided with limitations in essential IT infrastructure. Because
panchayats frequently possessed no reliable internet connection, *panchayat*
members had to make additional journeys to (sometimes distant) block headquarters to submit written records, which were then keyed into the IT system
by a block-level clerk, whose superiors are particularly well positioned to
derive further illicit income from this process.

Another important reason for the decline in person days worked was the
closer relationship enjoyed in recent years between elected *panchayat* members and two groups at the grassroots who are unhappy with NREGA: contractors (whose participation is banned) and landowners, who are aggrieved
because the existence of the programme can (1) erode bonds of dependence
which have long locked poor people into relationships of subordination, and
(2) drive up wages for agricultural labour. Landowners in many states have
worked to gain closer control over local *panchayats* as their resources and
powers have grown due to NREGA. Indeed, many *panchayat* members and
leaders are themselves substantial landowners or aspiring contractors, or in
some cases, both. By (illegally) reducing the supply of NREGA works, which
suits local labour-employing farmers (thus satisfying a grateful constituency),
elected councillors also benefit themselves by in effect raising the pressure on
NREGA job applicants to pay a higher share of their wages as kickbacks to
administrators who offer them one of the increasingly scarce jobs.

A third reason for the decline in person-days worked under NREGA was a
wave of fiscal dread within the upper reaches of the Government of India from

2011 onward. The finance ministry, whose senior officials never liked the NREGA concept when it was first floated as part of the coalition government's 'minimum programme' back in 2004, became increasingly assertive about the government's need to combat inflation, which (not coincidentally) was seen as potentially more damaging to a ruling party facing elections than perceived underperformance of NREGA. Since the programme accounted for something like 1 per cent of GDP, it was an attractive target for fiscal conservatives attempting to find budgetary savings. Of course, the finance ministry does not, in theory, possess the necessary authority to decide whether, under a demand-led programme, workers will be deprived of their right to work, and to be paid. In practice, however, the central government can use its bureaucratic leverage to slow down NREGA job-creating machinery. It has relied of late on an administrative procedure—not releasing new funds until all funds from previous works have been completely exhausted—that has had the effect of slowing down NREGA implementation in many states.

That the decline in NREGA employment is not the result of waning demand for work among poor people is apparent from the results of an initiative launched by the MoRD in New Delhi in late 2013. Its purpose was to encourage poor people to register their demands for NREGA employment with local authorities. It is called the *Kaam Mango Abhiyan* and was undertaken in one district in each of six states,[32] prior to a nation-wide roll-out on 2 February 2014. The initiative involves government officials working with national and local civil society organisations to acquaint poor villagers with their rights under the Act, but also to put pressure on *panchayat* leaders and bureaucrats at the block level to implement the programme more assiduously. During its first three months, this initiative triggered a marked increase in demand in the six districts where it began—in some cases, by as much as 150 per cent. Further evidence of latent demand emerged from the work of a young civil servant in Rajasthan who served as the Collector (chief bureaucrat) in two districts. His efforts to stimulate demand, and to press subordinate officials to respond to it, produced impressive results.[33] The demand is there. The problem is the unwillingness of powerful actors at multiple levels to permit NREGA to operate properly, and in particular to enforce rules that require disciplinary and further investigative action when audits reveal a persistent pattern of corruption.

Critics who claim that huge sums are being stolen from NREGA need to consider this evidence. If substantial profits were being made from the programme, would one really expect to see key actors at the local and sub-district levels reducing the number and scale of local works projects? To do so would be clearly to deprive themselves of opportunities for self-enrichment.

Another set of critics argues that direct cash transfers to poor people are preferable to NREGA, and should replace it. They claim that the programme is somehow patronising since its architects took it upon themselves to decide that poor villagers need opportunities to earn wages. We do not dispute the utility of cash transfers. One of us has co-authored a book which clearly demonstrates that in Brazil they have helped to reduce poverty.[34] But critics who propose that cash transfers should be made in place of NREGA misperceive NREGA's political intent. It seeks to do far more than to provide funds to poor people. If that were its only aim, then a reliable system of cash transfers would possibly be as good or better. But NREGA also targets other more overtly political dimensions of poverty. It attempts to encourage proactive demands for work and provides avenues for collective complaint—unlike cash transfers in which recipients are passive, isolated individuals. It therefore makes more sense to provide cash transfers in addition to NREGA rather than in place of it.[35]

Activists in India sometimes criticise conditional cash-transfer programmes, which link payments to desireable activities (such as keeping girls in school), as overly paternalistic and directive. NREGA does not incentivise household decision-making so minutely—it merely makes paid work universally available in rural areas.[36] Moreover, because modern society awards higher de facto citizenship status to workforce participants—as feminist scholars have argued[37]— NREGA has the advantage of indirectly conferring additional opportunities upon people who participate as workers. It is for these reasons that the ability of NREGA to improve the political capacities of poor people, and to challenge certain aspects of rural status hierarchies (a topic discussed in Chapter 6, on NREGA's non-material impacts), are vital to the creation of a self-sustaining dynamic of political mobilisation.[38]

Finally, it should be noted that the movement towards—which is to say the growing political acceptance of—cash-based schemes for such benefits as old-age pensions are building largely on an edifice constructed under NREGA. Because revised rules adopted in 2009 required NREGA wages to be paid to workers through bank (or post office) accounts, it triggered a massive increase in the degree to which people entered the formal financial sector. By late 2013, 93 million new accounts had been opened by poor people as a consequence of NREGA.[39] This change enabled poor villagers to gain access to other state and central government programmes that offer benefits only available through such accounts, including various forms of government-supported insurance.

The issue of NREGA's affordability, discussed earlier, must also be viewed from a political perspective, in which the reasons for the composition of the government's subsidy bill is also considered. As one commentator put it,

There has to be an understanding of where the subsidies really go. The government spends a little over 1 per cent of GDP on food security and employment generation (NREGA) but spends more than twice that much on subsidising electricity, cooking gas and other petroleum products, including diesel for luxury cars as well as fertiliser subsidies, which go primarily to rich farmers.[40]

In short, it is largely the political leverage, not the developmental or equity-based merits of their claims for support, that accounts for the success that these interest groups—well-off farmers and urban consumers—have had in making their own subsidies nearly untouchable.

A final, subtly worded but ultimately quite extreme critique of NREGA needs to be considered. A team at the World Bank argued that the programme is 'hurting economic development and poverty alleviation' because it erects 'policy barriers to internal mobility' within India. They focused specifically on mobility from villages to cities, which they see as the key way out of poverty for countries like India. The case is made in a complex geographical analysis and largely by implication, but the message is there. It should be stressed that many other World Bank analysts do not share this view, but this argument was set out quite prominently in the Bank's flagship annual publication, the *World Development Report, 2009: Reshaping Economic Geography*.[41]

Their analysis suggests that governments should avoid taking action to ease the misery of rural life, or to tackle rural poverty, because that would reduce migration to urban centres. No set of politicians in a democracy could contemplate that—especially in a democracy like India in which a large majority of the population (and thus of the electorate) resides in villages. Politicians from parties of the right, left, and centre feel increasingly compelled to address the needs of rural folk—both in order to survive politically, and because it is the right thing to do. They worry that large-scale migration to cities would disrupt the social composition of their constituencies (both rural and urban), which would make it more difficult for them to understand which social groups they need to cultivate in order to remain popular. They also believe that ever more rapid rural-urban migration would produce severe social dislocation, which would in turn pose dangers to democracy.

That sort of dislocation has occurred in recent decades in China, where over 200 million people have been enticed or forced off the land and into major cities—especially in the years before 2003, when the ruling elite imposed policies with a strong urban bias. China's leaders need not worry about votes, but the consequences of the ensuing social dislocation have proved deeply troubling to them. Collective protests have occurred on a massive scale—more massive than in India—not least in rural areas where those policies caused acute distress before 2003. To cope with this disorder, the authorities have created coercive agencies on which a larger share of their budget is spent than on national defence. When Hu Jintao and Wen Jiabao took power in 2003, they took numerous decisions to address the needs of rural dwellers—including putting an end to taxation on rural incomes. If even China's autocrats felt compelled to tackle rural poverty, then leaders in democracies like India can hardly be criticised for doing the same.

A far more nuanced approach is needed than the one offered by that World Bank team if we are to have a satisfactory assessment of NREGA's achievements and limitations. We propose such an approach in this book—one which accords particular weight to efforts that enhance the political capacity of poor people. And in using this approach, we have found more in NREGA to commend than to condemn. Despite many shortcomings, it is important to grasp the radical implications of NREGA in the non-material domains that include social relations. There must also be a greater acknowledgement that some of the very pro-poor policy proposals now being put forward as alternatives (or in some cases complements) to NREGA and other UPA-initiated efforts, would likely never have received serious consideration had NREGA (and programmes like it) not helped to build a consensus that welfare programmes need to be big, bold, and built to withstand constant attempts to both dilute and steal from them. In some cases, policy revisions adopted to improve NREGA's performance have become models for India's wider social welfare system—notably the payment of other forms of government assistance directly to the bank accounts of individual recipients.

Implications for the Study of Indian Political Economy

Our next two arguments connect aspects of the NREGA experience with important debates in the study of Indian politics and political economy. A perennial question in this field is how to characterise the nature of the Indian state. NREGA offers a unique window on the degree to which the Indian state is able to act with relative autonomy vis-à-vis social forces—that is, to pursue crucial human development goals in the face of opposition from powerful constituencies. Hence our third key argument:

3. *While the Indian state's porousness provides privileged access to business organisations and socially powerful constituencies, it also offers openings for voices seeking to effect progressive social change in the interests of non-elite groups.*

While states may be classified according to their primary ideological commitments, the nature of their political regimes, the means by which their officials are recruited, and many other variables, the axis of differentiation that most interests political scientists studying development has been the composition of the dominant interest coalition and how this affects the making and content of policy. The nature of the state in India over the years has often been described in rather stark, all-or-nothing terms—as controlled by powerful interests, impervious to fundamental change, or aligned with a particular vision of the world. Nehru's India, for instance, was portrayed as a state devoted to all-out industrialisation, secular democracy, and a non-aligned foreign policy. Over time these characterisations, and the dualities in which they are embedded, have softened, as scholars highlighted latent strains of thought and action. The ambivalence was captured best by the image of India as a 'strong-weak' state—endowed with certain capacities at the apex of the system, but hostage to special interests at the state level and below. More recent accounts of the Indian state cast it as one captured by big business[42] and in the thrall of a neo-liberal vision of government.[43]

Our analysis of the politics surrounding NREGA helps to moderate such a view. The scale of NREGA and other similar initiatives suggests that the Indian state is in no danger of withering. A government operating according to neo-liberal principles would not extend an open-ended financial commitment to such a large government-run programme—particularly one that represented such a major intervention in rural labour markets. Nor would a government controlled by a nexus between state elites and business interests have adopted the paradigm underlying NREGA, which involves empowering poor people to make specific claims on the state as a matter of right—and to mobilise collectively when the state fails to fulfil these legal and moral duties.

Atul Kohli's thoughtful examination of India's development process in recent decades, particularly the dynamics we have seen since 1980, highlights the progressive hold that business elites have gained over all aspects of state functioning. These include, most importantly, the economic policymaking apparatus (including key decision-making bodies, formal and informal), but also the conduct of India's relations with foreign governments and multilateral institutions (where delegations of business leaders are an increasingly visible presence), as well as arenas in which elected officials operate, such as political parties (largely funded by the corporate sector),[44] the news and entertainment media (owned mainly by corporate entities),[45] and the judiciary (where the shift in thinking about the place of business in the development process has led to an observable pro-business bias).[46] To those who recall the pre-liberalisation era, when private-sector industrialists enjoyed nothing like this level of public backing (and in some cases adulation), the high profile accorded to leading business figures in formulating policy, advising parties, and even running for office represents a jarring change.[47]

Yet, the process through which NREGA came into being demonstrates that the robust strategies for infiltrating key governmental structures and steering policy-making processes towards a set of preferred objectives has not been the sole preserve of elite interests. The 'porousness' of the Indian state can provide social activist constituencies, working with and on behalf of decidedly non-elite groups, the ability to shape the state's development paradigm, as well as specific laws, policies, and funding levels. The state's permeable membranes provide something akin to what social movement theorists call a 'political opportunity structure', allowing loosely allied networks of civic organisations, grassroots activists, academics, and other forces committed to social change to advance counter-hegemonic agendas through sustained and intensive engagement with state officials in devising the procedures that give governance rights their distinctive character.

Over the past decade (at least), advocates for rights-based approaches to securing human development have discovered multiple institutional channels through which to press for change. Parliamentary standing committees, for instance, were once a site of little substantive discussion, let alone action. Today they are used by ambitious politicians and assertive advocates alike to build and shape public and expert opinion in support of specific legislative proposals. Perhaps more visibly, as we saw in Chapter 2, bodies such as the NAC have served as forums within which activists dedicated to reengineering the state's approach to addressing poverty could have a substantial role in policymaking. Voices such as those of Harsh Mander, Aruna Roy, N.C. Saxena, Jean Dreze, Nikhil Dey, and many others, made the NAC a meeting ground between activists and political leaders such as the Congress's Jairam Ramesh. The NAC was a site for the development of such key reform initiatives as India's proposed Lok Pal (ombudsperson) Bill, the Right to Education Act, and the Right to Fair Compensation and Transparency in Land Acquisition, Rehabilitation, and Resettlement Act (LARRA) 2013.

Another institutional avenue for civil society penetration of agenda-setting and (in some cases) decision-making forums was India's Planning Commission. Until its abolition in 2014, the Planning Commission for many decades drew on the perspectives, insights, and policy recommendations of a wide range of development practitioners and social activists, as well as the usual mix of academic experts and policy analysts. There have been many complaints that the Planning Commission exceeded its mandate, or that it became a parallel centre of power—one with less accountability to voters or other stakeholders than parliament or the cabinet. These are not completely unfounded, though some critiques have exaggerated the problem considerably. The same set of critics, for instance, have complained noticeably less about other manifestations of 'state-civil society synergy'[48] (including various government advisory councils), which have been institutionalised in ways that provide deep and pervasive influence for representatives of particular industries, as well as for the corporate sector more broadly. In this context, the creation (or reinvention) of institutions that provide spaces for social activists to magnify the voices of poor and marginalised people should be seen as a balancing mechanism that signifies the Indian state's continuing struggle to overcome the elite biases that it inherited from its colonial past.[49]

At first glance, this interpretation may seem curious, since the members of the National Advisory Council who largely designed NREGA (and the Right to Information Act) emerged from what might be seen as elite positions in government and academe. But key actors, such as Aruna Roy, Jean Dreze, and Nikhil Dey, had spent many years working and living among marginalised people at the grassroots, and their proposals were based on insights derived from poor people's own struggles for justice, voice, and dignity. One recent study stressed the disconnect between their claims to represent a grassroots movement and their privileged backgrounds and positions.[50] The advantages that status and elite connections has conferred upon these very same activists—including the protection afforded by public visibility—has been noted by one of the authors of this volume in earlier research.[51] But rather than seeing this as a besetting contradiction, it is more fruitful to view the activists' efforts to bridge the divide between the largely urban middle class and the rural poor[52] as another of the hybrid forms of engagement that India's civil society has produced, blending vertical and horizontal dimensions of accountability in pursuit of both economic and political rights through a combination of movement and NGO forms of activism,[53] and harnessing the capacities of both civil servants and civic activists.

None of this, however, means that the political influence of organized industry is on the wane. Indeed, the result of the 2014 general election increased the direct access of business interests to government policymaking, not least through the appointment to key posts of several economists sympathetic to the laments of business stakeholders concerning regulatory burdens and policy instability. The Modi government—some of whose thinking on NREGA is discussed in the epilogue to this chapter—dismantled both the NAC and the Planning Commission, replacing the latter with the NITI Aayog, or 'Policy Commission'. It is not at all obvious, however, that the current constriction of policy space for progressive activists is permanent, or that recent institutional reforms will squeeze out pro-poor policymaking over the longer-term. This is in part because of the precedent, established by NREGA and other rights-based initiatives, that poor people and civil society groups working on their behalf have a legitimate claim to participate directly in governance activities formerly assigned to state agencies alone. In assessing their overall impact, moreover, it should also be noted that both the NAC and the Planning Commission were crucial to the many rounds of policy revision that NREGA was exposed to during the UPA government's decade in power. It was through the NAC that proposals for worker bank account payments were discussed and refined, and the Planning Commission was closely involved in the process of determining what the 'convergence agenda'—the centerpiece of NREGA 2.0 during the UPA's waning years—would look like in practice. Moreover, as we have seen, NREGA itself—like much of the government's rights-based legislation—included provisions to create even more government institutions that would provide a voice for ordinary citizens usually shut out of policymaking processes. These included the Central Employment Guarantee Council and other oversight bodies. Indeed, it was a key political insight of India's leading social activists—that policy implementation bodies almost always end up engaging in some form of policymaking—that drove them to insist on such mechanisms in the legislation that emerged from the NAC. Examples include the committees and oversight authorities created under LARRA and the Right to Education Act, both of which provided a durable platform for social activists seeking to influence the development agenda and to enhance the state's accountability to poor people.

Our next argument is closely connected to the question of which interest-group coalitions (if any) dominate state decision-making in India, and addresses another issue of longstanding interest to students of Indian politics: whether and how anti-poverty programmes can be used to build a pro-poor political constituency, without becoming subsumed in the patron-client networks that have dominated Indian politics. This is the basis for the book's fourth main argument:

4. *Various aspects of NREGA implementation—including efforts to make officials more accountable to poor and marginalised people—have demonstrated the complex process through which 'clientelist' politics in India is being transformed rather than eliminated.*

Over the past decade, a lively debate has emerged over whether—and, if so, to what degree—India has begun to transition from 'clientelist' politics (in which government benefits are distributed to the supporters of a particular candidate, faction, or party) to 'programmatic' politics (in which political backing is driven not by anticipation of partial treatment by those who assume government office, but by the wisdom and likely impacts of a party's ensemble of policy positions). This debate has been framed largely in terms of a shift in India's development strategy since the 1980s, from one in which the state played a more intrusive role in economic decision-making to a more market-oriented model. Increasing reliance on market mechanisms combined with a shrinking state sector should, in theory, reduce the ability of patrons to steer benefits to their chosen clients, thus reducing the incentives for rent-seeking of various types. But this process has taken place unevenly at best—in some sectors, but not others; in some places, but not others; under some parties, but not others. Government decision-makers (whether civil servants or the elected officials under whose direction they ostensibly operate) have retained great discretion over many aspects of economic policy. They are able to achieve this discretion in part because of the gradual, iterative, and long-lasting nature of India's reform process. As each new reform measure is assessed, enacted, and implemented, a range of official actors are lobbied to steer policymaking toward the decisions favoured by various interests. Also reinforcing the system of corruption that underlies clientelism is the heightened salience of government decision-making regarding access to (and control over) land and other natural resources.[54]

During the past two decades of policy change, it became increasingly apparent that the Indian state was pursuing it own unique brand of economic reform, and indeed, some saw the process as far more 'home grown' from the start.[55] Governments of the left, right, and centre have refused to radically withdraw the state in ways that had been witnessed in many of the countries that first liberalised their economies during the 1980s and early 1990s. Both the central and state governments have, for instance, been deeply involved in the process of promoting industrialisation—notably through tax incentives for the establishment of new production facilities and the acquisition of land on behalf of private firms willing to locate in Special Economic Zones.[56] In addition, governments at various levels of India's polity maintain and operate complex subsidy programmes and fund social welfare.

In this context, the emergence of NREGA represented something of a paradox for policy analysts. Guaranteeing even temporary employment in rural areas represented, without doubt, a marked expansion of the role of government, and thus the possibility of expanding patronage-based politics. Yet, at the same time, NREGA was explicitly designed to counter the kinds of abuses that generally allowed the benefits of anti-poverty schemes to be steered to the clients of one or another powerful patron in exchange for their political loyalty. Such clients, in the case of NREGA, would include those workers whose political allegiance would gain them a share of programme resources, as well as the officials (elected and bureaucratic) who are permitted to loot such programmes. The accountability provisions found in NREGA were meant to curb bureaucratic discretion in the selection of beneficiaries, and to disincentivise corruption by making illegality more apparent to local communities, who would be empowered to take action.[57]

As we have seen in the preceding chapters, neither bureaucratic discretion nor political interference by patrons has been effectively abolished. Work that should have been made available 'on demand' was rationed—based on broadly political (though not always partisan) factors, with the collusion of officials who benefited from the resultant opportunities for obtaining illicit income. In addition, powerful farming communities who faced higher agricultural wage bills due to the existence of competing NREGA worksites were, in some instances, able to influence whether, where, and how many NREGA works projects were undertaken. People from certain social groups, or from particular localities that were thought to support parties or factions other than those with de facto decision-making power, could be—and often were—excluded from NREGA work opportunities. In the absence of local civic movements capable of pressing for the implementation of NREGA's transparency and 'social audit' measures, certain forms of corruption-based clientelism were able to persist in many places.

Even so, the mechanisms for tracking the actions of individual officials—for instance, through the web-enabled MIS—made it risky for NREGA implementers to appropriate the wages of those NREGA workers who did get jobs, especially as additional safeguards were devised. The payment of wages via bank accounts was particularly effective in changing the cost-benefit calculus of officials who may have considered engaging in corrupt acts. Even if these and other measures could not stamp out NREGA corruption, even in places endowed with active movements for accountability, in many places the kind of brazen theft of workers' wages that had characterised precursor employment schemes became extremely rare.

At the same time, people's growing awareness of the theoretical 'guarantee' of temporary employment increased the need for politicians at the state level to be seen to be implementing the programme in a credible fashion. As a result, ruling party leaders in several states—including Madhya Pradesh and Rajasthan—engaged in the practice of identifying a small number of districts where systematic looting of NREGA could take place without endangering the party's electoral fortunes. Because this process was guided from the apex of each state's political system, it helped to swell the corpus of illicit funds available to party leaders—funds that could be used to buy the support of MLAs and other political actors. This form of patron-client politics, which centres on relations between members of the political elite at different levels of the system, is an example of how clientelist politics was being transformed rather than eliminated.[58] Thus, even if implementation of NREGA works was, in most cases, not consciously used to buy electoral support from particular groups of voters at the grassroots—and Schneider's recent research indicates that politicians are not particularly good at predicting the party affiliation of individual benefit claimants in any case[59]—clientelist politics was still alive and well.

NREGA offered politicians at high levels another kind of electoral payoff— that is, in addition to generating funds with which to buy political support among intermediaries who could, in theory, deliver votes for the ruling party. This second benefit was the ability of NREGA, if managed reasonably well, to convey to voters in 'best case' and 'ambiguous' districts (not in the 'worst case' districts where looting was systematic—see Chapters 4 and 5 for further details) the government's commitment to embracing a post-clientelist political future. Election surveys conducted since NREGA came into force suggested that, when the programme provided meaningful responses to a substantial number of ordinary people, voters were willing to reward leaders at both the central and state levels of the political system. Assessments of good NREGA performance were based on factors like the quantum of employment offered, the level and timeliness of the wages paid, the degree to which working conditions conformed to legal requirements, the durability of the physical assets created, and so forth. The important point is that people extended political support not merely to individual officials who dispensed patronage (in the form of temporary employment), but to parties and elected representatives that worked to make the scheme function creditably.

To advance this claim is not to argue that anti-poverty programmes like NREGA can achieve popularity that may prove decisive at election time. Many over-excited commentators analysing the re-election of the Congress-led UPA in 2009 attributed its victory to NREGA. A careful examination of reliable polling data yields a more restrained judgement. Surveys showed that people who had only heard of NREGA, without benefiting from it, voted less often for Congress and its allies than for other parties. However, people who had taken work under the programme voted more often for the UPA. The resulting gains that the ruling alliance made were modest: an edge of about 3 per cent of the overall vote. But in very close electoral contests—a small minority of the total—3 per cent could alter outcomes. It was therefore plausible to conclude that the UPA picked up between twelve and fifteen extra seats thanks to NREGA. In a parliament of 543 members, those gains were not great enough to decide which alliance would form the government. But because these vote shares also represented losses for rival parties, they made a difference. An additional twelve or fifteen MPs helped to ensure that the UPA would have a stable parliamentary majority for the ensuing five years.[60] Thus, the actual impact of NREGA at that election was far from trivial, but less than decisive. What mattered more after the 2009 election was the widely believed myth that the programme had won the election for the UPA. It ensured that NREGA would be sustained, and that the government would persist with efforts to make growth inclusive of poor rural people—efforts which met with limited but nevertheless important successes.

It is important to pay close attention to the details of how the political strategy of inclusive growth was pursued—and to the ambiguities and limitations that attended one key element in that strategy. NREGA is just one in a series of post-clientelist initiatives undertaken by senior politicians, albeit a large one. They have increasingly introduced such programmes because they recognise that the distribution of patronage is insufficient to win re-election; they need to supplement clientelism with programmatic initiatives that are protected from local bosses, who face strong incentives to overgraze the commons of patronage-based spending. The forms this takes can vary considerably across Indian states, with appeals to social groups being a particularly important element in some states, including Tamil Nadu.[61]

Implications Beyond the Indian Case

The third pair of arguments advanced in this book contribute to debates beyond India, particularly in theory-building in the comparative study of development politics. Hence our next claim:

5. *NREGA is emblematic of a new category of rights, pioneered in India over the past decade—a category we term 'governance rights', which are characterised chiefly by their hybridity, both in terms of what is being guaranteed and how these guarantees can be enforced.*

NREGA was the flagship in a flotilla of initiatives that represented a fundamental transformation in the nature of rights-based approaches to development in India. While rights-based development has been a popular rhetorical formulation since at least the late 1990s—having been a fad among European aid donors for much of that decade—it resulted in little by way of sustained practical action to combat poverty. But in India, recent years have witnessed the passage of a raft of rights-related laws, including the Forest Rights Act (2006),[62] which accords people who traditionally dwell in forests conditional title to forest land and the right to use forest products, and the Right to Education Act (2010),[63] which entitles all children fourteen years of age and under the right to attend school, which under the statute was also made compulsory. NREGA, along with the Right to Information Act—both passed in 2005—became the template for this new wave of legislation.

Three distinctive features of NREGA are significant in this context. First, it specifies a non-means-tested entitlement to advance a particular aspect of human well-being. Second, the Act requires the creation of a set of special-purpose institutions to ensure that state commitments are fulfilled. Third, NREGA includes a range of mechanisms through which ordinary people and their associations can engage directly in the process of holding the officials who implement it accountable for their actions and omissions. Taken together, these and other provisions amount to a novel hybrid of two categories of rights that are typically treated in isolation from one another: social and economic rights, and civil and political rights. The way in which NREGA was conceived recognises that, while these two categories may be theoretically distinct, in practice they are inseparable. To fulfil social and economic rights—such as the right to a decent livelihood—requires not just the general legal protections associated with liberal democracy, but institutional arrangements that encourage citizens to participate in the procedures through which state programmes operate. The right to engage directly in mechanisms through which officials are held accountable for their performance in delivering programme entitlements represents a hybrid category that we call 'governance rights'.

This book has argued that the conception of rights found in NREGA constitutes, in essence, the right to participate in purpose-built governance institutions to ensure the delivery of particular benefits essential to the fulfilment of social and economic rights. As manifestations of hybridity, governance rights are distinct from civil and political rights insofar as they are not about choosing representatives or protecting a zone of free speech. Instead, governance rights confer on citizens the right to engage directly in processes intended to ensure direct accountability of officials charged with delivering on state 'guarantees' (by making officials publicly answerable and sanctionable). This is consistent with Foweraker and Landman's framework for understanding the relationship between citizenship rights and social movements: NREGA activism, before and after the Act's passage, demonstrated that 'claims for universal rights ... create a direct challenge to the particularism of clientelistic control', which the authors recognise as rampant in many developing country contexts.[64] Moreover, 'insofar as social movements are able to press for civil and political rights, they both seek to defend fundamental liberties and come to contest the culturally specific delivery of social rights'.[65]

Let us now consider NREGA's influence upon an array of poverty reduction measures introduced by the UPA, and the impact of those measures on the poor. Three of the UPA government's five major rights-based initiatives—NREGA, the Right to Information Act, and the Forest Rights Act—were all passed into law at roughly the same time, in 2005–6. So the implementation of NREGA cannot be said to have influenced the creation of the other two. The Right to Information Act has had a significant impact in a political system plagued by an acute 'allergy' among power holders to transparency and downward accountability. That is evident from the murders of a number of activists seeking to make use of it.[66]

The Forest Rights Act, by contrast, has been a disappointment. Two problems—both of which connect to its 'rights-based' character—have loomed large. First, officials from two different ministries are responsible for implementation: the Ministry of Tribal Affairs (MTA), charged with carrying out laws related to the many Adivasis who reside in forests, and the Ministry of Environment and Forests, which oversees the Forest Service, whose traditional powers are challenged by the Act. The MTA has no employees in place at sub-district and local levels, so its sympathy for the Act cannot be brought to bear where poor people actually live. Employees of the Forest Service, by contrast, reach down to the grassroots, but tend to be unsympathetic and often obstructive.

The second problem arises out of the hasty and careless drafting of the Act. It contains a single, devastating sentence: 'the provisions of this Act shall be in addition to, and not in derogation of, the provisions of any other law for the time being in force'. In other words, the new Act does not override earlier legislation that the Forest Service has long used to deny forest dwellers the very rights the new Act sought to promote. This has not prevented nearly two million poor forest dwellers from gaining valuable certificates of ownership over plots of forest land, but they have gained little or nothing from numerous other provisions in the Act.[67] The point here is that the meticulous drafting of NREGA—especially of the sections which inserted potent (indeed unrivalled) transparency mechanisms into it—was not fully emulated when the Forest Rights Act was being prepared.

Let us now turn to two other rights-based initiatives undertaken in the UPA government's later years, which thus could reasonably be expected to have been influenced by the perceived political and developmental utility of NREGA. They were the Right to Education Act, passed into law three months after the 2009 national election, and the National Food Security Act (NFSA) of 2013, which was intended to fulfil poor people's right to food. The enactment of the Right to Education Act so soon after the 2009 election, when many entertained an exaggerated belief in the political impact of NREGA, was certainly facilitated by perceptions of the latter programme. The NFSA was passed much later, after an excruciatingly long process of political contestation that was a major embarrassment to the Congress-led government, which had fallen into paralysis after being engulfed in major corruption allegations beginning in late 2010. The NFSA represented a last, desperate attempt to revive the government's popularity. It thus qualifies as part of NREGA's 'wider impact'.

During its decade in power (2004–14), the Congress-led government also took other steps to address poverty that were not rights-based. Two were especially important: the Jawaharlal Nehru National Urban Renewal Mission (JNNURM); and a substantial increase in funding for an existing programme, the Integrated Child Development Services scheme (ICDS). The former fared rather badly, and the latter achieved little—partly because they were not designed with the care that went into the formulation of NREGA. The JNNURM was devised at roughly the same time as NREGA, but by people who had little or no contact with its architects. The decision to inject substantial new funds from surging revenues into the pre-existing ICDS was made slightly later, but before NREGA established a strong enough record to serve as an inspiration. Neither the JNNURM nor the better-resourced ICDS created fresh opportunities for poor people to engage actively in the public sphere as NREGA did. Key administrators of the JNNURM were so preoccupied with maximising the numbers of new houses built that they failed to pursue consultations with poor stakeholders that had originally been promised. As for the ICDS, an existing (and poorly functioning) programme, no substantial reform measures were introduced to make its operations more transparent or its decision-making structures more participatory. Substantial new funds were simply pumped into it.[68]

NREGA's worksite-based nature has driven some of the positive impacts documented in this book. Both the sharing of work duties across wide social divides, and the tendency of people who have earned wages to feel empowered to demand them (in a way that is perhaps not as true of transfer-payment beneficiaries), contributed to the broader trend of upending hierarchies and promoting assertiveness, which NREGA has done much to catalyse. The JNNURM did not have the same access-to-information, social audit, and demand-driven institutional features, and it was not an Act of Parliament. But perhaps just as important as these differences was the fact that NREGA made people into employees, however temporary, and was executed locally, where public officials—the targets of accountability—were more accessible.

The role of civil society organisations in attempting to make the officials responsible for implementing NREGA more accountable is complex and variable. As Scheingold's classic study of litigation-generated rights in the United States argued, such rights could serve as crucial mobilisational 'resources' for activists and ordinary citizens.[69] To take advantage of these opportunities was to engage in the 'politics of rights', something that India's NREGA activists had taken a step further by helping in the public articulation of rights through not only litigation (represented by the right to food case, discussed in Chapter 2), but also through legislation, including NREGA and the other rights-based laws passed during the UPA's decade in power. Indeed, we have emphasised the importance of civil society to achieving the potential of rights-based initiatives such as NREGA throughout this book. Yet, as evidence from many parts of

India has demonstrated, not all types of civic associations are equally effective in this respect. Conventional advocacy and service-delivery NGOs rarely adopt strategies or take actions necessary to improve NREGA performance. Our surveys of NREGA workers in Madhya Pradesh and Rajasthan suggest that organisations that possess other characteristics were more likely to show better results than ordinary NGOs. Much of this success had to do with the hybrid nature of these other groups: they combined efforts to mobilise people on the margins of society with a focus on concrete developmental activities—what Gandhians call 'constructive work'. This is by no means an easy balance to achieve. Movement-oriented groups are strikingly, though not surprisingly, thin on the ground in India. To mobilise people to demand their rights is to take serious risks, including financial ruin, social ostracism, and physical danger. Many activists seeking to expose misdeeds in NREGA and other development programmes have been threatened with violence, and some have been killed.[70] For poor people whose lives and livelihoods are fragile at best, the payoff from associating with, let alone actively joining, such movements can seem small and distant. This understandable reluctance has caused many promising and courageous activist groups to flounder. The characteristics and tactics employed by some of the groups that have managed to make inroads—through the opportunities provided by NREGA's rules, and the politics surrounding their implementation—were examined in detail in Chapters 4 and 5.

This book's sixth argument is also directed at debates of a comparative and theoretical nature, for which the Indian case is potentially of great importance—namely, the literature on democratic decentralisation:

6. *The NREGA-prompted devolution of resources to elected local councils made* gram panchayats, *despite their shortcomings, a site where poorer people's demands for accountability were legitimated—a process aided in some states (e.g. Rajasthan) by particularly well-positioned civil society organisations, and in others (e.g. Karnataka) by committed, capable state bureaucracies.*

The corruption under NREGA that has occurred at the district level and below has prompted, among other things, a renewed willingness among political analysts to dismiss the potential of *panchayats* as an instrument for empowering the poor and, ultimately, increasing government accountability to citizens. The quick capture of newly empowered local institutions by local elites is a familiar phenomenon, and it is hard to fault anyone for expecting this state of affairs to persist, regardless of changed circumstances. Most analyses now in print—including some by one of the authors of this volume[71]—are quite pessimistic.

But there are at least two important reasons why the NREGA experience calls for revising this narrative. First, much of the corruption that accompanied NREGA's implementation stemmed not from decentralisation itself, but from the incomplete form of decentralisation pursued. This finding may seem counterintuitive given that NREGA's rules extend not only to the *gram panchayat* but to the *gram sabha* as well. However, it was not the depth of its institutional reach that made decentralisation under NREGA incomplete. What was missing, at least in part, was sufficient devolution of authority to permit elected leaders at the sub-district level and below to check the power of field-level bureaucrats over crucial steps in the NREGA implementation process. Without this authority, even well-intentioned local leaders, including those competing for poor peoples' votes, would have to skim from the programme to bribe bureaucrats to deliver the clearances required to keep the works and wages coming. It was the unwillingness of state- and district-level politicians (ministers, party leaders, MLAs) to cede their power over the local bureaucracy, and the rents it commanded, that left the BDO and other crucial mid-level officials outside the purview of block-level elected officials.

A crucial reason why this institutional imbalance within local elected institutions (de jure political power, but de facto subordination to bureaucratic authority) was less damaging to NREGA than it might have been, lies in politics. Of particular significance are the incentives created by patterns of partisan competition at the state level. Because state-level parties seek to draw electorally successful local faction bosses into their spheres of influence, the more sophisticated among the *gram panchayat* leaders can exert considerable leverage in their battles with local officialdom. An MLA with whom a *sarpanch* has joined forces has, at the very least, the ability to threaten a recalcitrant BDO with a transfer to a grim job in an undesirable duty station, unless the BDO goes easy on the *sarpanch* who has called in this favour. While often effective, such tactics are a highly inefficient means for delivering a measure of governance autonomy to *gram panchayats*. Even so, this override mechanism helps to counteract the effects of incomplete decentralisation. Another mitigating factor is that the flow of NREGA funds has largely bypassed the block level.

A second reason to reassess the received wisdom about decentralisation and elite capture concerns the nature of corruption under NREGA, which is sufficiently visible at a local level to sometimes galvanise poor people to protest. Our analysis suggests that while many types of corruption have afflicted

NREGA projects, the transparency and accountability mechanisms built into NREGA have often provided a deterrent to the most brazen forms of corruption. This can have effects on people's willingness to participate in politics. While the Act's provisions have fallen far short in terms of detecting corruption and prosecuting perpetrators, the variety of methods for exposing misdeeds has made a substantial difference. In many places, the procedural requirements that NREGA imposed on local government institutions facilitated the asking of uncomfortable questions. Even when the answers from officials and political representatives were incomplete or unconvincing, the culture of questioning began to take hold.[72] Moreover, to misappropriate funds, officials often had to enlist the reluctant collusion of workers in order to adhere to NREGA guidelines. They could not rely on invisible skimming, which could take place unilaterally, thus making corruption more visible.

Third, in recent years, new (and as yet mostly unpublished) studies have emerged which demonstrate that there is less grounds for pessimism concerning the potential for local democratic institutions to combat poverty. Researchers in a broad cross-section of localities across India and in other countries have found that if elected local councils are allowed to function over extended periods, they can improve human development. There are many strands to this emerging literature, but among the most striking is the evidence that, over time, poor people grasp the opportunities that competitive *panchayat* politics offers. This means applying pressure on candidates in local elections to deliver concrete benefits rather than empty promises. Even leaders from elite social backgrounds are often forced to compete for the (usually abundant) votes of the poor, and to recognise that they are accountable to such people between elections as well. Local councils address poverty in ways that would not have been expected of a *gram panchayat* a decade or two earlier.[73]

Another set of findings that supports a more optimistic assessment of the relationship between decentralisation and poverty-reduction, with special reference to the Indian case, is contained in an authoritative collection of papers by three distinguished analysts. The authors apply sophisticated quantitative methods to a large national dataset to develop a rigorous assessment of the functioning of rural *panchayats*. Their research reveals that when local councils are permitted to operate for extended periods—since 1993 in India—poor villagers acquire substantial political awareness, confidence as political actors, political skills, and connections to allies: their 'political capacity' is significantly enhanced. That alone represents one form of poverty reduction. In addition, poor people in India have made use of that capacity to influence local councils to address their needs—to a greater extent than they have in the past—so that other dimensions of their 'poverty' (a severe lack of incomes and assets) are also tackled.[74] This is immensely important when we consider that NREGA has provided massive new resources to elected local councils. It suggests that elite capture is a much less serious problem than the extant literature might lead one to suspect, and that NREGA can serve the interests of the poor more effectively than the pessimists about democratic decentralisation would have us believe.

The book authored by these three scholars. candidly acknowledges the numerous problems associated with elected local councils in India: it is a 'warts and all' analysis. If it had offered nothing but good news about local councils, its remarkably positive findings on poverty reduction would have been less persuasive. But it sets out detailed evidence on many of the disappointments that we have found in our own research on NREGA: corruption, the centralisation of power in some councils, and the poor quality of the works created.[75] And yet the authors conclude that despite such problems, increased local democracy has had a significant positive impact on the prevalence of poverty. Its encouraging findings are consistent with those of another recent book on efforts to tackle poverty—in part through democratic decentralisation—in India (in the years before NREGA), Uganda, and Brazil.[76]

The ambiguous but still positive contribution of elected local councils to transparency and accountability compensates somewhat for disappointments on two other fronts: efforts to raise poor villagers' awareness of NREGA, and the conduct of *gram sabha*-based social audits. During NREGA's implementation, few state governments made more than perfunctory attempts to foster an awareness among poor people of key details of the programme: that they had the right to demand work and to receive compensation if it was not provided; that local-level mass meetings were supposed to influence and monitor NREGA works; that an IT system existed, against which they could check information found on their job cards; and that other transparency mechanisms were also there to protect them.[77] Nor did most state governments apply consistent pressure on bureaucrats at district and sub-district levels, and on elected leaders at the local level, to promote awareness, transparency, and accountability, and to punish corrupt practices.

Gram sabha-based social audits have also fallen short, but the picture is not entirely bleak. In Chapter 4, we reported survey results from Rajasthan showing that 'only' 27 per cent and 38 per cent of survey respondents in two districts said that their *gram sabhas* had met even once. Such findings must be placed in their proper perspective: the international norm for the proportion of people who have attended *gram sabha*-type meetings is close to zero. So 27 per cent should not cause undue dejection. And in some parts of India, over time, *gram sabhas* have occurred more often, thanks in part to efforts by NREGA administrators in New Delhi, and partly because poor villagers have gradually become more politically assertive.

Evidence from studies conducted in Andhra Pradesh suggests that trends in these two areas—rights awareness and social auditing—may well go together, and that a vicious cycle of poor performance can be reversed. One World Bank-funded study conducted in three districts (Cuddapah, Khammam, and Medak) found that, while worker awareness of programme entitlements, as well as their sense of their influence over programme officials was initially low, huge improvements were registered in both areas within six months of a functioning social-audit system being established.[78] It was a push by the state government, aided by social activists from Rajasthan, that helped to bring the Andhra Pradesh social audit mechanism into being. For all its faults—the Andhra Pradesh system gave far too little influence to Panchayati Raj Institutions, for instance—the state's experience is a vivid reminder that opportunities for effective citizen participation can unleash powerful forces that can transform people's relationship to politics. While 'enforcement' action to punish errant officials has not always taken place, Aiyar *et al.* note that in Andhra Pradesh the other aspect of accountability, 'answerability' (the requirement that officials answer difficult questions from workers), has been aided immensely by NREGA's focus on citizen participation.[79]

Given the importance of local representative institutions to the analytical narrative we are advancing in this book, it may strike some readers as odd that we are documenting ways in which Andhra Pradesh 'succeeded', despite side-lining *panchayats*. However, our argument is not that *panchayats* are essential for NREGA to yield benefits, just that the political competition unleashed when local democratic institutions are functioning tolerably well can be a crucial enabler of programme performance in some contexts. And in any case, *panchayats* themselves have tended to be enlivened by the introduction of NREGA. Andhra Pradesh was anomalous in the degree to which the state government simultaneously sought to institutionalise the social audit system, while vigorously undercutting the fiscal powers of *panchayats*. With respect to Andhra Pradesh's overall NREGA performance, a good case could be made that a kind of 'strategic path dependence' was at work. Chief Minister Y.S. Rajasekhara Reddy, whose reign coincided with the period when

NREGA was most vigorously promoted by the central government, was following a set of tactics pioneered in Andhra Pradesh by his predecessor, Chandrababu Naidu. While NREGA's social audit structures were of course a departure from earlier practices, many of the partner entities at the grassroots had been created under Naidu (local self-help groups, for example). Most importantly, the method—undercutting *panchayats* through the creation of parallel institutions—was retained. Working through a bureaucratic channel of communication built around NREGA, the CM was (like his predecessor) able to bypass the networks of his political clients and rivals to obtain reliable information on prevailing circumstances at the district level and below. YSR's monitoring system, while unique in its scope and intensity, demonstrated the possibilities of active state engagement in facilitating the emergence of popular accountability institutions.

Because NREGA structures in most states prevented *panchayat* representatives from completely masking the theft of peoples' wages (a more egregious practice in the eyes of local people than dipping into general public funds), sufficient outrage was sometimes generated to embolden workers to join campaigns launched by the kind of civil society groups mentioned above. In fact, NREGA often enables the preferences of ordinary (and poor) people to influence decisions. Local-level analyses by scholars and development analysts have focused mainly on the grassroots meetings (*gram sabhas*) and social audits, which are supposed to influence and monitor the programme. Those meetings deserve attention, but they are only part of the story. Increased accountability and transparency at the local level have, on the whole, been achieved largely within councils rather than between local citizens and elected officials through formal *gram sabhas* and NREGA-mandated social audits.

Epilogue: India's 2014 General Election and NREGA's Future

At the 2014 national election, the Congress Party and its allies suffered a crushing defeat at the hands of the BJP. Some commentators suggested that this represented a mass rejection of poverty-reduction programmes, including of course NREGA, by voters who were hungry for economic growth. They are mistaken, as most BJP leaders understand. The main explanations for the election result were a highly successful campaign mounted by the BJP, which stressed the 'good days' ahead if Narendra Modi were given a mandate to unleash India's entrepreneurial energies. Above all, the election result reflected the political ineptitude and paralysis of the Congress-led government in New

Delhi after late 2010, when it was engulfed in a firestorm of media criticism over various scandals which did not abate in the years that followed. That searing experience left Congress leaders badly rattled, and their actions became more hesitant and erratic. Sittings of Parliament became utterly chaotic, and little business could be transacted. Senior civil servants who had seen some of their colleagues mauled by the media concluded that inaction was the most prudent option under the circumstances. They and the ruling party politicians with whom they interacted grew paranoid, and became averse to signing any document that might later be exposed to their detriment. This is illustrated by an incident in the Prime Minister's Office in 2012, in which an official attached a small post-it note to a file, making a brief comment on a policy issue. He was hauled up before a superior and told that he should 'put nothing on paper'.[80]

Nirmala Sitharaman, who was an articulate national spokesperson for the BJP before becoming a minister in the Modi government, was sharply critical of NREGA during the campaign. That is to be expected from an opposition party, but the reckless and repeated inaccuracy of many of her claims reflected the extent to which villainising NREGA had become a mainstay of the BJP's self-image. During the 2014 election campaign, Sitharaman alleged that in its handling of NREGA, the UPA government exhibited a 'disregard for rules and good governance at every stage: planning, execution, monitoring, and accountability'. This was an odd claim given that most NREGA planning and almost all of its execution and monitoring were in the hands of state governments, several of which were controlled by the BJP. Some BJP state governments (including one in Madhya Pradesh) handled these tasks reasonably well, while one (Karnataka) performed poorly.[81] The aspiring prime minister of Sitharaman's party at the time her statements were made was the chief minister of Gujarat, another poorly performing state, both in terms of the number of days worked and the analyses found in reports of the Comptroller and Auditor General of India. So to blame Congress for such problems made little sense, except as part of a concerted effort to cast the programme as beyond redemption.

Sitharaman also claimed that the MoRD in New Delhi was 'only half hearted' in its monitoring of NREGA. She based this claim on a correct but narrow statement of fact: as monitoring body, the CEGC, had been unable to closely track programme performance. However, she completely ignored the constant efforts of dynamic officials in the MoRD to identify problems in the programme and to design interventions to address them. Sitharaman also added a serious and highly inaccurate rider: that the Ministry showed 'brazen disregard (for) targeted poverty reduction'. This accusation is based on evidence from three states—Bihar, Uttar Pradesh, and Maharashtra—which contain 46 per cent of India's rural poor but received only 20 per cent of NREGA funds.[82] Perhaps not surprisingly, she omits to mention that the central government sought to disburse NREGA funds generously to these states, but was prevented from doing so by problems at the state level that were beyond its control.[83] In Bihar, Chief Minister Nitish Kumar's government sought energetically to maximise the impact of the programme, but was thwarted by the legacy of fifteen years of feckless rule by his predecessor. Half of the key administrative posts at the sub-district level (which are essential to NREGA implementation) stood vacant. Bihar's archaic appointments procedures slowed the pace of filling those posts, and *panchayats* were all but controlled by interventionist bureaucrats in Patna.[84] In Uttar Pradesh, the state government showed far too little interest in NREGA, in part because of the restrictions on contracting it would incur. The central government was not to blame for these problems, as Sitharaman clearly knew, and if Congress-ruled Maharashtra had been receiving above-average NREGA allocations, Sitharaman would likely have complained of favouritism. But logic or consistency was not the point: blaming the central government for problems with NREGA not only allowed the BJP to further undercut whatever was left of Congress's pro-poor credentials; claims of overcentralisation also resonated with a key BJP campaign promise—to devolve more power to state governments, and to involve their officials more directly in central policy formulation, in a process BJP leaders termed 'cooperative federalism'.

In the run up to the 2014 election, it was never quite clear to the policy community, let alone voters, what Narendra Modi would do with NREGA were he to become prime minister. Both he and the BJP maintained a studied ambiguity on the topic throughout the campaign. This was, in a sense, consistent with the party's position since an early version of the NREG Bill first emerged in 2004. BJP MPs initially dismissed the idea as too costly, but later criticised the government for attempting to water down the original draft. This oscillation bears a striking resemblance to the BJP's approach to the National Food Security Bill (NFSB) introduced by the UPA government in 2011, and eventually passed in late 2013. BJP leaders—at state and central levels—dismissed the idea as fiscally irresponsible. But soon afterwards, Narendra Modi himself wrote an open letter to Prime Minister Manmohan Singh to complain that the entitlements spelled out in the NFSB were not generous enough. The office of BJP leader Arun Jaitley, who after the election became finance minister, was the source of the data analysis and argumentation contained in Modi's open letter.

Once NREGA was in force, the BJP relentlessly criticised its entire approach as the epitome of government waste, fraud, and abuse. The BJP nevertheless simultaneously claimed to have implemented the scheme effectively in the states that it governed. These two statements sit oddly alongside one another. To claim that BJP-ruled states did better in implementing a centrally sponsored scheme than Congress states is a potentially plausible proposition that could be empirically verified. It is not, however, a viable position to argue that what the BJP considers a fundamentally flawed, badly designed, and ultimately misconceived Act, was in fact carried out with very good results by BJP state governments. By eliding this distinction, the BJP managed to be both for and against NREGA at the same time. In his campaign oratory, Modi frequently expressed his disgust with UPA schemes such as NREGA that offered mere 'crumbs' to the poor, even as he bragged about the superior efficiency with which his government in Gujarat had delivered NREGA work to job-seekers. While campaigning in Assam, Modi criticised the Congress-run state government for not enlisting enough workers into NREGA, a programme that his party's economic advisors insisted was a symbol of all that was wrong with India's entitlement culture. This confusion persisted and, if anything, intensified as the campaign progressed. The BJP manifesto had but a single cryptic line on NREGA, calling for the programme to be more closely linked to agriculture. This implied an intention to keep NREGA operating in some form, but without saying so directly or indicating how this new emphasis might be realised.

Modi's first substantive utterance on NREGA, at a March 2013 meeting of business leaders, consisted of empty rhetoric. He said that NREGA should have been conceived as a 'development guarantee' programme, one based on service to the nation. It was difficult for either the electorate or India's policy analysts to know what to make of such statements, though the corporate audience to which Modi was speaking cheered his equally evasive punch line—that India needed 'actions not more Acts'. His vagueness about NREGA was tactically shrewd: why alienate those who had either benefited from NREGA—including not only poor rural labourers, but also the bureaucrats and politicians who continued to steal from it—and those who regard the programme as a symbol of political malaise?

Within a week of Prime Minister Modi taking office, it became clear that NREGA would not be killed off directly. The employment guarantee was designed as a legislative Act precisely to make it more difficult for a future government to scrap; another Act of Parliament would be needed to repeal it. The prime minister's advisors concluded that to immediately repeal NREGA would be to risk making the Modi government appear callous to the plight of the rural poor, and could even create political tensions that would make it more difficult to adopt the pro-business measures promised during the election campaign. The BJP's senior leadership clearly understood that it was in the party's interest to emphasise poverty reduction in its public rhetoric. In his first speech in the Central Hall of Parliament after his election victory, Prime Minister-designate Narendra Modi emphasised that his government 'exists for the poor ... is dedicated to the poor ... this is our responsibility'.[85]

That NREGA would not be central to the vision for meeting this responsibility was clear during Modi's first year in office. The prime minister's disdain for the programme was evident, even as he announced his government's intention to continue operating it. In a well publicised address, Modi maintained that the programme would continue primarily as a means of reminding the public—through the visible manual labour employed on NREGA projects—that the Congress Party, which had governed India for most of the years since independence, had failed to end poverty.[86] Unable to abolish NREGA, the Modi government instead found stealthy ways of cutting its cost and curtailing its significance. Some of these were used by the UPA government during its second term in office, though others were of its own devising. Among the first proposals quietly floated by the PMO was to reduce the proportion of programme funds dedicated to wages. While the Act specified that the labour-materials ratio could not fall below 60:40, the new government's senior economic advisors sought support for pushing the ratio to near parity, with 51 per cent of funds dedicated to wages, and 49 per cent to materials. Commentators noted that, in practice, more expenditure on materials would increase the incentive for implementing agencies to recruit construction contractors, whose reliance on machinery and lower-paid (and often less protected) workers would further undermine the interests of NREGA job-seekers.[87] The other potential programme reform that attracted critical attention was the idea of confining NREGA to India's 200 poorest districts, just as it had been in its early pilot phase. This idea was opposed by BJP leaders from states where, if the proposal was implemented, NREGA would all but vanish.

Throughout the Modi government's first year in office, debates over NREGA's utility continued. Evidence of the programme's generally positive performance continued to pour in. This included a much-discussed collection of studies, from the 2012–14 period, published by the United Nations Development Programme's Delhi office.[88] Another major part of the public conversation was a study produced by the respected National Council for Applied Economic Research (NCAER) entitled 'MGNREGA: A catalyst for rural transformation'. Despite caveats about implementation shortcomings, including corruption, these widely publicised studies provided a steady supply of detailed findings on NREGA's positive impacts—on poverty-reduction, women's 'financial inclusion', and so forth. Even more difficult for the BJP leadership to ignore was an October 2014 'open letter' to the prime minister, published by a group of prominent economists based in India and abroad.[89] They called on the government to augment, not undermine, NREGA, noting that fifty million households were at the time receiving at least some employment under the programme every year. Half of the workers were women, and almost half were Dalits or Adivasis. The open letter noted that, for the first time, the central government had imposed formal spending limits on state governments, which amounted to an assault on the programme's underlying commitment to a rights-based approach. The widespread publicity given to the open letter triggered a vehement response from government-connected economists, and a further reply from the original group of NREGA-supporting economists. This tussle, which received significant media coverage, was an extension of the Sen-vs.-Bhagwati feud of 2013 (discussed in Chapter 7), with many of the same names involved. The open letter imbroglio brought additional public attention to NREGA's unsettled fate—which may have been another reason why the Modi government did not act more forcefully to dismantle it.

The Modi government's decision to refrain from substantially overhauling NREGA—much less drastically scaling it back or abolishing it completely—has probably been driven more by pragmatic politics than anything else. At least one key BJP leader—Madhya Pradesh Chief Minister Shivraj Singh Chouhan—spoke out forcefully in support of NREGA, suggesting that the ruling party was not as united on the need to phase out NREGA as the rhetoric emanating from the PMO might have suggested.[90] Even more worryingly for the government, it faced unexpectedly fierce resistance to its plans to amend progressive land legislation that had been passed in the waning days of the UPA government. This was the centerpiece of its pro-business agenda during its first year in office.[91] The intention was to dilute procedural protections that had been established for people whose land had been identified for compulsory acquisition by the state for industrial or infrastructural purposes. The government expended considerable political capital in what, at least in the short term, was a losing effort: the amendments could not pass through parliament's upper chamber, and the temporary executive ordinance promulgated to give effect to the reforms lapsed. By the summer of 2015, the government's key economic advisors were informing the press that the Government of India would instead assist state governments in passing state-level amendments that would trump the landholder and community protections found in the national legislation. For the Modi government, the political costs of this failed effort included not only an impression that Modi was more concerned with the ability of business interests to gain access to land than with farming communities threatened with dislocation,[92] but also stark divisions within the Hindu nationalist movement on which the BJP's electoral success relied. Several movement- and party-affiliated organisations voiced their concerns about the rolling back of protections for farmers, including in representations submitted to a parliamentary committee.[93]

However the Modi government decides to proceed with NREGA, there is good reason to suspect that movement activists and other groups will continue to mobilise for its full implementation. Thanks in part to the Modi government's mis-steps in its first year in power, supporters of NREGA are well-positioned to resist efforts to repeal the Act. By promoting a pro-poor vision of the 'right to work', NREGA has achieved more, politically speaking, than virtually any other Indian social programme. By creating space for the exercise of 'governance rights', NREGA has helped to ensure that the process of 'democratic struggle', which informed its creation, is sustained.

NOTES

1. INTRODUCTION

1. The programme was renamed the Mahatma Gandhi National Rural Employment Guarantee Act in 2010. We use the term NREGA throughout this book.
2. Women performed just under half of the work every year. Source: 'DMU Reports' on the NREGA website, http://nrega.nic.in/netnrega/home.aspx
3. Arup Banerji & Ugo Gentilini, 'Social Safety Nets: Lessons from Global Evidence and Practice', paper prepared for the Bank of Namibia's Annual Symposium on Social Safety Nets in Namibia, Assessing Current Programmes and Future Options (Washington, DC: World Bank, September 2013).
4. Charles E. Lindblom, *Politics and Markets: The World's Political Economic Systems* (New York, NY: Basic Books, 1977).
5. Himanshu, 'Populism or Entitlement-based Populism', *Livemint*, 8 May 2014.
6. Jean Dreze, 'Employment Guarantee and the Right to Work', in Niraja Gopal Jayal & Pratap Bhanu Mehta (eds.), *The Oxford Companion to Politics in India* (Delhi: Oxford University Press, 2010), p. 516.
7. Merilee S. Grindle, *Audacious Reforms: Institutional Invention and Democracy in Latin America* (Baltimore, MD: Johns Hopkins University Press, 2000).
8. Shylashri Shankar & Raghav Gaiha, *Battling Corruption: Has NREGA Reached India's Poor?* (Delhi: Oxford University Press, 2013). See especially the section on the 'politicisation of the poor' (pp. 80–83), which employs concepts similar to those found in this book.
9. See James Manor, *The Political Economy of Democratic Decentralisation* (Washington, DC: World Bank, 1999), Chapter 6. On the difficulty in making social audits work under NREGA, see Mihir Shah's comments in the *Economic Times*, 27 May 2010, and *The Hindu*, 6 September and 13 December 2009.
10. Shankar & Gaiha, *Battling Corruption*, pp. 164–166.
11. This comment was made by some participants in a discussion at King's College, University of London in 2013.

12. See for example 'Cash Transfer and Social Protection', *Social Protection in Asia's Newsletter*, 7 June 2010. A case is made that employment schemes and cash transfers should be seen as 'complementary tools in addressing a variety of vulnerabilities faced by families and individuals'.

13. Lloyd I. Rudolph & Susanne Hoeber Rudolph, *In Pursuit of Lakshmi: A Political Economy of the Indian State* (Chicago, IL: University of Chicago Press, 1987).

14. See Michal Kalecki, *Selected Essays on the Economic Growth of the Socialist and the Mixed Economy* (Cambridge: Cambridge University Press, 1972). For an analysis of how best to interpret the Indian case, see K.N. Raj, 'The Politics and Economics of "Intermediate Regimes"', *Economic and Political Weekly*, 7 July 1973.

15. This was the thrust, for instance, of remarks presented by Prem Shankar Jha at a New School University seminar hosted by the India-China Institute, New York, April 2012.

16. Atul Kohli, *Poverty Amid Plenty in the New India* (Cambridge: Cambridge University Press, 2012).

17. Kanchan Chandra argues, in a different context, that patronage politics is being 'relocated' rather than abolished. See Kanchan Chandra, 'The New Indian State: The Relocation of Patronage in the Post-Liberalisation Economy', *Economic and Political Weekly*, 50(41), 10 October 2015, pp. 46–58.

18. The official title is the Scheduled Tribes and Other Traditional Forest Dwellers (Recognition of Forest Rights) Act, 2006.

19. The official title is the Right of Children to Free and Compulsory Education Act, 2010.

20. This was true in, for example, Madhya Pradesh, Karnataka, and Kerala.

21. Interview with a key NGO representative, Sirohi, 12 January 2009.

22. A research team led by Raghav Gaiha that studied NREGA found that this had happened much of the time. *Indian Express*, 23 April 2012.

23. Myron Weiner, *The Indian Paradox: Essays in Indian Politics* (New Delhi: Sage Publications, 1989); Lloyd I. Rudolph & Susanne Hoeber Rudolph, *The Modernity of Tradition: Political Development in India* (Chicago, IL: University of Chicago Press, 1967); Kohli, *Poverty Amid Plenty in the New India*.

2. ACT OF CREATION: THE CONTENT AND ORIGINS OF NREGA

1. The Act entered the statute books on 7 September 2005 when it was published by the Ministry of Law and Justice (Legislative Department) in the Gazette of India (Extraordinary), Registered No. DL—(N)04/0007/2003—5.

2. We should note that the Schedules included under NREGA were revised on a number of occasions.

3. Some, on the other hand, were more or less boilerplate, derived from normal legal constraints. Section 1(2), for instance, excludes the State of Jammu and Kashmir from the Act's purview.

4. Section 2(*o*).
5. Ratna Sudarshan, 'Impact of NREGA on Rural Labour Market in Kerala: Preliminary Findings on Women's Work', Presented at the conference *NREGS in India: Impacts and Implementation Experiences*, 16–17 September 2008, Delhi.
6. Sudha Narayanan, 'Employment Guarantee, Women's Work and Childcare', *Economic and Political Weekly*, 43(9), 2008, pp. 10–13
7. Section 2(*h*).
8. Section 3(3).
9. Section 7(1).
10. Section 7(2).
11. Section 7(3).
12. Section 7(4), 7(5), 7(6).
13. Section 8(2).
14. Section 8(3).
15. Section 10.
16. Section 11(1).
17. Section 11(2).
18. Section 12(1).
19. Section 12(3)(g) and 12(3)(b).
20. Section 20(1).
21. Section 22(2).
22. Section 22(1)(a).
23. Section 22(2)(a).
24. Section 15(6).
25. Section 15(7).
26. Section 14(3)(e).
27. Section 14(5)
28. Section 13(1).
29. Section 16(1) and 16(2).
30. Section 16(7).
31. Section 16(8).
32. Section 16(3) and 16(4).
33. Section 16(4) and 16(5).
34. Section 16(5).
35. Section 15(1).
36. Section 15(4).
37. Section 15(3).
38. Section 15(5)(b) and 15(5)(c).
39. Section 13(3)(a).
40. Section 13(4) and 14(3)(a).
41. Section 14(3)(b).

42. Section 15(5)(a).
43. Section 15(5)(d) and 15(5)(e).
44. Section 17(3).
45. Interview, New York, 16 February 2014.
46. S. Mahendra Dev, 'Experience of India's (Maharashtra) Employment Guarantee Scheme: Lessons for Development Policy', *Development Policy Review*, 14(3), September 1996, pp. 227–254.
47. See Anuradha Joshi & Mick Moore, 'The Mobilising Potential of Anti-Poverty Programmes', *IDS Discussion Paper No. 374* (Brighton, UK: Institute of Development Studies, 2009).
48. Martin Ravallion, 'Reaching the Rural Poor Through Public Employment: Arguments, Evidence, and Lessons from South Asia', *The World Bank Research Observer*, 6(2), July 1991, pp. 153–175.
49. The right to work is mentioned in Article 41.
50. Article 37.
51. Ibid.
52. Jean Dreze, 'Employment Guarantee and the Right to Work', in Niraja Gopal Jayal & Pratap Bhanu Mehta (eds.), *The Oxford Companion to Politics in India* (Delhi: Oxford University Press, 2010). This chapter was adapted from Dreze's 2007 Kapil Dev Singh Memorial Lecture (Patna, Bihar).
53. Harsh Dhobal (ed.), *Writings on Human Rights, Law and Society in India: A Combat Law Anthology* (New Delhi: Human Rights Law Network, 2011), p. 418.
54. These legislative acts were, respectively, The Rajasthan Right to Information Act, 2000 (Act No. 13 of 2000); and amendments to Chapter II, Section 7, among others, of The Rajasthan Panchayati Raj Act, 1994 (effected through Rajasthan Act No. 9 of 2000). For analysis of the movements that gave rise to these changes and their significance, see Anne Marie Goetz & Rob Jenkins, 'Hybrid Forms of Accountability: Citizen Engagement in Institutions of Public-Sector Oversight', *Public Management Review*, 3(3), 2001, pp. 363–384.
55. The petition alleged violation of the provisions of the Minimum Wages Act, 1948, as well as Articles 14 and 23 of the Constitution, through state government abuse of the provisions of Section 3 of the Rajasthan Famine Relief Works Employees (Exemption from Labour Laws) Act, 1964.
56. Neelabh Mishra, 'Drought and Deaths', *Frontline*, 14–27 April 2001; 'Hunger Deaths in Baran', *Frontline*, 19(24), 2002.
57. Mishra, 'Drought and Deaths'.
58. Jean Dreze, 'On Research and Action', *Economic and Political Weekly*, 37(9), 2–8 March 2002, pp. 817–819.
59. Ibid., p. 817.
60. Ibid.
61. The Akal Sangharsh Samiti was, according to one source, supposed to submit the

petition to initiate the PIL, but because office-holders of the Samiti were not physically present on the appointed day, the petition was signed by the leader of the
PUCL, who was there. The 'right to food' campaign, as such, emerged later, but
could be seen in large part as an outgrowth of the Samiti's work. (The authors are
grateful to the anonymous publisher's reviewer who provided this information.)
62. C. Gonsalves, P.R. Kumar, & A.R Srivastava (eds.), *The Right to Food* (New Delhi:
    Human Rights Law Network, 2005).
63. See also *Supreme Court Orders on the Right to Food: A Tool for Action*, 2nd edition
    (Delhi: Right to Food Campaign Secretariat, 2008), pp. 11–12.
64. *Supreme Court Orders on the Right to Food*, p. 14.
65. Jason Lakin & Nirmala Ravishankar, 'Working for Votes: The Politics of
    Employment Guarantee in India', Paper presented at the annual meeting of the
    American Political Science Association, Philadelphia, PA, 2006, pp. 11–12.
66. Ibid., p. 12.
67. Aruna Roy, Jean Dreze, and Nikhil Dey, 'The Right to Transparent Governance',
    Combat Law Magazine, 1 March 2007.
68. Dreze, 'Employment Guarantee and the Right to Work', p. 511.
69. Ibid.
70. Ibid., p. 512.
71. Ian MacAuslan, 'India's National Rural Employment Guarantee Act: A Case Study
    for How Change Happens', background paper for Oxfam International, *From
    Poverty to Power: How Active Citizens and Effective States Can Change the World*
    (Oxford, 2008), pp. 2–3.
72. She had been having private meetings with a leading advocate since at least 2000,
    according to one informed observer. Interview, Delhi, 18 December 2004.
73. MacAuslan, 'India's National Rural Employment Guarantee Act', p. 3.
74. 'Raj'n to set up commission to probe starvation deaths: Sonia', *PTI*, 9 November
    2002.
75. Mishra, 'Drought and Deaths'.
76. MacAuslan, 'India's National Rural Employment Guarantee Act', p. 13.
77. Ibid., p. 3.
78. For instance, 'TDP Government has neglected farmers: Sonia', *The Hindu*, 24 April
    2004.
79. Dreze, 'Employment Guarantee and the Right to Work', pp. 511–512.
80. The Congress's pre-poll allies in 2004 were the Rashtriya Janata Dal (RJD), Dravida
    Munnetra Kazhagam (DMK), Nationalist Congress Party (NCP), Pattali Makkal
    Katchi (PMK), Telangana Rashtra Samithi (TRS), Jharkhand Mukti Morcha
    (JMM), Lok Janshakti Party (LJP), Marumalarchi Dravida Munnetra Kazhagam
    (MDMK), All India Majlis-e-Ittehadul Muslimeen (AIMIM), People's Democratic
    Party (PDP), Indian Union Muslim League (IUML), Republican Party of India
    (Athavale) (RPI (A)), Republican Party of India (Gawai) (RPI (G)), and Kerala

Congress (Joseph) (KC(J)). The UPA depended on India's main Communist parties for 'outside' support.

81. 'The UPA government will immediately enact a National Employment Guarantee Act. This will provide a legal guarantee for at least 100 days of employment to begin with on asset-creating public works programmes every year at minimum wages for at least one able-bodied person in every rural, urban poor and lower middle-class household.' National Common Minimum Programme of the Government of India (May 2004), p. 3. Available at: pmindia.nic.in/cmp.pdf. Accessed 20 March 2011.

82. 'The Meaning of Verdict 2004', Editorial, *The Hindu*, 14 May 2004; 'The Other Bharat's Backlash', *Business Line*, 14 May 2004; 'India's rural voters seek a brighter future', *The Daily Telegraph*, 14 May 2004. See also Arundhati Roy, 'Let Us Hope the Darkness Has Passed', *The Guardian*, 14 May 2004; and Salman Rushdie, 'India's New Era', *The Washington Post*, 14 May 2004.

83. A more detailed version of this argument is found in James Manor, 'Did the Central Government's Poverty Initiatives Help to Re-elect it?', in Lawrence Saez and Gurharpal Singh (eds.), *New Dimensions of Politics in India: The United Progressive Alliance in Power* (London and New Delhi: Routledge, 2011). See also, Steven I. Wilkinson, 'Elections in India: Behind the Congress Comeback', *Journal of Democracy*, 16(1), January 2005, pp. 153–67; and Yogendra Yadav, 'The Elusive Mandate of 2004', *Economic and Political Weekly*, 39(51), 18 December 2004, pp. 5383–5398.

84. Lakin & Ravishankar, 'Working for Votes', p. 3.

85. Saxena and Mander have both had longstanding academic connections with the Institute of Development Studies, University of Sussex, including through research and publication. See their respective contributions to a special issue of the journal *IDS Bulletin* entitled 'Standing on the Threshold: Food Justice in India' (Brighton, UK: Institute of Development Studies, July 2012).

86. This is how three of the main leaders of this combined movement put it: 'the right to food, the right to work and the right to information were inextricably linked with each other. Each issue had its own "campaign", but these campaigns constantly informed and strengthened each other.' Roy, Dreze, & Dey, 'The Right to Transparent Governance', pp. 418–19.

87. See NAC communication, available at http://nac.nic.in/communication/FinancialREGA.pdf

88. R. Murgai & M. Ravallion, 'Employment Guarantee in Rural India: What Would It Cost and How Much Would It Reduce Poverty?', *Economic and Political Weekly*, 40 (31), 30 July 2005, pp. 3450–55.

89. According to Jeelani, 'the Commission's deputy chairman, Montek Singh Ahluwalia, formerly a senior official with the World Bank and the International Monetary Fund, resisted the "guarantee" component, arguing that it would make

implementation of the programme too costly'. See Mehboob Jeelani, 'NREGA's Reality Check', *Caravan*, 1 May 2010.

90. Roy, Dreze & Dey, 'The Right to Transparent Governance'. It has also been reported that the two complaints stressed by business groups such as the Confederation of Indian Industry (CII) were the impact on India's budget deficit and the likelihood of fraud and abuse in NREGA operations. See Jeelani, 'NREGA's Reality Check'.

91. Raghav Gaiha, 'The Employment Guarantee Scheme in India: Is It Mistargeted?', *Asian Survey*, 36(12), December 1996, pp. 1201–1212.

92. Roy, Dreze, & Dey, 'The Right to Transparent Governance'.

93. Ibid.

94. Ibid.

95. Ibid.

96. Ibid.

97. Ibid.

98. Ibid.

99. Ibid.

100. Ibid.

101. This section is based on our interviews with two members of the NAC, with a senior civil society leader who was a close associate of NAC members, and with officials who then worked within key central government ministries.

102. For more detail on the growing importance of such programmes in and beyond India in recent years, see J. Manor, 'Post-Clientelist Initiatives', in K. Stokke and O. Tornquist (eds.), *Transformative Politics* (London: Palgrave, 2012).

103. Manor, 'Did the Central Government's Poverty Initiatives Help to Re-elect it?'

104. MacAuslan, 'India's National Rural Employment Guarantee Act', p. 4.

105. Deepta Chopra, 'Policy Making in India: A Dynamic Process of Statecraft', *Pacific Affairs*, 84(1), March 2011, pp. 96–98.

106. Interview, Delhi, 18 December 2004.

107. Dreze, 'Employment Guarantee and the Right to Work', p. 512.

108. The NREGA GoM was chaired by Pranab Mukherjee (defence minister). Other members included: P. Chidambaram (Finance), Sharad Pawar (Food), H.R. Bhardwaj (Law), Mani Shankar Aiyar (Panchayati Raj), K. Chandrashekhar Rao (Labour), Kapil Sibal (Science and Technology), Raghuvansh Prasad Singh (Rural Development), and Montek Singh Ahluwalia (Planning Commision).

109. Jeelani, 'NREGA's Reality Check'.

110. Ibid.

111. Ibid.

112. Interview with a senior Congress leader from Rajasthan, Jaipur, 18 January 2009.

113. Jeelani, 'NREGA's Reality Check'.

114. Ibid.

115. These comments are based on interviews with N.C. Saxena and others who were present at that meeting, Delhi, 3 December 2010 and 18 January 2012.

116. The scale of the post-2003 increase in 'Gross Revenues of Central and State Governments' is apparent from the following Reserve Bank of India data (expressed in billions of rupees):

	Central Gov't	State Gov'ts
2002–3	2,162.66	2,577.07
2003–4	2,543.48	2,899.61
2004–5	3,049.58	3,291.53
2005–6	3,674.74	3,824.58
2006–7	4,735.12	4,561.84
2007–8	5,931.47	5,218.44
2008–9	6,052.99	5,483.18
2009–10	6,245.28	5,628.97
2010–11	7,868.88	7,358.20
2011–12	9,324.40	8,620.01

See Reserve Bank of India, 'Direct and Indirect Tax Revenues of Central and State Governments', Table 116, at: http://dbie.rbi.org/DBIE/dbie.rbi?site=publications. Accessed 20 August 2013.

117. Jean Dreze & Aruna Roy, 'Response to the "list of points" raised by the Standing Committee on Rural Development, about the National Rural Employment Guarantee Bill 2004', 31 May 2005. Available at http://www.righttofoodindia.org/rtowork/standingcte.html

118. Ibid.

119. Ibid., p. 3.

120. Dreze, 'Employment Guarantee and the Right to Work', p. 513.

121. James Manor, 'When Local Government Strikes It Rich', *Research Report No. 1* (Visby: Swedish International Centre for Local Democracy, 2013).

122. Dreze & Roy, 'Response to the "list of points"', p. 3.

123. Ibid., p. 4.

124. Ibid.

125. Ibid.

126. Ibid. Specific penalties would be used against officials who failed to provide work, supply the unemployment allowance, address complaints within a reasonable period, submit audit reports, and carry out required social audits.

127. Ibid.

128. See Meena Menon, 'On the trail of the Rozgar Adhikar Yatra', *The Hindu*, 30 May 2005.

129. See 'We Lost a Comrade', *The Hindu*, 7 December 2008.

130. *Jan Manch on Employment Guarantee Summary Report*, 2 July 2005. Available at http://www.righttofoodindia.org/rtowork/ega_keydocs.html. Accessed 7 April 2009.

131. Dreze, 'Employment Guarantee and the Right to Work', p. 512.

132. This was contained within section 27(2), which states that 'the Central Government may, on receipt of any complaint regarding the issue or improper utilisation of funds granted under this Act in respect of any Scheme if *prima facie* satisfied that there is a case, cause an investigation into the complaint made by any agency designated by it and if necessary, order stoppage of release of funds to the Scheme'.

133. At the time, the minister was Raghuvansh Prasad Singh of the Rashtriya Janata Dal.

134. Interview with a member of the National Commission for Enterprises in the Unorganised Sector, New Delhi, 10 April 2008.

135. 'Rural Employment Guarantee Act: People's Victory; Safeguard It', *People's Democracy* [weekly publication of the CPI (M)], 29(35), 28 August 2005; 'CPI(M) claims credit for job guarantee programme', *The Hindu*, 14 February 2006.

136. Lakin and Ravishankar argue that the Left's catalytic role was 'protecting the legislation from its detractors within the government and joining in solidarity with the civil society activists', concluding that 'pressure from the Left parties in Parliament helped to prevent complete dilution of the original legislation, and to force the UPA government to maintain its fidelity to the promise of NREGA it had made in the CMP'. See Lakin & Ravishankar, 'Working for Votes', p. 19.

137. 'Cabinet Nod for Rural Jobs Bill', *The Hindu*, 12 August 2005.

138. The press statement of the minister of rural development, reported in the news article cited by Lakin and Ravishankar ('Rural Job Bill Hits Wage Wall', *Indian Express*, 19 July 2005), gave the mistaken impression that there was a choice between rule-constrained priority setting by *panchayats* and constraint-free priority setting.

139. That the argument was (by July 2005) not over whether a list of MoRD-determined rules would constrain *panchayat* decisions on works to be undertaken, is in fact indicated by Lakin and Ravishankar themselves, when they point to Sonia's statement of 27 July 2005 on the need for a greater role for *panchayats*. Sonia's point was that *panchayats*, not local bureaucrats, should determine priorities—but, either way, they would have to conform to MoRD rules (see the article cited by Lakin and Ravishankar: 'Sonia Gandhi Pitches for Passage of NREGB', *Hindustan Times*, 27 July 2005).

140. Lakin & Ravishankar, 'Working for Votes', p. 23.

141. Ibid.

142. Ibid., p. 13.
143. Ibid., p. 12.
144. Lakin and Ravishankar also refer to Theda Skocpol's findings on the role of competitive patronage politics during the creation (and expansion) of pensions and other transfer payments in post-Civil War America.
145. Lakin & Ravishankar, 'Working for Votes', p. 26.
146. Ibid., p. 16.
147. MacAuslan, 'India's National Rural Employment Guarantee Act', p. 2.
148. Lakin and Ravishankar (in 'Working for Votes') do touch on this matter briefly in their concluding section, when they note that 'Court-appointed commissioners sought the advice of civil society groups on the ground throughout India to check on the status of the implementation of Court orders', a process which helped 'to resolve collective action problems' (pp. 28–29). See also N.C. Saxena, 'First Report of the Commissioner', in Gonsalves et al (eds.), *The Right to Food*.
149. Rob Jenkins, 'India's Unlikely Democracy', *Journal of Democracy*, 18(2), April 2007, pp. 55–69.
150. Deepta Chopra, 'Policy Making in India'.
151. Rob Jenkins, 'NGOs and Politics', in Niraja Gopal Jayal & Pratap Bhanu Mehta (eds.), *The Oxford Companion to Politics in India* (Delhi: Oxford University Press, 2010).
152. Chopra, 'Policy Making in India', p. 98.
153. Ibid., p. 101.
154. Ibid.
155. Ibid., p. 98.
156. Ibid., p. 100.
157. Dreze, 'Employment Guarantee and the Right to Work', p. 512.
158. Ibid.
159. Ibid.
160. Ibid.
161. Ibid., p. 513.

3. ALL POLITICS IS 'LOCAL'? NREGA IMPLEMENTATION AND MULTILEVEL GOVERNANCE

1. It is worth noting that some of these efforts—such as early initiatives to create 'Nigrani Committees' in Bihar to provide technical input into planning and to organise social audits—were undertaken with the best of intentions, notably to undercut local bosses who would subvert NREGA for their own ends, while appearing 'on paper' to have fulfilled all the procedural requirements. See *Evaluation and Impact Assessment of National Rural Employment Guarantee Scheme in Bihar* (Delhi: Institute for Human Development, October 2006), p. 82.

2. The Secretary to the Administrative Reforms Commission empaneled by the Rajasthan government in 1999 noted that almost immediately following the passage of the 73rd amendment, the Rajasthan government enacted a local government statute—the Rajasthan Panchayati Raj Act (1994)—that the government had 'chosen to delegate very few areas'. Even these were subjected to many 'conditions laid down by the [state] government'. No financial powers were transferred to PRIs, except committed expenditure on staff salaries. Even when income is generated by the PRIs themselves, their use is regulated by the state government. The overall assessment reads: 'in effect the *panchayats* function as agencies of the state government rather than as independent self-governing bodies'. Much of this changed following amendments passed by the state legislature in 2000. See Kiran Soni Gupta, 'Strengthening the Panchayats: Rajasthan Proposes to Revise Local Administration'. Available at: http://indiatogether.org/govt/local/articles/arc-rajasthan.htm

3. See James Manor, 'Epilogue: Caste and Politics in Recent Times', in Rajni Kothari (ed.), *Caste in Indian Politics* (Delhi: Orient Blackswan, 2010). For a reaction to this argument, see John Harriss, 'Reflections on Caste and Class, Hierarchy and Dominance', *Seminar*, 633, 2012.

4. The term 'sarpanch' is used in much of north India, but other labels are used elsewhere.

5. Society for Participatory Research in Asia, *A Study on the Role of Panchayati Raj Institutions in Implementation of NREGA, Phase—II* (New Delhi, 2007).

6. *The Pioneer*, 25 April 2010.

7. *The Pioneer*, 24 March and 14 April 2010.

8. Jean Dreze & Reetika Khera, 'The PEEP Survey: Water for the Leeward India', *Outlook*, 24 March 2014.

9. Some states have alternated between rotation and non-rotation-based systems for allocating reservations in local government. In 2010, the UP government returned to a rotational system after two election cycles, in which reserved seats for chief executives were distributed on the basis of local population proportions. See www.indlaw.com/guest/DisplayNews.aspx?B590F42E-F91A-4A1A-BF27–01AC5BC5AD92

10. For a more detailed assessment of these issues, see Manor, *When Local Government Strikes It Rich*.

11. Interview, Shivpuri District, Madhya Pradesh, 2 December 2009.

12. Subrata Mukherjee & Saswata Ghosh, 'What Determines the Success and Failure of "100 Days Work" at the Panchayat Level? A Study of Birbhum District', Institute of Development Studies, Kolkata, February 2009.

13. See, for example, Brinda Karat, 'Another Excuse to Cut Government Spending', *The Hindu*, 11 November 2011. Karat was a politburo member of the CPI-M, one of the parties that pushed for NREGA's enactment.

14. The idea of long-term political dominance must be distinguished from the shorter-term electoral incentives and dynamics addressed by authors such as Shylashri Shankar & Raghav Gaiha in *Battling Corruption: Has NREGA Reached India's Poor?* (Delhi: Oxford University Press, 2013), pp. 142–60.

15. Puja Dutta, Rinku Murgai, Martin Ravallion, & Dominique Van de Walle, 'Does India's Employment Guarantee Scheme Guarantee Employment?', *Economic and Political Weekly*, 47(16), 21 April 2012, pp. 55–64. When something far from normal occurred—the introduction of the requirement that workers be paid through bank accounts—a total denial of opportunities ensued for varying periods (some quite prolonged) across these states. It happened partly because some local- and block-level officials believed that it was illegal to offer work until accounts had been opened, but mainly because they sought (unsuccessfully) to devise tactics to get around this new impediment to theft.

16. The former term has been used by Anirudh Krishna in *Active Social Capital: Tracing the Roots of Development and Democracy* (New York: Columbia University Press, 2002); and the latter term by James Manor in 'Small-Time Political Fixers in India's States: "Towel Over Armpit"', *Asian Survey*, 40(5), 2000, pp. 816–35.

17. Manor, 'Small-Time Political Fixers'.

18. This distinction is elaborated in Rob Jenkins, 'Economic Reform, Clientelist Politics, and India's 2004 Elections', paper presented at the Annual Meeting of the American Political Science Association, Washington, DC, 1–4 September 2005, pp. 10–11.

19. Krishna, *Active Social Capital*.

20. These cases were described by a correspondent from the Udaipur edition of *Rajasthan Patrika*, one of the state's leading Hindi daily newspapers, 14 January 2009.

21. This paragraph is based on village-level field work and on a discussion with a group of civil society activists and local council leaders, Sehore, Madhya Pradesh, 10 December 2008.

22. This kind of arrangement was encountered by Indrajit Roy in Bihar and West Bengal. See Indrajit Roy, 'Guaranteeing Employment, Forging Political Subjectivities: Insights from the NREGS', paper delivered at a conference at the University of Sussex, June 2012, p. 37.

23. Roy, 'Guaranteeing Employment, Forging Political Subjectivities', pp. 35–36.

24. See, for example, evidence from Orissa in *The Pioneer*, 1 February and 2 April 2010.

25. Prabhu Ghate also encountered this practice in his 'A Quick Study of NREGA Implementation in Selected States', p. 50. Unpublished manuscript, no date.

26. The generic term for this intermediate tier of the system is the *Panchayati Samiti*, though it goes by different names in different states—the *Janapada Panchayat* in Madhya Pradesh, for instance, or the *Kshetra Samiti* in Uttar Pradesh.

27. We are grateful to S.S. Meenakshisundaram for confirming this point. Until his retirement, he was for many years the Government of India's leading authority on democratic decentralisation.
28. Interview, Bhopal, 21 July 2008.
29. This comment is based on extensive discussions in that region of the state in November and December 2008.
30. Interviews with civil society activists, Bhopal, 26 October 2010. Similar evidence has emerged from discussions with analysts of NREGA in several other states.

4. STATE POLITICS AND NREGA I: RAJASTHAN

1. P. Bhargava, 'Food Security and Public Distribution System in Rajasthan', *IDS Working Paper* (Jaipur: Institute of Development Studies, 2003).
2. P.C. Bansil, *Poverty Mapping in Rajasthan* (Delhi: Concept Publishing, 2006), p. 131.
3. Interview, New Delhi, January 2010.
4. A. Panagariya, 'A Mystical State Comes of Age', *The Economic Times*, 28 April 2010. Available at: http://articles.economictimes.indiatimes.com/2010-04-28/news/27620168_1_poverty-ratio-bimaru-state-rajasthan
5. Government of India (Planning Commission), *National Human Development Report 2001* (New Delhi, 2001), p. 143.
6. R. Vanneman & A. Dubey, 'Horizontal and Vertical Inequalities in India', in J. Gornick and M. Jantti (eds.), *Income Inequality: Economic Disparities and the Middle Class in Affluent Countries* (Stanford, CA: Stanford University Press, 2011), pp. 439–58.
7. Government of India (Planning Commission), *National Human Development 2001*, New Delhi, 2001, p. 46.
8. K.L. Kamal, 'Rajasthan: Politics of Declining Feudal Order', in Iqbal Narain (ed.), *State Politics in India* (Meerut: Meenakshi Prakashan, 1976).
9. Rob Jenkins, 'Where the BJP Survived: The Rajasthan Assembly Elections of 1993', *Economic and Political Weekly*, 29 (11), 12 March 1994, pp. 635–41.
10. P.C. Mathur & Iqbal Narain, 'The Thousand Year Raj', in Francine R. Frankel & M.S.A. Rao (eds.), *Dominance and State Power in Modern India* (Delhi: Oxford University Press, 1989).
11. M.N. Srinivas, 'Mobility in the Caste System', in M. Singer & B. S. Cohn (eds.), *Structure and Change in Indian Society* (Chicago, IL: Aldine Publishing Co., 1968).
12. R. Jenkins, 'Rajput Hindutva', in C. Jaffrelot & T.B. Hansen (eds.), *The BJP and Compulsions of Politics* (Delhi: Oxford University Press, 1998), pp. 101–20.
13. R. Jenkins, 'Reservation Politics in Rajasthan', paper presented at the annual meeting of the LSE Crisis States Programme, New Delhi, December 2004.
14. See Anirudh Krishna, *Active Social Capital* (New York, NY: Columbia University Press, 2002).

15. This was particularly the case in Rajasthan's state assembly elections of 2008.

16. A good deal of this history (which includes an important role for such institutions as the Indira Gandhi Panchayati Raj Institute in Jaipur) is recorded in Alka Srivastava, *A Long Journey Ahead—Women in Panchayati Raj: A Study in Rajasthan* (New Delhi: Indian Social Institute, 2006).

17. The findings from this survey are published in a series of articles contained within the special section, 'The Battle for Employment Guarantee', *Frontline*, 16 January 2009. The detailed methodology and survey instrument can be accessed at www. righttofoodindia.org

18. Jean Dreze, 'NREGA: Dismantling the Contractor Raj', *The Hindu*, 20 November 2007.

19. Ibid.

20. Ibid.

21. Ashok Pankaj & Rukmini Tankha, *Women's Empowerment through Guaranteed Employment* (New Delhi: Institute for Human Development, 2009).

22. Ibid.

23. Government of India, *Gendering Human Development Indices* (New Delhi: Ministry of Women and Child Development, 2009), pp. 9–13.

24. Madhu Kishwar's article on this topic remains relevant. See Madhu Kishwar, '"Naukri" as Property: Causes and Cures for Corruption in Government', *Manushi*, No. 100, May–June 1997.

25. This perception was conveyed in an interview that provided almost exactly the same view as one supplied twelve years earlier by another staff member of the same organisation. Interview, Udaipur, January 2010.

26. Interview, Sirohi, 14 January 2009.

27. Interview, Sirohi, 15 January 2009.

28. Herbert Kitschelt & Steven I. Wilkinson (eds.), *Patrons, Clients and Policies: Patterns of Democratic Accountability and Political Competition* (Cambridge: Cambridge University Press, 2007).

29. Rob Jenkins, 'NGOs and Indian Politics', in Niraja Gopal Jayal & Pratap Bhanu Mehta (eds.), *The Oxford Companion to Politics in India* (Delhi: Oxford University Press, 2010), pp. 409–26.

30. This refers to the title of a key text discussed in Chapter 3, Anirudh Krishna, *Active Social Capital* (New York: Columbia University Press, 2002).

31. Jean Dreze and Siddhartha Lal, 'Employment Guarantee: Unfinished Agenda', *The Hindu*, 13 July 2007.

32. Interview, Jaipur, 8 January 2009.

33. Pankaj & Tankha, *Women's Empowerment*.

34. We saw no direct evidence of this. The person making the claim, a district lawyer, was credible and had no perceptible advantage to gain from dissimulation.

35. Interview with key members of the *Abhiyan*, New York, September 2008.

36. Around this time, advertisements placed by the Government of Rajasthan began

to appear in the local press indicating that social audit forums within gram sab-has would be constituted throughout the state, as per the provisions of the NREGA Operational Guidelines.

37. 'Vasundhara Raje Government Backs Out of Banswara Social Audit', *The Hindu*, 26 December 2007.
38. Dreze and Lal, 'Employment Guarantee in Rajasthan...', 2008.
39. Ibid.
40. Rob Jenkins, 'In Varying States of Decay: The Politics of Anti-Corruption in Maharashtra and Rajasthan', in R. Jenkins (ed.), *Regional Reflections: Comparing Politics Across India's States* (Delhi: Oxford University Press, 2004), pp. 219–52.
41. See 'The Battle for Employment Guarantee', *Frontline*, 16 January 2009.
42. 'Jhalawar Social Audit Fails to Take Off', *The Hindu*, 2 February 2008.
43. 'Social and political dividends from NREGA', *The Hindu*, 18 October 2009.
44. Rozgar Evum Suchana Ka Adhikar Abhiyan (RESKAA), 'Bhilwara—District Social Audit Padyatra-Invitation and Background Note', 29 September 2009.
45. 'NREGA Audit: Bhilwara Shows the Way', *The Hindu*, 17 October 2009.
46. Sanjay Lodha, 'Rajasthan: Performance and Campaigning Pay Dividends', *Economic & Political Weekly*, 26 September 2009, p. 188.
47. 'CP Joshi: Rural Development and Panchayati Raj', *The Week*, 14 June 2009.
48. 'Cradle of Panchayati Raj Now Den of Corruption', *DNA*, 7 September 2010.
49. This is information supplied by the Jaipur correspondent for a national English-language daily newspaper.
50. Interview, Delhi, 12 January 2010.
51. Interview, Delhi, 15 January 2010.
52. It should be stressed, however, that by adopting an extremely top-down approach, Andhra Pradesh appears to have violated a key element of NREGA: failing to provide autonomy over fund-allocation to local *panchayats*.
53. Karuna Vakati Aakella & Soumya Kidambi, 'Social Audits in Andhra Pradesh: A Process in Evolution', *Economic & Political Weekly*, 24 November 2007, pp. 18–19.
54. Interview, Udaipur, 18 January 2012.
55. An oft-cited Supreme Court case that equates non-payment of minimum wages, even in the specific context of 'famine relief' works, to 'forced labour', is Sanjit Roy v. State of Rajasthan 1983 AIR 328, 1983 SCR (2) 271.
56. Reetika Khera, 'Group Measurement of NREGA Work: The Jalore Experiment', Conference Paper, Centre for Development Economics, Delhi School of Economics, 2008.
57. This scene was witnessed by one of the authors outside Tilonia, Rajasthan, 6 January 2009.
58. Interview, Jaipur, 15 March 2011.
59. 'MGNREGA Social Audit Opposed at Meet', *Times of India*, 30 July 2010.
60. Sarbeswar Sahoo, *Civil Society and Democratisation in India: Institutions, Ideologies and Interests* (Abingdon: Routledge, 2013).

5. STATE POLITICS AND NREGA II: MADHYA PRADESH

1. Average annual rainfall in western Madhya Pradesh is 1017 mm, more than three times that in western Rajasthan (313 mm). In the eastern portions of the two states, the differential drops to 2:1 (1339 mm in Madhya Pradesh compared to 675 mm in Rajasthan). These are 25-year averages compiled by www.rainwater-harvesting.org

2. This is discussed in more detail in chapter three of M.A. Melo, N. Ng'ethe, & J. Manor, *Against the Odds: Politicians, Institutions and the Struggle against Poverty* (London: Hurst, 2012).

3. Interview with two Ekta Parishad leaders, Bhopal, 7 November 2010.

4. These comments are based on James Manor's field research in these five states between 1998 and 2014.

5. Interview with a senior official who was involved in both programmes, Bhopal, 14 December 2008.

6. This emerged at a workshop, held at the India International Centre in New Delhi on 7 December 2010, at which draft versions of this chapter (and Chapter 4) were discussed. Participants' comments were 'not for attribution'.

7. These figures are for the period after 2000, when a new state, Chhattisgarh, was created by carving out a number of contiguous districts of Madhya Pradesh. Prior to 2000, Madhya Pradesh had been India's largest state in terms of area.

8. Government of India (Planning Commission), *National Human Development Report 2001* (New Delhi, 2001), p. 141. A similar calculation for 2001 placed Madhya Pradesh twelth of fifteen major states (p. 25). Rural Rajasthan came ninth.

9. Ibid., p. 143.

10. Ibid., p. 187.

11. Vanneman & Dubey, 'Horizontal and Vertical Inequalities in India'.

12. M.S. Ahluwalia, 'State Level Performance Under Economic Reforms in India', paper presented at Stanford University, May 2000, p. 26. Available at: www.planningcommission.gov.in/aboutus/speech/spemsa/msa007.pdf

13. Government of India (Planning Commission), *National Human Development Report*, p. 46.

14. Ibid., p. 159.

15. J. Manor, 'The Congress Defeat in Madhya Pradesh', *Seminar*, February 2009.

16. Ibid.

17. This is discussed in more detail in J. Manor, 'In Part a Myth: The BJP's Organisational Strength', in K. Adeney & L. Saez (eds.), *Coalition Politics and Hindu Nationalism* (London & New Delhi: Routledge, 2005); J. Manor, 'The Congress Defeat in Madhya Pradesh'.

18. This comment is based on extensive field research since 1998 at the village level in Madhya Pradesh and in several others where party loyalties are more intensely and widely held.

19. For more detail, see J. Manor, 'Beyond Clientelism: Digvijay Singh's Participatory, Pro-Poor Strategy in Madhya Pradesh', in A.E. Ruud & P. Price (eds.), *Leaders and Politics in South Asia* (London and New Delhi: Routledge, 2010).

20. This and Digvijay Singh's approach to governing are analysed in detail in Chapter 3 of Melo, Ng'ethe, & Manor, *Against the Odds*.

21. Even when winning the 2003 state election (which one of us witnessed), the BJP organisation in Madhya Pradesh was shown to be embarrassingly frail. Most mass contact with voters during that campaign was undertaken not by BJP activists but by members of the Rashtriya Swayamsevak Sangh (RSS), many of whom were brought into Madhya Pradesh from other states. See Manor, 'The Congress Defeat in Madhya Pradesh'.

22. The Congress government that ruled Madhya Pradesh between 1993 and 2003 relied to a considerable extent on *panchayat* institutions. The BJP, which has governed the state since December 2003, has relied on these bodies much less, and has undermined their authority.

23. We are grateful to S.S. Meenakshisundaram for stressing this point.

24. This is discussed in detail in Chapter 3 of Melo, Ng'ethe, & Manor, *Against the Odds*.

25. Interviews with Amitabh Singh, Bhopal, 15 December 2008, and with a group of civil society activists and *panchayat* chairpersons, Sehore, 12 December 2008.

26. The surveys in both states were conducted by the same team of survey specialists from the Institute of Development Studies, Jaipur. By using the same enumerators, we avoided variations that might have arisen if different teams had operated in the two states.

27. *Financial Express*, 26 May 2007.

28. Interview with *Samarthan* activists, Bhopal, 12 December 2008.

29. Centre for Budget and Governance Accountability, *Report on the Implementation of the NREGA in Andhra Pradesh, Chhattisgarh, Jharkhand and Madhya Pradesh* (New Delhi, June 2006), p. 26. Available at: www.nrega.nic.in

30. See also, for example, Government of India (Ministry of Rural Development), *National Rural Employment Guarantee Act (NREGA): Some Reports from the Field, 2006–07* (New Delhi, 2007), p. 12 and pp. 30–40.

31. See, for example, the views of Aruna Roy, set forth in *The Hindu*, 17 October 2009.

32. Jenkins, 'NGOs and Indian Politics'.

33. James Manor has seen this over several periods of field work in a number of those other districts since 2000.

34. In December 2003, the BJP won a state election by a large margin after ten years of rule by the Congress Party, its main rival in the (largely) two-party system that has long existed in Madhya Pradesh. In late 2008, it was re-elected with a reduced but workable majority.

35. Tariq Thachil, *Elite Parties, Poor Voters: How Social Services Win Votes in India* (New York: Cambridge University Press, 2014).

36. See, for example, *Times of India*,18 October 2006; *The Hindu*,1 August 2010; *Sanhati*, 7 August 2010.

37. These comments are based on interviews with Madhuri Behn and informants with close ties to government officials in Barwani, 9 and 10 December 2008.

38. Jean Dreze, 'Employment Guarantee and the Right to Work', in Niraja Gopal Jayal & Pratap Bhanu Mehta (eds.), *The Oxford Companion to Politics in India* (Oxford: Oxford University Press, 2010), p. 516.

39. Ibid.

40. Ibid.

41. Andhra Pradesh is an exception.

42. These comments are based in interviews with senior civil servants in Bhopal and New Delhi, December 2008.

43. Examples include the Indira Gandhi Old Age Pension Scheme, the Rajiv Gandhi Shramik Kalyan Yojana (an unemployment allowance programme), and the Jawaharlal Nehru National Urban Renewal Mission.

44. Interview with a member of the National Advisory Council, New Delhi, 8 May 2009.

45. Poorest Areas Civil Society [PACS], *Madhya Pradesh and Chhattisgarh* (New Delhi, 2006), p. 4.

46. One conspicuous exception is Tamil Nadu, where the government decided that 100 per cent of NREGA projects should be implemented through *panchayats*— although it is not entirely clear that 100 per cent of NREGA funds passed through *panchayat* accounts. Some funds have been channelled through line ministries with the proviso that *panchayats* be given some influence over their use.

47. Interview with Amita Sharma, senior administrator of NREGA, New Delhi, 8 April 2008.

48. This comment is based on numerous interviews with leaders of the Congress Party and the BJP in Bhopal since 2002, and on field work in Madhya Pradesh villages, where it is common to find that only two or three local residents are (often vaguely) identified as members of one or another party. In this respect, the state differs markedly from many others where partisan passions loom large in villages.

49. For more detail on this issue, see J. Manor, 'What Do They Know of India Who Only India Know?', *Commonwealth and Comparative Politics*, 48(4), 2010, pp. 505–16.

50. Samarthan has long sought to bolster the capacity of elected leaders and members of local councils, to strengthen networks that connect them and give them greater voice, to lobby the state government on their behalf, and to disseminate important information to them and through them to citizens—especially the poor and the socially excluded. It has made greater headway on this front than has been possible in Rajasthan—and in all but three other Indian states—because the Congress chief minister who held power in Madhya Pradesh between 1993 and 2003, Digvijay Singh, was an enthusiast for *panchayati raj*.

51. Interview with an analytically acute civil society activist, Bhopal, 21 July 2008.
52. This account is based on interviews with civil society leaders who took part in this discussion, Bhopal, 11 December 2008.
53. The exception is Ekta Parishad, a Gandhian organisation which—uniquely among civil society organisations in Madhya Pradesh—has a mass following. It was often sharply critical of the Congress Party when it governed between 1993 and 2003, but late in that decade, it forged an accommodation with Congress in exchange for concessions on land issues that affected poor people. For more details, see Chapter 3 of Melo, Ng'ethe, & Manor, *Against the Odds*.
54. This comment is based on interviews with several BJP leaders in Bhopal in 1999 and 2008.
55. See Chapter 3 of Melo, Ng'ethe, & Manor, *Against the Odds*.
56. National Council of Applied Economic Research, *NCAER-PIF Study Evaluating Performance of National Rural Employment Guarantee Act* (New Delhi: NCAER/Public Interest Foundation, 2009), pp. 12–16. The report attributes this to over-reporting, but in Madhya Pradesh, the explanation is actually excessive zeal on the part of the government. According to NREGA administrative data, in mid-2008, 7.24 million job cards had been issued, though the state had only 5.23 million rural households. This represented 135 per cent of rural households. In Shivpuri District, 267,158 job cards had been issued, amounting to 133 per cent of rural households. Our field research in Shivpuri found that this discrepancy was largely explained by households that obtained more than one job card, though it also partly reflected the creation of job cards for non-existent people.
57. Ibid., pp. 14–15.
58. Centre for Budget and Governance Accountability, *Report on the Implementation of NREGA*, p. 20 and 43.
59. *DNA*, 4 February 2010.
60. The results of this CNN-IBN-The Hindu Election Tracker Poll were reported in 'Will It Continue to be Advantage Chouhan?', *The Hindu*, 25 July 2013. Available at: www.thehindu.com/news/national/will-it-continue-to-be-advantage-chouhan/article4952708.ece
61. These points emerged from discussions with Yogendra Yadav and Sanjay Kumar at the Centre for the Study of Developing Societies, Delhi, which collected and analysed this evidence.
62. These figures come from the Centre for the Study of Developing Societies, Delhi.
63. See Manor, 'The Congress Defeat in Madhya Pradesh'.
64. Interview, Delhi, 30 May 2009.
65. These figures appear, along with a more detailed explanation, in J. Manor, 'Did the Central Government's Poverty Initiatives Help to Re-Elect it?', in L. Saez & G. Singh (eds.), *New Dimensions of Politics in India: The United Progressive Alliance in Power* (New Delhi and London: Routledge, 2011). They are derived from a

post-poll survey conducted by the National Election Study supervised by the Centre for the Study of Developing Societies, Delhi, to which we are grateful for assistance.

66. J. Manor, 'The Trouble with Yeddyurappa', *Economic and Political Weekly*, 13 March 2011, pp. 16–19.

67. Interview, Bhopal, 5 December 2008.

68. The quotation is from an interview with a *sarpanch* in Sehore District, where such control is exercised, 10 December 2008.

69. These comment are based on two prolonged discussions with separate groups of *sarpanches* and civil society activists in Sehore District (a 'best case'), 10 December 2008. In some Indian states—for example, Bihar—severe shortages of block-level officials have caused huge problems.

70. Sangeeta Kamat, *Development Hegemony: NGOs and the State in India* (Delhi: Oxford University Press, 2002).

6. NREGA'S IMPACT ON THE MATERIAL WELL-BEING AND POLITICAL CAPACITY OF POOR PEOPLE

1. One useful example is Government of India (Ministry of Rural Development), *MGNREGA Sameeksha* (New Delhi: Orient Blackswan, 2012).

2. They have made their case in several publications, but for a good summary, see S. Shankar, R. Gaiha, & R. Jha, 'Numbers to the Rescue', *Indian Express*, 20 October 2009. See also, R. Jha, R. Gaiha, S. Shankar, & K.S. Imai in *The Africa Report* (December 2009–January 2010), p. 57; R. Gaiha, S. Shankar, & R. Jha, 'Targeting Accuracy of the NREG: Evidence from Rajasthan, Andhra Pradesh and Maharashtra', *Working Paper 3* (Canberra: Australia South Asia Research Centre, 2010); and R. Jha, R. Gaiha, S. Shankar, & M.K. Pandey, 'Targeting Accuracy of the NREG: Evidence from Madhya Pradesh and Tamil Nadu', *Working Paper 19* (Canberra: Australia South Asia Research Centre, 2010).

3. P. Dutta, R. Murgai, M. Ravallion & D. van de Walle, 'Does India's Employment Guarantee Scheme Guarantee Employment?', *Economic and Political Weekly*, 21 April 2012, pp. 55–64. This paper was also published by the World Bank as *Policy Research Working Paper 6003* (March 2012).

4. *The Hindu*, 14 September 2009.

5. Ibid.

6. We are grateful to Grace Carswell and Geert de Neve for this information. The International Labour Organization has noted that NREGA helped Indians who suffered from the global economic crisis to cope with shocks such as this. *Economic Times*, 27 January 2010.

7. K. Banerjee & P. Saha, 'The NREGA, the Maoists and the Developmental Woes of the Indian State', *Economic and Political Weekly*, 45 (28), 10 July 2010, pp. 42–7.

8. R. Khera (ed.), *Battle for Employment Guarantee* (Delhi: Oxford University Press, 2011), pp. 43–81.

9. See table 1.2 in *MGNREGA Sameeksha*, p. 13.

10. R. Jha, R. Gaiha & S. Shankar, *The Tribune*, 1 November 2009. This finding emerged from their research in Rajasthan, a more typical state than Maharashtra (another of their cases), where the impact of NREGA has, as noted, been less constructive.

11. M. Shah, 'Employment Guarantee, Civil Society and Indian Democracy', *Economic and Political Weekly*, 17 November 2007, pp. 43–51.

12. Institute of Forest Management, Institute of Rural Management, & Institute of Social Science Research, 'Independent Evaluation of MGNREGA', 2012. Initially cited in *MGNREGA Sameeksha*.

13. *The Hindu*, 19 September 2009.

14. *Business Standard*, 9 July 2012.

15. *MGNREGA Sameeksha*, pp. 45–51 (quotation from p. 47). See also Brinda Karat's arguments in *The Hindu*, 11 November 2011.

16. *Business Standard*, 14 July 2012, citing findings from a study conducted by Oxford University and the Institute for Social and Economic Change, Bangalore.

17. See also *MGNREGA Sameeksha*, pp. 8–9.

18. E. Berg, S. Bhattacharyya, R. Durg, & M. Ramachandra, 'Can Rural Public Works Affect Agricultural Wages? Evidence from India', *Working Paper WPS/2012–15*, Centre for the Study of African Economies, University of Oxford, 2012.

19. *The Hindu*, 16 October 2010.

20. 'NREGA Spiked Rural Wages Only 10 per cent, Rest is Due to Rise in Minimum Support Price: Raghuram Rajan', *Economic Times*, 17 August 2014.

21. *MGNREGA Sameeksha*, p. 7, drawing on K. Deininger & K.H. Rao, 'Poverty Impacts of India's National Rural Employment Guarantee Scheme: Evidence from Andhra Pradesh', 2010.

22. Shamika Ravi & Monika Engler, 'Workfare as an Effective Way to Fight Poverty: The Case of India's NREGS', *World Development*, 67, 2015, pp. 57–71; V.S. Babu & K.H. Rao, *Impact of MGNREGS on Scheduled Castes and Scheduled Tribes: Studies Conducted in Eight States* (Hyderabad: National Institute of Rural Development, 2010); and Banerjee & Saha, 'The NREGA, the Maoists and the Developmental Woes of the Indian State'. All were initially cited in *MGNREGA Samseeksha*.

23. Ravi & Engler, *Workfare as an Effective Way to Fight Poverty;* Babu & Rao, 'Impact of MGNREGS'.

24. See, for example, ASCI, *Study for Quick Appraisal of NREGA in Andhra Pradesh* (Hyderabad, 2009), Part II, p. 6, 9.

25. Indira Armugam encountered this trend in Tamil Nadu.

26. *The Hindu*, 6 September 2009. The study was conducted in 2006–7 by the Institute of Applied Manpower Research, Delhi.

27. P. Ghate, 'A Quick Study of NREGA Implementation Issues in Selected States', Unpublished manuscript, p. 44.

28. Banerjee & Saha, 'The NREGA, the Maoists and the Developmental Woes of the Indian State'; D. Johnson, 'Can Workfare Serve as a Substitute for Weather Insurance? The Case of NREGA in Andhra Pradesh', *Working Paper 22*, Institute of Financial Management and Research (Chennai, 2009). All initially cited in *MGNREGA Sameeksha*.

29. Ghate, 'A Quick Study', p. 44.

30. Interview, Mysore, 12 November 2010.

31. *Frontline*, 3–16 January 2009.

32. This emerged from our interviews during field research in rural Madhya Pradesh. See also, P. Mistry & A. Jaswal, 'Study of the Implementation of NREGS: Focus on Migration' (Ahmedabad: DISHA, 2009). Available at www.knowledge.nrega.net

33. ASCI, *Study for Quick Appraisal of NREGA*, Part II, p. 3.

34. V. Uppal, 'Is NREGA a Safety Net for Children?', Paper for 'Young Lives', Department for International Development Project, Oxford University, 2009.

35. This emerged from field research in Karnataka and Bangladesh in preparation for the book, R.C. Crook & J. Manor, *Democracy and Decentralisation in South Asia and West Africa: Participation, Accountability and Performance* (Cambridge: Cambridge University Press, 1998).

36. J. Manor, 'Perspectives on Decentralisation', forthcoming in separate volumes to be published, respectively, by the International Food Policy Research Institute (Washington, DC) and the International Centre for Local Democracy (Sweden).

37. Interview with Digvijay Singh, former chief minister of Madhya Pradesh, New Delhi, 7 May 2010.

38. See Josy Joseph, 'I'm a Little Nervous About NREGA-2: Interview with Prof Jean Dreze', *DNA*, 17 August 2009; the views of some members of the Central Employment Guarantee Council (including Dreze) in *The Hindu*, 13 September 2010; and numerous references provided below. Note that Dreze has argued both that NREGA 'slows down' distress migration (*DNA*, 17 August 2009) and that distress migration has not declined as much as it would have if NREGA had been implemented more effectively (*Business Standard*, 14 July 2012).

39. Those studies were originally cited in the central government's volume, *MGNREGA Sameeksha*, p. 53. They are: T. Shah, S. Verma, R. Indu, & P Hemant, *Asset Creation through Employment Guarantee?: Synthesis of Student Case Studies of 40 MGNREGA Works in 9 States of India* (Anand: International Water Management Institute, 2010); and S. Verma, *MG-NREGA Assets and Rural Water Security: Synthesis of Field Studies in Bihar, Gujarat, Kerala and Rajasthan* (Anand: International Water Management Institute, 2011). See also National Consortium of Civil Society Organisations, *MGNREGA: Opportunities, Challenges and the Road Ahead* (New Delhi, 2011). Both sources were initially cited in *MGNREGA Sameeksha*.

40. One worth stressing is S. Verma, *Multiple Use Water Services in India: Scaling Up Community Based MUS through MGNREGA* (Anand: International Water Management Institute, 2011).

41. *The Hindu*, 6 September 2009.

42. Centre for Science and Environment, *An Assessment of the Performance of the National Rural Employment Guarantee Programme in Terms of its Potential for Creation of Natural Wealth in India's Villages* (New Delhi, 2008). Initially cited in *MGNREGA Sameeksha*, p. 51.

43. *Frontline*, 3–16 January 2009.

44. R. Kumar & R. Prasanna, 'Role of NREGA in Providing Additional Employment for Tribals and Curtailing Migration', in Government of India (Ministry of Rural Development), *National Rural Employment Guarantee Act (NREGA): Design, Process and Impact* (New Delhi, 2010).

45. *The Pioneer*, 21 December 2009 and 11 April 2010.

46. This was Vishal Naik of Samarthan in Bhopal.

47. *Economic Times*, 25 July 2010.

48. *The Pioneer*, 30 May 2010.

49. The quotation is from *MGNREGA Sameeksha*, p. 51. The source is K. Kareemulla, S.K. Reddy, C.A. Rao, S. Kumar, & B. Venkteswarlu, 'Soil and Water Conservation Works through National Rural Employment Guarantee Scheme (NREGS) in Andhra Pradesh—An Analysis of Livelihood Impact', *Agricultural Economics Research Review*, 2009, pp. 443–50.

50. ASCI, *Study for Quick Appraisal of NREGA*, Part II, pp. 3 and 5.

51. Note that despite this comment, Bihar is for the most part an exception to the pattern in nearly all other states, in that only 9 per cent of rural households did NREGA work in 2011–12 (*Business Standard*, 9 July 2012). The impact on 'distress migration' in Bihar was therefore less marked than in most other states. Despite energetic efforts by enlightened civil servants in Bihar's state government, this poor performance occurred because of a severe shortage of administrative staff at lower levels, a problem that could only be corrected slowly.

52. *Times of India*, 21 October 2009 and 13 June 2010.

53. A study in Chhattisgarh, for example, found that while NREGA states that workers should be paid for their labour within fifteen days, only 4 per cent of workers had been paid within that period, and almost 70 per cent had waited more than a month to be paid (*The Hindu*, 22 January 2011). See also, *Outlook*, 1 October 2007. Delays also put off potential job seekers—see for example, *The Hindu*, 25 April 2012; *Business Standard*, 14 July 2012.

54. S. Verma & T. Shah, 'Labour Market Dynamics in Post-MGNREGS Rural India', Water Policy Research Highlight, IWMI-TATA Water Policy Program, 2012 (initially cited in *MGNREGA Sameeksha*, p. 51); and P. Sainath, 'NREGS: Not Caste in Stone', *The Hindu*, 14 September 2009. See also Joseph, 'Interview with Prof Jean Dreze'.

55. *The Hindu*, 12 August 2010. For more on migration from that region to brick kilns in South India, see *The Hindu*, 24 September 2010.

56. *Business Standard*, 11 July 2010, drawing upon an analysis by Ashwani Kumar.

57. Perverse evidence of this is provided by a World Bank report which criticises NREGA because it had substantially reduced the rate of rural-to-urban migration that the World Bank regarded as essential for India to make a major developmental leap. The authors clearly regard the massive social dislocation seen in China as a preferable model—something which politicians in a democracy like India are disinclined to permit. The authors also fail to see that the wages and opportunities available to migrants arriving in Indian cities fall far short of what is required to raise their families' living standards (*Economic Times*, 15 March 2009). The report was sufficiently embarrassing to the World Bank's India Country Director for him to offer a much more positive view of NREGA a few weeks later (see *Economic Times*, 3 June 2009).

58. *MGNREGA Sameeksha*, p. 19. Figures were derived from the official website, www.mgnrega.nic.in

59. Ibid., pp. 18–19, drawing on Dutta et al., 'Does India's Employment Guarantee Scheme Guarantee Employment?'.

60. Ibid., p. 19, drawing on Jayati Ghosh, 'Equity and Inclusion through Public Expenditure: The Potential of the NREGS', paper for an international conference on NREGA, New Delhi, January 2009.

61. That is, Rs. 53,000 crores. Ibid., p. 18.

62. Dutta et al., 'Does India's Employment Guarantee Scheme Guarantee Employment?', p. 17.

63. R.M. Sudarshan, *India's National Rural Employment Guarantee Act: Women's Participation and Impacts in Himachal Pradesh, Kerala and Rajasthan* (Brighton, UK: Institute of Development Studies, 2011), cited in *MGNREGA Sameeksha*, p. 21.

64. Devaki Jain, 'Guaranteeing Employment: Immeasurable Benefits for Women', Unpublished paper (Bangalore, 2005), originally cited in Jean Dreze, 'Employment Guarantee and the Right to Work', in Niraja Gopal Jayal & Pratap Bhanu Mehta (eds.), *The Oxford Companion to Politics in India* (Oxford: Oxford University Press, 2010), p. 511.

65. Aruna Bagchee, 'Political and Administrative Realities of the EGS', *Economic and Political Weekly*, 40(42), 15 October 2005, pp. 41–50. Originally cited in Dreze, 'Employment Guarantee and the Right to Work'.

66. Joseph, 'Interview with Prof Jean Dreze'.

67. One study found that 35 per cent of female workers for private contractors had suffered harassment. The figure for NREGA work sites was not specified, but on all sites where contractors were not present (they are legally banned from involvement in NREGA), only 8 per cent had faced harassment (*Frontline*, 3–16 January

2009). The same study also found that contractors were operating in some places, despite the ban, in all of the states studied except Rajasthan. See also, *Sunday Pioneer*, 12 June 2010.

68. This emerged from our interviews during field research in Madhya Pradesh. Similar perceptions were found in Tamil Nadu by Grace Carswell and Geert de Neve. See Geert De Neve and Grace Carswell, 'NREGA and the Return of Identity Politics in Western Tamil Nadu, India', *Forum for Development Studies*, 38(2), 2011, pp. 2005–10.

69. National Sample Survey Office, 'India—Employment and Unemployment Survey: NSS 66th Round', July 2009–June 2010 (Delhi, 2011). Available at: http://www.ilo.org/surveydata/index.php/catalog/208/study-description; cited in *MGNREGA Sameeksha*, p. 21.

70. Sudarshan, *India's National Rural Employment Guarantee Act*, p. 21.

71. Khera (ed.), *The Battle for Employment*, pp. 43–81.

72. The quotation is from *MGNREGA Sameeksha*, p. 22, drawing on C. Dheeraja & Hanumantha Rao, *Changing Gender Relations: A Study of MGNREGA Across Different States* (Hyderabad: National Institute of Rural Development, 2010).

73. *MGNREGA Sameeksha*, p. 25, drawing on Reetika Kera & N. Nayak, 'Women Workers and Perceptions of the National Rural Employment Guarantee Act', *Economic and Politicval Weekly*, 44(43), 24 October 2009; Khera (ed.), *The Battle for Employment Guarantee*, pp. 43–81.

74. *Times of India*, 5 September 2009.

75. *MGNREGA Sameeksha*, p. 24, drawing on Dheeraja & Rao, 'Changing Gender Relations'.

76. *MGNREGA Sameeksha*, drawing on Khera & Nayak, 'Women Workers and Perceptions'.

77. ASCI, *Study for Quick Appraisal*, Part II, p. 3.

78. This emerged from survey research by our colleagues at the Institute of Development Studies, Jaipur, for the United Nations Development Programme.

79. Discussion with Indira Armugam, London, 28 April 2011.

80. See, for example, *MGNREGA Sameeksha*, p. 25.

81. This emerged from our field research in Madhya Pradesh and Rajasthan. See also, Dheeraja & Rao, 'Changing Gender Relations'.

82. See, for example, Crook & Manor, *Democracy and Decentralisation in South Asia and West Africa*, Ch. 2.

83. *The Hindu*, 30 April 2009.

84. Discussion with Indira Armugam, London, 28 April 2009.

85. A.K. Basu, 'Impact of Rural Employment Guarantee Schemes on Seasonal Labour Markets: Optimum Compensation and Workers' Welfare', *The Journal of Economic Inequality*, 11(1), 2011. Initially cited in *MGNREGA Sameeksha*.

86. ASCI, *Study for Quick Appraisal*, Part II, p. 6, 9.

87. See for example, M.N. Panini, 'The Political Economy of Caste', in M.N. Srinivas (ed.), *Caste: Its Twentieth Century Avatar* (New Delhi: Penguin, 1996), pp. 28–68; James Manor, 'Prologue: Caste and Politics in Recent Times', pp. xxii-xxvi (on the 'materiality of caste').

88. This change has occurred to varying degrees in different places. But for several years there has been evidence from a variety of regions to indicate that the trend was quite real. See for example, G.K. Karanth, 'Caste in Contemporary Rural India', in Srinivas (ed.), *Caste: Its Twentieth Century Avatar*, p. 106; A. Mayer, 'Caste in an Indian Village: Change and Continuity', in C.J. Fuller (ed.), *Caste Today* (Delhi: Oxford University Press, 1997), pp. 32–64; G.K. Karanth, *Change and Continuity in Agrarian Relations* (New Delhi: Concept, 1995); S.R. Charsley & G.K. Karanth (eds.), *Challenging Untouchability: Dalit Initiative and Experience from Karnataka* (London: Altamira Press, 1998); D. Gupta, *Caste in Question: Identity or Hierarchy?* (New Delhi: Sage, 2004); S.S. Jodhka, 'Caste and Untouchability in Rural Punjab', *Economic and Political Weekly*, 37(19), 11 May 2002, pp. 1813–23; and S.S. Jodhka & P. Louis, 'Caste Tensions in Punjab: Talhan and Beyond', *Economic and Political Weekly*, 38(28), 12 July 2003, pp. 2923–36.

89. The institution of caste exists among Muslims as well as Hindus. See Imtiaz Ahmed (ed.), *Caste and Social Stratification among Muslims in India* (Delhi: Manohar, 1973).

90. We are grateful to Hemlath Rao and his colleagues at ASCI for insights into this episode. See also, ASCI, *Study for Quick Appraisal of NREGA*, Part II, pp. 1–4. On poor people's use of wages to invest in their small plots of land, see p. 9.

91. The study was conducted by the Institute of Applied Manpower Research. See *The Hindu*, 6 September 2009.

92. ASCI, *Study for Quick Appraisal of NREGA*, pp. 1–9.

93. Interview, Hyderabad, 30 December 2011.

94. See Sainath, 'NREGS: Not Caste in Stone'. As one labourer put it to Sainath, 'We work together, all of us, and not on a caste basis'.

95. See, for example, J. Manor, 'Conflict and Accommodation Amid Waning Hierarchies', *Seminar* (May 2012).

96. This comment is based on James Manor's research in that district in 2011.

97. We Are grateful to Grace Carswell and Geert de Neve for this information.

98. Indrajit Roy, 'Guaranteeing Employment, Forging Political Subjectivities: Insights from the NREGS', Unpublished paper, June 2012, p. 26.

99. *The Hindu*, 14 September 2009.

100. Discussion with Indira Armugam, London, 28 April 2009.

101. K. Imai, R. Gaiha, V. Kulkarni, & M. Pandey, 'National Rural Employment Guarantee Scheme, Poverty and Prices in Rural India', *Economics Discussion Paper Series—EDP 908*, University of Manchester, 2009. Initially cited in *MGNREGA Sameeksha*.

102. See, for example, *DNA*, 17 August 2009.

103. See the report by Jean Dreze & Reetika Khera, *Frontline*, 3–16 January 2009. See also, *Sunday Pioneer*, 12 June 2010.

7. NREGA, NATIONAL POLITICS, AND POLICY EVOLUTION

1. See J. Dreze, 'Employment and the Right to Work', in R. Khera (ed.), *Battle for Employment Guarantee* (New Delhi: Oxford University Press, 2011).

2. See R. Jenkins, 'The Politics of "Permanent Reform"', in R. Jenkins, L. Kennedy & P. Mukhopadhyay (eds.), *Power, Policy and Protest: The Politics of India's Special Economic Zones* (Delhi: Oxford University Press, 2014).

3. J. Dreze & A. Sen, *An Uncertain Glory: India and Its Contradictions* (Princeton, NJ: Princeton University Press, 2013), p. 284.

4. 'Wake-up Call on Rural Employment Guarantee', *Economic and Political Weekly*, 43(4), 26 January 2008, pp. 5–6.

5. J. Dreze, 'Employment Guarantee and the Right to Work', in Jayal & Mehta (eds.), *The Oxford Companion to Politics in India*, p. 516.

6. Ibid.

7. M. Jeelani, 'NREGA's Reality Check', *Caravan*, 1 May 2010.

8. As a 2008 study of NREGA in Bihar and Jharkhand noted, the programme was being undertaken in the two states under severely trying circumstances, including a 'poor record of development delivery including public works and poverty alleviation', 'ineffective PRIs [Panchayati Raj Institutions] in Bihar and non-formation of formal PRIs in Jhankhand', and 'weak traditions of civil society mobilisation' in both states. Ashok K. Pankaj, *Processes, Institutions and Mechanisms of Implementation of NREGA: Impact Assessment of Bihar and Jharkhand* (Delhi: Institute for Human Development, 2008), p. 1.

9. Jeelani, 'NREGA's Reality Check'.

10. Ibid.

11. 'After Modi sniffs corruption in NREGA, Delhi flags state dossier', *Indian Express*, 27 July 2010.

12. 'Supreme Court nod for CBI probe into alleged irregularities in MNREGA', *The Economic Times*, 14 March 2014.

13. We make no comment here on differing views expressed about the quality of the public works produced under NREGA. Our research has not focused on that issue.

14. Bharat Bhatti, 'Aadhaar-Enabled Payments for NREGA Workers', *Economic and Political Weekly*, 47(49), 8 December 2012, pp. 16–19 (quote from p. 16).

15. Ibid.

16. For a balanced, survey-based analysis, see Anindita Adhikar & Kartika Bhatia, 'NREGA Wage Payment: Can We Bank on the Banks?', *Economic and Political*

Weekly, 45(1), 2 January 2010, pp. 30–37. Among the recommendations emerging from this study was that NREGA social audits should 'include verification of bank records including payment orders' (p. 37).

17. Dreze, 'Employment Guarantee and the Right to Work', pp. 516–17.

18. Ibid.

19. Ibid.

20. For examples other than those which we witnessed, see *The Pioneer*, 29 June and 9 July 2010; and *The Hindu*, 21 August and 13 September 2010.

21. For other examples, see *The Economic Times*, 10 May and 30 December 2010; *The Pioneer*, 1 July 2010; *The Hindu*, 28 July 2010; and *Business Standard*, 16 May 2010 and 17 July 2012. Also see the discussion earlier in this chapter of the recent interventions ('new checks') that have closed off opportunities to divert funds from NREGA.

22. Rajni Kothari, 'Non-Party Political Process', *Economic and Political Weekly*, 19(5), 1984, pp. 216–24.

23. *The Pioneer*, 1 July 2010.

24. Government of India (Planning Commission), *Towards Faster and More Inclusive Growth: Approach Paper to the 11th Five Year Plan (2007–2012)* (New Delhi, 2007), p. 72.

25. C.H. Hanumantha Rao, *Agriculture, Food Security, Poverty and Environment: Essays on Post-Reform India* (Delhi: Oxford University Press, 2005). Rao points out that population is not the main factor here, either: 'The rural labour force, whether in agriculture or non-agriculture, has been gowing at a faster rate than the population growth in rural areas', mainly because of the 'steep decline' in the share of people who are self-employed (p. 210).

26. One of the authors attended this event and noted that the finance minister reinforced the point about NREGA in the informal discussion that followed his prepared remarks.

27. The website of the Mazdoor Haq Satyagraha provides something like a manifesto for the groups that collectively drove the protest in 2010. See http://srabhiyan. wordpress.com/

28. 'Ensure minimum wages to NREGA workers: Activists', *Times of India*, 4 October 2010.

29. *The Hindu*, 7 January 2011.

30. Contrast the argument in an article by R. Gaiha, S. Shankar, & R. Jha in the *Indian Express*, 20 October 2010, with demands from members of the Central Employment Guarantee Council (CEGC) for increases in wages. *The Hindu*, 29 August 2010. For a sense of the debate, see also, *Deccan Chronicle*, 15 June 2010; and *The Hindu*, 23 October 2010 and 6 and 21 January 2011.

31. 'Need to have a parity of wage under MNREGA: Jairam', *India TV*, 2 February 2014. Available at: http://www.indiatvnews.com/politics/national/need-to-have-parity-of-wage-under-mnrega-jairam-14665.html

32. MoRD (Dept. of Rural Development), Notification, The Gazette of India, Extraordinary, New Delhi, 25 May 2006. GSR. 311(E). [Jt Secretary, Office Ref. No. J. 24011/5/2005-SGRY(M)].

33. MoRD (Dept. of Rural Development), Notification, The Gazette of India, Extraordinary, New Delhi, 23 March 2012. S.O. 578(E). [Jt Secretary, Office Ref. No. J-11011/1/2009/MGNREGA(Pt)].

34. Action for Employment Guarantee, 'Update 124: NREGA Audit of Scheme Rules, Action from the Field', 13 September 2011. Available at: http://www.nrega.net. in/content/update-124-nrega-audit-scheme-rules-action-field-uid-primer-and-more

35. Lakin & Ravishankar, 'Working for Votes'.

36. Ashutosh Varshney, *Democracy, Development and the Countryside: Urban-Rural Struggles in India* (Cambridge: Cambridge University Press, 1998), p. 176 (cited by Lakin & Ravishankar, 'Working for Voters', p. 24).

37. MoRD, 'Guidelines for Implementation of Works on Individual Land Under NREGA', January 2009. Draft.

38. This was voiced, though only conditionally endorsed, by Partha Mukhopadyay in a conversation with one of the authors, New York, 4 May 2012.

39. MoRD, 'Guidelines for Implementation of Works on Individual Land Under NREGA'.

40. MoRD, 'Minutes of the Meeting of Empowered Committee under MGNREGA regarding Bihar and Jharkhand held on 28th March, 2012', New Delhi, 19 April 2012, Director MGNREGA, Ref. No. J-11018/2/2012-MGNREGA, Section 3(a)(v).

41. Ibid.

42. New York, NY: Public Affairs, 2013.

43. Ibid., pp. 49–50.

44. Ibid., pp. 96.

45. Ibid., pp. 153.

46. Ibid., pp. 157–164.

47. Princeton, NJ: Princeton University Press, 2013.

48. Dreze is a native of Belgium who has lived in India for decades, eventually becoming an Indian citizen.

49. Bhagwati & Panagariya, *Why Growth Matters*, p. 154.

50. Ibid.

51. Dreze & Sen, *An Uncertain Glory*, p. 99.

52. Ibid., p. 105.

53. *Business Standard*, 9 July 2013.

54. *Business Standard*, 6 September 2013.

55. See Utsa Patnaik, 'Theorizing food security and poverty in the era of economic reforms', *Social Scientist* (July–August 2005).

56. Dreze, 'Employment Guarantee and the Right to Work', p. 14, footnote 12.

57. Aditya Dasgupta, Kishore Gawande, & Devesh Kapur, 'Anti-poverty Programmes Can Reduce Violence: India's Rural Employment Guarantee and Maoist Conflict', Mimeo, 13 September 2014.

58. 'MGNREGA Will Help Implement Direct Benefit Transfers', *Livemint.com*, 2 February 2013. Available at: http://www.livemint.com/Politics/7W9SWyur Cc3LWdcVrHadqM/MNREGA-will-help-implement-direct-benefit-transfers-PM.html

59. MoRD, Notification no. S.O. 2877 (E), 11 November 2009. The guidelines were issued in the form of a letter from the Secretary, Rural Development, to state government chief secretaries, dated 30 December 2009 (D.O. No. J. 11013/2/2009-NREGA).

60. Personal communication with the author, 22 October 2010.

61. *The Hindu*, 25 September 2011.

62. Jeelani, 'NREGA's Reality Check'.

63. 'Employment Guarantee Council Rejig Sidelines Dreze and Roy', *Business Standard*, 8 February 2011.

64. Ministry of Rural Development (Department of Rural Development), 'Minutes of the meeting of Empowered Committee under MGNREGA regarding Bihar and Jharkhand held on 28th March, 2012', New Delhi, 19 April 2012, Director MGNREGA, Ref. No. J-11018/2/2012-MGNREGA, Section 3(a)(i).

65. Ibid., Section 3(a)(iii).

66. Ibid., Section 3(a)(vii).

67. Principal Secretary, Rural Development Department, to All States/UTs, Annexure-A: e-MR Models implemented in States, GoI, MoRD, MGNREGA Division, 23 April 2012, RE: 'All States to move to e-Muster Rolls (e-MR) within 6 months'.

68. MoRD, 'Minutes of the meeting of Empowered Committee under MGNREGA regarding Bihar and Jharkhand held on 28th March, 2012', New Delhi, 19 April 2012, Director MGNREGA, Ref. No. J-11018/2/2012-MGNREGA, Section 3(a)(iii).

69. Principal Secretary, Rural Development Department, to All States/UTs, GoI, MorD, MGNREGA Division, 23 April 2012, RE: 'All States to move to e-Muster Rolls (e-MR) within 6 months', Paragraph 6.

70. Sarah Jewitt & Kamla Khanal, 'Tribes, Forest Rights, and Political Drivers in Koraput, Odisha', *Ballots and Bullets*, 29 April 2014. Available at: http://nottspolitics.org/2014/04/29/tribes-forest-rights-political-drivers-in-koraput-odisha/

71. Centre for Education of Research Development, *NREGA Processes in Andhra Pradesh and Madhya Pradesh: Appraisal and Research Study* (report submitted to the Ministry of Rural Development, no date).

72. 'Aruna Roy Walks out of Sonia Gandhi-Led National Advisory Council', *Indian Express*, 29 May 2013.
73. 'Need to Have Parity of Wage under NREGA: Jairam', *India TV News*, 2 February 2014.
74. 'Chartered Accountants May Audit NREGA', *The Hindu*, 20 July 2013.
75. Government of India (Ministry of Rural Development), Order No. L-12053/ 46/2011-MNREGA-I (FTS), RE: 'Relaxation for making wage payments through cash to MGNREGA workers in IAP Districts' (New Delhi, November 2011). Available at http://nrega.nic.in/netnrega/Administrative.aspx
76. Dreze, 'Employment Guarantee and the Right to Work', p. 11.
77. Ibid., p. 12
78. There are, however, ways in which certain forms of corruption can in fact be useful in securing political backing for economic liberalisation. See Rob Jenkins, *Democratic Politics and Economic Reform in India* (Cambridge: Cambridge University Press, 1999).

8. IMPLICATIONS

1. *Indian Express*, 30 March 2013.
2. It was made up of scholars from India's National Council of Applied Economic Research and the University of Maryland. The project was entitled 'The India Human Development Survey'. See www.ihds.umd.edu. Accessed 11 May 2014.
3. *The Hindu*, 5 April 2014. No figures were given in that report for a sixth group, other religious minorities.
4. *The Hindu*, 30 March 2014.
5. *Indian Express*, 20 October 2009. Their detailed analyses appear in S. Shankar & R. Gaiha, *Battling Corruption: Has the NREGA Reached India's Poor?* (Delhi: Oxford University Press, 2013).
6. *Indian Express*, 30 March 2013.
7. Administrative Staff College of India, *Study for Quick Appraisal*, Part II (Hyderabad 2009) pp. 1–9, and interviews in October 2010 with Hemlath Rao, who led the research team.
8. These figures are drawn from the World Bank (data.worldbank.org/indicator/ NY.GDP.MKTP.KD.ZG) and from official figures for 2013–14, reported in *Bloomberg Business Week*, 8 February 2014.
9. The World Bank office in India made no public statement on the matter, but was said to have expressed its doubts directly to the Finance Ministry in late 2004. Interview with a senior civil servant, New Delhi, 17 December 2004.
10. World Bank, *World Development Report 2009: Reshaping Economic Geography* (Washington, DC: World Bank, 2009), p. 163. The WDR notes that '[t]he economic benefits of migration are not always recognised by policy makers'. It then

cites NREGA as an example of this syndrome because one of its aims was to counter distress-driven rural-urban migration. The Bank's position was widely seen among NREGA's supporters as lacking in compassion.

11. World Bank, *World Development Report 2013—Jobs* (Washington, DC: World Bank, 2013), p. 271.

12. World Bank, *World Development Report 2014—Risk and Opportunity: Managing Risk for Development* (Washington, DC: World Bank, 2014), p. 156.

13. UN Women, *Progress of the World's Women 2015–2016: Transforming Economies, Realizing Rights* (New York: United Nations, 2015), pp. 146–47. Because the report advocates an entitlement-based employment programme as a second-best option if unconditional unemployment allowances are not feasible in a given country context, the recommendations for using NREGA-like programmes to advance gender equality were outlined in the chapter on 'social policy' (Chapter 3) rather than the chapter on 'transforming work' (Chapter 2).

14. These comments are based on interviews with officials who participated in the discussions, New Delhi, 7 and 9 January 2014.

15. A. Siddle & T.A. Koelbe, *The Failure of Decentralisation in South African Local Government* (Cape Town: UCT Press, 2012); J. Manor, 'Local Government in South Africa: Potential Disaster amid Genuine Promise', Paper prepared for the UK Department for International Development for a project managed by the Institute of Development Studies, University of Sussex, 2000.

16. These comments are based on a draft case study, 'Community Work Programme', by a South African team for the BRICS Project, School of Advanced Study, University of London, 2013.

17. Himanshu, 'Populism or Entitlement-based Populism', *Livemint.com*, 8 May 2014.

18. This is found in many of Dreze's writings and public statements. See Jean Dreze & Reetika Khera, 'The PEEP Survey: Water for the Leeward India', *Outlook*, 24 March 2014, which noted that the benefits of rights-based schemes had been achieved 'mainly through democratic struggle'.

19. Merilee S. Grindle, *Audacious Reforms: Institutional Invention and Democracy in Latin America* (Baltimore: Johns Hopkins University Press, 2000).

20. Government of India (Ministry of Rural Development), *Mahatma Gandhi National Rural Employment Guarantee Act, 2005: Report to the People, 2nd Feb. 2006—2nd Feb 2010* (New Delhi, 2010), p. 31.

21. NTUI took a particular interest in organising NREGA workers and supporting their agitations. In early 2007 it published *Handbook on Rural Workers' Rights under the National Rural Employment Guarantee Act* (New Delhi: New Trade Union Initiative, 2007).

22. Rina Agarwala & Ronald J. Herring (eds.), *Whatever Happened to Class?— Reflections from South Asia* (Lanham, MD: Rowman and Littlefield, 2008), p. 18.

23. 'Hike in NREGA Wages Sought', *The Hindu*, 17 March 2011.

24. This comment was made by some participants in a discussion at Kings College, University of London, in 2013.
25. Surjit Bhalla has likened it and other UPA poverty programmes to 'doles'. See *Indian Express*, 26 October 2013. *The Economist* scorned the UPA's 'welfare handouts' in its 24 May 2014 report on the national election outcome. An ill-informed participant in a seminar at Kings College London in 2013 described the NREGA as 'only a subsidy'.
26. See, for example, Bhalla's comment in the *Indian Express*, 26 October 2013.
27. See J. Manor, *The Political Economy of Democratic Decentralisation* (Washington, DC: World Bank, 1999), Chapter 6. On the difficulty in making social audits work under NREGA, see Mihir Shah's comments in the *Economic Times*, 27 May 2010; and *The Hindu*, 6 September and 13 December 2009. Evidence (from India, Bangladesh, Cote d'Ivoire, and Ghana) that local-level mass meetings have generally had little success at drawing large numbers of poor people into direct and meaningful forms of participation is presented in Richard Crook & James Manor, *Democracy and Decentralisation in South Asia and West Africa: Participation, Accountability and Performance* (Cambridge: Cambridge University Press, 1998). pp. 29–32, 34–35, 94–96, 153–57, 216–23, 228–33 and 273–76.
28. These points were made to one of the authors in a telephone interview with a former CEGC member, 24 April 2013, but pertained primarily to the UPA-1 period (2004–2009).
29. Deepta Chopra, '"They Don't Want to Work" versus "They Don't Want to Provide Work": Seeking Explanations for the Decline of MGNREGA in Rajasthan', *ESID Working Paper No. 31* (Effective States and Inclusive Development Research Centre, University of Manchester, July 2014).
30. See, for example, *Economic Times*, 10 June 2012.
31. These comments are based on a telephone conversation with Nikhil Dey in Rajasthan, 1 February 2014; and communications with Yogesh Kumar in Madhya Pradesh, 3 February 2014.
32. They are Odisha, Karnataka, Uttar Pradesh, Maharashtra, Jharkhand, and Bihar. See *The Hindu*, 2 December 2003.
33. They were Dungarpur and Hanumangarh. Telephone interview with Nikhil Dey in Rajasthan, 1 February 2014.
34. See Chapter 5 of M.A. Melo, N. Ng'ethe, & J. Manor, *Against the Odds: Politicians, Institutions and the Struggle against Poverty* (London: Hurst, 2012).
35. See, for example, 'Cash Transfer and Social Protection', Social Protection in Asia's *Newsletter*, 7 June 2010, where a case is made that employment schemes and cash transfers should be seen as 'complementary tools in addressing a variety of vulnerabilities faced by families and individuals'.
36. Discussion with a Maharahstra-based activist with extensive knowledge of NREGA's operation in the state, 17 November 2014, Mumbai.

37. Alice Kessler-Harris, *In Pursuit of Equity: Women, Men, and the Quest for Economic Citizenship in 20th Century America* (Oxford: Oxford University Press, 2003).

38. It must also be acknowledged that many versions of workfare, of which NREGA is a particular subspecies, are seen to be attractive yet impractical. See, for instance, Maeve Quaid, *Workfare: Why Good Social Policy Ideas Go Bad* (Toronto: University of Toronto Press, 2002).

39. Ministry of Rural Development, *Mahatma Gandhi National Rural Employment Guarantee Act, 2005: Report to the People.*

40. 'Shedding communal image a challenge to BJP', *The Hindu*, 30 April 2014.

41. See Chapter 5 of that report, especially p. 163—and the commentary on it in the *Economic Times*, 15 March 2009, from which the quotations in this paragraph come. See also, for a slightly more measured document, World Bank, *Global Monitoring Report, 2013: Rural-Urban Dynamics and the Millennium Development Goals* (Washington, DC: World Bank, 2013), especially Chapter 3.

42. Atul Kohli, *Poverty Amid Plenty in the New India* (Cambridge: Cambridge University Press, 2012).

43. This was the thrust, for instance, of remarks presented by Prem Shankar Jha at a New School University seminar hosted by the India-China Institute, New York, April 2012.

44. An analysis conducted by the Association for Democratic Reforms (ADR), a leading activist group, found that, between 2004 and 2011, by one measure, 87 per cent of donations to India's parties were from businesses, either individually or collectively. See ADR, *Political Party Watch Report 2014*. Available at: adrindia.org/ research-and-report/political-party-watch/combined-reports/2014/corporates-made-87-total-donations-k

45. See, for instance, Paranjoy Guha Thakurta, 'The Business of Politics: Sun TV and the Maran Brothers', *Economic and Political Weekly*, 50(35), 29 August 2015.

46. Possible pro-business inclinations are among the potential biases carefully examined in Shylashri Shankar, *Scaling Justice: India's Supreme Court, Social Rights and Civil Liberties* (Delhi: Oxford University Press, 2009).

47. Kanchan Chandra provides an excellent account of many of the ways in which business leaders, through mechanisms of patronage, have been able to influence policy. See Kanchan Chandra, 'The New Indian State: The Relocation of Patronage in the Post-Liberalisation Economy', *Economic and Political Weekly*, 50(41), 10 October 2015, pp. 46–58.

48. Peter Evans (ed.), *State-Society Synergy: Government and Social Capital in Development* (Berkeley, CA: Research Series/International and Area Studies, University of California at Berkeley, 1997).

49. John Ackerman calls this 'Co-Governance'. See John Ackerman, 'Co-Governance for Accountability: Beyond "Exit" and "Voice"', *World Development*, 32(3), 2004, pp. 447–463.

50. Prashant Sharma, *Democracy and Transparency in the Indian State: The Making of the Right to Information Act* (Abingdon: Routledge, 2015), Chapter 3.

51. R. Jenkins, 'In Varying States of Decay: The Politics of Anti-Corruption in Maharashtra and Rajasthan', in R. Jenkins (ed.), *Regional Reflections: Comparing Politics Across India's States* (Delhi: Oxford University Press, 2004).

52. The linkage between the poor and the middle class in India's anti-corruption activism was noted in R. Jenkins, 'Democracy, Development and India's Struggle Against Corruption', *Public Policy Research*, 13(3), September–December 2006, pp. 155–163.

53. R. Jenkins, 'NGOs and Indian Politics', in Niraja Gopal Jayal & Pratap Bhanu Mehta (eds.), *The Oxford Companion to Politics in India* (Delhi: Oxford University Press, 2010).

54. The current Governor of the Reserve Bank of India has pointed to the significance of what he has called the transition from the 'license raj' to the 'resource raj'. See Raghuram Rajan, 'What Happened to India?', *Project Syndicate*, 8 June 2012. Available at: http://www.project-syndicate.org/commentary/what-happened-to-india

55. Rahul Mukherjee, 'Ideas, Interests, and the Tipping Point: Economic Change in India', *Review of International Political Economy*, 20(2), 2013, pp. 363–89.

56. For an analysis of how India's SEZ policy relates to ongoing processes of economic reform and 'state rescaling', see the 'Introduction' in R. Jenkins, L. Kennedy, & P. Mukhopadhyay (eds.), *Power, Policy and Protest: The Politics of India's Special Economic Zones* (Delhi: Oxford University Press, 2014).

57. At least some activists hoped that this might, in turn, generate an ethical shift on the part of implementing officials at the grassroots—what Jennifer Davis has called 'a change in the work environment that increases the moral cost of misconduct'— a phenomenon she observed in a number of bureaucratic niches in South Asia. Jennifer Davis, 'Corruption in Public Service Delivery: Experience from South Asia's Water and Sanitation Sector', *World Development*, 32(1), 2004, pp. 53–71.

58. Kanchan Chandra argues, in a different context, that patronage politics is being 'relocated' rather than abolished. See Kanchan Chandra, 'The New Indian State'.

59. Mark Schneider, 'Does Clientelism Work? A Test of Guessability in India', *CASI Working Paper Series*, No. 13–01 (Philadelphia, PA: Center for the Advanced Study of India, University of Pennsylvania, September 2014).

60. For further details, see J. Manor, 'Did the Central Government's Poverty Initiatives Help to Re-Elect It?', in L. Saez & G. Singh (eds.), *New Dimensions of Politics in India: The United Progressive Alliance in Power* (London and New Delhi: Routledge, 2011).

61. See Geert De Neve & Grace Carswell, 'NREGA and the Return of Identity Politics in Western Tamil Nadu, India', *Forum for Development Studies*, 38(2), 2011, pp. 205–10.

62. The official title is the Scheduled Tribes and Other Traditional Forest Dwellers (Recognition of Forest Rights) Act, 2006.

63. The official title is the Right of Children to Free and Compulsory Education Act, 2010.

64. Joe Foweraker & Todd Landman, *Citizenship Righs and Social Movements: A Comparative and Statistical Analysis* (Oxford: Oxford University Press, 1997), p. 16.

65. Ibid., pp. 16–17.

66. See, for example, *The Hindu*, 20 September 2010.

67. These comments are based on interviews with numerous people who were involved in the formulation of the Act, New Delhi, January 2014—most crucially with Videh Upadhyay, a Supreme Court lawyer. A full-scale analysis of the Act's formulation and implementation has been conducted by one of the authors of this volume, as part of a research project comparing government efforts to tackle poverty and inequality in Brazil, India, China, and South Africa (The BRICS Project, School of Advanced Study, University of London). See J. Manor, 'The Forest Rights Act, 2006', unpublished manuscript.

68. These comments are based on analyses by a team coordinated out of the University of London which has compared anti-poverty programmes in India with those in Brazil, China, and South Africa. Their findings will be published in 2016.

69. Stuart A. Scheingold, *The Politics of Rights: Lawyers, Public Policy and Political Change*, 2nd Edition (Ann Arbor, MI: University of Michigan Press, 2004). See especially Chapter 6 on 'Rights as Resources', and Chapter 9 on 'Legal Rights and Political Mobilisation', which identifies three key stages in this process: political activation, organisation, and realignment—something that activists in India have been engaged in throughout the struggle for the right to work.

70. 'Activist Beaten to Death for Exposing NREGA Scam in Jharkhand', *NDTV.com*, 3 March 2011.

71. See, for example, Crook & Manor, *Democracy and Decentralisation in South Asia and West Africa;* and Manor, *The Political Economy of Democratic*, Chapter 6.

72. Interview with a key NGO representative, Sirohi, 12 January 2009.

73. A research team led by Raghav Gaiha that studied NREGA found that this had happened much of the time. *Indian Express*, 23 April 2012.

74. H.K. Nagarajan, H.P. Binswanger-Mkhize, & S.S. Meenakshisundaram, *Decentralisation and Empowerment for Rural Development: The Case of India* (Delhi: Foundation Books, 2014).

75. On that latter point, see also, J. Manor, *When Local Government Strikes It Rich* (Visby: International Centre for Local Democracy, 2013).

76. Melo, Ng'ethe, & Manor, *Against the Odds.*

77. This contrasted with the proactive measures that characterised information campaigns in primary education in Uttar Pradesh, where outcomes were nevertheless

variable. See Abhijit Banerjee, Rukmini Banerji, Esther Duflo, Rachel Glannerster, & Stuti Khemani, 'Can Information Campaigns Spark Local Participation and Improve Outcomes: A Study of Primary Education in Uttar Pradesh, India', *World Bank Policy Research Working Paper 3967* (Washington, DC: World Bank, July 2006).

78. Yamini Aiyar & Salimah Samji, 'Transparency and Accountability in NREGA: A Case Study of Andhra Pradesh', *Accountability Initiative Working Paper Series*, 1(1), (Delhi: Centre for Policy Research, 2009).

79. Yamini Aiyar, Soumya Kapoor Mehta, & Salimah Samji, 'India: Implementing Social Audits', in Kalanidhi Subbarao, Carlo del Ninno, Colin Andrews, & Claudia Rodriquez-Alas (eds.), *Public Works as a Safety Net: Design, Evidence and Implementation* (Washington, DC: World Bank, November 2012), pp. 249–68.

80. Interview with that official, New Delhi, 18 November 2013.

81. On the poor performance in Karnataka, see the Planning Commission report summarised in the *Economic Times*, 26 March 2010. The wretched record of that government is examined in detail in J. Manor, 'Lucky in Its Adversaries: A Slipshod Congress Gains a Majority in the Karnataka Election', *Economic and Political Weekly*, 48(47), 23 November 2013, pp. 51–59.

82. She based her remarks on reports by the Comptroller and Auditor-General which focus very narrowly on patterns in the release of NREGA funds, and which reveal next to nothing about the impact of the programme on poor people.

83. *Indian Express*, 9 May 2014.

84. This comment is based on discussions with a senior civil servant in Bihar who helped to administer NREGA there. New Delhi, 7 December 2013. See also, Jean Dreze's comments on this problem in *The Hindu*, 23 April 2010.

85. *The Hindu*, 21 May 2014.

86. 'PM Narendra Modi attacks Congress; says MNREGS "living monument" of poverty', *Financial Express*, 12 March 2015.

87. A particularly vivid complaint along these lines, contained in an editorial published in Delhi's leading English language daily newspaper, was that lowering the labour-materials ratio would 'open the flood gates for the entry of the construction lobby'. 'NREGA Scheme is Not Broken, So Govt Need Not Fix It', *Hindustan Times*, 16 October 2014.

88. United Nations Development Programme, *MGNREGA Sameeksha-II: An Anthology of Research Studies, 2012–2014* (New Delhi, 2015).

89. 'Full Text of Leading Economists' Letter to PM Modi on NREGA', *NDTV.com*, 14 October 2014.

90. 'Shivraj Singh Chouhan Calls MGNREA "One of the Best Programmes"', *Indian Express*, 21 April 2015.

91. The Modi government's efforts to amend the Right to Fair Compensation and Transparency in Land Acquisition, Rehabilitation and Resettlement Act 2013 are

discussed in Rob Jenkins, 'Advice and Dissent: The Federal Politics of Reforming India's Land Acquisition Legislation', in R. Nagaraj & S. Motiram (eds.), *Towards a Political Economy of Contemporary India* (Cambridge: Cambridge University Press, forthcoming).

92. '78 per cent don't want land bill, 63 per cent say Modi's image anti-poor: Survey', *Deccan Herald*, 11 May 2015.

93. 'Swadeshi Jagran Manch opposes land Bill, slams "undue hurry"', *Indian Express*, 2 July 2015.

BIBLIOGRAPHY

Aakella, Karuna Vakati and Soumya Kidambi (2007), 'Social Audits in Andhra Pradesh: A Process in Evolution', *Economic and Political Weekly*, 42(47), 24 November, pp. 18–19.

Ackerman, John (2004), 'Co-Governance for Accountability: Beyond "Exit" and "Voice"', *World Development*, 32(3), pp. 447–463.

'Activist Beaten to Death for Exposing NREGA Scam in Jharkhand' (2011), *NDTV. com*, 3 March. (Available at: http://www.ndtv.com/india-news/activist-beaten-to-death-for-exposing-nrega-scam-in-jharkhand-448910)

Adhikar, Anindita and Kartika Bhatia (2010), 'NREGA Wage Payment: Can We Bank on the Banks?', *Economic and Political Weekly*, 45(1), 2 January, pp. 30–37.

Administrative Staff College of India (2009), *Study for Quick Appraisal of NREGA in Andhra Pradesh* (Hyderabad: ASCI).

'After Modi sniffs corruption in NREGA, Delhi flags state dossier' (2010), *Indian Express*, 27 July.

Agarwala, Rina and Ronald J. Herring (eds.) (2008), *Whatever Happened to Class? Reflections from South Asia* (Lanham, MD: Rowman and Littlefield).

Ahluwalia, M.S. (2000), 'State Level Performance under Economic Reforms in India', Paper presented at Stanford University, May. (Available at: http://www.planningcommission.gov.in/aboutus/speech/spemsa/msa007.pdf)

Ahmed, Imtiaz (ed.) (1973), *Caste and Social Stratification among Muslims in India* (Delhi: Manohar).

Aiyar, Yamini and Salimah Samji (2009), 'Transparency and Accountability in NREGA: A Case Study of Andhra Pradesh', *Accountability Initiative Working Paper Series*, 1(1) (Delhi: Centre for Policy Research).

Aiyar, Yamini, Soumya Kapoor Mehta, and Salimah Samji (2012), 'India: Implementing Social Audits', in Kalanidhi Subbarao, Carlo del Ninno, Colin Andrews, and Claudia Rodriquez-Alas (eds.), *Public Works as a Safety Net: Design, Evidence and Implementation* (Washington, DC: World Bank), pp. 249–268.

'Aruna Roy Walks out of Sonia Gandhi-Led National Advisory Council' (2013), *Indian Express*, 29 May.

Association for Democratic Reforms (2014), *Political Party Watch Report 2014* (Hyderabad, ADR). (Available at: http://www.adrindia.org/research-and-report/political-party-watch/combined-reports/2014/corporates-made-87-total-donations-k)

Babu, V.S. and K.H. Rao (2010), *Impact of MGNREGS on Scheduled Castes and Scheduled Tribes: Studies Conducted in Eight States* (Hyderabad: National Institute of Rural Development).

Bagchee, Aruna (2005), 'Political and Administrative Realities of Employment Guarantee Scheme', *Economic and Political Weekly*, 40(42), 15 October, pp. 41–50.

Banerjee, Abhijit, Rukmini Banerji, Esther Duflo, Rachel Glannerster, and Stuti Khemani (2006), 'Can Information Campaigns Spark Local Participation and Improve Outcomes: A Study of Primary Education in Uttar Pradesh, India', *World Bank Policy Research Working Paper 3967* (Washington, DC: World Bank).

Banerjee, K. and P. Saha (2010), 'The NREGA, the Maoists and the Developmental Woes of the Indian State', *Economic and Political Weekly*, 45(28), 10 July, pp. 42–7.

Banerji, Arup and Ugo Gentilini (2013), 'Social Safety Nets: Lessons from Global Evidence and Practice', paper prepared for the Bank of Namibia's Annual Symposium on Social Safety Nets in Namibia, Assessing Current Programmes and Future Options (Washington, DC: World Bank).

Bansil, P.C. (2006), *Poverty Mapping in Rajasthan* (Delhi: Concept Publishing).

Basu, A.K. (2013), 'Impact of Rural Employment Guarantee Schemes on Seasonal Labour Markets: Optimum Compensation and Workers' Welfare', *The Journal of Economic Inequality*, 11(1), pp. 1–34.

Berg, E., S. Bhattacharyya, R. Durg, and M. Ramachandra (2012), 'Can Rural Public Works Affect Agricultural Wages? Evidence from India', *Working Paper WPS/2012–15*, Centre for the Study of African Economies (Oxford: University of Oxford).

Bhagwati, Jagdish and Arvind Panagariya (2013), *Why Growth Matters: How Economic Growth in India Reduced Poverty and the Lessons for Other Developing Countries* (New York: PublicAffairs).

Bhargava, P. (2003), 'Food Security and Public Distribution System in Rajasthan', *IDS Working Paper* (Jaipur: Institute of Development Studies).

Bhatti, Bharat (2012), 'Aadhaar-Enabled Payments for NREGA Workers', *Economic and Political Weekly*, 47(49), 8 December, pp. 16–19.

'Cabinet Nod for Rural Jobs Bill' (2005), *The Hindu*, August 12.

Centre for Budget and Governance Accountability (2006), *Report on the Implementation of the NREGA in Andhra Pradesh, Chhattisgarh, Jharkhand and Madhya Pradesh*, New Delhi, June. (Available at: http://www.nrega.net)

Centre for Education of Research Development (2010), *NREGA Processes in Andhra*

Pradesh and Madhya Pradesh: Appraisal and Research Study (Report submitted to the Ministry of Rural Development).

Centre for Science and Environment (2008), *An Assessment of the Performance of the National Rural Employment Guarantee Programme in Terms of its Potential for Creation of Natural Wealth in India's Villages* (New Delhi).

Chandra, Kanchan (2015), 'The New Indian State: The Relocation of Patronage in the Post-Liberalisation Economy', *Economic and Political Weekly*, 50(41), 10 October, pp. 46–58.

Charsley, S.R. and G.K. Karanth (eds.) (1998), *Challenging Untouchability: Dalit Initiative and Experience from Karnataka* (London: Altamira Press).

'Chartered Accountants May Audit NREGA' (2013), *The Hindu*, 20 July.

Chopra, Deepta (2011), 'Policy Making in India: A Dynamic Process of Statecraft', *Pacific Affairs*, 84(1), March, pp. 89–107.

―――― (2014), '"They Don't Want to Work" versus "They Don't Want to Provide Work": Seeking Explanations for the Decline of MGNREGA in Rajasthan', *ESID Working Paper No. 31* (Effective States and Inclusive Development Research Centre, University of Manchester).

'CP Joshi: Rural Development and Panchayati Raj' (2009), *The Week*, 14 June.

'CPI(M) claims credit for job guarantee programme' (2006), *The Hindu*, 14 February.

'Cradle of Panchayati Raj now den of corruption' (2010), *DNA: Daily News and Analysis (Jaipur)*, 7 September.

Crook, R.C. and J. Manor (1998), *Democracy and Decentralisation in South Asia and West Africa: Participation, Accountability and Performance* (Cambridge: Cambridge University Press).

Davis, Jennifer (2004), 'Corruption in Public Service Delivery: Experience from South Asia's Water and Sanitation Sector', *World Development*, 32(1), pp. 53–71.

De Neve, Geert and Grace Carswell (2011), 'NREGA and the Return of Identity Politics in Western Tamil Nadu, India', *Forum for Development Studies*, 38(2), pp. 205–10.

Deininger, K. and K.H. Rao (2010), *Poverty Impacts of India's National Rural Employment Guarantee Scheme: Evidence from Andhra Pradesh* (New Delhi: Government of India, Ministry of Rural Development).

Desai, Sonalde, Prem Vashishtha, and Omkar Joshi (2015), *Mahatma Gandhi National Rural Employment Guarantee Act: A Catalyst for Rural Transformation* (New Delhi: National Council of Applied Economic Research).

Dev, S. Mahendra (1996), 'Experience of India's (Maharashtra) Employment Guarantee Scheme: Lessons for Development Policy', *Development Policy Review*, 14(3), pp. 227–254.

Dheeraja, C. and Hanumantha Rao (2010), *Changing Gender Relations: A Study of MGNREGA across Different States* (Hyderabad: National Institute of Rural Development).

Dhobal, Harsh (ed.) (2011), *Writings on Human Rights, Law and Society in India: A Combat Law Anthology* (New Delhi: Human Rights Law Network).

Dreze, Jean (2002), 'On Research and Action', *Economic and Political Weekly*, 37(9), 2 March, pp. 817–819.

—— (2007), 'NREGA: Dismantling the Contractor Raj', *The Hindu*, 20 November.

—— (2010), 'Employment Guarantee and the Right to Work', in Niraja Gopal Jayal and Pratap Bhanu Mehta (eds.), *The Oxford Companion to Politics in India* (Delhi: Oxford University Press).

—— (2011), 'Employment Guarantee and the Right to Work', in Reetka Khera (ed.), *The Battle for Employment Guarantee* (Delhi: Oxford University Press).

Dreze, Jean and Amartya Sen (2013), *An Uncertain Glory: India and Its Contradictions* (Princeton, NJ: Princeton University Press).

Dreze, Jean and Aruna Roy (2005), 'Response to the "list of points" raised by the Standing Committee on Rural Development, about the National Rural Employment Guarantee Bill 2004'. (Available at: http://www.righttofoodindia. org/rtowork/standingcte.html)

Dreze, Jean and Reetika Kheva (eds.) (2014), 'The PEEP Survey: Water for the Leeward India', *Outlook*, 24 March.

Dreze, Jean and Siddhartha Lal (2007), 'Employment Guarantee: Unfinished Agenda', *The Hindu*, 13 July.

Dutta, P., R. Murgai, M. Ravallion, and D. van de Walle (2012), 'Does India's Employment Guarantee Scheme Guarantee Employment?', *Economic and Political Weekly*, 47(16), 21 April, pp. 55–64.

'Employment Guarantee Council Rejig Sidelines Dreze and Roy' (2011), *Business Standard*, 8 February.

'Ensure minimum wages to NREGA workers: Activists' (2010), *Times of India*, 4 October.

Evans, Peter (ed.) (1997), *State-Society Synergy: Government and Social Capital in Development* (Berkeley, CA: Research Series/International and Area Studies, University of California).

Foweraker, Joe and Todd Landman (1997), *Citizenship Rights and Social Movements: A Comparative and Statistical Analysis* (Oxford: Oxford University Press).

Gaiha, Raghav (1996), 'The Employment Guarantee Scheme in India: Is It Mistargeted?' *Asian Survey*, 36(12), pp. 1201–12.

Gaiha, Raghav, Shylashri Shankar, and Raghbendra Jha (2010), 'Targeting Accuracy of the NREG: Evidence from Rajasthan, Andhra Pradesh and Madhya Pradesh', *Working Paper 3* (Canberra: Australia South Asia Research Centre).

Ghate, Prabhu (n.d.), 'A Quick Study of NREGA Implementation in Selected States' (New Delhi).

Goetz, Anne Marie and Rob Jenkins (2001), 'Hybrid Forms of Accountability: Citizen Engagement in Institutions of Public-Sector Oversight', *Public Management Review*, 3(3), pp. 363–84.

Gonsalves, C, P.R. Kumar, and A.R Srivastava (eds.) (2005), *The Right to Food* (New Delhi: Human Rights Law Network).

Government of India (2009), *Gendering Human Development Indices* (New Delhi: Ministry of Women and Child Development).

Government of India (Ministry of Rural Development) (2006), 'Notification', *The Gazette of India, Extraordinary*, 25 May (New Delhi). GSR. 311(E). [Jt Secretary, Office Ref. No. J. 24011/5/2005-SGRY(M)].

—— (2007), *National Rural Employment Guarantee Act (NREGA): Some Reports from the Field, 2006–07* (New Delhi).

—— (2009), 'Guidelines for Implementation of Works on Individual Land Under NREGA', January, Draft.

—— (2009), Letter from the Secretary of Rural Development, to state government chief secretaries, 30 December (D.O. No. J. 11013/2/2009-NREGA).

—— (2009), Notification no. S.O. 2877 (E), 11 November.

—— (2010), *Mahatma Gandhi National Rural Employment Guarantee Act, 2005: Report to the People, 2nd Feb. 2006—2nd Feb 2010* (New Delhi).

—— (2011), 'Update 124: NREGA Audit of Scheme Rules, Action from the Field', *Action for Employment Guarantee*, 13 September. (Available at: http://www.nrega. net.in/content/update-124-nrega-audit-scheme-rules-action-field-uid-primer-and-more)

—— (2012), 'Letter from Principal Secretary, Rural Development Department, to All States/UTs, Annexure-A: e-MR Models implemented in States, GoI, MoRD, MGNREGA Division', 23 April.

—— (2012), 'Notification', *The Gazette of India, Extraordinary*, 23 March (New Delhi). S.O. 578(E). [Jt Secretary, Office Ref. No. J. 11011/1/2009/ MGNREGA(Pt)].

—— (2012), 'Minutes of the meeting of Empowered Committee under MGNREGA regarding Bihar and Jharkhand held on 28th March, 2012', 19 April (New Delhi). Director MGNREGA, Ref. No. J-11018/2/2012-MGNREGA, Section 3(a)(v).

—— (2012), *MGNREGA Sameeksha* (New Delhi: Orient Blackswan).

—— (2013), 'Order No. L-12053/46/2011-MNREGA-I (FTS), RE: 'Relaxation for making wage payments through cash to MGNREGA workers in IAP Districts', 18 November (New Delhi). (Available at: http://nrega.nic.in/netnrega/Adminis-trative.aspx).

—— (2014), *National Rural Employment Guarantee Act, 2005: Report to the People, 2nd February 2014* (New Delhi: Government of India).

Government of India (Planning Commission) (2001), *National Human Development Report 2001* (New Delhi).

—— (2007), *Towards Faster and More Inclusive Growth: Approach Paper to the 11th Five Year Plan (2007–2012)* (New Delhi).

BIBLIOGRAPHY

Government of India, Ministry of Law and Justice (Legislative Department) (2005), Gazette of India (Extraordinary), Registered No. DL—(N)04/0007/2003—05, item: National Rural Employment Guarantee Act 2005 (New Delhi).

Government of India, Prime Minister's Office (2004), *National Common Minimum Programme of the Government of India*, May. (Available at: http://pmindia.nic.in/cmp.pdf)

Grindle, Merilee S. (2000), *Audacious Reforms: Institutional Invention and Democracy in Latin America* (Baltimore, MD: Johns Hopkins University Press).

Gupta, D. (2004), *Caste in Question: Identity or Hierarchy?* (New Delhi: Sage).

Gupta, Kiran Soni (2002), 'Strengthening the panchayats: Rajasthan proposes to revise local administration', *India Together*, August. (Available at: http://indiatogether.org/govt/local/articles/arc-rajasthan.htm)

Hanumantha Rao, C.H. (2005), *Agriculture, Food Security, Poverty and Environment: Essays on Post-Reform India* (Delhi: Oxford University Press).

Harriss, John (2012), 'Reflections on caste and class, hierarchy and dominance', *Seminar*, 633.

'Hike in NREGA Wages Sought' (2011), *The Hindu*, 17 March.

Himanshu (2014), 'Populism or Entitlement-based Populism', *Livemint.com*, 8 May.

Imai, K., R. Gaiha, V. Kulkarni, and M. Pandey (2009), 'National Rural Employment Guarantee Scheme, Poverty and Prices in Rural India', *Economics Discussion Paper Series—EDP 908*, University of Manchester.

'India's rural voters seek a brighter future' (2004), *The Daily Telegraph*, May 14.

Institute for Human Development (2006), *Evaluation and Impact Assessment of National Rural Employment Guarantee Scheme in Bihar* (New Delhi).

Institute of Development Studies (2012), *Standing on the Threshold: Food Justice in India* (Brighton: Institute of Development Studies, UK).

Institute of Forest Management, Institute of Rural Management, and Institute of Social Science Research, (2012), 'Independent Evaluation of MGNREGA', in Ministry of Rural Development, Government of India, *MGNREGA Sameeksha: An Anthology of Research Studies on the Mahatma Gandhi National Rural Employment Guarantee Act 2006–2012* (New Delhi).

Jain, Devaki (2005), 'Guaranteeing Employment: Immeasurable Benefits for Women', unpublished paper.

Jan Manch on Employment Guarantee Summary, Report (2005), 2 July. (Available at: http://www.righttofoodindia.org/rtowork/ega_keydocs.html)

Jeelani, Mehboob (2010), 'NREGA's Reality Check', *Caravan*, 1 May.

Jenkins, Rob (1994), 'Where the BJP Survived: The Rajasthan Assembly Elections of 1993', *Economic and Political Weekly*, 29 (11), 12 March 1994, pp. 635–41.

——— (1998), 'Rajput Hindutva', in C. Jaffrelot and T.B. Hansen (eds.), *The BJP and the Compulsions of Politics* (Delhi: Oxford University Press).

——— (1999), *Democratic Politics and Economic Reform in India* (Cambridge: Cambridge University Press).

—— (2004), 'In Varying States of Decay: The Politics of Anti-Corruption in Maharashtra and Rajasthan', in R. Jenkins (ed.), *Regional Reflections: Comparing Politics Across India's States* (New Delhi: Oxford University Press).

—— (2004), 'Reservation Politics in Rajasthan', paper presented at the annual meeting of the LSE Crisis States Programme, New Delhi, December.

—— (2005), 'Economic Reform, Clientelist Politics, and India's 2004 Elections', paper presented at the Annual Meeting of the American Political Science Association, Washington, DC, 1–4 September.

—— (2006), 'Democracy, Development and India's Struggle Against Corruption', *Public Policy Research*, 13(3), September–December, pp. 155–163.

—— (2007), 'India's Unlikely Democracy', *Journal of Democracy*, 18(2), April, pp. 55–69.

—— (2010), 'NGOs and Indian Politics', in Niraja Gopal Jayal and Pratap Bhanu Mehta (eds.), *The Oxford Companion to Politics in India* (Delhi: Oxford University Press).

—— (2014), 'The Politics of "Permanent Reform"', in R. Jenkins, L. Kennedy, and P. Mukhopadhyay (eds.), *Power, Policy and Protest: The Politics of India's Special Economic Zones* (Delhi: Oxford University Press).

—— (2016), 'Advice and Dissent: The Federal Politics of Reforming India's Land Acquisition Legislation', in R. Nagaraj and S. Motiram (eds.), *Towards a Political Economy of Contemporary India* (Cambridge: Cambridge University Press).

Jenkins, R., Loraine Kennedy, and Partha Mukhopadhyay (2014), 'Introduction', in R. Jenkins, L. Kennedy, and P. Mukhopadhyay (eds.), *Power, Policy and Protest: The Politics of India's Special Economic Zones* (Delhi: Oxford University Press).

Jewitt, Sarah and Kamla Khanal (2014), 'Tribes, Forest Rights, and Political Drivers in Koraput, Odisha', *Ballots and Bullets*, 29 April. (Available at: http://nottspolitics. org/2014/04/29/tribes-forest-rights-political-drivers-in-koraput-odisha/)

Jha, R., R. Gaiha, S. Shankar, and K.S. Imai (2010), *The Africa Report* (January)

Jha, R., R. Gaiha, S. Shankar, and M.K. Pandey (2010), 'Targeting Accuracy of the NREG: Evidence from Madhya Pradesh and Tamil Nadu', *Working Paper 19*, (Canberra: Australia South Asia Research Centre).

'Jhalawar Social Audit Fails to Take Off' (2008), *The Hindu*, 2 February.

Jodhka, S.S. (2003), 'Caste and Untouchability in Rural Punjab', Economic and Political Weekly, 37(19), 11 May, pp. 1813–1823.

Jodhka, S.S. and P. Louis (2003), 'Caste Tensions in Punjab: Talhan and Beyond', Economic and Political Weekly, 38(28), 12 July, pp. 2923–2936.

Johnson, D. (2009), 'Can Workfare Serve as a Substitute for Weather Insurance? The Case of NREGA in Andhra Pradesh', *Working Paper 22*, (Chennai: Institute of Financial Management and Research).

Joseph, Josy (2009), 'I'm a Little Nervous about NREGA-2: Interview with Prof Jean Dreze', *DNA*, 17 August.

Joshi, Anuradha and Mick Moore (2009), 'The Mobilising Potential of Anti-Poverty Programmes', *IDS Discussion Paper No. 374* (Brighton, UK: Institute of Development Studies).

Kalecki, Michal (1972), *Selected Essays on the Economic Growth of the Socialist and the Mixed Economy* (Cambridge: Cambridge University Press).

Kamal, K.L. (1976), 'Rajasthan: Politics of Declining Feudal Order', in Iqbal Narain (ed.), *State Politics in India* (Meerut: Meenakshi Prakashan).

Kamat, Sangeeta (2002), *Development Hegemony: NGOs and the State in India* (Delhi: Oxford University Press).

Karanth, G.K. (1995) *Change and Continuity in Agrarian Relations* (New Delhi: Concept).

——— (1996), 'Caste in Contemporary Rural India', in M.N. Srinivas (ed.), *Caste: Its Twentieth Century Avatar* (New Delhi: Penguin).

Karat, Brinda (2011), 'Another Excuse to Cut Government Spending', *The Hindu*, 11 November.

Kareemulla, K., S.K. Reddy, C.A. Rao, S. Kumar, and B. Venkteswarlu (2009), 'Soil and Water Conservation Works through National Rural Employment Guarantee Scheme (NREGS) in Andhra Pradesh—An Analysis of Livelihood Impact', *Agricultural Economics Research Review*, 22, pp. 443–50.

Kessler-Harris, Alice (2003), *In Pursuit of Equity: Women, Men, and the Quest for Economic Citizenship in 20th Century America* (Oxford: Oxford University Press).

Khera, Reetika (2008), '"Group Measurement" of NREGA Work: The Jalore Experiment', Conference Paper, Centre for Development Economics, Delhi School of Economics.

——— (ed.) (2011), *The Battle for Employment Guarantee* (New Delhi: Oxford University Press).

Kishwar, Madhu (1997), '"Naukri" as Property: Causes and Cures for Corruption in Government', *Manushi*, 100, pp. 13–24.

Kitschelt, Herbert and Steven I. Wilkinson (eds.) (2007), *Patrons, Clients and Policies: Patterns of Democratic Accountability and Political Competition* (Cambridge: Cambridge University Press).

Kohli, Atul (2012), *Poverty Amid Plenty in the New India* (Cambridge: Cambridge University Press).

Kothari, Rajni (1984), 'Non-Party Political Process', Economic and Political Weekly, 19(5), 4 February, pp. 216–224.

Krishna, Anirudh (2002), *Active Social Capital: Tracing the Roots of Development and Democracy* (New York: Columbia University Press).

Kumar, R. and R. Prasanna (2010), 'Role of NREGA in Providing Additional Employment for Tribals and Curtailing Migration', in Government of India (Ministry of Rural Development), *National Rural Employment Guarantee Act (NREGA): Design, Process and Impact* (New Delhi).

Lakin, Jason and Nirmala Ravishankar (2006), 'Working for Votes: The Politics of Employment Guarantee in India', Paper presented at the annual meeting of the American Political Science Association, Philadelphia, PA.

Lindblom, Charles E. (1977), *Politics and Markets: The World's Political Economic Systems* (New York: Basic Books).

Lodha, Sanjay (2009), 'Rajasthan: Performance and Campaigning Pay Dividends', *Economic and Political Weekly*, 44(39), 26 September, pp. 186–90.

MacAuslan, Ian (2008), 'India's National Rural Employment Guarantee Act: A Case Study for How Change Happens', background paper for Oxfam International, *From Poverty to Power: How Active Citizens and Effective States Can Change the World* (Oxford: Oxfam International).

Manor, James. (1999), *The Political Economy of Democratic Decentralization* (Washington, DC: World Bank).

—— (2000), 'Local Government in South Africa: Potential Disaster Amid Genuine Promise', paper prepared for the UK Department of International Development, Institute of Development Studies, University of Sussex.

—— (2000), 'Small-Time Political Fixers in India's States: "Towel Over Armpit"', *Asian Survey*, 40(5), pp. 816–835.

—— (2005), 'In Part a Myth: The BJP's Organisational Strength', in K. Adeney and L. Saez (eds.), *Coalition Politics and Hindu Nationalism* (London and New Delhi: Routledge).

—— (2009), 'The Congress Defeat in Madhya Pradesh', *Seminar* (February).

—— (2010), 'Beyond Clientelism: Digvijay Singh's Participatory, Pro-Poor Strategy in Madhya Pradesh', in A.E. Ruud and P. Price (eds.), *Leaders and Politics in South Asia* (London: Routledge).

—— (2010), 'What Do They Know of India Who Only India Know?', *Commonwealth and Comparative Politics*, 48(4), pp. 505–516.

—— (2011), 'Epilogue: Caste and Politics in Recent Times', in Rajni Kothari (ed.), *Caste in Indian Politics*, revised edition (New Delhi: Orient Longman).

—— (2011), 'Did the Central Government's Poverty Initiatives Help to Re-elect it?', in Lawrence Saez and Gurharpal Singh (eds.), *New Dimensions of Politics in India: The United Progressive Alliance in Power* (London and New Delhi: Routledge).

—— (2011), 'The Trouble with Yeddyurappa', *Economic and Political Weekly*, 46(13), 13 March, pp. 16–19.

—— (2012), 'Post-Clientelist Initiatives', in K. Stokke and O. Tornquist (eds.) *Transformative Politics* (London: Palgrave, 2012).

—— (2012), 'Conflict and Accommodation Amid Waning Hierarchies', *Seminar* (May).

—— (2013), 'Lucky in Its Adversaries: A Slipshod Congress Gains a Majority in the Karnataka Election', *Economic and Political Weekly*, 48(47), 23 November, pp. 51–59.

—— (2013), 'When Local Government Strikes It Rich', *Research Report No. 1*, (Visby, Sweden: Swedish International Centre for Local Democracy).

Mathur, P.C. and Iqbal Narain (1989), 'The Thousand Year Raj', in Francine R. Frankel and M.S.A. Rao (eds.), *Dominance and State Power in Modern India* (Delhi: Oxford University Press).

Mayer, A. (1997), 'Caste in an Indian Village: Change and Continuity', in C.J. Fuller (ed.) *Caste Today* (Delhi: Oxford University Press), pp. 32–64.

Melo, M.A., N. Ng'ethe, and J. Manor (2012), *Against the Odds: Politicians, Institutions and the Struggle Against Poverty* (London: Hurst).

Menon, Meena (2005), 'On the Trail of the Rozgar Adhikar Yatra', *The Hindu*, 30 May.

'MGNREGA Social Audit Opposed at Meet' (2010), *Times of India*, 30 July.

'MGNREGA Will Help Implement Direct Benefit Transfers' (2013), *Livemint.com*, 2 February.

Mishra, Neelabh (2001), 'Drought and Deaths', *Frontline*, 18(8), 14 April.

—— (2002), 'Hunger Deaths in Baran', *Frontline*, 19(24), 23 November.

Mistry, P. and A. Jaswal (2009), 'Study of the Implementation of NREGS: Focus on Migration', Mimeo, August. (Available at: www.knowledge.nrega.net)

Mukherjee, Rahul (2013), 'Ideas, Interests, and the Tipping Point: Economic Change in India', *Review of International Political Economy*, 20(2), pp. 363–389.

Mukherjee, Subrata and Saswata Chosh (2009), 'What Determines the Success and Failure of "100 Days Work" at the Panchayat Level? A Study of Birbhum District' (Kolkata: Institute of Development Studies).

Murgai, R and M. Ravallion (2005), 'Employment Guarantee in Rural India: What Would It Cost and How Much Would It Reduce Poverty?', *Economic and Political Weekly*, 40(31), 30 July.

Nagarajan, H.K., H.P. Binswanger-Mkhize, and S.S. Meenakshisundaram (2014), *Decentralization and Empowerment for Rural Development: The Case of India* (New Delhi: Foundation Books).

Narayanan, Sudha (2008), 'Employment Guarantee, Women's Work and Childcare', *Economic and Political Weekly*, 43(9), 1 March, pp. 10–13.

National Consortium of Civil Society Organisations (2011), *MGNREGA: Opportunities, Challenges and the Road Ahead* (New Delhi).

National Council of Applied Economic Research (2009), *NCAER-PIF Study Evaluating Performance of National Rural Employment Guarantee Act* (New Delhi: NCAER/Public Interest Foundation).

'Need to Have Parity of Wage under NREGA: Jairam' (2014), *India TV News*, 2 February. (Available at: www.indiatvnews.com/politics/national/need-to-have-parity-of-wage-under-mnrega-jairam-14665.html)

New Trade Union Initiative (2007), *Handbook on Rural Workers' Rights under the National Rural Employment Guarantee Act* (New Delhi).

'NREGA Audit: Bhilwara Shows the Way' (2009), *The Hindu*, 17 October.

'NREGA Scheme is Not Broken, So Govt Need Not Fix It' (2014), *Hindustan Times*, 16 October.

'NREGA Spiked Rural Wages Only 10%, Rest is Due to Rise in Minimum Support Price: Raghuram Rajan' (2014), *Economic Times*, 17 August.

Panini, M.N. (1996), 'The Political Economy of Caste', in M.N. Srinivas (ed.) *Caste: Its Twentieth Century Avatar* (New Delhi: Penguin), pp. 28–68.

Pankaj, Ashok K. (2008), *Processes, Institutions and Mechanisms of Implementation of NREGA: Impact Assessment of Bihar and Jharkhand* (Delhi: Institute for Human Development).

Pankaj, Ashok and Rukmini, Tankha (2009), *Women's Empowerment through Guaranteed Employment* (New Delhi: Institute for Human Development).

Patnaik, Utsa (2005), 'Theorizing food security and poverty in the era of economic reforms', in Gladys Lechini (ed.), *Globalization and the Washington Consensus: Its Influence on Democracy and Development in the South* (Buenos Aires: CLACSO).

Poorest Areas Civil Society [PACS] (2006), *Madhya Pradesh & Chhattisgarh* (New Delhi).

Quaid, Maeve (2002), *Workfare: Why Good Social Policy Ideas Go Bad* (Toronto: University of Toronto Press).

Raj, K.N. (1973), 'The Politics and Economics of "Intermediate Regimes"', *Economic and Political Weekly*, 49(37), 7 July.

'Raj'n to set up commission to probe starvation deaths: Sonia' (2002), *PTI*, 9 November.

Rajan, Raghuram (2012), 'What Happened to India?', *Project Syndicate*, 8 June. (Available at: http://www.project-syndicate.org/commentary/what-happened-to-india)

Ravallion, Martin (1991), 'Reaching the Rural Poor Through Public Employment: Arguments, Evidence, and Lessons from South Asia', *The World Bank Research Observer*, 6(2), pp. 153–175.

Ravi, Shamika and Monika Engler (2015), 'Workfare as an Effective Way to Fight Poverty: The Case of India's NREGS', *World Development*, 67, pp. 57–71.

Reserve Bank of India (multiple years), 'Direct and Indirect Tax Revenues of Central and State Governments', in Reserve Bank of India, *Handbook of Statistics on Indian Economy*. (Available at: https://www.rbi.org.in/scripts/PublicationsView.aspx?id=16556)

Right to Food Campaign Secretariat (2008), *Supreme Court Orders on the Right to Food: A Tool for Action*, 2nd edition (New Delhi).

Roy, Aruna, Jean Dreze, and Nikhil Dey (2007), 'The Right to Transparent Governance', *Combat Law Magazine*, 1 March.

——— (2011), 'The Right to Transparent Governance', in Harsh Dhobal (ed.), *Writings on Human Rights, Law and Society in India: A Combat Law Anthology* (New Delhi: Human Rights Law Network).

BIBLIOGRAPHY

Roy, Arundhati (2004), 'Let Us Hope the Darkness has Passed', *The Guardian*, 14 May.

Roy, Indrajit (2012), 'Guaranteeing Employment, Forging Political Subjectivities: Insights from the NREGS', paper for a conference at the University of Sussex, June.

Rudolph, Lloyd I. and Susanne Hoeber (1987), *In Pursuit of Lakshmi: A Political Economy of the Indian State* (Chicago, IL: University of Chicago Press).

'Rural Employment Guarantee Act: People's Victory; Safeguard It' (2005), *People's Democracy* (weekly publication of the CPI (M)), 29(35), 28 August.

'Rural Job Bill Hits Wage Wall' (2005), *Indian Express*, 19 July.

Rushdie, Salman (2004), 'India's New Era', *The Washington Post*, 14 May.

Sahoo, Sarbeswar (2013), *Civil Society and Democratization in India: Institutions, Ideologies and Interests* (Abingdon: Routledge).

Sainath, P. (2009), 'NREGS: Not Caste in Stone', *The Hindu*, 14 September.

Sanjit Roy v. State of Rajasthan (1983), AIR 328, 1983 SCR (2) 271.

Saxena, N.C. (2005), 'First Report of the Commissioner', in Gonsalves, C., P.R. Kumar, and A.R Srivastava (eds.), *The Right to Food* (New Delhi: Human Rights Law Network).

Scheingold, Stuart A. (2004), *The Politics of Rights: Lawyers, Public Policy and Political Change*, 2nd Edition (Ann Arbor, MI: University of Michigan Press).

Schneider, Mark (2014), 'Does Clientelism Work? A Test of Guessability in India', *CASI Working Paper Series*, 13(1) (Philadelphia, PA: Center for the Advanced Study of India, University of Pennsylvania). (Available at: https://casi.sas.upenn.edu/sites/casi.sas.upenn.edu/files/research/Does%20Clientelism%20Work%20-%20Mark%20Schneider%20(CASI%20Working%20Paper)_0.pdf)

'Seventy-Eight percent don't want land bill, 63 percent say Modi's image anti-poor: Survey' (2015), *Deccan Herald*, 11 May.

Shah, M. (2007), 'Employment Guarantee, Civil Society and Indian Democracy', *Economic and Political Weekly*, 42(45–6), 10 November, pp. 43–51.

Shah, T., S. Verma, R. Indu, and P. Hemant (2010), *Asset Creation through Employment Guarantee?: Synthesis of Student Case Studies of 40 MGNREGA Works in 9 States of India* (Anand: International Water Management Institute).

Shankar, S. (2009), *Scaling Justice: India's Supreme Court, Social Rights and Civil Liberties* (Delhi: Oxford University Press).

Shankar, S., R. Gaiha, and R. Jha (2009), 'Numbers to the Rescue', *Indian Express*, 20 October.

Shankar, S. and R. Gaiha (2013), *Battling Corruption: Has NREGA Reached India's Poor?* (Delhi: Oxford University Press).

Sharma, Prashant (2014), *Democracy and Transparency in the Indian State: The Making of the Right to Information Act* (Abingdon: Routledge).

'Shivraj Singh Chouhan Calls MGNREA "One of the Best Programmes"' (2015), *Indian Express*, 21 April.

Siddle, A. and T.A. Koelbe (2012), *The Failure of Decentralisation in South African Local Government* (Cape Town: UCT Press).

BIBLIOGRAPHY

'Social and political dividends from NREGA' (2009), *The Hindu*, October 18.

Social Protection in Asia Programme (2010), 'Cash Transfers and Social Protection', *SPA Newsletter*, 7 June (Brighton, UK: Institute of Development Studies).

Society for Participatory Research in Asia (2007), *A Study on the Role of Panchayati Raj Institutions in Implementation of NREGA, Phase—II* (New Delhi).

'Sonia Gandhi Pitches for Passage of NREGB' (2005), *Hindustan Times*, 27 July.

Srinivas, M.N. (1968), 'Mobility in the Caste System', in M. Singer and B. S. Cohn (eds.), *Structure and Change in Indian Society* (Chicago, IL: University of Chicago Press).

Srivastava, Alka (2006), *A Long Journey Ahead—Women in Panchayati Raj: A Study in Rajasthan* (New Delhi: Indian Social Institute).

Sudarshan, R.M. (2011), *India's National Rural Employment Guarantee: Women's Participation and Impacts in Himachal Pradesh, Kerala and Rajasthan* (Brighton, UK: Institute of Development Studies, 2011).

Sudarshan, Ratna (2008), 'Impact of NREGA on Rural Labour Market in Kerala: Preliminary Findings on Women's Work', paper presented at the conference *NREGS in India: Impacts and Implementation Experiences*, 16–17 September, New Delhi.

'Swadeshi Jagran Manch Opposes Land Bill, Slams "Undue Hurry"' (2015), *Indian Express*, 2 July.

'TDP Government has neglected farmers: Sonia' (2004), *The Hindu*, April 24.

Thachil, Tariq (2014), *Elite Parties, Poor Voters: How Social Services Win Votes in India* (New York: Cambridge University Press).

Thakurta, Paranjoy Guha (2015), 'The Business of Politics: Sun TV and the Maran Brothers', *Economic and Political Weekly*, 50(35), 29 August.

'The Battle for Employment Guarantee' (2009), special section, *Frontline*, 16 January.

'The Meaning of Verdict 2004' (2004), Editorial, *The Hindu*, 14 May.

'The Other Bharat's Backlash' (2004), *Business Line*, 14 May.

UN Women (2015), *Progress of the World's Women 2015–2016: Transforming Economies, Realizing Rights* (New York: UN Women).

United Nations Development Programme (2015), *MGNREGA Sameeksha-II: An Anthology of Research Studies, 2012–2014* (New Delh).

University of London (School of Advanced Study) (2013), 'Community Work Programme: A Case Study', Report of the South Africa Research Team, BRICS Project.

'Supreme Court nod for CBI probe into alleged irregularities in NREGA' (2014), *Economic Times*, 14 March. (Available at: http://articles.economictimes.indiatimes. com/2014-03-14/news/48222160_1_cbi-probe-alleged-irregularities-misappropriation)

Uppal, V. (2009), 'Is NREGA a Safety Net for Children?', background paper for the 'Young Lives' Project, Oxford University.

Vanneman, R. and A. Dubey (2011), 'Horizontal and Vertical Inequalities in India', in J. Gornick and M. Jantti (eds.), *Income Inequality: Economic Disparities and the Middle Class in Affluent Countries* (Stanford, CA: Stanford University Press), pp. 439–58.

Varshney, Ashutosh (1998), *Democracy, Development and the Countryside: Urban-Rural Struggles in India* (Cambridge: Cambridge University Press).

'Vasundhara Raje Government Backs Out of Banswara Social Audit' (2007), *The Hindu*, 26 December.

Verma, S. (2011), *MGNREGA Assets and Rural Water Security: Synthesis of Field Studies in Bihar, Gujarat, Kerala and Rajasthan* (Anand: International Water Management Institute).

––––––– (2011), *Multiple Use Water Services in India: Scaling Up Community Based MUS through MGNREGA* (Anand: International Water Management Institute).

'Wake-up Call on Rural Employment Guarantee' (editorial) (2008), *Economic and Political Weekly*, 43(4), 26 January, pp. 5–6.

'We Lost a Comrade' (2008), *The Hindu*, 7 December.

Weiner, Myron (1989), *The Indian Paradox: Essays in Indian Politics* (New Delhi: Sage Publications).

Wilkinson, Steven I. (2005), 'Elections in India: Behind the Congress Comeback', *Journal of Democracy*, 16(1), pp. 153–67.

'Will It Continue to be Advantage Chouhan?' (2013), *The Hindu*, 25 July.

World Bank (2009), *World Development Report 2009: Reshaping Economic Geography* (Washington, DC).

––––––– (2013), *Global Monitoring Report, 2013: Rural-Urban Dynamics and the Millennium Development Goals* (Washington, DC).

––––––– (2013), *World Development Report 2013: Jobs* (Washington, DC).

––––––– (2014), *World Development Report 2014—Risk and Opportunity: Managing Risk for Development* (Washington, DC).

Yadav, Yogendra (2004), 'The Elusive Mandate of 2004', *Economic and Political Weekly*, 39(51), 18 December.

INDEX